Work in Progress
A Guide to Academic Writing and Revising

FIFTH EDITION

Work in Progress

A Guide to Academic Writing and Revising

LISA EDE

Oregon State University

BEDFORD/ST. MARTIN'S

Boston ◆ New York

For Bedford/St. Martin's

Executive Editor: Marilyn Moller
Developmental Editor: Diana M. Puglisi
Editorial Assistant: Belinda Delpêche
Senior Production Editor: Shuli Traub
Senior Production Supervisor: Dennis J. Conroy
Marketing Manager: Brian Wheel
Art Direction/Cover Design: Lucy Krikorian
Text Design: Wanda Kossak
Copy Editor: Rosemary Winfield
Composition: Stratford Publishing Services
Printing and Binding: R. R. Donnelley & Sons Company

President: Charles H. Christensen
Editorial Director: Joan E. Feinberg
Editor in Chief: Nancy Perry
Marketing Director: Karen Melton
Director of Editing, Design, and Production: Marcia Cohen
Managing Editor: Erica T. Appel

Library of Congress Catalog Card Number: 00–104680

Manufactured in the United States of America.

6 5 4 3
f e d c

For information, write: Bedford/St. Martin's, 75 Arlington Street, Boston, MA 02116 (617–399–4000)

ISBN: 0–312–25085–1

Acknowledgments
Acknowledgments and copyrights can be found at the back of the book on pages 461–63, which constitute an extension of the copyright page.

To my students
and
(of course)
to Gregory

Preface

With the first edition of *Work in Progress,* I wanted to write a theoretically sophisticated but commonsensical textbook, one grounded both in the centuries-old rhetorical tradition and in recent theoretical and pedagogical research on writing. I wanted to write a textbook that would enrich but not dominate the life of the classroom. Traditional textbooks too often place students and teachers in opposition: The teacher acts as the provider of knowledge, while students are positioned as passive absorbers of this wisdom. *Work in Progress* would, I hoped, foster the development of a genuinely collaborative community, grounded in mutual respect and a shared commitment to inquiry. Learning and teaching are, after all, both works in progress.

Fortunately, *Work in Progress* has been successful enough to warrant subsequent editions, and thus it continues as my own work in progress. With each new edition, I have attempted to build on the strengths of earlier editions and to respond to the needs and suggestions of instructors and students who have used the text. The fourth edition, for instance, recognized the increasing importance of collaborative writing and online technologies by adding two new chapters on these subjects. This new fifth edition expands the discussion of online writing by incorporating discussions of this subject throughout the text and by adding a new section on document design (in Chapter 9, "Strategies for Planning, Drafting, and Document Design").

The most significant changes in this fifth edition are all intended to clarify and enrich the text's treatment of academic writing. *Work in Progress* has always provided a solid foundation for students entering the academy, for its rhetorical approach encourages students to learn how to analyze and address different disciplinary contexts and expectations. Two new chapters — Chapter 4, "Understanding the Research Process" and Chapter 15, "Putting It All Together: Writing Academic Arguments" — build on and enrich this strong foundation. A reorganization of the text also foregrounds the centrality, and interconnections, among the processes of reading, writing, and research. These interconnections are further supported by a new "Writers' References" section at the back of the book, which provides information students need to engage effectively in academic argument and research-based writing. This edition of *Work in Progress* also includes a significantly expanded number of student essays. *Work in Progress*, Fourth Edition, included five student essays. Twenty student essays appear in the fifth edition. As a result, this edition provides both more — and more diverse — examples of academic writing across the disciplines.

These additions will, I hope, increase the usefulness and timeliness of *Work in Progress* — as well as reinforce the text's central goals. These goals continue to be reflected in a number of key features:

- a focus on the concept of the rhetorical situation (Chapters 5 and 6)

- explicit support for and reinforcement of collaborative learning and writing activities (Chapter 12)

- a broad range of examples of successful student writing in the disciplines (Chapter 15)

- attention to the impact of new technologies for student writers (Chapter 7)

- inclusion of a mini-anthology of readings focused on online writing technologies and situations (Chapter 3)

- extensive attention to the processes of reading and research, and to reading, writing, and research as dynamic, interdependent activities (Chapters 3 and 4)

- full discussion of the demands of academic writing (Chapters 13, 14, and 15)

- a strong emphasis on the importance of social context and textual conventions of writing (Chapter 6)

NEW TO THIS EDITION

A new chapter on the research process.   Chapter 4, "Understanding the Research Process," presents the strategies that writers need to master to conduct research effectively — whether they are looking for a few details to enrich an essay or working on an extensive research paper. This chapter presents research, in other words, as central to academic writing, rather than as an isolated activity. Chapter 4 teaches students how to carry out the most critical activities researchers undertake — from assessing their goals as researchers to developing appropriate search strategies to evaluating print and online sources. It also includes an annotated sample student research paper. Information about MLA and APA documentation styles is provided in a readily accessible section at the back of the book.

A new chapter on academic argument.   Chapter 15, "Putting It All Together: Writing Academic Arguments," presents a detailed case study of a student's writing and revising to strengthen the argument in an academic essay. Included are the student's analysis of her rhetorical situation and notes about her writing process. The chapter concludes with a "Miscellany of Student Essays" from the disciplines. The eight essays represented in this miscellany represent such diverse disciplines as biology, philosophy, political science, English, chemistry, history, anthropology, and ethnic studies.

A substantially increased — and substantially diversified—selection of student essays.   The fourth edition of *Work in Progress* included five student essays, most from first-year writing classes. This fifth edition includes twenty student essays, both in chapters throughout the text and in the "Miscellany of Student Essays." Many of these essays have been drawn from disciplines across the curriculum; as a consequence, students will have a better introduction to — and examples of — the kinds of writing they will be asked to undertake as they progress in their studies.

A new "Writers' References" section.   This provides information students need to become successful academic writers and researchers. The section includes MLA Documentation Guidelines, APA Documentation Guidelines, Web Resources, and Developing a Portfolio of Your Written Work.

A new discussion of document design.   Chapter 9, "Strategies for Planning, Drafting, and Document Design," now includes a rhetorical approach to document design. The section begins with a discussion of the historical trends — trends that include but are not limited to online technologies — that have increased the role of visual elements in communication. The section concludes with guidelines that enable students to make effective decisions about document design.

A new organization.   To emphasize the significant interconnections among the processes of reading, writing, and research, *Work in Progress* is now divided into four major parts and the chapter on reading is presented earlier (Chapter 3, formerly Chapter 11).

A companion Web site.   Additional resources for students and instructors can be found at <http://www.bedfordstmartins.com/workinprogress>.

ORGANIZATION

Part One is an introduction to the interdependent processes of writing, reading, and research. The four chapters in Part One approach these processes from a rhetorical perspective, one that calls attention to the situated nature of any act of communication. Rather than presenting students with formats or rules to follow, these chapters encourage students to build upon their commonsense understanding of communication through reading, writing, and researching. In keeping with this approach, detailed documentation guidelines have been provided in a separate section of the book.

Part Two, which includes three chapters, focuses on the concept of the rhetorical situation. The first chapter in Part Two introduces students to the concept of the rhetorical situation and encourages them to take a strategic, situated approach to writing. Such an approach encourages students to ask questions about their role as writers, about their readers, and about the textual conventions that come into play in any particular rhetorical situation. The second chapter builds on the first by looking at textual conventions as socially constructed, socially negotiated understandings between readers and writers. It includes three articles on the same topic by psychologist John H. Flavell. Because these articles are directed toward quite different audiences, they provide a powerful case study of what it means to both address and invoke an audience. The final chapter in Part Two applies these understandings to online writing situations.

Part Three offers practical strategies for writing. The five chapters in Part Three cover the topics of invention, planning, drafting, and document design, revision, and collaboration. These chapters introduce students to a variety of practical strategies they can use as they plan, draft, and revise. Rather than emphasizing a single, prescribed series of steps or strategies that students must follow, *Work in Progress* encourages students to develop a repertoire of strategies they can use (working alone and with others, on- and offline), depending on their purpose and situation.

Part Four initiates students into the reading and writing they will do as members of the academic community. The first of the three chapters in Part Four articulates a rhetorical approach to academic argument. This chapter offers suggestions for analyzing disciplinary conventions and for understanding what is expected for assignments. The second chapter discusses the relationship between academic analysis and arguments and provides several student examples that clarify this relationship. And the final chapter presents an extended case study of one student's experience writing an essay on a poem by Emily Dickinson. It includes three drafts of the essay, as well as the student's analysis of her rhetorical situation and notes about her writing process. This chapter closes with a miscellany of eight examples of student writing across the disciplines.

As previously noted, this fifth edition of *Work in Progress* includes a new "Writers' References" section at the back of the book. The topics covered in this section are MLA Documentation Guidelines, APA Documentation Guidelines, Web Resources, and Developing a Portfolio of Your Written Work.

I have attempted to make *Work in Progress* an innovative textbook — but also to be sure it remains a practical textbook. It provides a conceptual framework and activities that stimulate effective classroom instruction, yet it also offers teachers considerable autonomy and flexibility. Some teachers will particularly appreciate the book's emphasis on reading and on academic writing, for instance, while others may draw more heavily on its numerous interactive, collaborative, workshop-oriented activities. Still other instructors will appreciate the ways in which *Work in Progress*'s rhetorical approach supports an emphasis on cultural and/or literacy studies. The *Instructor's Notes* to *Work in Progress* provide further elaboration of ways in which the text can be used and the book's companion Web site offers additional resources.

ACKNOWLEDGMENTS

Before I wrote *Work in Progress*, acknowledgments sometimes struck me as formulaic or conventional. Now I recognize that they are neither; rather, acknowledgments are simply inadequate to the task at hand. Coming at the end of the preface — and hence twice marginalized — acknowledgments can never adequately convey the complex web of interrelationships that make a book like this possible. I hope that the people whose support and assistance I acknowledge here not only note my debt of gratitude but also recognize the sustaining role that they have played, and continue to play, in my life.

I would like to begin by thanking my colleagues at the Center for Writing and Learning at Oregon State University. I could accomplish little in my teaching, research, and administration without the support and friendship of Moira Dempsey, Saundra Mills, Matt Yurdana, and Wayne Robertson. They, along with our writing assistants, have taught me what it means to collaborate in a sustaining, productive fashion. Others in the OSU English department, my second academic home, supported me while I wrote and revised this text. I am indebted to my colleagues Chris Anderson, Vicki Tolar Burton, and Anita Helle for their friendship and their commitment to writing over the years.

I have dedicated this book to my students, and I hope that it in some way reflects what *they* have taught me over the years. I also owe a great debt of gratitude to another friend and teacher, Suzanne Clark, who allowed me to persuade her to interrupt her own important works in progress to collaborate with me on the *Instructor's Notes*.

I also wish to acknowledge Carole Ann Crateau, instructor at OSU's Honors College, who generously helped me identify a number of new student essays for this edition. And I want very much to thank Matthew Johnston, whose writing is featured in Chapter 7, "Negotiating Online Writing Situations," as well as the seventeen other students whose essays appear throughout the fifth edition of *Work in Progress*.

Colleagues and students play an important role in nurturing any project, but so do those who form the intangible but indispensable community of scholars that is one's most intimate disciplinary home. Here, it is harder to determine who to acknowledge; my debt to the composition theorists who have led the way or "grown up" with me is so great that I hesitate to list the names of specific individuals here for fear of omitting someone deserving of credit. I must, however, acknowledge my friend and frequent coauthor Andrea Lunsford, who writes with me even when I write alone. I owe Andrea a particularly strong debt of gratitude for an important role she played in this fifth edition of *Work in Progress*. For when she learned that this edition would include extensive discussions of MLA and APA documentation style, Andrea insisted that there was no need to reinvent the wheel, and thus generously shared examples developed for *The Everyday Writer*. The material that appears on pages 419–50 of *Work in Progress* is adapted from *The Everyday Writer*.

I would also like to thank the many dedicated teachers of composition I have worked and talked with over the years. By their example, comments, suggestions, and questions, they have taught me a great deal about the teaching of writing. A number of writing instructors took time from their teaching to read and comment on drafts of this edition. Their observations and suggestions have enriched and improved this book. These reviewers include: Linda Bensel-Meyers, University of Tennessee; David Blakesley, Southern Illinois University–Carbondale; Thomas Burkdall, Occidental College; Donna Dunbar-Odom, Texas A&M–Commerce; Anne Farmer, Allen County Community College; Ron Fortune, Illinois State University; Robert Holderer, Edinboro University; Kate Massey, California Polytechnic State University; Tim Miank, Lansing Community College; Donna Niday, Iowa State University; Jonna Perrillo, New York University; George Sebouhian, SUNY College–Fredonia; and Heide-Marie Weidner, Tennessee Technological University.

I wish to thank the dedicated staff of Bedford/St. Martin's, particularly Diana Puglisi, whose editorial expertise — and wonderful sense of humor — helped make a difficult, deadline-ridden process both more manageable and more enjoyable. Marilyn Moller and Nancy Perry, who each edited earlier editions of *Work in Progress*, also provided insight and assistance at critical moments. It is a pleasure — and a gift — to continue collaborating with (and learning from) them. In addition, I want to thank project editor Shuli Traub, whose patient attention to detail proved especially valuable.

As this book goes to press, teachers and scholars of composition are mourning the loss of Robert Connors, who died in an accident on June 22, 2000. I was fortunate enough to know Bob and to collaborate with him on several projects. Bob was a person and scholar of great intelligence, generosity, and wit. The loss to his family and friends — and to the field of composition studies — is inestimable.

Finally, I want to (but cannot adequately) acknowledge the support of my husband, Gregory Pfarr, whose passionate commitment to his own work, and to our life together, sustains me.

Lisa Ede

Contents

WRITING, READING, AND RESEARCH: AN INTRODUCTION

PART ONE

On Writing

A *college student in mathematics education* decides to keep a journal during his student-teaching practicum. He uses his journal to reflect on his students' problems, to record observations about the school where he is teaching, to analyze the effectiveness of his lesson plans, and to cope with the inevitable highs and lows of his first experience in the classroom. At the end of the term, for an advanced seminar in his major, he draws on the journal to write an essay on the relationship between theory and practice in mathematics education. "It's a good thing I kept that journal," he tells a friend. "It helped me get beyond clichés about teaching to what I really know works in the classroom."

A *businessperson* who is chairing his local school board learns that a group of parents plans to petition the board to have several young adult books removed from the middle-school library. Aware that petitions such as this can develop into major controversies if not handled properly, he decides to ask others how they have responded on similar occasions, so he logs into SchoolBoard, an electronic bulletin board for members of school boards and others interested in local educational issues, and types in his query. His question provokes a lively exchange. After reading the responses, he prints a number of suggestions, types in his thanks, and adds his own comments to the ongoing conversation.

Two *students in an introduction-to-literature class* learn that they must write an analysis of Mrs. Ramsey, a character in Virginia Woolf's *To the Lighthouse.* They meet to discuss possible essay topics. At first their conversation moves slowly; they both liked the novel and found Mrs. Ramsey interesting, but they're not sure how to move from a general response to a specific topic. Finally one of them suggests that they write down all the questions they have about Mrs. Ramsey. They do so and are reassured by their list. But what to do next? Why not try to imagine how different characters in Woolf's novel might respond to their questions, one of them suggests. Perhaps the characters' responses will help them see something that they might otherwise overlook. They quickly make a list of characters, divide them up, and agree to meet the next day to discuss their experiment. As they say goodbye, they comment with relief on how good it feels to have gotten started.

A *consulting engineer* meets with colleagues to begin work on a proposal for a major construction project. Knowing they have just a month to meet the deadline, she assigns duties to group members. Some will begin research on technical issues; others will consult with resource people within the firm; and still others will begin writing nontechnical sections of the draft. Her role will be to organize and monitor the group effort and edit the final proposal. After the meeting, she works out a schedule for preliminary reports, emails it to her colleagues, and reminds them that thanks to their new groupware computer program, they will be able to generate, revise, and edit text together. This will be much more efficient, she observes, than their former practice of sending sections of text via email.

A *team of government safety inspectors* visits a meat-processing plant for its annual inspection. After three days of interviews and observations, they compile an annotated list of problems that have appeared since their last visit and fax it to their main office.

A *grandmother* realizes that her grandchildren know very little about their family's history, so she embarks on a family genealogy project. She begins by writing all that she remembers about her parents and grandparents. After printing and reading her first draft, she realizes that over the years she has forgotten many details, so she emails her draft to her brother and sister and asks for corrections and additions. Then she begins searching the World Wide Web for genealogy sites. Who knows? She might unearth some information about their family. And even if she doesn't, she is sure to locate both images and information that will enrich her project. She's tried to tell her grandchildren about her father's experiences in the war — but World War II is hard for twenty-first-century children to grasp. If she can find a photograph of the bombing of Pearl Harbor — a bombing her father experienced firsthand — that might make the war, and her father, more real to them. Thank goodness she invested in a new desktop publishing program and color printer recently! She'll need them for this important project.

A *senior majoring in sociology* meets with her adviser to discuss her senior honors thesis. The student is interested in the relationship of rap and hip hop music to recent cultural, political, and economic developments in North America. The student and her adviser talk about the lengthy process involved in writing a thesis. The adviser recommends a two-pronged approach. "Look inward at your own interests and understandings by keeping a notebook of ideas and reading notes about your project," the adviser recommends. "Eventually, this notebook will lead to a proposal for your thesis — but for now just explore your ideas and respond to things you read. Be sure to look outward also. Obviously, you'll be collecting resources in the library, but you should also gather information online." They move to the adviser's computer and begin to surf the Web, looking for sites and bookmarking several that look promising. As they wrap up their conference, the adviser reminds the student that at the end of her project she'll give an oral presentation on her thesis. "As you look at Web sites, be sure to look for multimedia clips that you can use in your presentation," the adviser recommends.

People write for a variety of reasons. Many people write because they are required to. Term papers, business letters, reports, proposals, magazine articles — most are written by a person or a group asked to take on the responsibility for the project. Sometimes this writing simply reports the results of analysis or observations, as in the safety inspectors' list. But often the writing functions as a means for solving problems, making decisions, or coming to understand complex situations.

People also write to fulfill important personal needs. The grandmother describing her parents, bringing them to life for her grandchildren, writes because she wants to record her family's history. The student teacher uses his journal to help make sense of — and survive — his first year in the classroom. People write to solve problems and to communicate with others, but they write to look inward as well.

■ ■ ■

FOR EXPLORATION

What do you typically write, and why? Make a list of all the kinds of writing you regularly do — shopping lists, class notes, whatever. What kinds of writing do you do most often? Least often? What are your usual reasons for writing? Which of your writing experiences are generally productive and satisfying? Unproductive and unsatisfying? In a paragraph or two explore why some writing experiences are productive and satisfying while others are not.

UNDERSTANDING HOW WRITING WORKS

At first glance, the writers described at the beginning of this chapter might seem to have little in common. But if you look more closely, you can see a number of similarities — similarities that can tell you something about how writing works.

The writing that these people do matters; it helps determine how successful they are in school or on the job or how they feel about themselves.

None of these writers works in isolation. They may spend some time thinking and writing alone, but all interact regularly with others. Sometimes they do so to generate ideas or to get responses. On other occasions, they actually write with others.

Whether writing alone or collaboratively, they all write in a specific context or situation. As writers, they are influenced by such factors as these:

Their reason for writing and the nature of their writing project

The issues they want to explore and the points they want to make

The readers for whom they are writing

Textual conventions, like report or business letter formats, that help define the form their writing takes

Their feelings about their writing

The amount of practice they have had with a particular kind of writing

External factors, such as deadlines and access to computers and online technologies

No matter what they write, from the moment they begin to think about their writing, these writers face a complex series of *choices*. Some of these choices will involve the writing process. To make practical decisions about their writing, these writers ask themselves questions such as

Do I know enough about my subject? Do I need to do additional research? Should I consult online as well as print sources? Interview authorities on my topic?

When should I begin writing? How much time should I spend planning, drafting, and revising?

How might I benefit from working with others?

Other questions involve the writing itself:

What do I hope to accomplish? Are my goals realistic, and do they meet the needs and expectations of my readers?

How can I organize and develop my ideas most effectively?

How much supporting detail do I need to provide?

What tone or style is appropriate, given my subject, purpose, and audience?

How can I most effectively share my ideas with others? Through a conventional printed essay or report? Through a PowerPoint presentation? Or should I consider putting this online via the World Wide Web?

They all recognize the significant role that writing plays in their personal and professional lives. Writing doesn't necessarily come easily, but they willingly spend the time and energy necessary to write well. Writing, they know, is important *work in progress.*

■ ■ ■

FOR EXPLORATION

Recall one successful writing experience. (Don't limit yourself to academic writing, by the way.) What factors enabled you to complete this writing successfully? Write a paragraph or more describing this experience and analyzing the reasons you consider it successful.

DEVELOPING RHETORICAL SENSITIVITY

How do writers make choices as they compose? Experienced writers like those described at the beginning of this chapter draw on *all* their resources when they write. They learn about writing from their reading, and they also analyze their own situation as writers. They think about their writing purposes — the meaning they wish to communicate, their reasons for writing — and their readers. They explore their own ideas, challenging themselves to express their ideas as clearly and carefully as possible. They play with words and phrases, sentences and paragraphs, to make their writing stylistically effective. And they take advantage of the resources available to them thanks to online technologies. In all of these activities, experienced writers practice *rhetorical sensitivity* — even though they might not use this phrase to describe their thinking and writing.

You may not be familiar with this phrase, either. It derives from the word *rhetoric,* the art of effective communication. Rhetoric is one of the oldest fields of intellectual study in Western culture; it was first formulated by such Greek and Roman rhetoricians as Isocrates (436–338 B.C.), Aristotle (384–322 B.C.),

Cicero (106–43 B.C.), and Quintilian (A.D. 35–96). Originally developed to meet the needs of speakers, rhetoric quickly came to be applied to written texts as well.

In your daily life, you already practice considerable rhetorical sensitivity. As you make decisions about how you wish to interact with others, you naturally (if unconsciously) draw on your commonsense understanding of effective communication. Imagine, for instance, that you are preparing to interview for a job. In deciding what to wear, how to act, and what to say during the interview, you will make a number of decisions that reflect your rhetorical sensitivity. Much of your attention will focus on how you can present yourself best, but you also recognize the importance of being well prepared and of interacting effectively with your interviewers. If you are smart, you will consider the specific situation for which you are applying. Someone applying for a position in a bank might well dress and act differently than someone applying for a job as a swim coach. Successful applicants know that all that they do — the way they dress, present themselves, respond to questions, and interact with interviewers — is an attempt to communicate their strengths and persuade their audience to employ them.

As a "reader" of contemporary culture, you also employ rhetorical sensitivity. As a consumer, for instance, you are bombarded with advertisements urging you to purchase various products or services. How you respond to these advertisements will depend primarily on how you "read" them. Wise consumers know that advertisements are designed to persuade, and they learn ways to read them with a critical eye (even as they appreciate, say, a television commercial's humor or a magazine ad's design). You read other aspects of contemporary culture as well. Much of the time you may do so for entertainment: While watching sports or other programs on television, for instance, your primary goal may be to relax and enjoy yourself. If you find the plot of a detective show implausible or the action of the Monday night football game too slow, you can easily click to a more interesting program.

At times, however, you may choose to take a more critical, distanced perspective on such forms of popular culture as television, music, and magazines. After arguing with a friend about whether the music group Limp Bizkit advocates violence, you may well watch their videos with a careful eye; you may compare them with other rock groups. When you compare different musicians' lyrics, type of dress, and movements, you are considering the ways in which these groups attempt to appeal to and communicate with their audience. Though you probably would not have used this term to describe your analysis, you are analyzing the rhetoric of their performances.

When you think rhetorically, you consider the ways in which words and images are used to engage — and sometimes to persuade — others. Writers who think rhetorically apply their understanding of human communication in general, and of written texts in particular, to the decisions that will enable effective communication within a specific writer-reader situation.

Seeing the Key Elements of Rhetoric in Context

As applied to written texts, rhetoric involves three key elements:

- One or more *writers* who have (or must discover) something to communicate

- One or more *readers* with whom the writer would like to communicate

- A *text* — an essay, poem, Web site, report, email, or other verbal (and, increasingly, also visual) communication — that makes this exchange of information possible

The relationship among these three elements is dynamic. Writers select and arrange language to express their meanings, but readers are equally active. Readers don't simply decipher the words on the page; they draw on their own experiences and expectations as they read. As a student, for instance, you naturally read your economics textbook differently than you read a popular novel. You also know that the more experience you have reading certain kinds of writing — science fiction novels or the sports or financial pages of the newspaper, for example — the more you will get out of them.

And what about the third rhetorical element, the text? As Chapter 7, "Negotiating Online Writing Situations," explains more fully, changes in the technologies of writing — the technologies writers use to share their writing with readers — hold powerful implications for contemporary writers. A Midwestern farmer writing to a parent in the mid-nineteenth century would have had few choices to make about his text. He would have known that he would write a letter (following the conventions of that genre) by hand to his parents. A student living in the Midwest in the twenty-first century who wishes to communicate with his parents has many more options. He could still write a letter by hand — for even in our technologically advanced culture handwritten letters are still highly valued. (Indeed, the infrequency with which we write letters makes them all the more prized.) But the student could also call, email, or fax his parents. If the student has constructed a Web site, his parents might interact with him by visiting his site. If they have their own site, they could acknowledge their connection with their son by linking their two sites. Such a link is quite different from the letter that nineteenth-century parents might send to a child, but in its own way it still communicates important information to readers (in this case, those surfing the Web).

As this example indicates, writing and reading do not occur in a vacuum. The language you grow up speaking, the social and cultural worlds you inhabit, the technologies of writing available to you: These and other factors all play important roles in your writing. If you grow up speaking a language other than English, for instance, you may find English speakers' direct, concise prose style puzzling. Communication is central to all human cultures, but the form this communication takes can vary in significant ways: What feels natural to a member of one community may feel strange or even uncomfortable to someone else.

Precisely because writing is a distinctly human activity, writers can sometimes experience difficulties and dilemmas. Students whose first language is not English often must work hard to understand and adapt to North American oral and written communication preferences. Even those who have grown up in American culture may find that the writing they are asked to do in college differs considerably from the language they use in their everyday lives. The United States is, after all, a country of many cultures, ethnic groups, languages, and dialects. The language that feels comfortable and natural to you when you speak with your family and friends may differ considerably from that required in academic reading and writing assignments.

■ ■ ■

FOR EXPLORATION

Take a few moments to freewrite about the language you speak in your home community and the language you use at school. If you speak several dialects or languages, feel free to include this in your reflection. To what extent do academic forms of writing feel comfortable or uncomfortable? Why? If you have found academic writing difficult or uncomfortable, what steps, if any, have you taken to meet this challenge?

Here is a second option for your consideration. Instead of writing about the relationship between your home and school languages, take this opportunity to reflect on your feelings about and uses of recent online writing technologies, such as email and the Web. How comfortable are you with these technologies? Has it been a struggle to learn to use them, or have they come more or less naturally to you? Do you find yourself missing such older writing practices as handwriting letters? Spend a few minutes writing about these and related questions.

Like life, writing involves negotiation. When you prepare for a job interview, you must decide how much you are willing to modify your everyday way of dressing to meet the expected demands of the situation. Similarly, when you write — whether in college, at work, or for civic or other activities — you must consider the expectations of others. At times it can be difficult to determine — let alone meet — these expectations. In your first weeks at a new job, for instance, you probably felt like the new kid on the block. Gradually, however, you became sensitive to the expectations of those with whom you worked. Likewise, as a college student you may at times feel like a new *writer* on the block. Both *Work in Progress* and your composition course will help you build on the rhetorical sensitivity that you already have, so that you can suc-cessfully complete your reading and writing assignments.

As you develop this rhetorical sensitivity, you will understand that writing offers many opportunities for self-expression. Unless you are writing entirely for yourself, however — as you do when you are writing in a journal — you must always consider the situation in which you are writing. Neither students nor businesspersons, to cite two examples, are free to write whatever they wish. Their participation in larger institutions brings constraints, just as it also provides opportunities for communication with others. A student writing an essay about a controversial issue and a middle-level manager writing an annual sales report are both taking advantage of institutionally sanctioned opportunities to communicate their own ideas. If the student and the manager wish to have their ideas taken seriously, if they wish to be effective with their intended audience, they must write in a form acceptable to their readers.

How do forms become "acceptable" to readers? Such forms as the essay, business letter, scientific report, and email develop over time, responding to the needs of readers and writers. The scientific report and the business letter, for instance, evolved along with and in response to the rise of modern science and of Western capitalism. Different forms of writing thus have histories, just as languages and countries do.

As a writer, you cannot ignore the situation within which you are writing or the forms and conventions your readers expect you to follow. But unless you are writing a legal contract or filling out a renter's agreement, you also have considerable flexibility and opportunities for self-expression. An example from my experience writing *Work in Progress* may help clarify this point. When I started, I knew that I needed to follow certain conventions. Some of these conventions — such as the requirement that a textbook have headings, sub-headings, and activities at the end of each chapter — are very general; others are more specific to composition textbooks. I didn't feel burdened or limited by these conventions; in fact, they reassured me, for they provided a frame-work that helped me develop my ideas. When you write, you, too, must work within conventions appropriate to your situation, purpose, and subject, but these conventions are generally enabling.

Demonstrating Rhetorical Sensitivity

Writers who demonstrate rhetorical sensitivity consider all the elements of rhetoric when they compose. They think about their own purposes and inten-tions — the meanings they want to convey to readers. They reflect on the image of themselves, the writer's *persona,* that they want to create in their writ-ing. They consider the needs, interests, and expectations of their readers. And they draw on the knowledge they have gained about language through speak-ing, listening, reading, and writing.

All writers — you included — have some degree of rhetorical sensitivity. Because you learned language as a child and have used it in your daily life ever since, you have already developed sensitivity to oral language. When you converse with others, you automatically adjust your language to the situation. You naturally speak differently when you chat with friends than when you talk with your minister, employer, or teacher.

If you are like many students, you may be more confident of your ability to communicate effectively through oral language than through written discourse. How can you increase your rhetorical sensitivity as a writer? You can do so by reading broadly, writing often, and discussing your writing with others. Helping you achieve this rhetorical sensitivity is a major goal of this textbook and of your composition course.

■ ■ ■

FOR EXPLORATION

Take a few moments to reflect on your understanding of the terms *rhetoric* and *rhetorical sensitivity*. You may find it helpful to recall and describe an incident in your daily life when you were called on to demonstrate rhetorical sensitivity. Then write a paragraph or so stating your current understanding of these terms. Finally, write one or two questions that you still have about *rhetoric* and *rhetorical sensitivity*.

UNDERSTANDING WRITING "RULES"

Writing is hard but rewarding work. Sometimes people think that they can make that hard work just a little easier by establishing rigid rules. You may have been warned, for instance, never to use the pronoun *I* in your college writing. This rule may have confused you; you may have wondered what's so terrible about having a few *I*'s sprinkled throughout your essay.

If you think commonsensically about how language works, drawing on the rhetorical sensitivity you have developed as a reader and a writer, you can begin to understand how rules like this got established. More important, you can decide when this and other rules make sense and when they are overly rigid or unnecessarily limiting.

Let's look at the rule just mentioned: "Never use *I* in your writing." Teachers sometimes discourage students from using *I* because most academic writing is intended to focus on the subject being discussed, on arguments and evidence, rather than on the writer's individual experiences and opinions. A history professor who assigns an essay exam on the causes of the civil rights movement of the 1950s and 1960s will want you to demonstrate your ability to define and explain those causes rather than to express your personal feelings about the movement.

There's a kernel of commonsense wisdom, then, in the prohibition some teachers have against using *I*. The problem is that there are times when *I* is exactly the right pronoun to use — when you're describing a personal experience, for example, or when you want to show that an observation truly is your own opinion. Rather than adhering rigidly to rules like this one, you can use your rhetorical sensitivity to decide what makes sense in a specific situation.

■ ■ ■

FOR EXPLORATION

Think of several writing "rules" that you've never understood or fully accepted. List as many of these rules as possible, and then choose one rule and write a brief explanation of why you question it.

FOR GROUP WORK

Bring your response to the preceding Exploration to class. Working with a group of classmates, discuss your lists, and select one writing rule that you all question. Consider the following questions, with one person recording all your answers:

1. Why do you all think that this writing rule may be questionable? Identify a situation when following this rule might not be preferable or wise.

2. What arguments in favor of this rule can your group identify? At what times would following this rule make good sense?

Be prepared to discuss your conclusions with your class.

THINKING — AND ACTING — LIKE A WRITER

As you've just seen, thinking commonsensically about writing can help you understand some of the basic conventions of writing. Later chapters focus more specifically on ways to increase your rhetorical sensitivity and thus become a more *effective* writer. But you may also wish to improve your *efficiency* as a writer — your ability to manage your time well, to cope with the inevitable frustrations of writing, and to use all your personal energies and resources when you write. How can commonsensical thinking about writing help you in that respect as well?

Writing is a *process,* and stopping to think about how your own writing process may affect the quality of your writing can prove illuminating. One of my students, for example, formulated an analogy that helped us all think very fruitfully about how the writing process works. "Writing," he said, "is actually a lot like sports."

Writing — like sports? Let's see what this comparison reveals about the writing process.

Writing and sports are both performance skills. You may know who won every Wimbledon since 1950, but if you don't actually play tennis, you're not a tennis player — just somebody who knows a lot about tennis. Similarly, you can know a lot about writing, but to demonstrate (and improve) your skills, you must *write.*

Writing and sports both require individuals to master complex skills and to perform these skills in an almost infinite number of situations. Athletes must learn specific skills, plays, or maneuvers, but they can never execute them routinely or thoughtlessly. Writers must be similarly resourceful and flexible. You can learn the principles of effective essay organization, for instance, and you may write a number of essays that are, in fact, well organized. Nevertheless, each time you sit down to write a new essay, you have to consider your options and make new choices about your writing. This is a primary reason why smart writers do not rely on formulas or rules but instead use rhetorical sensitivity to analyze and respond to each particular situation.

Experienced athletes and writers know that a positive attitude is essential. Some athletes "psych" themselves up before a game or competition, often with the help of a sports psychologist. But any serious athlete knows that's only part of what having a positive attitude means. It also means running five miles when you're already tired at three or doing twelve repetitions during weight training when you're exhausted and no one else would know if you did only eight. A positive attitude is equally important in writing. If you approach a writing task with a negative attitude — "I never was good at writing" — you create obstacles for yourself. Keeping a positive, open attitude is essential in tennis, skiing — and writing.

To maintain a high level of skill, both athletes and writers need frequent practice and effective coaching. "In sports," a coach once said, "you're either getting better or getting worse." Without practice — which for a writer means both reading and writing — your writing skills will inevitably slip (as will your confidence). Likewise, coaching is essential in writing because it's hard to distance yourself from your own work. Coaches —

your writing instructor, a tutor (or writing assistant) at a writing center, or a fellow student — can help you gain a fresh perspective on your writing and make useful suggestions about revision as well.

Experienced athletes and writers continually set new goals for themselves. Athletes who believe that they are either getting better or getting worse continually set new challenges for themselves and analyze their performance. They know that coaches can help them but that they are ultimately the ones performing. Experienced writers know this too, so they look for opportunities to practice their writing. And they don't measure their success simply by a grade. They see their writing always as work in progress.

■ ■ ■

FOR EXPLORATION

Freewriting is a technique used to generate and explore ideas. Here is a description of freewriting by Peter Elbow, the professor who created this technique:

> To do a freewriting exercise, simply force yourself to write without stopping for [a certain number] of minutes. Sometimes you will produce good writing, but that's not the goal. Sometimes you will produce garbage, but that's not the goal either. . . . Speed is not the goal, though sometimes the process revs you up. If you can't think of anything to write, write about how that feels or repeat over and over "I have nothing to write" or "Nonsense" or "No." If you get stuck in the middle of a sentence or thought, just repeat the last word or phrase till something comes along. The only point is to keep writing.*

Use this technique to freewrite about your attitude toward writing. Write for five or ten minutes, perhaps beginning with one of the following phrases:

When I write, I feel. . . .

Writing means. . . .

Writing is like. . . .

---

*This description is excerpted from Peter Elbow, *Writing with Power: Techniques for Mastering the Writing Process* (New York: Oxford UP, 1981), 13.

BECOMING PART OF A COMMUNITY OF WRITERS

For many people, one big difference between writing and sports is that athletes often belong to teams. Writers, they think, work in lonely isolation — tucked away in a carrel at the library or seated at the kitchen table or computer with only books and notes as companions. But does writing actually require isolation and loneliness? Let's go back to the writers described at the beginning of this chapter. Only the government safety inspectors actually write together — sitting together and jointly composing their list of problems. Like many in business, industry, and the professions, however, the consulting engineer works as part of one or more teams. Much of the time she composes alone, but her work is part of a group effort: Her drafts will be responded to, and perhaps changed, by members of the group. Several of the other writers talk extensively with friends and coworkers — sometimes in person and sometimes via email — before and while writing. And the businessperson takes advantage of an electronic bulletin board as he considers how the school board might best respond to a request to remove several books from a school library. Later, he and other school board members will work collaboratively to draft a response to the petition.

As these examples indicate, the romanticized image of the writer struggling alone until inspiration strikes is hardly accurate. Most writers alternate between periods of independent activity, composing alone at a desk or computer, and periods of social interactions — meeting with friends, colleagues, or team members for information, advice, or responses to drafts. They may also correspond with others in their field, or they may get in touch with people doing similar work through their reading, research, or online writing technologies.

Finally, people who take their writing seriously are just like other people who share an interest. They like to develop social relationships or networks with others who feel as they do. They realize that these networks will help them learn new ideas, improve their skills, and share their interest and enthusiasm. Sometimes these relationships are formal and relatively permanent. Many poets and fiction writers, for instance, meet regularly to discuss work in progress. Perhaps more commonly, writers' networks are informal and shifting, though no less vital. A new manager in a corporation, for instance, may find one or two people with sound judgment and good writing skills to review important letters and reports. Similarly, students working on a major project for a class may meet informally but regularly to compare notes and provide mutual support.

Unfortunately, college life generally does not encourage the development of informal networks like these, especially among undergraduates. Students juggling coursework, jobs, families, and other activities can find it difficult to get together or to take the time to read and respond to one another's writing.

Luckily, many colleges and universities have established writing centers, where you can go to talk with others about your writing. If your campus has a writing center, take advantage of the opportunity to get an informed response to your work.

■ ■ ■

FOR EXPLORATION

If your campus has a writing center, make an appointment to interview a writing assistant about the services the center provides. You may also want to ask the writing assistant about his or her own experiences as a writer. Your instructor may ask you to present the results of your interview orally or to write a summary of your discussion.

Whether you have access to a writing center or not, you can still participate in an informal network with others who, like you, are working to improve their writing skills. Because you are in the same class and share the same assignments and concerns, you and your classmates constitute a natural community of writers. The following guidelines can help you participate effectively in group activities. These suggestions apply whether you work with the same group of students all term or participate in a variety of groups.

■ GUIDELINES FOR GROUP WORK

1. *Develop Effective Team-Working Skills.* Good teamwork doesn't come naturally; you may need to develop or strengthen the skills that will contribute to effective group work. As you work with others in your class, keep these suggestions in mind:

   ■ *Remember that people have different styles of learning and interacting.* Some of these differences represent individual preferences: Some students work out their ideas as they talk, for instance, while others prefer to think through their ideas before speaking. Other differences are primarily cultural and thus reflect deeply embedded social practices and preferences. Effective groups value diversity and find ways to ensure that *all* members can comfortably participate in and benefit from group activities.

(continued)

(continued)

- *Balance a commitment to "getting the job done" with patience and flexibility.* Time is usually limited, and responsible group members will recognize the need to "get the job done" but will also be flexible and patient.

- *Work with your peers to articulate group goals and monitor group processes.* To work together successfully, group members must take the time to clarify goals and procedures; otherwise, valuable time is wasted. Similarly, effective groups develop some means (formal or informal) of evaluating group activities. If you are part of a group that is meeting regularly, you might decide to begin meetings by having each person state one way in which the group is working well and one way in which it could be improved. The time spent discussing these comments and suggestions could contribute to better group dynamics.

- *Deal immediately and openly with any problems in the group process, such as a dominating or nonparticipating member.* It's not always easy to discuss problems such as these openly, but doing so is essential to effective group work.

2. *Be Ready to Assume Various Roles.*

- Sometimes you may function as your group's leader, either informally or formally. At other times you may be called on to act as a mediator, to help the group reach a consensus. Or your main responsibility may be keeping the group on task so that you can achieve your goals in the time allotted. Effective group members assume the roles necessary to a specific task and situation, and they recognize the need for flexibility and variety.

3. *Take Time at the Start to Review Your Assignment and to Agree on Relevant Procedures.*

- *For brief collaborative activities,* such as a fifteen-minute group discussion in class, you may need to spend only a few minutes reviewing your teacher's instructions and establishing basic ground rules.

(continued)

(continued)

■ *For more extended projects* — particularly those that will involve group meetings outside of class — plan to spend the first ten or fifteen minutes of your meeting reviewing your assignment and setting goals for your meeting. Begin by having group members discuss the assignment and the tasks it involves. Which tasks need to be accomplished now, and which ones can wait until later? How should these responsibilities be divided among group members?

4. *Develop Ways to Encourage Productive Conflict.*

■ "Two heads are better than one," the proverb reminds us — and that's because when two or more people get together to discuss an issue or solve a problem, they naturally have different ways of analyzing a topic or of approaching a problem. The diverse perspectives and strategies that people bring to a problem or task are one of the main reasons why group activities are so productive. Capitalize on these differences. Encourage the discussion of new ideas. Consider alternative approaches to your subject. Don't be afraid to disagree; doing so may enable your group to find a more creative solution to a problem, to discover a new and stimulating response to a question. Just be sure that your discussion remains both friendly and focused on the task at hand.

Not all conflict is productive, of course. If personality conflicts prevent effective discussion about the writing to be done, your group is wasting time that could be better used for writing. Unproductive conflict erodes the effectiveness of your group; productive conflict enables your group to maximize your creativity and draw on all of your shared resources.

5. *Be Realistic about the Advantages and Disadvantages of Group Learning Activities.* No method is perfect, and group work is no exception. But group learning does bring many benefits:

■ Groups inevitably have greater resources than individuals.

■ Groups can employ more complex problem-solving methods than individuals.

(continued)

(continued)

- Working in groups can help you learn more effectively and efficiently.

- Participating in group activities can help prepare you for on-the-job teamwork.

- By responding as writers and readers, groups can give members immediate and meaningful responses to their writing and helpful suggestions for revision.

Group learning also brings potential disadvantages:

- It can take longer to achieve consensus or solve a problem, usually because members of a group examine more options and look at a problem from more angles than a single person would.

- Individual group members may not always be prepared, or they may try to dominate or withdraw from discussion.

- Group members may not share responsibility for a project equitably.

Most problems can be avoided if all participate fully in group activities and respond to problems when they occur. Groups are, after all, a bit like friendships or marriages: They develop and change; they require care and attention. Problems can arise, but if you're committed to keeping the group going, alert to signs of potential trouble, and willing to talk problems out, you can all benefit from group work.

FOR GROUP WORK

If your instructor has divided your class into groups, meet with your group to discuss how you can most effectively work as a team. Begin your meeting by exchanging names, phone numbers, and (if you have them) email addresses; take time just to chat and get to know each other. You might also see if your group can formulate some friendly rules to guide group activities. You might all agree, for instance, to notify at least one member if you can't make a group meeting. Try to anticipate some of the problems you may have working together, such as coordinating schedules, and discuss how to resolve them.

FOR THOUGHT, DISCUSSION, AND WRITING

1. Now that you have read this first chapter, set some goals for yourself as a writer. Make a list of several goals you'd like to accomplish in your composition class this term. Then write a paragraph or more discussing how you plan to achieve these goals.

2. Interview one or more students in your current or prospective major. Ask about student writing in this field:

   > What kinds of writing are students required to do in classes in this field? Is this writing similar to the writing done professionally in this field? If not, how is it different?

   > How is their writing evaluated by their professors?

   > How well do the students interviewed feel that their composition classes prepared them for the writing they now do?

   > What advice about writing would they give to other students taking classes in this field?

   Your instructor may ask you to report the results of this interview to your class. Your instructor may also ask you to write an essay summarizing the results of your interview.

3. Reflect on your past experiences with group activities, and then freewrite for five to ten minutes in response to these questions: How would you describe your experience with group activities in the past? What factors contribute to making group activities successful or unsuccessful? What strengths do you feel you bring to group activities? What weaknesses? Your freewrite should give you valuable information that you can draw on when you work with others in your class or that you might share with other members of your group. Discussion of these questions should enable you to work together more productively and efficiently.

Understanding the Writing Process

Writing is hardly a mysterious activity, yet it is sometimes viewed as if it were. Many people seem to think that those who write well possess a magical power or talent. According to this view, people are either born with the ability to write well or not, and those who do write well find writing easy. They just sit down and the words and ideas begin to flow.

My own experiences as a writer, and those of my students, indicate that this popular stereotype simply isn't accurate. Successful writers work as hard on their writing as anyone else. Unlike less accomplished writers, however, successful writers develop strategies that enable them to cope with the complexities of writing and thus to experience the satisfaction of a job well done.

Here are two essays, one by a student writer, Mary Ellen Kacmarcik, and one by a professor of English, Burton Hatlen. In different ways, Kacmarcik and Hatlen each discuss what it means to be a writer and comment on their own development as writers. They also each make the point that, as Hatlen says, "writing is a craft, which can be learned by anyone willing to work at it." As you read their essays, ask yourself to what extent your own assumptions about writing and experiences as a writer resemble theirs. How are they different? See if you can recall specific experiences, such as those Kacmarcik and Hatlen describe in their essays, that played a critical role in your development as a writer or your understanding of writing.

A WRITER IS FORMED
by Mary Ellen Kacmarcik

The woman at the front of the room hardly resembled my idea of an English teacher. Her raggedy undershirt, heavy flannel jacket, disheveled pants, and braided, stringy hair gave her the appearance of having just returned from a backcountry expedition. And she was huge; she must have tipped the scales at well over two hundred pounds.

"My name is Harriet Jones," she said, "and this is English 111."

This was my introduction to college writing. Ten students had enrolled in this beginning composition class at Islands Community College. Like most of my classmates, I was returning to education after a period in the work force. I had spent one year at Western Washington University but had avoided writing classes. I discovered later, when I sent for my transcripts to apply to Oregon State University, that I had withdrawn from a writing course at Western. I have no memory of this. Did I drop it the first day, or did I struggle with an essay or two before giving up?

At any rate, I went to Alaska that summer to work in the seafood canneries. It was a trip I had planned with two friends during my senior year in high school. I expected to return to college in the fall with thousands of dollars in my bank account. The work was miserable, but I fell in love with remote Sitka, and I stayed. Time passed with adventures enough to fill a novel. I eventually landed a job I really wanted at Northern Lights Natural Foods, a small, family-owned natural foods store. That job inspired me to take a nutrition course at the community college. I realized during the course that some biology would help me understand nutrition, so I took biology the following semester. I began to consider a career in nutrition, which led me to apply to the Department of Foods and Nutrition at OSU. I wasn't ready to leave Sitka, however; I would work one more year and take a few more classes on the side.

That is how I came to be sitting in Ms. Jones's class, preparing myself for a relationship with an English grammar handbook. We were to respond to short stories, an exercise which in my experience was limited to junior high school book reports. Although I have always been an avid reader, I had given little thought to characters, conflicts, plots, and settings. So those early essays were on topics that did not interest me. I had never heard of a comma splice either, but Ms. Jones assured us that any paper containing one would be promptly rewarded with an E grade. I would agonize over blank pages, afraid to begin, afraid of saying the wrong thing, afraid of committing some technical error. I somehow managed to fill up the pages and hand in those early essays. Fortunately, Ms. Jones encouraged us to revise after she had graded our papers.

It turned out that she was also very willing to talk with us about writing. I discovered that this formidable woman was actually a caring, humorous person. The writing did not instantly become easier, though. During the second term, we worked on longer papers that required some research. We also did in-class assignments such as freewriting and essay exams. By the end of the term, I had finally become comfortable with putting my ideas on paper.

The year with Ms. Jones was great preparation for my studies at OSU. I learned the importance of editing my work and following conventions. I gained confidence in stating my views. I also learned that teachers are human and that most of them enjoy discussing projects with students outside of class.

In thinking about my history as a writer for this essay, I realized that I have always been a writer — even when I felt unconfident and out of practice. Letters to aunts, uncles, and grandparents were my earliest writings outside of schoolwork, and they have been the main link between my parents' families on the East Coast and my nuclear family here in the Northwest. These letters followed a set format for years:

Dear Aunt _____ (or Grandma),

How are you? I am fine. Thank you for the _____
_____ .

Love,
Mary Ellen

My letters have matured with me, and I consider them a sort of journal except that I mail this journal off in bits and pieces instead of keeping it to read later. My letters describe what I have been doing, how I feel about things, and what I plan to do. When I lived in Alaska, letters were my link to family and friends in Washington.

Another early writing experience was an expanded form of passing notes in school. A friend and I wrote notes to each other that often went on for pages, much of it nonsense and gossip. We would work on these packets for days before exchanging them. Now I can see that we were flexing and developing our writing muscles as well as building our friendship through the sharing of ideas.

Currently, I write the newsletter for a club I belong to, an activity I volunteered for to gain experience and to stay involved with writing. I would like to combine writing with nutrition as a career. (I considered a major in journalism, but I have a strong desire to learn everything I can about nutrition.) I would like to help people improve their health by sharing this knowledge with them. I still think of myself as someone who is going to write someday. But I have been writing because I wanted to ever since I learned how.

WRITING IS A CRAFT THAT CAN BE LEARNED, NOT AN EFFORTLESS OUTPOURING BY GENIUSES
by Burton Hatlen

A writer — that's what I would be when I grew up. I made that decision in 1952, when I was 16, along with what now seems to be half the people I knew at the time. We were all going to be "writers," whatever we meant by that.

I can't speak for my friends, but in my case, at least, being a writer meant living a certain kind of life. The setting would be Paris, *la rive gauche:* a sidewalk café. A man (with a beard, a beret dropping over his right eye, a turtleneck sweater, sandals, a pipe) is seated at a round table, a half-empty glass of red wine before him. There are other people around the table, but they are a little dim. And there is talk. Jung. Kafka. Anarchism. The decline of the West. But mostly there is that man. Me. Someday.

I didn't need anyone to tell me that the road from a dusty farming town in the Central Valley of California to that Paris café would be a long and difficult one. In fact, it was *supposed* to be long and difficult. "You must suffer, suffer" — so said a cartoon character of my youth to a would-be artist. And I had a real-life example of such suffering. When I was 10, my cousin brought her new husband, George, to town. George had actually been to Paris, and he was going to write a novel before returning there. Later, I heard my aunt tell my mother that she had read the manuscript of his novel. According to her, it was "filthy," and what was more, she whispered, she was sure George "drank." In any case, his novel remained unpublished and George never made it back to Paris. At some level I realized that his sad story augured ill for my own dreams of living the life of a writer in a 1950's version of Paris in the 20's.

Nevertheless, in 1956, after my junior year at Berkeley, I decided that if I was ever to become a writer, I'd better try to write. I spent five months working at various jobs, and when I had saved $500 I moved into a one-room apartment in San Francisco. By then the "renaissance" there was in full flower, and the city seemed to me a reasonable facsimile of Paris. In North Beach there were real cafés, where real poets — Kenneth Rexroth, Robert Duncan, Lawrence Ferlinghetti (who actually wore a beret) — sat around and talked. If location had anything to do with becoming a writer, San Francisco seemed the right place to be.

For three months, until my money ran out, I spent my evenings in North Beach and my days at the oilcloth-covered kitchen table in my apartment, writing. Or at least that's what I told myself I was doing. In fact, in those three months I managed to write only about three pages of what I called a novel. It was about a young man living alone in a San Francisco apartment, who looked into the sky one day, saw it split open, and went mad. I fussed for the first week or two over those pages, making sure that every word was *juste*. But I had never worked out a plot, and once the young man went mad, I didn't know what else to do with him.

I stopped writing, and devoted my days to reading — all of Dreiser, among other things. What I remember best about that time is not the few paragraphs I wrote, but the wonder I felt as I read the yellowing pages of my second-hand copy of *The Genius*.

In January I went back to Berkeley, and that spring, at the suggestion of one of my teachers, applied to graduate school. Over the next few years, the sidewalk café began to seem no more than an adolescent fantasy, and, before I knew it, I had become not a writer in Paris, but a teacher entangled in committee meetings and bureaucratic infighting.

What brought all this back to me was a conversation I had earlier this year with a one-time colleague of mine, the author of a respectable university-press book on Sir Thomas Browne and, in the days when we taught together, a tenured associate professor and a popular teacher of Shakespeare. A few years ago, at 44, he suddenly resigned his teaching position and moved to Boston, where, I heard later, he was working a couple of days a week as a waiter and spending the rest of his time writing. When I went to Boston last winter I looked him up.

We talked about his novel and my work. Then the conversation turned to our respective children, all of whom, we realized, had not only decided to become artists of one sort or another but, unlike us at their age, were actually *doing* so. I thought about the Paris café, and then I asked him what he had wanted to do with his life when he was 20.

"Actually," he said, "I wanted to live the way I'm living now — working at a nothing job that doesn't take anything out of me, and writing."

That was a pretty fair description of my own dream when I moved to that apartment in San Francisco. What had happened to it? I think the main reason that I never realized the dream was my mistaken notion of what it means to be a writer, which I had picked up partly from media images of Hemingway and Fitzgerald, Sartre and Camus, and partly from my teachers. Those influences had suggested that writing was something geniuses were somehow able to do without thinking about it; ordinary people dabbled at their peril. That writing is also a craft that can be learned, that a young person might decide to write and then systematically learn how to do so, was never so much as hinted at by anyone I knew. So, when the words for my novel did not automatically come pouring out of me, I had concluded that I must not be a writer.

In fact, I have over the years written enough poetry to make a good-sized book, and enough prose — if it were all gathered together — to make two or three. Yet I feel uncomfortable saying I'm a writer who teaches, preferring instead to see myself as a teacher who writes. Nevertheless, writing is clearly a major part of my life. Yes, I do feel some envy of my friend in Boston, who is at last doing what he dreamed of when he was 20. And no, I've never written that novel, because I still don't know how to go about it. If most of what I write is about other people's writing, that's all right, because through it I've found a way to share with others the wonder I felt 30 years ago as I read Dreiser.

Since then, I have gradually come to see that writing takes manifold forms, that the conception of writing as a hermetic mystery, which I picked up from my reading and my teachers in the 1950's, is not only wrong, but pernicious. It dishonors the writing that nongeniuses do and denies the hard work at the craft that is essential to all writing, even the writing of "geniuses." It caused my cousin's husband to decide that if he couldn't be a writer, he didn't want to be anything, and I think it caused me to waste several years chasing illusions.

The myth that real writing is the effortless outpouring of geniuses did not die in the 1950's. There is abundant evidence that it still persists — at least among my students, most of whom also dream that someone, someday, will find a spark of "genius" in what they write. As a teacher who writes (or a writer who teaches), I am becoming more and more convinced that it's my job to nurture the writer in every student, while at the same time making it clear that writing is a craft, which can be learned by anyone willing to work at it.

■ ■ ■

FOR EXPLORATION

After reading Kacmarcik's and Hatlen's essays, reflect on your own assumptions about writing and your experiences as a writer. To do so, set aside at least half an hour to respond (either by freewriting or jotting down notes) to the following questions:

1. What are your earliest memories of learning to write? Of reading?

2. How was writing viewed by your family and friends when you were growing up?

3. What role did reading play in your development as a writer?

4. Can you recall particular experiences in school or on the job that influenced your current attitude toward writing?

5. If you were to describe your history as a writer, what stages or periods in your development would you identify? Write a sentence or two briefly characterizing each stage or period.

6. What images come to mind when you hear the term *writer*?

7. What images come to mind when you think of yourself as a writer? You may find it easiest to draw up a list of metaphors, such as "As a writer, I'm a turtle — slow and steady" or "As a writer, I'm a racehorse — fast out of the gate but never sure if I've got the stamina to finish." Write two or three sentences that use images or metaphors to characterize your sense of yourself as a writer.

8. What kinds of writing have you come to enjoy? To dislike?

9. What do you enjoy most about the process of writing? What do you enjoy least?

10. What goals would you like to set for yourself as a writer?

FOR EXPLORATION

Using the information generated by the previous Exploration, write a letter to your classmates and teacher in which you describe who you are as a writer today — and how you got to be that way.

FOR GROUP WORK

Bring enough copies of the above letter to share with members of your group. After you have all read one another's letters, work together to answer the following questions. Choose one person to record the group's answers so that you can share the results of your discussion with the rest of the class.

1. To what extent are your attitudes toward writing and experiences as writers similar? List three to five statements about your attitudes toward and experiences as writers with which all group members can agree.

2. What factors account for the differences in your attitudes toward writing and experiences as writers? List two or three factors that you agree account for these differences.

3. What common goals can you set for yourselves as writers? List at least three goals you can agree on.

MANAGING THE WRITING PROCESS

Writing is not a magical process. Rather, it is a craft that can indeed be learned. But how do writers actually manage the writing process? Notice how differently the following six students say that they proceed.

> My writing starts with contemplation. I let the topic I have chosen sink into my mind for a while. Then I brainstorm on paper, coming up with words, phrases, and sentences that relate to my topic. It is usually during the brainstorming process that I find whether or not I have chosen the right topic. If I am not satisfied with my topic, I start over. Then I make a

simple plan for my essay, and then I start on my rough draft. Peer responses, final drafts, and revisions follow, sometimes with more brainstorming in between.

— EDITH CASTERLINE

I have to sit down with pen in hand and just write whatever comes out naturally. I then go back and work with what I've written.

— MICHELLE COLLUM

I have to think my ideas out in detail before I begin drafting. Only then can I begin writing and revising.

— MARSHA CARPER

When I write, I first brainstorm for an idea. This may take only a few minutes or days, depending on the kind of paper I'm working on. Once I get an idea, I then sit down and start writing. This seems to be the best way for me to get started. After I've written the rough draft, I then go back and do some major revision. I revise and have others check for mistakes I might have missed, and then I type it out.

— DAVE GUENTHER

As a writer, I am first a thinker and then a doer. I first think about my topic carefully, and then I write what I wish to say.

— GARY ETCHEMENDY

I write by coming up with a sketchy rough draft and then filling it in or changing it.

— PAUL AUSTIN

On the surface, these students' writing processes seem to have little in common. Actually, however, all involve the same three activities: planning, drafting, and revising. These activities don't necessarily occur in any set order. Michelle Collum postpones most of her planning until after she has generated a rough draft, for example, whereas Marsha Carper plans extensively before she writes her first word. To be successful, however, all these writers must sooner or later think critically and make choices about words, ideas, and anticipated responses of readers. Then they must try out these choices in their heads, on paper, or at the computer, evaluate the effects of these choices, and make appropriate changes in their drafts. Rather than being a magical or mysterious activity, then, writing is a process of planning, drafting, and revising.

Identifying Composing Styles

The preceding description of planning, drafting, and revising may make writing sound neater and more predictable than it actually is. Writing is, in fact, a messy and often unpredictable process. Even though all writers engage in planning, drafting, and revising, they do so in a variety of ways. Furthermore, no one approaches every writing task in the same way. (For this reason, it is more accurate to refer to writing *processes* rather than the writing process.) Instead, a writer will decide how to approach a writing assignment based on such factors as the nature and importance of the writing task, the schedule, the experience the writer has with a particular kind of writing, and so on.

Most experienced writers do, however, have a preferred way of managing the writing process. Some writers devote the most energy to planning, while others focus more on revising. Still others focus equally on planning, drafting, and revising.

Heavy Planners. Like Marsha Carper and Gary Etchemendy, heavy planners generally consider their ideas and plan their writing so carefully in their heads that their first drafts are often more like other writers' second or third drafts. As a consequence, they often revise less intensively and frequently than other students. Many of these students have disciplined themselves so that they can think about their writing in all sorts of places — on the subway, at work, in the garden pulling weeds, or in the car driving to and from school.

Some heavy planners write in this way because they prefer to; others develop this strategy out of necessity. Marsha Carper, for instance, says that she simply has to do a great deal of her writing "in her head" rather than on paper because she lives fifty miles from the university and must spend considerable time commuting. In addition, she's a mother as well as a student, and at home she often has to steal odd moments to work on her writing. As a result, she's learned to use every opportunity to think about her writing while she drives, cooks, or relaxes with her family.

Heavy Revisers. Like Michelle Collum and Paul Austin, heavy revisers need to find out what they want to say through the act of writing itself. When faced with a writing task, they prefer to sit down at a desk or computer and just begin writing.

Heavy revisers often state that writing their ideas out in a sustained spurt of activity reassures them that they have something to say and helps them avoid frustration. These students may not seem to plan because they begin drafting so early. Actually, however, their planning occurs as they draft and especially as they revise. Heavy revisers typically spend a great deal of their writing time revising their initial drafts. To do so effectively, they must be able to read their work critically and be able, often, to discard substantial portions of first drafts.

As you've probably realized, in both of these styles of composing, one of the components of the writing process is apparently abbreviated. Heavy planners don't seem to revise as extensively as other writers. Actually, however, they plan (and, in effect, revise) so thoroughly early in the process that they often don't need to revise as intensively later. Similarly, heavy revisers may not seem to plan; in fact, though, once they write their rough drafts, they plan and revise simultaneously and often extensively.

Sequential Composers.   A third general style of composing is exemplified by Dave Guenther and Edith Casterline. These writers might best be called sequential composers because they devote roughly equivalent amounts of time to planning, drafting, and revising. Rather than trying out their ideas and planning their writing mentally, as heavy planners do, sequential composers typically rely on written notes and plans to give shape and force to their ideas. And unlike heavy revisers, sequential composers need to have greater control over form and subject matter as they draft.

Sequential composers' habit of allotting time for planning, drafting, and revising helps them deal with the inevitable anxieties of writing. Like heavy revisers, sequential composers need the reassurance of seeing their ideas written down: Generating a volume of notes and plans gives them the confidence to begin drafting. Sequential composers may not revise as extensively as heavy revisers, for they generally draft more slowly, reviewing their writing as they proceed. But revision is nevertheless an important part of their composing process; like most writers, sequential composers need a break from drafting to be able to critique their own words and ideas.

Each of these composing styles has advantages and disadvantages. Heavy planners can be efficient writers, spending less time drafting and revising than do other writers, but they must have great mental discipline. An unexpected interruption when they are working out their ideas — a child in tears, a phone call — can cause even the most disciplined thinker to have a momentary lapse. Because so much of their work is done in their heads, heavy planners are less likely to benefit from the fruitful explorations and revisions that occur when writers review notes and plans or reread their own texts. And because heavy planners put off drafting until relatively late in the composing process, they can encounter substantial difficulties if the sentences and paragraphs that had seemed so clearly developed in their minds don't look as coherent and polished on paper.

Heavy revisers experience different advantages and disadvantages. Because they write quickly and voluminously, heavy revisers aren't in danger of losing valuable ideas. Similarly, their frequent rereading of their drafts helps them remain open to new options that can improve their writing. However, heavy revisers must learn how to deal with emotional highs and lows that occur as they discover what they want to say through the process of writing itself. They must be able ruthlessly to critique their own writing, discarding large portions of text or perhaps starting over if necessary. And because they revise so extensively, heavy revisers must be careful to leave adequate time for revision or the quality of their work can suffer.

What about sequential composers? Because they plan to spend time planning, drafting, and revising — and do so primarily in writing — they have more external control over the writing process than heavy planners and revisers have. Sequential composers are also unlikely to fool themselves into thinking that a quickly generated collection of ideas is an adequate rough draft or that a plan brainstormed while taking the subway is adequate preparation for writing. Sequential composers can, however, develop inefficiently rigid habits — habits that reflect their need to have external control over their writing process. They may, for instance, waste valuable time developing detailed written plans when they're actually ready to begin drafting.

Good writers are aware of their preferred composing style — and of its potential advantages and disadvantages. They take responsibility for decisions about how to manage their writing, recognizing the difference, for instance, between the necessary incubation of ideas and procrastination. Good writers are also flexible; depending on the task or situation, they can modify their preferred approach. A person who generally is a heavy reviser when writing academic essays, for instance, might write routine business memos in a single sitting because that is the most efficient way to get the job done. Similarly, heavy planners who prefer to do much of the work of writing mentally must employ different strategies when writing collaboratively with others, or when engaged in research-based writing.

There is one other common way of managing the writing process — though it might best be described as management by avoidance — procrastination. All writers occasionally procrastinate, but if you habitually put off writing a first draft until you have time only for a *final* draft (and this at 3 A.M. on the day your essay is due), your chances of success are minimal. Though you may have invented good reasons for putting off writing — "I write better under pressure"; "I can't write until I have all my easier assignments done first" — procrastination makes it difficult for you to manage the writing process in an efficient and effective manner.

Is procrastination always harmful? Might it not sometimes be a period of necessary incubation, of unconscious but still productive planning? Here's what one thoughtful student writer discovered about her own tendency to procrastinate:

> For me, sometimes procrastination isn't really procrastination (or so I tell myself). Sometimes what I label procrastination is really planning. The trouble is that I don't always know when it's one or the other. . . .
>
> How do I procrastinate? Let me count the ways. I procrastinate by doing good works (helping overtime at my job, cleaning house, aiding and abetting a variety of causes). I procrastinate by absorbing myself in a purely selfish activity (reading paperbacks, watching TV, going to movies). I procrastinate by visiting with friends, talking on the telephone,

prolonging chance encounters. I procrastinate by eating and drinking (ice cream, coffee, cookies — all detrimental). Finally, I procrastinate by convincing myself that this time of day is not when I write well. I'd be much better off, I usually conclude, taking a nap. So I do.

Part of my difficulty is that I can see a certain validity in most of my reasons for procrastinating. There are some times of day when my thoughts flow better. I have forced myself to write papers in the past when I just didn't feel fluid. Not only were the papers difficult to write, they were poorly written, inarticulate papers. Even after several rewrites, they were merely marginal. I would much rather write when I am at my mental best.

I need to balance writing with other activities. The trouble is — just how to achieve the perfect balance!

— HOLLY HARDIN

Holly's realistic appraisal of the role that procrastination plays in her writing process should help her distinguish between useful incubation and unhelpful procrastination. Unlike students who tell themselves that they should never procrastinate — and then do so anyway, feeling guilty every moment — Holly knows that she has to consider a variety of factors before she decides to invite a friend to tea, bake a batch of chocolate chip cookies, or take a much-needed nap.

Analyzing Your Composing Process

The poet William Stafford once commented that "a writer is not so much someone who has something to say as he is someone who has found a process that will bring about new things he would not have thought if he had not started to say them." Stafford's remarks emphasize the importance of developing a workable writing process — a repertoire of strategies that you can draw on in a variety of situations.

■ GUIDELINES FOR ANALYZING YOUR COMPOSING PROCESS

The following guidelines provide questions you can use to describe and evaluate your current composing strategies. Respond in writing to each of these questions.

(continued)

(continued)

1. What is your general attitude toward writing? How do you think this attitude affects the writing you do?

2. Which of the composing styles described in this chapter best describes the way you compose? If none seems to fit you, how do you compose?

3. How do you know when you are ready to begin writing? Do you have a regular "start-up" method or ritual?

4. How long do you typically work on your writing at any one time? Are you more likely to try to write an essay in a single sitting, or do you prefer to work on your writing over a number of days (or weeks)?

5. Has the availability of word processing and online technologies such as the Internet influenced your composing process? How?

6. What planning and revising strategies do you use? How do you know when you have spent enough time planning and revising?

7. What role do exchanges with others (such as conversations about your writing or responses to work in progress) typically play in your writing?

8. How do you procrastinate? (Be honest! All writers procrastinate occasionally.)

9. Are you aware of having preferred writing habits and rituals? What are they? Which are productive and supportive? Which interfere with or lessen the efficiency of your writing process?

10. Thinking in general about the writing you do, what do you find most rewarding and satisfying about writing? Most difficult and frustrating? Why?

FOR GROUP WORK

Meet with classmates to discuss your responses to the composing process questions. Begin your discussion by having each person state two important things he or she learned as a result of completing the analysis. (Appoint a recorder to write down each person's statements.) Once all members of your group have spoken, ask the recorder to read their statements aloud. Were any statements repeated by more than one member of the group? Working as a group, formulate two conclusions about the writing process based on your discussion that you would like to share with the class. (Avoid vague and general assertions, such as "Writing is difficult.") Be prepared to discuss your conclusions with your classmates.

Keeping a Writer's Notebook

Many writers keep journals or notebooks. Some writers may focus on work in progress, jotting down ideas, descriptions, or bits of conversation. Others use their journals or notebooks to reflect on their own experiences as writers. Holly Hardin's discussion of procrastination was, in fact, an entry from her notebook. You may want to record your responses to the Exploration exercises in this book in your own writer's notebook. Your teacher may also ask you to include entries from your writer's notebook in a portfolio of your written work.

Whatever is recorded, a writer's notebook serves a single purpose — to help the writer — so if you keep a notebook, it should reflect your own interests and needs. Your notebook may be a nicely bound blank book or a spiral notebook, whatever seems most inviting to you. If you write on a computer, you might want to keep your notebook on a disk and print copies at regular intervals. The following guidelines suggest possible uses for your writer's notebook.

■ GUIDELINES FOR KEEPING A WRITER'S NOTEBOOK

Use your writer's notebook to

- Ask yourself questions
- Reflect on your writing process
- Record your thoughts about current writing projects
- Brainstorm in response to an assignment
- Record possible ideas for future writing projects
- Note details, arguments, or examples for particular writing projects
- Try out various introductions or conclusions

(continued)

(continued)

- Play with imagery or figurative language such as similes or metaphors

- Map out a plan for a writing project

- Express your frustrations or satisfactions with your writing

- Keep schedules for writing projects

- Preserve random thoughts about work in progress

- Freewrite about an idea or a topic

- Copy phrases, sentences, or passages that impress you as particularly effective models for imitation or analysis

- Think about what you have learned about writing

- Reflect on the relationship between your reading and writing processes

FOR EXPLORATION

If you are not already doing so, try keeping a writer's notebook for two weeks. At the end of this period, consider the following questions: Did keeping a notebook help you come up with ideas for writing? (Can you find two or three entries that you could possibly develop into an essay?) Has your notebook given you any insights into how you manage the writing process? Did you enjoy writing in your notebook?

Developing Productive Writing Habits and Rituals

Scratch a writer and you'll discover a person with decided habits and rituals. Professional writers are often particularly conscious of their writing habits and rituals. All writers, however, have some predispositions that affect their writing. Some people write best early in the morning; others, late at night. Some require a quiet atmosphere; others find the absence of noise or music distracting. Some people can compose only by writing longhand; others can't imagine writing without a computer. People have different ways of telling themselves that they are ready to write. Clearing my desk of its usual clutter is one way that I tell myself it's time to get serious. Here is how two students describe their start-up writing rituals:

Exercise immediately before working on a paper seems to provide me mental, as well as physical, stimulation. After I run, I tackle a first draft with incredible PMA (positive mental attitude). The head of steam I build during my run (the natural "runner's high") tides me over to at least the second or third page of my first draft. Finishing most papers after that point is usually not a big problem. While I exercise, I spend as much time as I can thinking about new analogies or visualizing the paper's organization and flow. I think about the most basic message that I want my reader to get. If I were to summarize each paragraph in one sentence, I think to myself, what would the sentence say? Is there anything I can eliminate?

Sometimes I think about a chosen audience for the topic. If I were to tell them about the subject face-to-face would my message change? What would I say? What would they most easily understand?

Near the end of my run, I think about how good the paper will be — I hone my expectations. This cheerleading pushes me through the front door and straight to my desk. I can hardly wait to get started. I'm almost afraid the ideas I generated will escape me before I can corner them on paper.

I don't know whether the final product of this process is any better than it might otherwise have been, but it eases the pain of first-draft compositions. I produce a draft more confidently and more quickly than I would by sitting down and hacking away at it.

— HOLLY HARDIN

Most of my writing begins at the kitchen sink. After the dishes are drying in the rack and the living room is in order, I head for my bedroom — where I do my writing — and make the bed, fold socks, empty the trash, and straighten anything that looks at all out of order. Throughout the final stage of this ritual I am spiraling inward toward my writing desk, the last place I clean. When the desk is bare except for my computer, a handbook, and two dictionaries (a paperback for quick spelling references and a hardcover for bigger jobs), I sit down and begin contemplating the task at hand. Following the premise that the mind will take up the discipline put on the body and surroundings, the process of organization moves from the outside inward until I'm sitting in front of the computer sharpening a pencil with my pocketknife. Cleaning house is also a good way to work out the "prewrite jitters" and let me think casually about what I want or need to write. With the house straight at a quiet hour, I start on the first drafts of an introductory paragraph. Now the process has moved out again in a form that I can store, mull over, scribble on, and type again in a new draft. I'm off!

— TOM GRENIER

Though Holly and Tom take two very different approaches, they both emphasize the ways in which their particular rituals help them cope with the "prewrite jitters." Productive writing rituals like these are a positive way of pampering yourself — of creating the environment most conducive to writing.

WRITING IN AN AGE OF COMPUTER AND ONLINE TECHNOLOGIES

As a student, you are undoubtedly already aware of the many ways that electronic technologies are influencing our lives. Chapter 7, "Negotiating Online Writing Situations," discusses some of the opportunities and constraints inherent in such media as email and hypertext. You may be aware, for instance, that users of email have developed an elaborate "netiquette" to guide their communications. Chapter 7 helps you understand the *rhetorical* reasons why these conventions have developed and provides guidelines you can employ as you take advantage of these new opportunities to communicate with others.

Whether you have explored email or the World Wide Web, you have probably already benefited from computers' word processing capabilities. Those who find pen or pencil drafting a slow process often marvel at the ease with which word processing enables them to generate text. Many writers report that composing at the computer encourages them to be creative and to revise more easily and effectively. And as companies produce increasingly sophisticated and powerful computers and software, word processing programs offer a variety of options in addition to such traditional features as a spellchecker and a thesaurus. Programs with window or split-screen capability, for instance, allow you to look at two sections of a text at the same time, and computer graphics programs allow you to include computer-generated charts, graphs, diagrams, and even artwork in your writing. The following suggestions will make the process of writing with a computer especially productive.

■ GUIDELINES FOR WRITING WITH A COMPUTER

---

1. *Find Your Own Best Way.* Some people reserve the computer for typing up and printing documents they have already written by hand. They may make minor revisions at the computer, but they generally make major revisions on their printed texts by hand and then enter the changes into the computer. Others actually compose at the computer. A writer might brainstorm at the computer, for instance, and then use the word processing program's split-screen option to keep these notes onscreen as a guide while writing. As you might expect, heavy revisers adapt particularly easily to

(continued)

(continued)

composing at the keyboard. Take the time to explore the options available to you and find those best suited to your own needs.

2. *Recognize the Limitations of Onscreen Revision.* Computers can make revision easier and faster, but they have potential limitations as well. Sometimes writers, seduced by the ease with which they can change things on the computer, focus too much on minor stylistic modifications instead of organization or development of ideas. Many writers find that to evaluate these more global aspects of their writing, they must work with hard copy. Because of the small size of the computer monitor's screen, it can be difficult to grasp the big picture — yet effective writing depends on just this ability.

   When you print drafts of an essay to read and revise, be sure to save these earlier versions. You may decide that an introduction that you rejected in favor of a later version was best after all. Leaving a "paper trail" makes it easy to reinsert your original introduction.

3. *Take Advantage of the Useful Features That Many Word Processing Programs Provide.* Some writers use their computers as glorified typewriters, primarily to ease the burden of producing neatly printed texts. But most computer programs offer a number of features that can make writing easier and more productive. In addition to window or split-screen options, some programs allow you to write notes or directions that appear onscreen but not in the printed text; this feature allows you to interact with your own writing without cluttering up drafts with comments that must be deleted later. Your program's BLOCK and MOVE (or CUT and PASTE) functions enable you to move sections of text easily, and the SEARCH function makes it possible to locate every instance of a word or phrase. You can use this function when editing to check that you haven't overused a word or to correct a misspelled word used several times in a draft. Many word processing programs have SAVE AS functions that enable you to try a potentially risky revision without endangering your original. Finally, if you are fortunate enough to have access to networked computers, you can benefit from electronic collaboration. Such networks enable you to get onscreen responses to work in progress; they also make group-writing projects easier and more productive.

(continued)

(continued)

4. *Use the Resources Available to You on the World Wide Web — but Use Them Responsibly.* Ten years ago, most personal computers were used primarily for word processing, desktop publishing, and related activities. But with the rise of the Internet and World Wide Web, computers increasingly serve as information conduits, bringing previously unimaginable resources to writers and readers. A student writing an essay on the Pre-Raphaelite painter Dante Gabriel Rossetti can easily locate a reproduction of one of his paintings on the Web, download it, and include it in an essay. If the student is constructing a Web site on this topic, he has access to even greater resources. He could, for instance, find a multimedia presentation on the textile workshop of William Morris, a fellow Pre-Raphaelite and friend of Rossetti's. The student could download this presentation and include it on his site.

The student could do this — but *should* he? To answer this question, writers need to understand that just as print texts can be — and often are — protected by copyright laws, so are online texts and multimedia documents. The exact nature of this protection is still unclear: The development of the Web has raised many questions about the applicability of copyright laws to Web-based materials. These questions will be addressed by the courts in coming years. For the present, you should probably assume that most materials on the Web fall under copyright protection — unless the site clearly indicates otherwise.

Does this mean that you can't include a film clip or a reproduction of an artwork in your writing after all? Not necessarily. Some Web sites, including many government sites, specifically state that information and images presented therein can be downloaded and used. Moreover, just as print documents and images that are more than seventy-five years old are considered to be "in the public domain" and can be used by anyone, so too is the case for such materials reproduced on the Web. The Web includes also many sites devoted to "clip art" — icons, backgrounds, and textures. These items are designed specifically for others to use, though some require acknowledgment of the source. Finally, if a site contains information or images that may be copyright-protected but could enrich your writing, you always have the option of writing to the person or organization that has posted the Web site and requesting permission to use the items in which you are interested.

The development of online technologies provides new opportunities, as well as potential dangers and difficulties, for writers. But has it changed the essential nature of writing or simply provided new possibilities for and means of expression? To answer this question, I contacted Mary Ellen Kacmarcik Gates and Burton Hatlen, the authors of the essays you read at the start of this chapter. I asked these writers to reflect on the ways in which computer and online technologies have changed their writing practices — and their sense of themselves as writers. Here are their responses to this question. (Before presenting their comments, I should note that after graduating from Oregon State University, Mary Ellen married, had two daughters, and worked for a time in the field of foods and nutrition. Most recently, Mary Ellen has been a stay-at-home mother homeschooling her daughters and participating in a variety of volunteer activities. Burton Hatlen continues to teach at the University of Maine.)

WRITING IN THE AGE OF THE INTERNET
by Mary Ellen Kacmarcik Gates

I think of a dozen beginnings for my first formal essay since college. Then I get stuck, so I sit down at the keyboard and jot ideas. Over the next week or two I open up the document and add to it — deleting this, moving that. As I do so, I become increasingly aware of how dependent I have become not only on word processing but on having access to the Internet and the World Wide Web. In my daily life, I do a fair amount of writing, including editing a monthly newsletter for a homeschool support group. Producing the newsletter has challenged me to increase my computer and online skills. Now I can send attachments via email, download materials from the World Wide Web, and insert them into word processed texts. I've become acquainted with folders, jpeg files, and hyperlinks.

Reading and writing email has become an essential part of my daily routine. Early in the morning, when my husband has left for work and the girls are still asleep, I turn on my computer. "Would you like to check to see if you have any new mail now?" the computer asks me. I click yes and wait eagerly for the messages. Email is great — it's like a post card. I can write a few sentences or a one-word reply and send it off. I worry sometimes, though, that email is too easy. I read a message, write a reply, send it — and it's out there for all the world to see. Sometimes after sending a message I realize that I didn't say what I meant to or that I said something that I really wouldn't want anyone else but the person I'm emailing to read, but it's too late. Of course, when I write to my mother, other family members, and friends, the stakes aren't too high. When I'm participating in an online discussion among members of my La Leche League group or some other sort of public forum, I try to be much more careful.

Email has become an essential part of my life, but I also do a good deal of reading online. I subscribe to an online newsletter for homeschoolers. The hostess of my monthly book club has a Web site where she sells discussion guides for members. I appreciate getting her guides online — but I appreciate even more getting together with the other members of my group to talk about the book we're discussing. I like the fact that when we get together there is no right or wrong answer. (What is the significance of the snow in *Snow Falling on Cedars*? I don't know. I don't care!) We use the discussion guides as springboards for discussion; it is assigned reading I look forward to.

Thinking about my book club reminds me that although reading and writing online have become central to my life, I have hardly abandoned print texts. At home there is so much to read — books, journals, newsletters (not to mention the ever present junk mail) — that it piles up everywhere. I am usually reading two library books at a time, one by the bed and another on the coffee table. My daughters don't know how to fall asleep without having a story read to them. I read some things — like the two bimonthly journals I receive from the La Leche League — with great care. Others, such as the newspaper, are skimmed. A letter from a friend is always a treasured gift.

When I think of letters, I think of my grandmother — and of a very special gift she left me. My grandmother died a few months ago, and when I learned that she had left me money in her will, I decided immediately to use the money to buy a better computer. This gift allows me to work faster and more efficiently online and to keep in touch with family and friends through email. Sometimes when I'm at the computer, I think of my grandmother. Snail mail letters, not emails, were the link that kept our relationship going. I'd seen my grandmother only once since 1962, so it was our letters over the years that created a bond between us.

What would my grandmother think of email? In recent years she was aware of computers, but she preferred not to learn how to use them. It would have been convenient to be able to email my grandmother, rather than writing my thoughts out longhand. But I don't think it would have changed our relationship or the thoughts I shared with her. For as much as having access to computer and online technologies has affected who I am as a writer and the processes I use when I write, some things remain the same. Whether I'm emailing a friend or writing a handwritten letter, what is most important to me are the ideas I am sharing.

Recently, a friend asked me to write words of wisdom for her daughter Brittany. She is collecting them in a special book to present to her daughter on her thirteenth birthday. My friend is younger than I am, yet she is years ahead of me in her parenting journey. I look to her as a mentor in my mothering. What will her daughter think of my advice? I struggle to think of what to say and how to say it. The pressure of writing something not just clever but wise hangs over me. That is when I remember that I don't have to get my writing perfect the first time. I just have to think, write, think, write, produce a draft, revise, think some more, write some more. Some writing takes more time, more drafts. (In situations like this, I'm especially grateful for word processing.) Some texts — like most of my emails — are written quickly. But despite computers, despite the Internet and all that it allows me to do, the basic process hasn't changed that much. The things that are are difficult about writing, like struggling to articulate my ideas in the clearest and most persuasive way, remain difficult. And the pleasures of accomplishing the task remain as well.

FROM OLIVETTI TO iMAC: TECHNOLOGY AS MEANS, NOT END
by Burton Hatlen

In 1953, when I left home for college (home was a farmhouse in the Central Valley of California, and college was Occidental College in Los Angeles), my parents gave me an Olivetti portable typewriter. I wrote all my college papers on this typewriter, along with weekly letters home to my parents, always composing directly on the machine; and five years later, I carried my Olivetti with me when I went east to graduate school, first at Columbia and then at Harvard. The Olivetti was a state-of-the-art machine in 1953, but it regularly jammed up when one of my large and clumsy fingers hit two keys simultaneously, and over the years the "e" wore away until it was almost illegible. Eventually, therefore, other typewriters entered my life. In the late 1960s I acquired an IBM electric typewriter, which employed a then-revolutionary technology: rather than a separate arm for each type slug, all the letters were on a single round ball, which spun and danced across the page, in response to my keystrokes. Between 1967 and 1971 I wrote my doctoral dissertation on this machine, at a desk in the living room of a farmhouse in Maine. And yes, the writing process extended to four years, at least in part because I found it impossible to let go of a page until it was free of all typing errors: if I chanced to hit the "r" when I was aiming for the "t" key, I compulsively retyped the entire page. I managed to finish the dissertation, eventually, and in the early 1970s I got tenure in the English department of the University of Maine. But for several years thereafter I wrote little prose because it was simply too much work. Instead I wrote poetry, where my typing habits actually served me well, as I carefully weighed each keystroke.

Somewhere around 1975, however, the English department secretary, Marilyn Emerick, let it be known that she was willing to type manuscripts for faculty, and suddenly I was liberated from the typewriter. She had a miraculous new machine, a correcting typewriter. And she was willing to decipher page after page of my handwritten scrawl. I can type, whether on a typewriter or on a computer, much faster than I can write by hand, but Marilyn's assistance meant that I no longer needed to worry about producing immaculate pages of text. Furthermore, the sheer muscular experience of propelling the ballpoint pen across the page seemed gloriously liberating, and the words began to pour out of me. I still had a typewriter in my office, but I rarely used it. For nearly ten years, Marilyn, who could type 140 words per minute, served as the essential intermediary for everything that I wrote.

And then, in 1983, during a summer of teaching at the Bard College Institute of Writing and Thinking, I met my first computer. Macintosh had donated a dozen or so computers to Bard, to be used for writing instruction; and, of course, if we on the faculty were to teach our students how to use these machines, we ourselves had to learn how to write on them. Within three weeks I was hooked, and I returned to the University of Maine that fall as a dedicated apostle of the computer revolution. Quite simply, the computer allowed me to write at full speed, without the hand cramps that would sometimes afflict me in my handwriting period, but it *also* allowed me to correct freely: not merely to clean up typos but also to engage in real revision, as I added, deleted, or moved about entire blocks of text. By 1985 I was doing all of my writing on a computer, and my writing habits have not changed significantly since then. Occasionally, I will still make a few notes in longhand, but these days when I am moved to write, I shift over almost immediately to the computer: at the moment, an iMac at home and a Macintosh G4 in the office.

And then there's email. Today, a Sunday, I've sent off three personal email messages, responded to three inquiries from students, and posted a boilerplate letter of invitation to twelve potential participants in a conference that I am organizing. Now, as the day draws to a close, I'm writing a few paragraphs on my writing habits, in response to a request from the author of this book, and I'll post these comments to her via email. That's a relatively light email day for me: I estimate that I normally spend at least two hours a day on email, sending and receiving from ten to twenty messages. I organize email conferences in all of my courses; and in one course that I am currently teaching, a distance education course, I communicate with the students largely by email. I edit a scholarly journal, and I communicate with contributors largely via email. As secretary of the Ezra Pound Society, a group devoted to the study of this poet's work, I am the "owner" of a listserv that generates from three or four to a dozen or so postings every day. I chair two university committees, and I organize our meetings via email. I regularly use email to organize panels at national conferences. These days, when I write an article, I often send it to an editor via email. Email has brought about a communications revolution, radically increasing the speed at which we can communicate information, person to person, around the world.

But has email changed the way I write? I don't believe so. In fact, I find myself resisting certain modes of discourse that seem to me too characteristic of the email culture: a tendency to shoot from the hip, a failure to think through issues carefully. Still, every day I'm online, trying to keep up with a world that seems to be spinning faster and faster.

Trying to keep up — that, I suppose, is what I've mostly been doing, all along. That Olivetti typewriter on which, almost fifty years ago now, in a dormitory room at Occidental College, I typed out letters to my parents back on the farm or essays that tried to puzzle out why Raskolnikov murdered those old women, seems today like a quaint relic of a world before the flood. (And what *did* happen to that typewriter, anyway? Did I give it away? Abandon it in a closet, when I left Boston for basic training at Fort Dix? I can't remember.) Still, the young man who wrote those letters and essays wasn't, as far as I can tell, so very different from the students who arrive, year after year, in my classrooms. Like them, he was trying to figure out how to do the right thing, in a world where that's never easy. Technology is always a means, never an end. Email can send our words around the world in a flash, but it cannot ensure that these words will be worth reading. "Ripeness is all," says Edgar to his dying father in Shakespeare's *King Lear,* and it still takes a lifetime to ripen into something like wisdom.

As these two writers' essays suggest, though computer and online technologies certainly offer many new opportunities for writers, they do not change the basic facts of a writer's life. Whether you are writing a letter by hand, word processing an essay, or composing an email message, as a writer you still need to take responsibility both for your writing process and for the results of that process. By reflecting on your own writing process and developing productive writing habits and rituals, you can meet the challenges you will face as a writer. As you do so, you will have the satisfaction of knowing (as Burton Hatlen observed earlier in this chapter) that writing is indeed a craft that can be learned, not an effortless outpouring by geniuses.

■ ■ ■

FOR THOUGHT, DISCUSSION, AND WRITING

1. You can learn a great deal about your own composing process by observing yourself as you write. To do so, follow these steps:

Choose an upcoming writing project to study. Before beginning this project, reflect on it and its demands. How much time do you expect to spend working on this project, and how do you anticipate allocating your time? What challenges does this project hold for you? What particular strengths and resources do you bring to this project?

As you work on the project, keep track of how you spend your time. Include a record of when you started and ended each work section as well as a description of your activities and a paragraph commenting on your process. What went well? What surprised you? What gave you problems? What might you do differently next time?

After you have completed the project, draw on your prewriting analysis and process log to write a case study of this specific project. In developing your case study, consider questions such as these: To what extent was your prewriting analysis of your project accurate? How did you actually allocate your time when working on this project? What strategies did you rely on most heavily? What went well with your writing? What was difficult? Conclude by reflecting about what you have learned from this case study about yourself as a writer.

2. All writers procrastinate occasionally — some just procrastinate more effectively than others. After brainstorming or freewriting about your favorite ways of procrastinating, write a humorous or serious essay on procrastination.

3. You can learn a great deal about writing by reading interviews with professional writers. Choose one of the following collections, and read two interviews. While reading them, try to think of the ways the statements these writers make might — and might not — apply to your own writing.

> *The True Subject: Writers on Life and Craft.* Edited by Kurt Brown. St. Paul: Greywolf Press, 1993.

> *Writers at Work: The Paris Review Interviews.* First series. Edited by Malcolm Cowley. New York: Viking, 1958.

> *Writers at Work: The Paris Review Interviews.* Subsequent series edited by George Plimpton. New York: Viking, 1963, 1967, 1976, and 1981.

> *The Writer on Her Work.* Edited by Janet Sternburg. New York: Norton, 1980.

The Writer on Her Work. Vol. 2, *New Essays in New Territory.* Edited by Janet Sternburg. New York: Norton, 1991.

The Writer's Craft. Edited by John Hersey. New York: Knopf, 1974.

4. The Exploration activities on pp. 27 and 28 encouraged you to reflect on your assumptions about writing and your experiences as a writer. Drawing on these activities and on the rest of the chapter, write an essay in which you reflect on this subject.

Understanding the Reading Process

Why do people read? Not surprisingly, people read for as many different reasons and in as many different contexts as they write. They read to gain information — to learn how to program their VCR or to make decisions about whether to attend a movie or purchase a new product. They read for pleasure. Whether surfing the Web or reading a novel, people enjoy immersing themselves in the lives and words of others. They read to engage in extended conversations with others about issues or questions of importance to them, such as ecology, U.S. policy in the Middle East, or contemporary music. In all of these ways, people read to enlarge their world, to experience new ways of thinking and also of being and acting.

Recent developments in such online technologies as email and the World Wide Web provide a striking confirmation of the preceding observation. As anyone who has ever participated in the whirl of a chat-room conversation knows, those communicating online can — and sometimes do — use the anonymity of email to try out new identities, including genders. Many find that the experience of reading online differs considerably from that of reading print texts. In the intense exchange characteristic of chat-room conversations, for instance, the conventional distinction between reading and writing almost blurs. This blurring also characterizes the experience of reading hypertext documents on the Web, for the Web provides new opportunities for readers to take charge of — or "author" — their reading.

In one sense, of course, readers have always been free to move around in traditional print texts: They could choose to read ahead to the conclusion of a mystery novel, for instance, or to skim a single section of a how-to book. But the physical structure of most print texts encourages a linear reading, either of the entire text (as is the case with novels and of many nonfiction books) or of sections within the larger text (as occurs with car and home repair manuals). Such is not the case with the Web. Although Web sites do have homepages that provide an introduction to the site, they offer readers a multitude of options for both entering and navigating the site. You might begin a period of Web reading by entering the Web address (or URL — Uniform Resource Locator) of a site for those interested in the sport of spelunking, or exploring underground caves. But perhaps a hotlink to a site on the Mammoth Cave in Kentucky will catch your eye, and before you know it, you're reading about its early exploration and development. And then a hotlink to a company advertising a sale on spelunking equipment might draw your attention. As you move from site to site, you — not the creators of the Web sites — are determining what and how you read.

Online technologies provide new opportunities for readers to interact in powerful and exciting ways with texts. But experienced readers and writers have always understood that reading and writing are mutually reinforcing acts. Both are acts of *composing,* of constructing meaning through language.

When you first read an essay for an anthropology class, for instance, you engage in a preliminary or "rough" reading. The process of grappling with an essay for the first time — of attempting to determine where the writer is going and why — is similar to the process of writing a rough draft. When you reread an essay with an eye on the strategies used, or the arguments, you are "revising" your original reading, much as you revise a draft when you write.

Both writing and reading challenge you to construct or compose the meaning of a specific text; both also engage you in dialogue with others, even if you are reading alone at the computer or in the library. Precisely because they involve dialogue, reading and writing are best understood as rhetorically, culturally, and socially situated activities. The purposes you bring to your reading, the processes you use to engage with a text, your understanding of the significance of your reading: These and other aspects of your reading grow out of your understanding of your particular situation as a reader.

An example might help to clarify this point. Imagine two people sitting in a café reading and drinking tea. One person is reading an accounting textbook; the person at the next table is reading a zine he picked up from a bench by the cash register. Both persons are reading texts — but they are undoubtedly reading them in quite different ways. The differences reflect these readers' social and cultural understanding of the texts they are reading. The student reading the accounting textbook for a course in which she is enrolled has many reasons for believing the textbook is authoritative. As a result, the student reads the textbook slowly and with care. If asked what she is doing, the student might say that she is studying rather than reading — a statement that reflects both the attentive nature of her reading and her relationship with her text.

The person reading the zine is reading with a different set of understandings and expectations. He knows that zines represent a backlash against the typical magazines that characterize popular culture. Some zines are hand drawn and lettered rather than word processed, for instance. And even if word processed, they often have an intentionally crude, in-your-face sense of design. Whereas textbooks go through a multilevel review process, one that adds to their credibility, anyone with the time and inclination can "publish" a zine. A zine found in a café could be a well-written and thought-provoking reflection on a contemporary issue, a poorly written diatribe — or simply boring. So the reader of the zine quickly skims the text to see if the topics are interesting and the writing worth reading.

Two readers surfing the Web might also read in quite diverse ways. Imagine a reader who has just learned that she has an illness and wishes to gather information about her illness online. This reader is likely to approach her online reading with seriousness and to search systematically for sites, such as the federally supported National Institutes of Health, that contain authoritative, scientifically supported studies. Though she is reading on the Web, she is approaching this online reading in the same way that she might read an important print text. And, in fact, she may well print many of the texts that she locates for more careful reading.

Contrast her situation with that of a second person who is also reading online. This person has recently taken up mountain biking and is interested in identifying possible places to vacation. Arriving at work a few minutes early, he decides to ease into his day by surfing the Web for possible vacation spots. This reader might move quickly — even almost randomly — from official sites, such as that of the American Mountain Biking Association, to homepages of mountain bikers (where he quickly scans for links to favorite vacation spots), to business and community sites, such as the visitors' information site for Moab, Utah, a hot vacation destination for mountain bikers.

As these examples indicate, whether you are reading traditional print texts or reading online, you are making rhetorical judgments about the texts that you are reading. These judgments are often unconscious and intuitive: The reader looking for mountain biking vacation spots did not ponder his situation at great length but rather just got online and began surfing. Even so, these judgments play an important role in your reading.

Perhaps because writing requires the physical activity of drafting, you are generally aware of the active role you play as writer. You may be less aware of the work you do when you read a text, but reading is an equally active process. For instance, look at the "Harper's Index" for December 1999 (see Figure 3.1 on p. 51). As you read, notice how you forge connections among the items listed. If you are like most readers, you will discover that certain themes or issues emerge from your reading.

■ ■ ■

FOR EXPLORATION

Freewrite for five minutes about the experience of reading the "Harper's Index." What strategies did you use as you read these "telling facts"? Reread the "Index," and list the major themes that your reading stimulated. Reviewing this list, consider the extent to which your own background and experiences influenced your reading.

HARPER'S INDEX

Chance that an American favors the resumption of any form of nuclear-weapons testing: 1 in 10

Total number of nuclear weapons worldwide when the first nuclear test ban negotiations began in 1958: 10,713

Percentage by which the number had changed by the time the Limited Test Ban Treaty was signed in 1963: +220

Percentage by which it has changed since then: –7

Number of U.S. nuclear reactors that have reported safety violations since 1996: 102

Percentage of federal nuclear-safety inspectors that the Senate proposed laying off last year: 37

Number of countries that have not made public their assessment of the Y2K readiness of their computer systems: 91

Number of countries besides Australia that have ever formally recognized Indonesia's sovereignty over East Timor: 0

Year in which Congress banned the State Department's military training program for Indonesian troops: 1992

Year in which the Pentagon's military training program for Indonesian troops ended: 1998

Average number of U.S. cruise missiles launched per month during the Clinton Administration: 11

Estimated number of the 222,200 "armor-piercing bomblets" dropped on Kosovo last spring that remain unexploded: 11,110

Chance that a Serb has left Kosovo since NATO troops took it over last June: 1 in 2

Chance that an ethnic Albanian left Kosovo while Serbian troops controlled the region last spring: 1 in 2

Percentage change in the number of Israelis living on the West Bank since the signing of 1993's Oslo peace accords: +50

Number of dogs and whores of whom Yasir Arafat is the son, according to Syria's defense minister: 120,000

Average number of death threats received each week this year by New York City Mayor Rudolph Giuliani: 2

Number of objects in the Brooklyn Museum's permanent collection that are made with human dung: 4

Number of toxic spills reported within one mile of the Clintons' new house in Chappaqua, New York: 43

Square miles of errant Antarctic icebergs being tracked by the National Ice Center in Washington, D.C.: 10,000

Number of coffins unearthed by floods in North Carolina last September: 110

Chance that an American without health insurance earns at least $50,000 per year: 1 in 4

Percentage of U.S. children who say their greatest wish for their parents is that they make more money: 23

Percentage who say their greatest wish for their parents is that they "spend more time with me": 11

Percentage of parents who predicted that their children would prefer more time with them: 56

Chance that a U.S. juvenile offender on death row is in Texas: 1 in 3

Chance that a black man living in Alabama cannot vote because of a felony conviction: 1 in 3

Billions in new federal poverty spending that the President proposed during his poverty tour last July: $1

Billions cut from the five-year federal food stamp budget in 1996: $24

Amount by which the U.N.'s estimate of what the U.S. owes it exceeds the Senate's estimate: $774,000,000

Estimated revenue that the U.N. generates each year for New York City: $3,300,000,000

Percentage change in the number of joint ventures signed between Cuba and foreign companies since 1992: +886

Days before Time Warner's Fortune Global Forum opened in China last fall that China banned *Time*'s special China issue: 6

Percentage of Americans who believe that the media "hurt democracy": 38

Percentage who say they would vote for Donald Trump for president over Al Gore or George W. Bush: 5

Percentage who say they would vote for Heather Locklear: 6

Year in which New York's Marriott Marquis hotel began taking reservations for New Year's Eve 1999: 1983

Year in which the hotel opened: 1985

Price of a bottle of Czar Nicholas II's champagne salvaged last year from a ship sunk in 1916: $4,922

Number of titles for "horseless carriages" issued to new car owners in Maine last spring due to a Y2K error: 2,000

Figures cited have been adjusted for inflation and are the latest available as of October 1999. Sources are listed on page 116.
"Harper's Index" is a registered trademark.

Figure 3.1

This "Harper's Index" appeared in the December 1999 issue of *Harper's Magazine*.

Reading, like writing, is a *situated* activity. When you read, you draw not only on the words on the page but on your own experiences as well. The connections that you perceived among the first six items in the "Harper's Index," for instance, were undoubtedly influenced by your views on nuclear safety and arms control. Reading is situated in additional ways. Just as you approach different writing tasks in different ways depending on your rhetorical situation, your approach to reading varies depending on the specific relationship of writer, reader, and text. Consider, for instance, how you read the introduction to a psychology text differently than you read a mystery novel or the sports page.

■ ■ ■

FOR EXPLORATION

Read the following two texts. The first, "Girl," is a brief short story set in the Caribbean by the contemporary writer Jamaica Kincaid. The second is the first two paragraphs of the introduction to *Language and Woman's Place,* a scholarly work by the linguist Robin Lakoff.

GIRL

by Jamaica Kincaid

> Wash the white clothes on Monday and put them on the stone heap; wash the color clothes on Tuesday and put them on the clothesline to dry; don't walk barehead in the hot sun; cook pumpkin fritters in very hot sweet oil; soak your little cloths right after you take them off; when buying cotton to make yourself a nice blouse, be sure that it doesn't have gum on it, because that way it won't hold up well after a wash; soak salt fish overnight before you cook it; is it true that you sing benna in Sunday school?; always eat your food in such a way that it won't turn someone else's stomach; on Sundays try to walk like a lady and not like the slut you are so bent on becoming; don't sing benna in Sunday school; you mustn't speak to wharf rat-boys, not even to give directions; don't eat fruits on the street — flies will follow you; *but I don't sing benna on Sundays at all and never in Sunday school;* this is how to sew on a button; this is how to make a buttonhole for the button you have just sewed on; this is how to hem a dress when you see the hem coming down and so to prevent yourself from looking like the slut I know you are so bent on becoming; this is how

you iron your father's khaki shirt so that it doesn't have a crease; this is how you iron your father's khaki pants so that they don't have a crease; this is how you grow okra — far from the house, because okra tree harbors red ants; when you are growing dasheen, make sure it gets plenty of water or else it makes your throat itch when you are eating it; this is how you sweep a corner; this is how you sweep a whole house; this is how you sweep a yard; this is how you smile to someone you don't like too much; this is how you smile to someone you don't like at all; this is how you smile to someone you like completely; this is how you set a table for tea; this is how you set a table for dinner; this is how you set a table for dinner with an important guest; this is how you set a table for lunch; this is how you set a table for breakfast; this is how to behave in the presence of men who don't know you very well, and this way they won't recognize immediately the slut I have warned you against becoming; be sure to wash every day, even if it is with your own spit; don't squat down to play marbles — you are not a boy, you know; don't pick people's flowers — you might catch something; don't throw stones at blackbirds, because it might not be a blackbird at all; this is how to make a bread pudding; this is how to make doukona; this is how to make pepper pot; this is how to make a good medicine for a cold; this is how to make a good medicine to throw away a child before it even becomes a child; this is how to catch a fish; this is how to throw back a fish you don't like, and that way something bad won't fall on you; this is how to bully a man; this is how a man bullies you; this is how to love a man, and if this doesn't work there are other ways, and if they don't work don't feel too bad about giving up; this is how to spit up in the air if you feel like it, and this is how to move quick so that it doesn't fall on you; this is how to make ends meet; always squeeze bread to make sure it's fresh; *but what if the baker won't let me feel the bread?;* you mean to say that after all you are really going to be the kind of woman who the baker won't let near the bread?

LANGUAGE AND WOMAN'S PLACE
by Robin Lakoff

Language uses us as much as we use language. As much as our choice of forms of expression is guided by the thoughts we want to express, to the same extent the way we feel about the things in the real world governs the way we express ourselves about these things. Two words can be synonymous in their denotative sense, but one will be used in case a speaker feels favorably toward the object the word denotes, the other if he is unfavorably disposed. Similar situations are legion, involving unexpectedness, interest, and other emotional reactions on the part of the speaker to what he is talking about. Thus, while two speakers may be talking about the same thing or real-world situation, their descriptions may end up sounding utterly unrelated. The following well-known paradigm will be illustrative.

(*a*) I am strong-minded.

(*b*) You are obstinate.

(*c*) He is pigheaded.

If it is indeed true that our feelings about the world color our expression of our thoughts, then we can use our linguistic behavior as a diagnostic of our hidden feelings about things. For often — as anyone with even a nodding acquaintance with modern psychoanalytic writing knows too well — we can interpret our overt actions, or our perceptions, in accordance with our desires, distorting them as we see fit. But the linguistic data are there, in black and white, or on tape, unambiguous and unavoidable. Hence, while in the ideal world other kinds of evidence for sociological phenomena would be desirable along with, or in addition to, linguistic evidence, sometimes at least the latter is all we can get with certainty. This is especially likely in emotionally charged areas like that of sexism and other forms of discriminatory behavior. This book, then, is an attempt to provide diagnostic evidence from language use for one type of inequity that has been claimed to exist in our society: that between the roles of men and women. I will attempt to discover what language use can tell us about the nature and extent of any inequity; and finally to ask whether anything can be done, from the linguistic end of the problem: Does one correct a social inequity by changing linguistic disparities? We will find, I think, that women experience linguistic discrimination in two ways: in the way they are taught to use language, and in the way general language use treats them. Both tend, as we shall see, to relegate women to certain subservient functions: that of sex object, or servant; and therefore certain lexical items mean one thing applied to men, another to women, a difference that cannot be predicted except with reference to the different roles the sexes play in society.

Now use the following questions to analyze your reading experience.

1. What were your expectations when you began to read each of these texts? Did you expect to find one or the other easier or more interesting

to read? Why? To what extent did your expectations derive from your own previous experiences as a reader?

2. Each of these texts comments on the situation of women in society and the role that language plays in women's lives. How did your assumptions and values about these issues influence your reading? Did you approach these texts as a sympathetic reader, or were you resistant to the general subject at the start? Why?

3. Just as writers often shift goals and strategies while writing, readers too sometimes revise their goals and strategies while reading. Did you find yourself doing so while reading either passage? Why? What caused these shifts, if they occurred?

4. How would you describe each author's relationship with her readers? Did these texts invite you to play a different role as reader? Describe your role as you read these texts. How did your awareness of this role influence your reading? List several features of each text that encourage readers to adopt a particular role.

5. What factors made each of these texts more or less difficult to read? Did the two texts require you to draw on different skills and different prior knowledge about the subject matter? How?

6. If you found reading either of these texts difficult or unenjoyable, can you imagine someone else who would find them easy and pleasurable to read? What values, knowledge, and skills would this person have? In what ways would this person differ from you? If you found one of these passages easy and enjoyable reading, can you identify the reasons why?

Now reread these two texts. How did this second reading differ from your first? To what extent do you find yourself "revising" your first reading? List several ways that the second reading differed from the first.

FOR GROUP WORK

Meet with a group of classmates to discuss your responses to the preceding Exploration. (Appoint a member of the group to act as a recorder so you can share the results of your discussion with the rest of the class.) Begin by comparing your answers to each of the preceding six questions. Formulate two or three responses to the following questions:

1. In what ways do your answers to these questions differ?

2. What do these differences reveal about the reading process?

READING VISUAL TEXTS

As the discussion thus far has emphasized, reading is as active — and as rhetorically, socially, and culturally situated — a process as writing. Skimming a magazine certainly demands less of our attention than reading a textbook full of complex calculations and scholarly references, but in either case the reader is intentionally (if often intuitively) choosing to engage a text in a specific manner. For just as writers draw on their rhetorical sensitivity when writing — sensitivity that they have gained in their years of reading, writing, speaking, and listening — so too do readers draw on their rhetorical sensitivity when reading.

But what role does *looking* — at texts, images, movies, television shows — play in the development of rhetorical sensitivity? As an experiment, turn back to the "Harper's Index" presented on p. 51. When you originally looked at this, did you notice the varying line indentations? Even if you were aware of them in your first reading, take a few moments to reread this text, taking particular care to observe the role that the indentations play in helping to define relationships among the statements included in the "Index." Notice, for instance, the sharp contrast between the third and fourth items. The sudden shift in level of indentation between these two statements emphasizes this contrast.

If something as simple as the indentation of a line can influence our response to and interpretation of a text, imagine the important role that images (such as photographs and drawings) and such design features as color, font size, and graphics can play in human communication. Think about the full range of reading that you do. If you are like me, you can easily identify a number of texts, such as magazines and Web pages, where visual elements are at least as important as the words on the page. If you want to be an engaged and critical reader, then, you must develop the ability to read visual texts with the same insight you bring to written texts.

For instance, look at the black and white reproductions of two magazine covers (Figures 3.2 and 3.3, pp. 57–58). (The original covers not surprisingly took advantage of color as part of the overall design; I will describe the use of color in the covers as I discuss them.) The first cover is from the December 1999 issue of *Wired* magazine. As you may already know, *Wired* magazine is a nationally distributed, advertisement-filled magazine (in this issue, for instance, the first seventy of the issue's 430 pages are devoted to ads) for those interested in computers and online technologies. The second cover is from the summer-fall 1999 issue of a magazine called *The Bear Deluxe;* this magazine is published quarterly by Orlo, a nonprofit organization located in Portland, Oregon, that explores environmental issues through the creative arts.

Each cover provides important cues to readers, cues that attentive readers will notice as they read both image and text. Each cover also assumes that

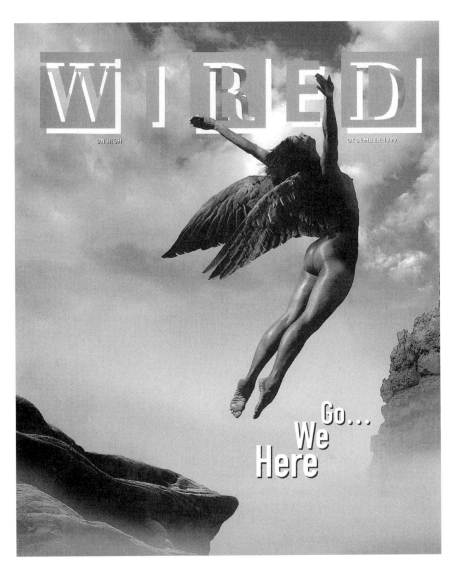

Figure 3.2

Figure 3.3

those looking at the cover will "read" the images and words presented there in sophisticated ways. The *Wired* cover, which shows a female figure with angel wings jumping off a rock into a cloud-filled blue sky, uses both photographic and digital technologies to create a dramatic end-of-the-millennium statement about the future. Those familiar with the history of art will recognize that the cover looks both backward and forward. Though this cover was created through a blend of photography and digital technology, it strongly evokes the paintings of Maxfield Parrish, an American artist whose often-reproduced images have become a part of popular culture. Parrish's paintings, which combined a photographic realism with romantic semiclassical or mythological settings, were particularly influential in the 1920s and 1930s. Color prints of Parrish's work sold by the millions during that time, and despite the ascendency of other, very different styles of painting throughout most of the twentieth century, Parrish's images never disappeared completely from the public consciousness.

For the editors of *Wired* to look forward to the future by looking back to the artwork of Parrish is a surprising move. But as readers of *Wired* are aware, this magazine delights in flaunting traditional print expectations and standards. It does so through the use of unconventional internal design features, such as unusual colors, fonts, margins, and photographs. In this case, the implied visual reference to Parrish raises interesting questions about how we bring cultural perspectives to our ways of seeing and of reading. In his time, Parrish painted utopian fantasies that did not (and, given their classical mythological content, could not) come to pass. What does this suggest about the millennium beginning January 1, 2000? And note the potential ambiguity inherent in the figure of the young female angel jumping off a rock. Are her wings spread fully enough to enable her to fly? What world is she flying to as she greets the new millennium? Is there a sense of danger, as well as possibility, in the words "Here We Go . . ." that appear beneath the angel on the cover?

The cover of *The Bear Deluxe* contrasts strongly with that of *Wired*. While the *Wired* cover is printed on glossy paper, this cover is printed on brown paper that looks very much like the paper that grocery store bags are made of. While the *Wired* cover depends on complex photographic and digital technologies, this cover appears to be simply and crudely drawn. (The artist who designed the cover may well have used clip art available on a CD or on the Internet, which was then incorporated into the overall image.) The cover presents basic information about the magazine in the upper left corner. In the center — in a sort of bull's eye that in the original cover is orange-red — appear two male figures dressed in suits reminiscent of the 1930s or 1940s shaking hands. Around them are, respectively, repeated images of a rabbit running, a gun, and a maple leaf. At the bottom are the words "Good Will Hunting."

Unless a person looking at this cover is a regular reader of *The Bear Deluxe,* he or she will bring little if any knowledge about the publication to their reading of the cover. This is significant, for as readers we often draw on our knowledge of the nature and contents of publications to provide a context for a reading. Readers must look at information provided alongside the issue's table of contents to discover that *The Bear Deluxe* is a regional, rather than a national publication. It is free to interested readers and is distributed in restaurants, bookstores, cafés — and even a few bowling alleys and laundromats. I picked up this issue of *The Bear Deluxe,* for instance, at a vegetarian restaurant in my town. This restaurant has a space where it offers announcements and free publications of potential interest to patrons.

A glance at the table of contents helps explain the cover, for one of the feature stories is, in fact, titled "Good Will Hunting." Readers who turn to the article discover a banner below the title that says: "Hunters and environmentalists have formed an uneasy alliance to save wildlife and its habitat." This information helps to explain the cover, but as was the case with the cover of *Wired,* ambiguities — intentional ambiguities — remain. The expressions on the faces of the two men shaking hands suggest the possibility that they have just completed a shady interaction, for instance. Are these expressions meant to suggest editorial suspicion of a possible alliance between hunters and environmentalists? And why did the designers of this cover choose to evoke the 1930s and 1940s rather than the present time and to echo the title of a popular movie from the late 1990s?

Not all magazine covers invite the kind of in-depth reading that I have just given these covers. Most Americans know, for instance, that the covers of such magazines as *Time, Newsweek,* and *People* generally present a photograph of a person or persons or of a news event such as a natural disaster. The familiarity of such design features helps reassure readers that they know what to expect in these magazines. If the photograph of a person appears on the cover of *Newsweek,* for instance, readers know that one of the issue's major stories — perhaps even the cover story — focuses on this person. Such knowledge increases the readability of the cover and of the following story. The implicit message that the cover sends to readers is this: If a person or event is important in the United States or to Americans, our magazine will feature it.

Why is it important to be able to "read" visual images and to understand the potentially powerful role that design and visual elements can play in written texts? Perhaps the most important reason has to do with the increasingly pervasive role that images have come to play in modern life. Driving down the street, watching television, skimming a magazine: In these and other situations we are continually presented with images and texts — many of which are designed to persuade us to purchase, believe, or do certain things. Often these images can be a source of pleasure and entertainment. (Someone who knows the history of art in America and recognizes the allusion to Maxfield Parrish's work in the cover of *Wired* can enjoy reflecting on the connections between Parrish's time and work and the new millennium.) But given the persuasive intent of many images, critical readers will develop ways to not just "read" but "read into" these images. The following guidelines present questions you can ask to analyze visual texts.

■ GUIDELINES FOR ANALYZING VISUAL TEXTS

1. How would you characterize your overall impression of the general design and presentation of words and images in this piece? Is the presentation cluttered or spare? Colorful or subdued? Carefully organized or (apparently) randomly presented? Calm or "busy"? Traditional, contemporary, or cutting-edge?

2. What images or design features play a particularly important role in this piece? Does it present a single dominant image or a variety of images? If the latter, how are these images related? What is your eye drawn to when you first look at this piece? Why?

3. In what ways do the design and presentation of words and images in this piece appeal to logic and to reason? To emotion? What role (if any) does the credibility of a company or individual play in this piece? Does the piece assume that readers would recognize a trademark or corporate name, for instance, or recognize a photograph or drawing of a well-known figure?

4. What is the relationship between image and text in this piece? Does one predominate? Is their relationship explicit or implicit? Does the text function primarily to present information or to reinforce or extend — or even to subvert or undermine — the image?

5. Does the visual text assume prior knowledge about an image (as was the case with the *Wired* cover)? What sort of knowledge? Historical? Artistic? Cultural? Political? What role does this prior knowledge play in helping the visual text to achieve its impact? Does it work differently depending on the reader's prior knowledge?

6. If you were to translate the impact or message of the visual text into words, how would you describe it? What do you think that those who constructed this piece intend, in other words, for its visual impact to be? Do you believe that it achieves its intended impact? Why?

FOR EXPLORATION

Look at the advertisements presented on pp. 166–68 at the end of Chapter 5. Choose the ad that most intrigues, moves, or puzzles you, and analyze it according to the questions presented above, writing your responses to each question. Finally, write one or two paragraphs about what you have learned as a result of this analysis.

RECOGNIZING THE NEED FOR DIVERSE READING STRATEGIES

As a college student, you read many different kinds of texts for a wide variety of purposes. You may skim a magazine or surf the Web for fun and relaxation. You may read a novel for pleasure and for its insight into human emotions. When you read a textbook for, say, your Introduction to Western Civilization class, you may read primarily for information. On other occasions, you read not simply to gain information but to engage in the process of inquiry. Professors David Bartholomae and Anthony Petrosky call this kind of reading "strong reading":

> Reading involves a fair measure of push and shove. You make your mark on a book and it makes its mark on you. Reading is not simply a matter of hanging back and waiting for a piece, or its author, to tell you what the writing has to say. In fact, one of the difficult things about reading is that the pages before you will begin to speak only when the authors are silent and you begin to speak in their place, sometimes for them — doing their work, continuing their projects — and sometimes for yourself, following your own agenda.

> — DAVID BARTHOLOMAE AND ANTHONY PETROSKY,
> *WAYS OF READING*

Strong readers evaluate their reading in terms of what they are able to *do* with their reading. If you are like many students, you may feel more confident reading for information than engaging in a strong reading of an essay, advertisement, poem, political treatise, engineering report, or Web site. Yet the ability to "make your mark" on a verbal or visual text, rather than simply allowing it to "make its mark on you," represents one of the most important goals of a college education. Such engaged, critical reading is intrinsically satisfying, for it enables you to engage in genuine inquiry. Strong reading naturally leads to — and benefits — writing; one of the best ways to strengthen your writing ability is thus to become adept at strong reading.

Just as successful writers develop a repertoire of writing strategies they can draw on in various situations, successful readers develop a repertoire of reading strategies. Here are a number of general guidelines to help you read both printed and online texts effectively and productively.

■ GUIDELINES FOR EFFECTIVE READING

1. *Recognize That Effective Readers Are Flexible Readers.* Effective readers understand that different reading situations and mediums call for different reading strategies — and that their purpose in reading should help them determine how to approach a text. Researching an essay on the homeless in urban centers in the Northeast, for instance, you might skim a number of print and online studies to become familiar with resources available on the subject. Once you have clearly defined your topic and purpose, you would then begin reading in a more focused and critical manner.

2. *Analyze the Text You Are Reading for Cues about Its Rhetorical, Social, and Cultural Contexts.* Earlier in this chapter you looked at the cover of a regional publication, *The Bear Deluxe*, with which you were almost certainly unfamiliar. You saw that by moving back and forth among the cover, table of contents, information about the journal, and lead article and by drawing on your general cultural knowledge (about men's fashions, for instance, and the title of the movie *Good Will Hunting*) you could nevertheless begin to understand and evaluate the cover. A similar process of inquiry can help you to better understand the rhetorical, social, and cultural contexts of print and online texts. Here are some questions you can ask yourself:

   Questions about the author, editor, or (in the case of Web sites) Webmaster What did this person (or persons) hope the text would accomplish? How might those goals have influenced the form, content, and design of the text? To what extent does the text call attention to the role that the author, editor, or Webmaster played? Is it an obvious role, as is the case with personal essays and homepages? Is it a more distanced and even hidden role, as is the case with editors and Webmasters?

   (continued)

(continued)

Questions about readers   Who are the intended readers of this text? A general audience (of a magazine, for instance, or a Web site)? An audience of specialists (as for scientific or professional journals and industry-specific publications)? Or is the audience composed of students (as is the case with college textbooks)? What role does the text invite readers to adopt as they read (study, surf, scan, or otherwise engage with) this text? Does the text assume that readers will bring considerable prior knowledge to their reading? What cultural or social understandings and preferences does the text assume? Does it assume, for instance, that readers won't read large passages of prose unless they are interrupted by images or other design features? That they will recognize a person whose photograph appears in an ad? That readers will share certain values and beliefs?

Questions about the text   When was this text published — and where? In a traditional print publication? (The comparison of the *Wired* and *The Bear Deluxe* covers should remind you that print publications are anything but equal.) On the Web? On an institutional site? A business site? A personal site? What can you infer about the reasons for publication? To inform? Entertain? Persuade?

3. *Develop Strategies for Reading against the Grain of a Text.* To read critically and actively, it sometimes helps to deliberately resist a text or to read "against the grain." For example, while reading an essay on abortion intended for a general audience, you might consider the essay from the perspective of a health-care provider or from that of a woman who has experienced an abortion. How would those readers respond to the author's arguments and strategies? You might read the essay paying particular attention to issues or examples that the author *doesn't* mention. Or you might focus on your own experience and how it supports or does not support the author's arguments. Such probing, resistant readings can help you determine not only what an essay says and does but also what it doesn't say and do and can thus provide an opening for fruitful questioning and analysis.

(continued)

(continued)

4. *Find Productive Ways to Respond to Challenging Texts.* As a college student, you will inevitably find some reading challenging. You may be unfamiliar with the research discussed or with the vocabulary or methodology used. You could have trouble determining what exactly is at stake in a particular argument. The following strategies will help you work through these and similar difficulties:

- Try to identify reason(s) a text seems difficult, and then turn these reasons into questions you can use as you read the text. Rather than becoming frustrated when a writer is commenting at length on an issue that seems unimportant to you, for instance, ask yourself *why* scholars in this field might find this issue worthy of attention.

- Interact with the text. Pose questions. Speculate about the implications of a line of argument. Look for gaps or absences in the presentation of evidence or ideas. Use your personal experience as a lens to consider the issues raised by a text — and then imagine how someone quite different from you might approach this issue or topic.

- Be patient. Just as the process of writing often requires rough drafts, so too can the process of reading require "rough readings." A text that on first reading seems difficult will often, on rereading, prove rewarding or more engaging.

DEVELOPING CRITICAL READING STRATEGIES

Reading critically means reading *actively,* reading not just to gather facts or information but to evaluate, analyze, appreciate, understand, and apply what you read. As a critical reader, you engage in a dialogue with the author. Rather than automatically accepting the author's perspective or arguments, you subject the author's ideas to careful examination.

To read critically, you need to develop a repertoire of reading strategies. The following discussion presents a number of strategies for critical reading and provides an opportunity for you to apply these strategies to a specific text, an article that considers the significance of the Internet.

Previewing

When you preview a text, you survey it quickly to establish or clarify your pur- pose and context for reading, asking yourself questions such as those included in the following guidelines. As you do so, recognize that print and online sources may call for different previewing strategies. With print sources, for instance, it is easy to determine the author and publisher. To learn the author of a homepage on the World Wide Web, however, you need to know how to read Web addresses. You also need to recognize that homepages include links to many disparate materials and that materials on the Internet and World Wide Web can appear, and disappear, with disconcerting frequency. Hence, determining the accuracy, authority, and currency of online resources can prove challenging. Whereas such print texts as scholarly journals and books have generally undergone extensive review and editing, such may not be the case with online sources.

■ GUIDELINES FOR PREVIEWING A TEXT

1. Where and when was this text published? If this text appears on the World Wide Web, how recently was it updated? What do this source and date suggest about the accuracy, authority, and cur- rency of this text?

2. What, if anything, do you know about the author of this text?

3. What can you learn from the title?

4. What can you learn by quickly surveying this text? Is the text divided into sections? If so, how do these sections appear to be organized? What links does a Web site provide? How useful do these links seem to be? Can you easily perceive the general approach the author is taking? What predictions about this text can you make on the basis of a quick survey? What questions can you now formulate to guide your subsequent reading of this text?

5. What is your personal response to the text, based on this preview?

FOR EXPLORATION

Using the preceding guidelines, preview the following article: "The Inter- net and Gutenberg," by Robert J. Samuelson, reprinted from the January 24, 2000 issue of *Newsweek*.

THE INTERNET AND GUTENBERG
by Robert J. Samuelson

In our self-absorbed age, everything is the newest New Thing or the biggest Big Thing. This spirit inevitably invests the Internet with transcendent significance. Steve Case of America Online already calls the new century "the Internet Century," and some authorities whisper that the Internet rivals the importance of Gutenberg's invention of the printing press in the 15th century. We suffer from historical amnesia.

Suppose you were born in 1900. You wouldn't yet watch movies (the first big silent hit, "The Great Train Robbery," showed in 1903), let alone imagine global TV. The airplane hadn't been invented, and Henry Ford wouldn't produce the first Model T until 1908. Fewer than 10 percent of U.S. homes had phones, and fewer than 8 percent had electricity. Antibiotics hadn't been discovered. As yet the Internet isn't in the same league with these developments.

Each changed lifestyles and popular beliefs. The automobile suburbanized America and inaugurated mass travel. Antibiotics, vaccines and public-health advances helped raise life expectancy from 47 in 1900 to 77 today. The explosion of prosperity — a consequence of electricity, other technologies and modern management — shortened working hours and expanded leisure. Movies and TV transformed popular culture.

The Internet is too young for anyone to foretell its ultimate significance — and time might vindicate the brashest prophecies. But some present claims aren't true. It is not true that no major innovation has spread so quickly. In 1990 only a handful of computer buffs used the Internet; by 1999 perhaps 38 percent of households were connected, reports Morgan Stanley Dean Witter. This roughly matches the adoption of the radio (which went from 0 to about 46 percent of households in the 1920s) and lags TV (which went from 9 percent of households in 1950 to 87 percent in 1960). . . .

Technologies acquire historical weight by reshaping the human condition. Gutenberg's press led to mass literacy, fostered the Protestant Reformation (by undermining the clergy's theological monopoly) and, through the easy exchange of information, enabled the scientific revolution. In the 19th century railroads created a truly national American market that favored mass production and the consumer society. To join this league, the Internet must be more than e-mail or a marketing platform. If you buy a book or car on the Net, the critical part of the transaction is still the book or car. Especially in business-to-business commerce, the Internet may improve efficiency through more price competition and supplier choice. But these are changes of degree, not kind.

Thoughtful Internet enthusiasts offer plausible speculations about its greater meaning. "Over the past 200 years, we have built up industrial economies of mass production . . . and mass markets," says Esther Dyson, editor of *Release 1.0,* a newsletter. By providing so much information, the Internet empowers consumers to escape mass markets; by making information so easy to dispense, it enables people to become independent producers. "The major impact is to give individuals more power over their lives," she says, while making it "tougher for governments, businesses — anyone — to operate in secrecy."

Kevin Kelly of *Wired* magazine, author of "New Rules for the New Economy," argues that the "Internet is actually being underhyped. Of all the people online in 10 years, only a tenth are online today." (Note: in 1999, there were 58 million worldwide connections, says Dataquest.) This could accelerate global commerce and weaken (for good or ill) national governments.

All the large issues remain unsettled. Will the Net enhance individual autonomy — or infringe on privacy? Will it increase people's economic independence — or expand corporate power? . . . Before answers become clear, the Internet will have to attain economic viability. Though booming, it is now largely a capitalist charity. Almost everything on it is being given away or sold at a loss. Retail e-commerce is puny. In 1999 it amounted to less than .5 percent of U.S. consumer spending. Ditto for advertising. In 1999 Internet ads amounted to $1.8 billion out of total U.S. advertising of $215 billion, estimates Robert Coen of Universal McCann.

The great Internet fortunes arise mainly from stock speculation or building the infrastructure — supplying computers, software and fiber optics. In 1999 this spending was $366 billion, says Nortel Networks, a major supplier. Sooner or later, the investment must pay a return, or it will stop. Even if the Internet flourishes, it may remain smaller than earlier Big Things. Our historical amnesia could benefit from the words of a Tennessee farmer at a church meeting in the 1940s. "Brothers and sisters, I want to tell you this," he said. "The greatest thing on earth is to have the love of God in your heart, and the next greatest is to have electricity in your home." Can the Internet really top that?

Annotating

When you annotate a text, you highlight important words or passages and write comments or questions that help you establish a dialogue with the text or remember important points. Different readers have different styles of annotating. Some people are heavy annotators, highlighting many passages and filling the margins with comments and questions. Others annotate more selectively, preferring to write few comments and to highlight only the most important passages or key words. In thinking about your own annotating strategies, remember that your purpose in reading should influence the way you annotate a text. You would annotate a text you are reading primarily for information differently than you would an essay you are reading for an assignment or a poem you are reading for pleasure.

Many readers annotate directly on the text as they read. If you have borrowed the text or prefer not to mark up your own book, however, you can use a separate piece of paper or computer to copy important passages and to write questions and comments.

How can you know the most effective way to annotate a text? The questions provided in the following guidelines can help you make appropriate choices as you read — and annotate — texts.

■ GUIDELINES FOR ANNOTATING A TEXT

1. What is your purpose in reading this text? What do you need to annotate to accomplish this purpose?

2. Where does the writer identify the purpose and the thesis (or main idea) of the text?

3. What are the main points, definitions, and examples? Would it be useful to number the main points or make a scratch outline in the margin?

4. What questions does this text suggest to you?

5. Can you identify key words that play an important role in this discussion? Does the text provide enough information so that you can understand these key words and appreciate their significance, or do you need to get further explanation?

6. Can you identify passages that seem to play a particularly crucial role in this text? What is your response to these passages?

7. Can you identify passages where your personal experience and values or knowledge of the subject cause you to question the author's assertions, evidence, or method?

FOR EXPLORATION

Annotate "The Internet and Gutenberg" (pp. 67–68) as you would if you expected to write an essay responding to it for your composition class.

Summarizing

Never underestimate the usefulness of writing clear, concise summaries of texts you read. Writing a summary allows you to restate the major points of a book or essay in your own words. Summarizing is a skill worth developing, for it requires you to master the material you are reading and make it your own. Summaries can vary in length, depending on the complexity and length of the material being summarized. Ideally, however, they should be as brief as possible. Here are suggestions to follow as you write your own summaries.

■ GUIDELINES FOR SUMMARIZING A TEXT

1. Reread the material, trying to identify the main ideas.

2. Highlight or number the main points.

3. Generally stick to main points. Leave out examples and anecdotes.

4. Before writing, try to form a coherent mental outline of the most important ideas.

5. State the main ideas in your own words, as briefly and clearly as you can.

FOR EXPLORATION

Following the preceding guidelines, write a brief summary of "The Internet and Gutenberg" (pp. 67–68).

Analyzing the Argument of a Text

Previewing, annotating, and summarizing can all help you determine the central informative or argumentative points made in a text. Sometimes, the central argument of a text is explicitly stated. Robin Lakoff begins her introduction to *Language and Woman's Place*, for instance, with this assertion: "Language uses us as much as we use language." Similarly, in his *Newsweek* column, Robert J. Samuelson asserts that "the Internet is too young for anyone to foretell its ultimate significance." Samuelson acknowledges that "time might vindicate the brashest prophecies," but he encourages readers to look at the development of the Internet in a broad historical and cultural context.

Not all authors are so direct. Someone writing about the consequences of contemporary feminism for life in North America may raise questions rather than provide answers or make strong assertions. Whether an author articulates a clear position on a subject or poses a question for consideration, critical readers attempt to determine for themselves if the author's analysis is valid — if the author provides good reasons in support of a position or line of analysis.

■ GUIDELINES FOR ANALYZING THE ARGUMENT OF A TEXT

1. What is the major claim or thesis of this text? Is it explicitly stated at any point, or is it implicit, requiring you to "read between the lines"?

2. What interests or values may have caused this writer to support this particular thesis? (Information about the writer from other sources, as well as clues from the writing itself, may help you determine this.)

3. What values and beliefs about this subject do you bring to your reading of this text? How might these values and beliefs affect your response to the writer's argument?

4. Does the writer define key terms? If not, what role do these unstated definitions play in the argument?

5. What other assumptions does the writer rely on in setting up or working through the argument? In texts on the World Wide Web, for instance, what choices and organizing principles do the links provided by the writer suggest?

6. What kind of evidence does the writer present? Is the evidence used logically and fairly? Has the writer failed to consider any significant evidence, particularly evidence that might refute his or her claims?

7. In what ways does the writer try to put the reader in a receptive frame of mind? Does the writer attempt to persuade the reader through inappropriately manipulative emotional appeals?

8. How does the writer establish his or her credibility? What image or *persona* does the writer create for himself or herself?

FOR EXPLORATION

Using the guidelines for analyzing the argument of a text, analyze the argument of "The Internet and Gutenberg" (pp. 67–68). Be sure to answer all of the questions for analyzing an argument.

FOR GROUP WORK

By comparing your responses to the Explorations with those of your peers, you can gain a helpful perspective on the effectiveness of your critical reading strategies. You can also better understand how different purposes and practices influence the reading of and responses to texts.

Bring your responses to the previous four exploration activities in this chapter to class. Meeting with a group, compare your responses. After you have shared your responses, work together to describe briefly the extent to which your responses were similar or dissimilar. Then discuss what these similarities and differences have helped you understand about the process of critical reading, coming to two or three conclusions to share with your classmates.

FOR THOUGHT, DISCUSSION, AND WRITING

1. Analyze the first chapter of two textbooks you are reading this term (including this one, if you like). Do these textbooks share certain textual conventions? How do you think the writers of these textbooks have analyzed their rhetorical situation? These textbooks are written for you and other students. How effective are they? How might they be more effective?

2. Earlier in this chapter you read "The Internet and Gutenberg" by Robert J. Samuelson. The readings at the end of this section focus on the benefits and limitations of the Web and of the Internet, the worldwide network of computers that support the Web and a variety of online forums. These readings, which have been selected from a number of print and online sources, range from the serious to the humorous. First skim the various texts, and then read them more carefully. Afterward, answer the following questions:

   ■ As you skimmed these texts, what were your expectations? To what extent did the form of a text and your knowledge of its original means and place of publication influence your expectations?

   ■ After reading each text more carefully, what was your response? To what extent did this response represent a deepening of or shift from your earlier expectations?

- How did your own assumptions and values about the Web and the Internet influence your readings of these texts?

- How would you describe the author's stance or relationship with readers in each of these texts? What role does each text invite you to play as reader? Did you find yourself reading the downloaded Web texts differently from texts first published in traditional print form?

- How did the fact that you were reading these texts together, rather than separately, influence your reading process? Did you find that you substantially revised your goals and strategies as a reader as you moved from text to text? In what ways? Did some of these texts invite or elicit stronger reading than others? Why or why not?

- How did you respond to the content of these texts? Which texts did you find more or less persuasive? Why?

- How did reading these texts influence your own views about the Internet?

- What other observations about reading or about the subject of the Internet and the Web did these texts stimulate in you?

3. After reading the selections on the Internet and the Web, reread Samuelson's *Newsweek* article. How has your reading of these additional texts influenced your response to Samuelson's article?

4. Once you have read the following selections, you will have read a number of texts that focus on the Internet and the Web. Write an essay articulating your own views on this subject. Alternatively, write an essay that responds to one or more of the previous readings.

UNDERSTANDING THE ALLURE OF THE INTERNET

By Joseph B. Walther and Larry D. Reid. (The Chronicle of Higher Education,
Feb. 4, 2000.)

A few well-placed conference presentations, a book or two, a couple of
chapters in other volumes, and an overwhelming number of stories in the
mass media have brought the phenomenon of Internet addiction to the
public's attention. We are told that the problem — sometimes called pathological Internet use, Internet dependency, and even onlineaholism — is
widespread. [...]

Despite the increasing attention to Internet addiction, nobody knows
whether it really exists, or what the theoretical or conceptual nature of
such an addiction might be. Certainly, some individuals who have spent a
great deal of time online have had serious problems in their lives: People
have gotten divorced, gone into debt, or lost their jobs. But we must be
careful not to use pathological labels for what may be someone's passing
immersion in the Internet. And we must guard against directing someone
who does have deep-seated problems to therapy that deals primarily with
Internet addiction, rather than looking for underlying psychological
issues. Above all, we must avoid launching a technological witch-hunt
instead of conducting substantive research about whether the Net causes
addiction or dependence.

Unfortunately, responding to some frightening cases of people whose
Internet use seemed to be out of control, a handful of researchers have
attempted to define and classify Internet addiction, using criteria from
other fields: gambling addiction, and drug and alcohol dependency (scholars in those fields now consider the term "addiction" too vague and politi-
cized to be of much use).

Mark Griffiths, a psychologist at Nottingham Trent University, in England, listed the core criteria for Internet addiction in a chapter in *Psychology and the Internet,* edited by Jayne Gackenbach (Academic Press, 1998).
Those criteria included considering Internet use your most important
activity; feeling good when you use the Internet; needing to use it more and
more to achieve the same satisfaction that you had before, with less use;
feeling symptoms of withdrawal, such as uneasiness, when you don't use it;
and allowing Internet use to interfere with your normal life.

Other researchers have used such criteria to develop questionnaires,
and sought volunteers who were interested in the topic to complete them,
to see how widespread Internet addiction might be. For instance, in 1994,
in one of the first and best known efforts, Kimberly Young, a psychologist
at the University of Pittsburgh at Bradford, posted notes around her campus and online, requesting that frequent Internet users complete her survey. She reported that 80 percent of her 496 respondents were addicted to
the Internet.

More recently, in late fall of 1998, the psychologist David Greenfield invited those interested in the topic of cyberspace addiction who came upon ABC News's World Wide Web site (www.abcnews.com) to answer Yes or No to 10 questions about Internet use. Almost 6 percent of the 17,251 people who took the survey answered Yes to five questions, which meant that they met Greenfield's criteria for Internet addiction. Extrapolating to the estimated number of Internet users, Greenfield suggested that 11.4 million people might be addicted to the Internet, a conclusion that the Associated Press reported widely. Since then, Greenfield has posted on his Web site (www.virtual-addiction.com) numerous disclaimers about the tentative nature of his data and conclusions, but he still offers — for a fee — cybertherapy for Internet addiction.

Skeptics responded quickly to those studies, suggesting that almost anything could be classified as addictive, using such criteria. In response to Kimberly Young's study, *The New Yorker* observed that breathing meets her criteria. One of us suggested, in a tongue-in-cheek talk at last summer's meeting of the American Psychological Association, that Internet addiction might actually be a new manifestation of a more insidious compulsion: to communicate by any means possible. The talk cited James C. McCroskey and Virginia P. Richmond's analysis of "talkaholism" in a 1995 article in *Communication Quarterly*.

Cheap shots, perhaps. But such responses come out of a well-warranted frustration that — no matter how noble their motivations — researchers and practitioners have not conducted more-rigorous work before offering scary statements about Internet addiction.

We should not use value-laden terms such as addiction to label something we know so little about. We need more information before we start monitoring the amount of time that our students are online, and taking action when their Internet use exceeds a certain level. And it is troubling that some researchers are offering online therapy to treat Internet addiction — which seems, as the reporter Anne Federwisch put it, to make as much sense as celebrating someone's success in Alcoholics Anonymous by throwing a cocktail party.

The next round of Internet studies must include more-solid questions. First, it is extremely important to consider the nature of people's activities on the Internet, rather than simply the extent of their use of the Net. People are obviously using the Internet to do things, but we have yet to focus on what those things are. Do people do basically the same things offline? The common presumption is that offline activities are better — healthier, or more natural — than online behavior, but we haven't examined whether that is so.

Are people using the Internet to do the online equivalent of flirting with strangers in bars? Or are they doing research, making new friends, collaborating on projects, expressing themselves artistically, learning computer programming, and exchanging social support? We have no reason to believe that if people were not able to use the Internet, they wouldn't engage in basically the same activities offline.

There is one catch: Typing has been shown to require four to five times as long as talking, and an hour's worth of socializing offline might take four hours online. Internet use may be a time sink, but it isn't necessarily pathological behavior.

Second, we need a formal and theoretical understanding of the Internet's particular allure. Researchers so far have focused on symptoms rather than causes. Only recently have some scholars speculated about the properties of the Internet that may make it attractive. For example, Young has tried to explain the gratification of cybersex with her "A.C.E." model: anonymity, convenience, and escape. Storm King, a student at the Pacific Graduate School of Psychology, is investigating whether people with addiction-prone personalities are using the Internet more than members of the general public are; if so, something about the Internet — perhaps its lack of face-to-face contact, which encourages uninhibited communication — may be particularly attractive to some people. Those hypotheses, however, still await verification.

In addition, researchers need to do a better job of collecting and analyzing data about Internet use. Most surveys of users have recruited their subjects by asking for volunteers who use the Net frequently, or who suspect that they might be addicted. By ignoring a broader range of subjects, that approach makes excessive use appear more common than it really is. Few studies have tried to show whether a great deal of use actually corresponds with other problems in the subjects' lives — as either a cause or an effect.

Next to none of the research has examined the accuracy of the questionnaires' measurements, or their consistency over time. Yet Lynn Roberts, a graduate student in social psychology at Curtin University of Technology, in Australia, has shown that online chat activity goes in phases, with initial exploration of chat rooms followed by seemingly obsessive enchantment, followed in turn by disillusionment and a sharp decline in use. Moderate use, or equilibrium, is the typical final stage. If Roberts is correct, it's important for researchers to retest their subjects who report that they spend a great deal of time on the Net.

Researchers must also understand that spending a lot of time online may be productive, rather than dysfunctional, behavior. The journalist Howard Rheingold related numerous stories about productive and moving uses of the Net in *The Virtual Community: Homesteading on the Electronic Frontier*. Malcolm Parks, of the University of Washington, and his coauthors have reported that online newsgroups and chat rooms simply function like many offline public places in which people meet and form friendships. Friendships formed online are no less valuable in several respects — such as commitment and understanding — than face-to-face ones, and a significant number of them move from virtual to physical acquaintance.

In a widely noted 1998 study published in *American Psychologist*, linking Internet use to depression, Robert Kraut and his colleagues at Carnegie Mellon University speculated that virtual friendships and online social-support networks were poor substitutes for face-to-face connections, undermining users' real-life support systems. However, their data do not support such a claim. Not only did they fail to assess the strength of online friendships, as Parks and his colleagues did, but Kraut and his coauthors actually found no deleterious effects on people's social support as a result of their Internet use.

In fact, Internet activities may be exceedingly beneficial to people in certain circumstances. Even Kimberly Young points out that the Net might be a good place to meet people for individuals who have low self-esteem and find it difficult to initiate conversations face to face, or those with a severely distorted body image. The face-to-face realm may be less attractive than cyberspace to other kinds of people: someone with a rare medical condition, who can find fellow sufferers online but not in his or her home town; the beautiful junior executive whose male coworkers look her in the chest instead of in the eye; and the college student who would rather discuss postmodernism to excess online than drink to excess with his roommates offline.

That is not to say that we should dismiss people who have problems with their Internet use. But it seems prudent to suggest that, even in some of those cases, we should focus on the sources of maladjustment that led them to the Net, rather than on the Net itself.

In sum, we mustn't forget that the Net has actually improved the lives of many people. We need more and different research before we say that Internet addiction exists, and before we use questionable criteria to diagnose thousands of people as addicted.

18 speed bike: $525

portable pup tent: $90

the longest paperback you could find: $9.99

seven days without email:

priceless

there are some things money can't buy.
for everything else there's MasterCard.®

Copyright 1994–2000. Reproduced courtesy of MasterCard International Incorporated.

AMERICANS WHO AREN'T YET WIRED ARE LURED TO THE NET

By David E. Kalish. (Corvallis Gazette Times, Dec. 18, 1999.)

Though it seems everybody's getting on the Web these days, two-thirds of Americans have yet to do so because of the expense or because of a lack of easy access. That may be about to change.

A campaign led by Wal-Mart and Kmart is under way to bridge the digital gap and bring Internet service to the poor and people living in rural towns. Until now, they've been largely ignored by Internet businesses.

Kmart and Yahoo! said this week they would launch a free Internet service, offering links to Kmart's online store and Yahoo's news, entertainment, financial and other services. Wal-Mart, in a deal with America Online, plans to offer discounted Internet access by next spring to people who may not have affordable hookups.

Wal-Mart says 840 towns in which it has stores are without a local Internet service provider, forcing anyone who wants to hook up to pay hefty long-distance charges.

"This will help accelerate what was an existing trend of rural households coming online," said Dylan Brooks, an analyst with Jupiter Communications, an Internet research firm in New York.

A Commerce Department report in July found that households earning $75,000 or more in urban areas are more than 20 times as likely to have Internet access as rural households at the lowest income levels. Black and Hispanic households are two-fifths as likely to have Internet access as white households.

In interviews this week, more than a dozen shoppers outside Wal-Mart stores indicated a reluctance to get wired, citing costs or worries about Web content.

Kathy Ledford of Johnson City, Tenn., said she bought a computer two years ago but refuses to go online for fear of exposing her children to pornography, profanity and violence.

"I have three children, and I just feel like I can't supervise them at all times," she said.

Vicky Cobb of Clever, Mo., also worries that some Internet content isn't appropriate for her teen-agers.

"All of our relatives are connected, but we just haven't decided yet whether it's a good or a bad thing," she said.

Andy Hogenmilles, a 25-year-old farmer in the small southwest Missouri town of Republic, shuns the Web, saying he doesn't need a computer to run his dairy farm. Hogenmilles, standing outside a Wal-Mart, said he might be interested in free or discounted Internet service if a free computer were offered along with it.

People living in rural towns or low-income areas, where museums, libraries and quality schools may be few and far between, are precisely the sort of users who could benefit the most from the cultural, entertainment and educational opportunities on the Internet. Medical-oriented sites can bring health care advice to people who may live far from doctors, hospitals and research centers.

Bob Pittman, president of AOL, suggested that some people simply need a little nudge.

"The majority of people (who aren't online) are people who procrastinate," he said. "We want them to encounter us in every place they are."

PAGING DOCTOR WEB

HOW TO KNOW WHEN THE INTERNET IS OFFERING
HEALTHY ADVICE
Dr. Web, *Prevention Magazine,* Sept. 1999.

Imagine browsing through a library to find some information on hangnails and finding several publications on the topic. One offers a hundred
different color pictures of a hundred different hangnails. Another says
that you can cure them by wearing an onion on your head. A third offers
suggestions for treating and preventing the condition, but there's no author
credited. Some books have pages missing, others can't even be opened.
And there's no librarian to help.

In some ways, that's what the Internet is like. As George D. Lundberg,
MD, editor of the *Journal of the American Medical Association,* explains,
"The Internet is a medium in which anyone with a computer can serve as
author, editor, and publisher" (*Journal of the American Medical Association,* April 16, 1997). The result: vast chunks of incomplete, misleading, or
inaccurate information. That's no big deal if you just want to catch up on
the latest gossip about Bill Gates. But if you're looking for health information, a bum steer can be a literal headache, or worse.

Dr. Lundberg suggests asking four questions to separate fact from
cyberbunk.

1. Who wrote the information?

2. What sources did they use?

3. Who owns, runs, or sponsors the Web site?

4. How long ago was the information posted?

The answers tell you a lot about how much you can trust the information you've found. And if you can't find the answers to those questions,
chances are it's not the place to answer your health questions either.

"Dilbert" by Scott Adams. May 5, 1997 and Feb. 3, 1997. Reprinted by permission of United Features Syndicate, Inc.

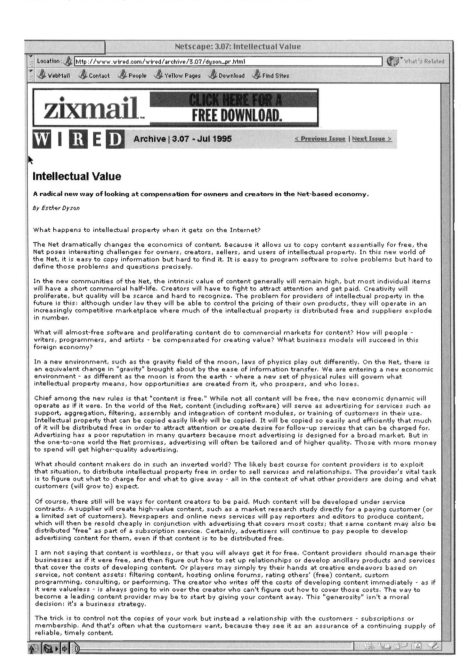

By Esther Dyson. ("Intellectual Value." From *Wired*, July 1995. Reprinted by permission of Conde Nast Publications, Inc.)

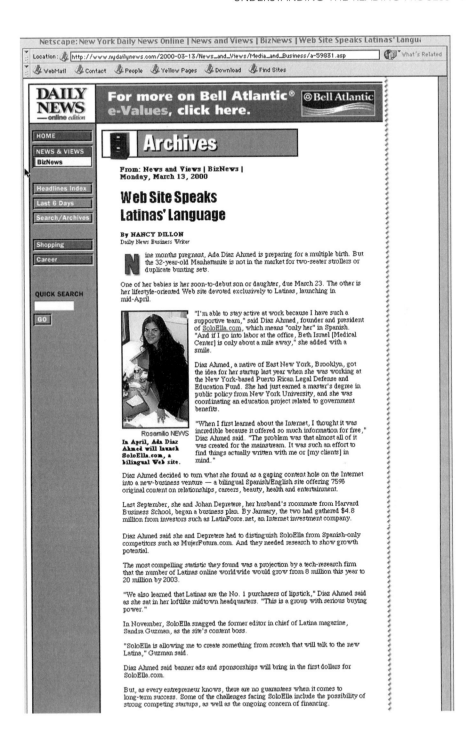

DAILY NEWS — online edition

- HOME
- NEWS & VIEWS
  - BizNews
- Headlines Index
- Last 6 Days
- Search/Archives
- Shopping
- Career

QUICK SEARCH

[   ] GO

Archives

From: News and Views | BizNews |
Monday, March 13, 2000

Web Site Speaks Latinas' Language

By NANCY DILLON
Daily News Business Writer

Nine months pregnant, Ada Diaz Ahmed is preparing for a multiple birth. But the 32-year-old Manhattanite is not in the market for two-seater strollers or duplicate bunting sets.

One of her babies is her soon-to-debut son or daughter, due March 23. The other is her lifestyle-oriented Web site devoted exclusively to Latinas, launching in mid-April.

"I'm able to stay active at work because I have such a supportive team," said Diaz Ahmed, founder and president of SoloElla.com, which means "only her" in Spanish. "And if I go into labor at the office, Beth Israel [Medical Center] is only about a mile away," she added with a smile.

Diaz Ahmed, a native of East New York, Brooklyn, got the idea for her startup last year when she was working at the New York-based Puerto Rican Legal Defense and Education Fund. She had just earned a master's degree in public policy from New York University, and she was coordinating an education project related to government benefits.

"When I first learned about the Internet, I thought it was incredible because it offered so much information for free," Diaz Ahmed said. "The problem was that almost all of it was created for the mainstream. It was such an effort to find things actually written with me or [my clients] in mind."

Rosamilio NEWS
In April, Ada Diaz Ahmed will launch SoloElla.com, a bilingual Web site.

Diaz Ahmed decided to turn what she found as a gaping content hole on the Internet into a new-business venture — a bilingual Spanish/English site offering 75% original content on relationships, careers, beauty, health and entertainment.

Last September, she and Johan Depretere, her husband's roommate from Harvard Business School, began a business plan. By January, the two had gathered $4.8 million from investors such as LatinForce.net, an Internet investment company.

Diaz Ahmed said she and Depretere had to distinguish SoloElla from Spanish-only competitors such as MujerFutura.com. And they needed research to show growth potential.

The most compelling statistic they found was a projection by a tech-research firm that the number of Latinas online worldwide would grow from 8 million this year to 20 million by 2003.

"We also learned that Latinas are the No. 1 purchasers of lipstick," Diaz Ahmed said as she sat in her loftlike midtown headquarters. "This is a group with serious buying power."

In November, SoloElla snagged the former editor in chief of Latina magazine, Sandra Guzman, as the site's content boss.

"SoloElla is allowing me to create something from scratch that will talk to the new Latina," Guzman said.

Diaz Ahmed said banner ads and sponsorships will bring in the first dollars for SoloElla.com.

But, as every entrepreneur knows, there are no guarantees when it comes to long-term success. Some of the challenges facing SoloElla include the possibility of strong competing startups, as well as the ongoing concern of financing.

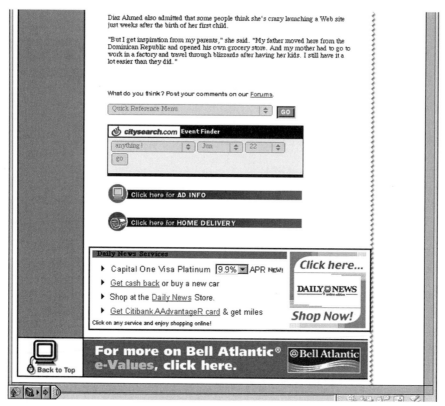

By Nancy Dillon. (From *The Daily News,* March 13, 2000.)

MY TURN

YOU CALL THIS PROGRESS?

By Seth Shostak. (Newsweek, "In My Opinion" column, Jan. 18, 1999.)

It's as ubiquitous as winter damp, a pernicious miasma that brings rot and ruin to society's delicate underpinnings. I speak of e-mail, the greatest threat to civilization since lead dinnerware addled the brains of the Roman aristocracy.

A technical byproduct of the Internet, e-mail lets 10 million Americans pound out correspondence faster than you can say QWERTY. One twitch of the finger is all it takes to dispatch missives to the next continent or the next cubicle at light speed. The result is a flood of what is loosely called communication, a tsunami of bytes that is threatening to drown white-collar workers everywhere. Masquerading as a better way to put everyone in touch, e-mail has become an incessant distraction, a nonstop obligation and a sure source of stress and anxiety. I expect that a public statement by the surgeon general is in the offing.

Mind you, e-mail started out cute and cuddly, an inoffensive spinoff from a government defense project. The technically inclined used it to send personal messages to colleagues without the need for a stamp or a wait. Only a small group of folks — mostly at universities — were plugged in to this select network. The amount of traffic was manageable. E-mail was something to be checked every week or so. But technology marches on. Today access to the Internet is widespread, as common and accessible as a cheap motel. Everyone's wired, and everyone has something to say.

Unfortunately, this is not polite correspondence, the gentle art of letter writing in electronic form. E-mail is aggressive. It has a built-in, insistent arrogance. Because it arrives more or less instantaneously, the assumption is that you will deal with it quickly. "Quickly" might mean minutes, or possibly hours. Certainly not days. Failure to respond directly usually produces a second missive sporting the mildly critical plaint, "Didn't you get my last e-mail?" This imperative for the immediate makes me yearn for old-style written communication, in which a week might lapse between inquiry and response. Questions and discussion could be considered in depth. A reply could be considered (or mentally shelved, depending on circumstance). Today, however, all is knee-jerk reaction.

In addition, there is the dismaying fact that electronically generated mail, despite being easy to edit, is usually prose at its worst. Of every 10 e-mails I read, nine suffer from major spelling faults, convoluted grammar and a stunning lack of logical organization. ASCII graffiti. For years I assumed this was an inevitable byproduct of the low student test scores so regularly lamented in newspaper editorials. Johnny can't read, so it's not surprising that he can't write either. But now I believe that the reason for all this unimpressive prose is something else: e-mail has made correspondents of folks who would otherwise never compose a text. It encourages messaging because it is relatively anonymous. The shy, the introverted and the socially inept can all hunker down before a glowing computer and whisper to the world. This is not the telephone, with its brutally personal, audible contact. It's not the post, for which an actual sheet of paper, touched by the writer and displaying his imperfect calligraphic skills, will end up under the nose of the recipient. E-mails are surreptitiously thrown over an electronic transom in the dead of night, packaged in plain manila envelopes.

Still, it is not these esthetic debilities that make e-mail such a threat. Rather, it's the unstoppable proliferation. Like the brooms unleashed by the sorcerer's apprentice, e-mails are beginning to overwhelm those who use them. Electronic correspondence is not one to one. It is one to many, and that's bad news on the receiving end. The ease with which copies of any correspondence can be dispensed to the world ensures that I am "kept informed" of my co-workers' every move. Such bureaucratic banter was once held in check by the technical limitations of carbon paper. Now my colleagues just punch a plastic mouse to ensure my exposure to their thoughts, their plans and the endless missives that supposedly prove that they're doing their jobs.

Because of e-mail's many-tentacled reach, its practitioners hardly care whether I'm around or not. I'm just another address in a list. So the deluge of digital correspondence continues irrespective of whether I'm sitting in my cubicle doing the boss's business or lying on the Côte d'Azur squeezing sand through my toes. Either way the e-mail, like a horde of motivated Mongolians, just keeps a-comin'. Vacations have lost their allure, and I hesitate to leave town. Consider: if I disappear for two weeks of rest and recreation, I can be sure of confronting screenfuls of e-mail upon my return. It's enough to make a grown man groan. The alternative is to take a laptop computer along, in the desperate hope of keeping up with e-mail's steady drip, drip, drip. Needless to say, there's something unholy about answering e-mails from your holiday suite. A friend recently told me that he can't afford to die: the e-mail would pile up and nobody could handle it.

Today I will receive 50 electronic messages. Of that number, at least half require a reply. (Many of the others consist of jokes, irrelevant bulletins and important announcements about secret cookie recipes. I actually like getting such junk e-mails, as they allow the pleasure of a quick delete without guilt.) If I spend five minutes considering and composing a response to each correspondence, then two hours of my day are busied with e-mail, even if I don't initiate a single one. Since the number of Internet users is doubling about once a year, I expect that by the start of the new millennium, I — and millions like me — will be doing nothing but writing e-mails. The collapse of commerce and polite society will quickly follow.

I'm as much in favor of technology as the next guy. Personally, I think the Luddites should have welcomed the steam looms. But if you insist on telling me that e-mail is an advance, do me a favor and use the phone.

DIGITAL LAND GRAB

By Henry Jenkins. (Technology Review, March/April 2000.)

Between 1869 and 1930, some 200 writers imitated, revised or parodied Lewis Carroll's *Alice in Wonderland*. Some sent Carroll's plucky protagonist into other imaginary lands; others sent different protagonists to encounter the Mad Hatter or the Cheshire Cat. Some promoted conservative agendas, others advocated feminism or socialism. Among Carroll's imitators were literary figures such as Christina Rossetti, Frances Hodgson Burnett and E. Nesbit. Literary critic Carolyn Sigler argues that Alice parodies contributed considerably to Carroll's subsequent reputation. Today, after Shakespeare's work and the Bible, Lewis Carroll's writings are the most often cited in the English-speaking world.

Now try a thought experiment. Imagine that the Wonderland stories were first appearing in 2000 as products of Disney or Viacom, and Rossetti, Burnett and Nesbit were publishing their parodies on the Internet. How long would it be before they were shut down by "cease-and-desist" letters? How many people would download "A New Alice in the Old Wonderland" before a studio flack asserted Disney's exclusive control over Humpty Dumpty™, The Cheshire Cat™ or The Red Queen™?

Rossetti's descendants, now called "fans," borrow characters, situations and themes from pre-existing works (more often television series than novels) and use them as resources for their own stories. Sometimes, such stories offer ideological critiques. Other times, fans recenter the plots around secondary characters or simply provide back story. These modern-day "scribblers" are housewives, secretaries, librarians, students, average citizens; their parodies are labors of love, paying public tribute to popular narratives that capture their imagination.

These fans are also shock troops in a struggle that will define the digital age. On the one hand, the past several decades have seen the introduction of new media technologies (from the VCR to MP3) that empower consumers to archive, annotate, appropriate and recirculate cultural materials. On the other, the emergence of new economic and legal structures makes tight control over intellectual property the basis for the cross-media exploitation of "branded" materials. We can already see bloody skirmishes over intellectual property as these two trends collide. Not long ago, Fox's lawyers took down dozens of *Buffy the Vampire Slayer* fan sites, and nobody even blinked because such saber rattling has become a regular occurrence.

A year or so ago, J. Michael Straczynski, executive producer of the cult television series *Babylon 5,* was speaking to the students in my science fiction class at MIT. One student asked him what he thought about "fans," and after a pause, he replied, "You mean, copyright infringers." The remark was met with nervous laughter and mutual misunderstanding.

So far, most discussions of intellectual property in cyberspace are preoccupied with calming corporate anxieties about controlling the flow of images and information. Technologists have touted new automated enforcement mechanisms that allow owners to ferret out infringements, and digital watermarks for tracing the precise origins of appropriated images. Yet we rarely ask whether such tight regulation of intellectual property is in the public interest. Who speaks for the fans? No one.

That doesn't mean they don't have a case. Indeed, there's much to be said on the scribblers' behalf. Fan critics might be covered by the same "fair use" protections that enable journalists or academics to critically assess media content, or by recent Supreme Court decisions broadening the definition of parody to include sampling. Fans don't profit from their borrowings, and they clearly mark their sites as unofficial to avoid consumer confusion. Fan sites don't diminish market value, often actively organizing letter-writing campaigns to keep floundering programs on the networks.

Sadly, none of this matters. If you are a housewife in Nebraska and you receive a letter from Viacom's attorneys telling you to remove your Web site or they will take away your house and your kid's college fund, you don't think twice about your alternatives. You fold.

As a result, although cease-and-desist orders are routine corporate practice, not a single case involving fan fiction has ever reached the courts. No civil-liberties organization has stepped forward to offer pro bono representation. Presumably, the right to free expression doesn't extend to the right to participate in your culture. As currently understood, the First Amendment protects media producers, but not media consumers. Copyright and trademarks are legal "rights" granted to property owners, while fair use is a "defense" which can only be asserted and adjudicated in response to infringement charges. And most of the people being caught in these battles lack the financial resources to take on a major corporation in court.

Disney, Fox and Viacom understand what's at stake here. The proliferating media mergers attest to their recognition that media convergence transforms intellectual property into solid gold. Viacom calls a television series like *Star Trek* a franchise that can generate a seemingly infinite number of derivative products and revenue streams in many media channels. What they can't produce and market directly, they license to another company.

Preparing for this new era, media companies are expanding their legal control over intellectual property as far and as wide as possible, stripmining our culture in the process. They have made inventive uses of trademark law to secure exclusive rights to everything from Spock's pointy ears to Superman's cape, pushed policies that erode the remaining protections for fair use, and lobbied for an expansion of the duration of their copyright protection and thus prevented works from falling into the public domain until they've been drained of value. In the end, we all suffer a diminished right to quote and critique core cultural materials. Imagine what our holiday season would look like if Clement Moore had trademarked Santa Claus!

For most of human history, the storyteller was the inheritor and protector of a shared cultural tradition. Homer took plots, characters, stories, well known to his audiences, and retold them in particularly vivid terms; the basic building blocks of his craft (plots, epithets, metaphors) were passed from one generation to another. The great works of the western tradition were polished like stones in a brook as they were handed off from bard to bard. This process of circulation and retelling improved the fit between story and culture, making these stories central to the way a people thought of themselves. King Arthur, for example, first surfaces as a passing reference in early chronicles and only over the course of several centuries of elaboration becomes complex enough to serve as the basis for *Le Morte D'Arthur.*

Contemporary Web culture is the traditional folk process working at lightning speed on a global scale. The difference is that our core myths now belong to corporations, rather than the folk.

And that kind of exclusive ownership cuts directly against the grain of the technology in question. From the start, computers were seen as tools of collaboration, designed to facilitate brainstorming and data sharing. If one follows the flow of ideas on a Web forum for more than a few posts, it becomes harder and harder to separate one person's intellectual property from another's. We quote freely, incorporating the original message into our own. When Netizens discuss television, we quote equally freely, pulling chunks of aired material into our posts, and adding our own speculations. Other people respond, add more material, and pretty soon the series as viewed by list participants differs radically from the series as aired. In other words, webbers approach television content as "shareware."

Still, what one originates, the law insists, one should have the right to control and profit from. The legal fiction is that no one is harmed by this land grab on the cultural commons. Tight control over intellectual property isn't ultimately a question of author's rights, because without much discussion, control has shifted from individual artists to media corporations — authors now have little say over what happens to their creations. The corporate attorneys rule.

If trademarks are used too broadly and without a history of legal enforcement, companies will lose exclusive claims to them — so Coca-Cola sends out spies to make sure nobody gets served a Pepsi when they order a Coke, Xerox insists that we call a photocopy a photocopy and Fox scans the Web to make sure nobody puts an *X-Files* logo on an unauthorized homepage. Attacking media consumers damages relationships vital to the future of their cultural franchises, but corporations see little choice, since turning a blind eye could pave the way for competitors to exploit valuable properties.

Copyright law was originally understood as a balance between the need to provide incentives to authors and the need to ensure the speedy circulation and absorption of new ideas. Contemporary corporate culture has fundamentally shifted that balance, placing all the muscle on one side of the equation. Media companies certainly have the right to profit from their financial investments, but what about the "investments" — emotional, spiritual, intellectual — we consumers have made in our own culture?

Through its "associates" program, the online book dealer Amazon.com encourages amateur critics to build book-oriented Web sites. If they link back to Amazon's homepage, they will get profit points from every sale made to consumers who follow that link. Amazon has discovered that revitalizing a grassroots book culture increases public demand for books. Perhaps media producers should follow Amazon's example and find ways to transform media consumers from "copyright infringers" into niche marketers, active collaborators in the production of value from cultural materials.

Intellectual property law didn't matter much as long as amateur culture was transmitted through subterranean channels, under the corporate radar, but the Web brought it into view by providing a public arena for grassroots storytelling. Suddenly, fan fiction is perceived as a direct threat to the media conglomerates.

One can, of course, imagine that fans should create original works with no relationship to previously circulating materials, but that would contradict everything we know about human creativity and storytelling. In this new global culture, the most powerful materials will be those that command worldwide recognition, and for the foreseeable future, those materials will originate within the mass media.

For the past century, mass media have displaced traditional folk practices and replaced them with licensed products. When we recount our fantasies, they often involve media celebrities or fictional characters. When we speak with our friends, sitcom catchphrases and advertising jingles roll off our tongues. If we are going to tell stories that reflect our cultural experiences, they will borrow heavily from the material the media companies so aggressively marketed to us. Let's face it — media culture is our culture and, as such, has become an important public resource, the reservoir out of which all future creativity will arise. Given this situation, shouldn't we be concerned about the corporations that keep "infringing" on our cultural wellspring?

HOW THE WEB DESTROYS THE QUALITY OF STUDENTS' RESEARCH PAPERS

By David Rothenberg. (The Chronicle of Higher Education, Aug. 15, 1997.)

Sometimes I look forward to the end-of-semester rush, when students' final papers come streaming into my office and mailbox. I could have hundreds of pages of original thought to read and evaluate. Once in a while, it *is* truly exciting, and brilliant words are typed across a page in response to a question I've asked the class to discuss.

But this past semester was different. I noticed a disturbing decline in both the quality of the writing and the originality of the thoughts expressed. What had happened since last fall? Did I ask worse questions? Were my students unusually lazy? No. My class had fallen victim to the latest easy way of writing a paper: doing their research on the World Wide Web.

It's easy to spot a research paper that is based primarily on information collected from the Web. First, the bibliography cites no books, just articles or pointers to places in that virtual land somewhere off any map: http://www.etc. Then a strange preponderance of material in the bibliography is curiously out of date. A lot of stuff on the Web that is advertised as timely is actually at least a few years old. (One student submitted a research paper last semester in which all of his sources were articles published between September and December 1995; that was probably the time span of the Web page on which he found them.)

Another clue is the beautiful pictures and graphs that are inserted neatly into the body of the student's text. They look impressive, as though they were the result of careful work and analysis, but actually they often bear little relation to the precise subject of the paper. Cut and pasted from the vast realm of what's out there for the taking, they masquerade as original work.

Accompanying them are unattributed quotes (in which one can't tell who made the statement or in what context) and curiously detailed references to the kinds of things that are easy to find on the Web (pages and pages of federal documents, corporate propaganda, or snippets of commentary by people whose credibility is difficult to assess). Sadly, one finds few references to careful, in-depth commentaries on the subject of the paper, the kind of analysis that requires a book, rather than an article, for its full development.

Don't get me wrong, I'm no neo-Luddite. I am as enchanted as anyone else by the potential of this new technology to provide instant information. But too much of what passes for information these days is simply *advertising* for information. Screen after screen shows you where you can find out more, how you can connect to this place or that. The acts of linking and networking and randomly jumping from here to there become as exciting or rewarding as actually finding anything of intellectual value.

Search engines, with their half-baked algorithms, are closer to slot machines than to library catalogues. You throw your query to the wind, and who knows what will come back to you? You may get 234,468 supposed references to whatever you want to know. Perhaps one in a thousand might actually help you. But it's easy to be sidetracked or frustrated as you try to go through those Web pages one by one. Unfortunately, they're not arranged in order of importance.

What I'm describing is the hunt-and-peck method of writing a paper. We all know that word processing makes many first drafts look far more polished than they are. If the paper doesn't reach the assigned five pages, readjust the margin, change the font size, and . . . *voilà*! Of course, those machinations take up time that the student could have spent revising the paper. With programs to check one's spelling and grammar now standard features on most computers, one wonders why students make any mistakes at all. But errors are as prevalent as ever, no matter how crisp the typeface. Instead of becoming perfectionists, too many students have become slackers, preferring to let the machine do their work for them.

What the Web adds to the shortcuts made possible by word processing is to make research look too easy. You toss a query to the machine, wait a few minutes, and suddenly a lot of possible sources of information appear on your screen. Instead of books that you have to check out of the library, read carefully, understand, synthesize, and then tactfully excerpt, these sources are quips, blips, pictures, and short summaries that may be downloaded magically to the dorm-room computer screen. Fabulous! How simple! The only problem is that a paper consisting of summaries of summaries is bound to be fragmented and superficial, and to demonstrate more of a random montage than an ability to sustain an argument through 10 to 15 double-spaced pages.

Of course, you can't blame the students for ignoring books. When college libraries are diverting funds from books to computer technology that will be obsolete in two years at most, they send a clear message to students: Don't read, just connect. Surf. Download. Cut and paste. Originality becomes hard to separate from plagiarism if no author is cited on a Web page. Clearly, the words are up for grabs, and students much prefer the fabulous jumble to the hard work of stopping to think and make sense of what they've read.

Libraries used to be repositories of words and ideas. Now they are seen as centers for the retrieval of information. Some of this information comes from other, bigger libraries, in the form of books that can take time to obtain through interlibrary loan. What happens to the many students (some things never change) who scramble to write a paper the night before it's due? The computer screen, the gateway to the world sitting right on their desks, promises instant access — but actually offers only a pale, two-dimensional version of a real library.

But it's also my fault. I take much of the blame for the decline in the quality of student research in my classes. I need to teach students how to read, to take time with language and ideas, to work through arguments, to synthesize disparate sources to come up with original thought. I need to help my students understand how to assess sources to determine their credibility, as well as to trust their own ideas more than snippets of thought that materialize on a screen. The placelessness of the Web leads to an ethereal randomness of thought. Gone are the pathways of logic and passion, the sense of the progress of an argument. Chance holds sway, and it more often misses than hits. Judgment must be taught, as well as the methods of exploration.

I'm seeing my students' attention spans wane and their ability to reason for themselves decline. I wish that the university's computer system would crash for a day, so that I could encourage them to go outside, sit under a tree, and read a really good book — from start to finish. I'd like them to sit for a while and ponder what it means to live in a world where some things get easier and easier so rapidly that we can hardly keep track of how easy they're getting, while other tasks remain as hard as ever — such as doing research and writing a good paper that teaches the writer something in the process. Knowledge does not emerge in a vacuum, but we do need silence and space for sustained thought. Next semester, I'm going to urge my students to turn off their glowing boxes and think, if only once in a while.

INTERNET GENDER GAP CLOSES IN U.S., STUDY SAYS
By Jube Shiver Jr. (The Los Angeles Times, May 11, 2000.)

The once-yawning gender gap in cyberspace among U.S. consumers has closed, according to a study to be released today.

Drawn by the communications flexibility of e-mail as well as burgeoning opportunities for shopping and entertainment, more than 9 million women went online for the first time in the last six months, according to a study by the Washington-based Pew Research Center.

The huge increase brings women's total online presence to parity with men, said the center, whose findings echo those of a separate report released last month by market research firm Angus Reid Group of Vancouver, Canada.

The two studies are the latest evidence that the Internet, once a niche medium that served the mostly male academic and scientific communities, has become, with unprecedented speed, an indispensable communications tool widely embraced by Americans.

"The Internet has clearly become a part of the nation's social fabric," said Lee Rainie, the Pew Research Center official who oversaw the study. "The online population is increasingly looking like the rest of America."

But contrary to some other reports, the Pew study said Internet users are not social misfits and "are more likely than nonusers to have robust social worlds." Much of the social interaction is facilitated by e-mail. On a typical day, 33% of those who go online send five to 20 e-mail messages, and 6% send more than 20 messages.

The Internet's impact on social behavior has been hotly debated in the wake of several highly publicized incidents, including the Columbine High School shootings in Colorado last year, in which Web sites were cited as fueling social isolationism and violence among the perpetrators of the crimes.

Some studies have claimed that hovering over a computer keyboard all day fosters isolated social misfits. But some say the Internet's global reach and burgeoning community deepen and expand users' relationships.

"The Internet is not isolationist; it's 'connectionist,'" said Rainie, coining a term.

Rainie said his study, which surveyed 3,533 adults by telephone during March, showed a dramatic increase in Internet use since the research center first began studying the Web five years ago.

Both the Pew report and the Angus study, which surveyed 21,000 people in the U.S. and 34 other countries, say American women and men surf the Internet in equal measure and place an equal share of the online shopping orders.

Not surprisingly, women and men use the global computer network in different ways.

Women frequent health and medical sites more than men, the Pew and Angus studies said. Men, meanwhile, spend more time researching product information online as well as trading stocks, the Pew study said. And perhaps because men on average earn more than women, they account for two-thirds of online spending, according to the Angus report.

Despite the throngs of women going online (rising to 46% of Web users from just 18% in 1996), in fact about half of Americans remain offline. And in general, the Pew study said, these nonusers tend to be older, female, poorer, less educated and less likely to be employed than Internet users as a whole.

Understanding the Research Process

The previous chapters have emphasized the mutually reinforcing nature of the processes of reading and writing. Although it is common to think of writing as a more active process than reading, both are acts of *composing* — of constructing meaning through language. When we write, we read and revise our text as we put words to paper. When we read, we construct the ongoing meaning of the text as our eyes move from word to word. The writing and reading relationship is a powerful example of synergy in action, for together these two processes accomplish results that neither could attain alone. Think of how much your writing depends on your reading. Much of your knowledge of the world — and also your knowledge of the structures of written language — is gained by reading. Through writing, you express that knowledge and share it with others.

Writing and reading are primary means of learning both new ideas and new skills, which is why they play such a central role in the work of the academy. But what role does research play in the reading and writing process? When you first think about research, you may think immediately of searching for articles and books in the library or of surfing the World Wide Web. Both libraries and the Web are valuable sources of information about many subjects, but research is actually a much more common activity in all of our lives — one that is an integral part of the writing and reading that we do. You are conducting research, for instance, if you consult a current issue of *Consumer Reports* before purchasing a new compact disc player. You are conducting research if you read *Bride* magazine to help plan your own or a friend's wedding. You are conducting research if you use the World Wide Web to locate the Web pages of the American Kayaking Association so that you can find out about kayaking opportunities in your area.

Both writing and reading can stimulate research. While writing an essay on cloning, for instance, you may realize that you don't understand this process as clearly as you thought you did, so you consult a print or online source to clarify your understanding. Reading can also create questions for which we seek answers. While reading *The English Patient,* a novel by Michael Ondaatje set in Italy during World War II, I realized that I did not have a clear understanding of the relationship between Italy and Germany at the end of the war. Germany and Italy were allies in the war, so why were the Germans setting mines on Italian soil? Because I enjoyed reading the novel and wanted to be sure that I understood it, I consulted an encyclopedia and several online sources about this subject.

As these examples indicate, research is rooted in curiosity. We all conduct research to make decisions, enrich our understanding, and become better informed about the world around us. Research, then, is a natural human activity — one that complements and reinforces the processes of reading and writing as well as those of observing and listening. As a student, you may need to learn certain research techniques, such as using library databases or evaluating sources on the Web, but you already understand many basic principles of research.

This chapter provides strategies that you can use to become an effective researcher. These strategies will be helpful whether you are spending an hour or so gathering information to enrich an essay or undertaking a more substantial research paper. In either case you need to know three things: the kind of information you need for your project, the most efficient and productive way to locate that information, and how to make the most effective use of the information you have located.

■ ■ ■

FOR EXPLORATION

Think back to your previous experiences conducting academic research. First identify an experience that you found both satisfying and productive. Freewrite or brainstorm several paragraphs about this experience. What made this research satisfying and productive? Now identify an experience that was frustrating, unproductive, or in other ways difficult. Freewrite or brainstorm several paragraphs about this experience. Now stop to reflect on these two experiences. Write one paragraph reflecting on what you have learned by thinking and writing about them. Based on these reflections, articulate two or three suggestions you would give yourself to make future research more satisfying and productive.

ASSESSING YOUR GOALS AS A RESEARCHER

Like writing and reading, research is a goal-driven activity. In some cases, your goals as a researcher may be limited. You may simply need to clarify or confirm information that you already have or to gather some supplementary information. Perhaps you are writing an essay about your father's experiences in the military during the Vietnam War. In writing your essay, your focus is primarily on your father's experiences. But you may want to gather information that will enrich your essay's historical and political context. This is very different from a formal research paper, which might focus, for instance, on the ethics of using Agent Orange to defoliate the jungle during the Vietnam War or on the impact of antiwar protests in the United States on the military's approach to the war. Projects like these, which could be addressed only in a paper of considerable length, would require an extensive research effort.

Whether you are writing an informal essay about your father and the Vietnam War or a more formal research paper, you need to know how to locate, evaluate, use, and document sources: the basic knowledge of research required is the same. But the *process* you follow will differ according to your research goals. For instance, you may consult just three or four sources for information that will enrich your essay on your father's experiences during the Vietnam War, so the process of documenting your sources — presenting bibliographic information in an appropriate format — will be relatively simple. For more formal research papers, you'll need to keep track of a wide variety of sources: you might consult twenty to thirty print and online sources and perhaps also engage in field research (such as interviewing). Given these different levels of research, perhaps the most important things to keep in mind when you conduct research are the question you want to answer (your goal as a writer) and the scope and nature of your project. The following guidelines present questions that you can use to assess your goals as a researcher.

■ GUIDELINES FOR ASSESSING YOUR GOALS AS A RESEARCHER

1. What role does research play in this writing project? Will your research provide supplementary details and examples? Or will your research inquire in depth into a subject and present the results of that inquiry to readers?

2. What questions — what need to know — drives your research? How focused are these questions? Are you still at a relatively exploratory stage where you need to do some general reading, Web surfing, and talking with others to help narrow and focus your topic? Or are you prepared to engage in in-depth research?

3. Does the nature of your topic require you to use certain research strategies or explore particular sources? Someone writing about the evolution of guitar styles from the southern and country blues

(continued)

(continued)

musicians of the 1920s and 1930s to the rock 'n' roll guitarists of today would certainly have to consult early recordings of this music, for instance.

4. What "process" implications does your research topic or question hold for you? A student who wants to gather information through field research as well as through print and online research must build in time for this activity.

DEVELOPING AN APPROPRIATE SEARCH STRATEGY

Whether you are conducting research to fill in a few holes in your understanding of a subject or are beginning a substantial research project, you need to develop an appropriate search strategy, one that will enable you to gather the information that you need and to do so in a timely fashion. If you are writing a substantial research paper, you will undoubtedly begin with a general topic that interests you, but your research will be more efficient once you have turned the topic into a goal-driven question. If you are investigating the media's coverage of AIDS, you will proceed differently than if you are investigating the adequacy of AIDS services provided in your community. The nature of your project influences not only how you conduct your inquiry but also what kinds of sources you consult.

Electronic technologies have dramatically increased the available sources of information. If you are writing an essay on the French artist Paul Cézanne for an art history class, for instance, you can use a search engine such as Infoseek to locate the Web site of the Louvre Museum in Paris. With just a few more clicks you can view — and even download and print — reproductions of some of Cézanne's best-known paintings, as well as commentaries written by art historians. Opportunities such as these give you access to information that might not otherwise be available. But there can be such a thing as too much information, particularly if you are not sure whether it is authoritative and relevant to your project.

Even before the advent of electronic technologies, establishing an effective search strategy required considerable thought. A student researching an environmental issue such as the adequacy of national legislation regulating water quality would need to decide whether to begin her investigation by consulting current federal legislation, by reviewing relevant articles in environmental and industry publications, or by reading several studies of this subject. Now that same student would also need to consider which online resources to consult.

To make appropriate decisions about how best to research your topic, you need to understand the strengths and limitations of the resources available to you. Subscribing to a discussion group (listserv) or consulting an Internet newsgroup on your topic can provide you with a broad and stimulating array of contemporary views; a carefully worded online query may identify additional resources. But to gain an adequate historical perspective on legislation governing water quality you would also need to consult scholarly books and articles as well as government documents. In addition, you might want to interview several scientists and legislators who are experts in this area. (Interviewing and other forms of field research are discussed later in this chapter.)

Particularly in substantial research projects, you may find it helpful to develop a multipronged research strategy. You might begin your research by reading postings to an Internet newsgroup, consulting your library's catalogue (whether in print or online), and surfing the Web looking for sites on your subject. But you would also want to consult more specialized sources, such as electronic databases or primary documents relevant to your topic. The following guidelines will enable you to develop an appropriate research strategy.

■ GUIDELINES FOR DEVELOPING AN APPROPRIATE RESEARCH STRATEGY

1. *If You Are Not Already Familiar with Your Library's Resources, Take the Time to Learn about Them.* Many campus libraries and computer services programs offer workshops and online tutorials designed to familiarize users with print and electronic resources. You also may want to consult such sources as Andrew Harnack and Eugene Kleppinger's *Online! A Reference Guide to Using Internet Sources* or Eric Crump and Nick Carbone's *English Online: A Student's Guide to the Internet and the World Wide Web.*

2. *Make Appropriate Use of Primary and Secondary Sources on Your Topic.* Scholars distinguish between primary sources (such as diaries, letters, data from experiments, and historical documents) and secondary sources (such as encyclopedias, scholarly books, biographies, and scientific experiments). Depending on your purpose, a source may be either primary or secondary. If as part of your research for an essay on the Arctic you read contemporary writer Barry Lopez's *Arctic Dreams: Imagination and Desire in a Northern Landscape,* Lopez's book would be considered a secondary source. If, however, you were writing an essay about

(continued)

(continued)

Lopez's prose style or career as a writer, then *Arctic Dreams* would serve as a primary source.

Different kinds of writing projects require different kinds of sources. If you are researching a specific person or event, for instance, you would undoubtedly want to consult such primary sources as newspapers or magazines. Later in this chapter you will read an essay by Brenda Shonkwiler on the collapse of the Tacoma Narrows Bridge. Brenda's essay is enlivened by her use of contemporary newspaper accounts of the disaster. Brenda knew, however, that given her interest in discovering why the bridge collapsed, secondary sources would play the most important role in her research. Her essay nicely balances the immediacy and power of primary sources with the perspective and insight of secondary materials.

3. *Learn the Ins and Outs of Effective Keyword Searching.* Keyword searches — whether on electronic databases in your library or on the Web — can be an efficient way to locate sources. Choosing appropriately narrow topics or keywords and experimenting with synonyms or other alternative terms for your topic can help you develop a manageable and relevant list of resources. If you are interested in the French Revolution, in other words, you might also search for "Marie Antoinette," "Louis XIV," or "Maximilien Robespierre." Often, a series of focused keyword searches can produce more helpful results than a single search using a broader term.

Be sure to take advantage of Boolean keyword search strategies. Boolean searches allow you to refine the ways that you look for information. You can use the term "and" to narrow and "or" to broaden a search, for instance. Some search engines, such as AltaVista, use both "and" and "or" and such symbols as "+" and "–" to allow you to conduct more powerful and focused searches. Here is an example of the difference such a strategy can make. A search on Google for the phrase "French Revolution" identified 76,100 Web sites, or "hits." When I narrowed the search by requesting information on "French+Revolution+Marie+Antoinette," the number of hits was reduced to 2,630, while a similar search of "French+Revolution+ Maximilien+Robespierre" resulted in 446 hits. This is still a large and unwieldy number of Web sites. You may be able to locate helpful information as a result of such a search —

(continued)

(continued)

but you may also want to further limit your search. A search on Google requesting sites with "French+Revolution+Marie+Antoinette+court+entertainment" generated 160 hits. An additional search with the added descriptor "Versailles" (French+Revolution+Marie+Antoinette+court+entertainment+Versailles) identified 55 sites. Because different search engines employ different keyword search strategies, it is a good idea to review the information they provide on conducting effective searches.

4. *Consult with Librarians, Teachers, and Others Who Can Help You in Your Inquiry.* Most college and university libraries employ both general and specialized (or subject matter) reference librarians. I have heard many librarians state that they wished that more students consulted them about ongoing research. The librarian will be better able to help you, however, if you pose specific questions. If you ask how to get information on a particular endangered species, the librarian at the reference desk can do little more than to suggest that you consult the library catalogue or other databases. If instead you inform the librarian that you are looking for recent congressional reports on a particular endangered species, you are likely to get a more focused and helpful response.

Remember, too, that your instructor can be a source of information not only about your assignment but also about possible research strategies to investigate it. And teachers in other areas, as well as persons working in business and industry, are potential resources. While researching her essay on the Tacoma Narrows Bridge disaster, for instance, Brenda Shonkwiler interviewed professors in civil engineering and physics.

Managing the Logistics of Research Projects

Logistical problems can torpedo an otherwise feasible project. When you're working on an extensive research project — a fifteen-page paper for your political science class, for example — it's good to take the following as your motto: Anything that can go wrong will go wrong. I don't say this to discourage you but to remind you of some of the factors that are outside of your control or that require careful planning. Issues of access can play a critical role in research. If your project requires considerable work with primary sources, such as newspapers, do you have the time necessary to obtain microfiched copies and work your way through them? You will probably need to set aside an hour or more for each research session. For that matter, are you sure that microfiched copies of the newspapers you wish to consult are readily available through your college library? If they are not, you will want to inquire at the start of your project about your library's interlibrary loan policies and request those items that are most central to your project at the earliest possible moment. Some colleges participate in consortiums that guarantee easy and quick access to shared resources; others require considerable time for interlibrary loan requests to be processed.

There are additional logistical issues to keep in mind. Suppose that you are writing a paper on current college students' attitudes toward body piercing and you want to survey the opinions of students in your sociology class. For your survey results to have merit — to contribute to your overall inquiry — you would have to spend five to six weeks developing, testing, implementing, and interpreting your survey. If you have only two weeks, perhaps you should conduct informal interviews with several students. These interviews would not give you as much information as a formal survey would — but they could add specificity and liveliness to your discussion.

Even in less complex situations where you are relying primarily on sources in your library or on the Web and are not engaged in field research, the demands of major research projects can seem overwhelming. Library books, photocopies of articles, printouts of Web sites, and notes you have taken can quickly accumulate into a mass of material that seems more like a confusing maze than an entryway to knowledge. As these examples demonstrate, time management and organizational skills are essential for research to proceed effectively. The following guidelines provide strategies you can use to make your research an enjoyable and exciting — rather than a frustrating and difficult — process.

■ GUIDELINES FOR MANAGING THE LOGISTICS OF RESEARCH PROJECTS

1. *Establish a Timetable for Your Research — and Review It Periodically to See If It Is Realistic.* One of the best ways to keep track of the work you need to do is to list the activities that are essential to your project in the order in which they should be completed. Here's what a sample list might look like:

   ■ Analyze the assignment and assess research goals.

   ■ Choose a preliminary topic.

   (continued)

(continued)

- Develop a preliminary search strategy.

- Conduct the research needed to narrow the topic.

- Finalize the topic.

- Finalize a search strategy.

- Conduct print and Internet research; start a bibliography.

- Develop an outline for the paper.

- Do additional research, if necessary.

- Draft the research paper.

- Get a response to the draft.

- Revise the draft; prepare a list of works cited.

- Proofread the final draft.

Set tentative dates for each of these activities. If you regularly review your list and dates, you'll have a good sense of when you need to extend or limit the amount of time for a particular activity.

2. *Employ a Research Log to Track What You Have Accomplished, to Make Notes, and So On.* A research log supplements the timetable that the previous guideline encouraged you to establish. You can keep a handwritten research log. Some writers prefer, for instance, to purchase a small pocket-sized notebook for each research project. In this notebook, you can record daily entries for work accomplished, keywords you have used in successful searches, to-do lists, ideas to follow up, and so on. You can also use your computer for this purpose, particularly if you have a portable notebook computer. In this case, set up a folder that can hold the kind of information suggested above. You could even establish subfolders about specific tasks or subjects. You could title these subfolders with such headings as "keyword searches," "books consulted," "articles consulted," "working bibliography," and so on. Whether you keep a handwritten or electronic research log, the point is to bring order to what can otherwise be a chaotic process.

3. *Build a Working Bibliography as You Go to Avoid Scrambling to Document All Your Sources at the End of the Project.* Sure, it takes time

(continued)

(continued)

to create a complete bibliographic entry for each source as you consult it, but you'll be glad you did when you reach the final stages of your research project. Nothing is more frustrating than searching through a floor littered with books, photocopies of articles, and printouts of Web pages — particularly when it's 3 A.M., your paper is due at 8 A.M., and you can't find the bibliographic information you need for several of your most important citations.

When consulting sources on the Web, you will find that some information published there (such as government documents) is permanently available but that much is temporary. A Web site that you search Monday afternoon may be substantially revised by Tuesday morning — and the page you wish to cite deleted. If you locate information of interest to you on the Web, be sure to download, save, and print it and also to gather all the information you will need to cite this source in your bibliography.

In the past, most writers kept entries for their working bibliography on three-inch by five-inch cards. Some writers still use these cards because they like the physical ease of manipulating the cards — by topic or by alphabetical order. But increasingly writers are using computer programs to organize their sources. Whichever method you use, be sure to check to see which documentation style your assignment requires before you begin your working bibliography. Later sections of this book provide essential information for the Modern Language Association (MLA) and American Psychological Association (APA) documentation styles.

EVALUATING SOURCES

The scholarly work of the academy is like an ongoing conversation. Even an apparently "original" discovery depends on the previous work of others. This is true whether that discovery involves identifying the molecular structure of DNA or developing a new reading of Freud's psychological theories. When scholars publish their research, they do so not to have the final word on their subject but to invite responses; it is through such responses that knowledge in the academy progresses.

The same holds true for other forms of inquiry. Discussions of political, environmental, cultural, economic, and other issues occur in many forums: in the popular press, special-interest groups, government and nonprofit educational bodies, and so on. These discussions, like those within the academy, can best be viewed as ongoing dialogues that occur in particular times and places. Contemporary debates over smoking differ in many ways from those that occurred in previous decades, for instance. In the 1980s, few tobacco companies were willing to state publicly that tobacco has harmful health effects. Now both those who wish to regulate or even ban tobacco in its various forms and those who grow tobacco and make cigarettes and other related products acknowledge tobacco's dangerous properties.

As these examples suggest, the question of what it means for a particular source to be authoritative is both complex and situated. Although a scientist who in 1978 published a scholarly essay on the potential side effects of tobacco might well have been considered authoritative by his peers at that time, his or her research would likely have limited value to today's scientists.

Evaluating Print Sources

As a student, you already have considerable experience evaluating print sources. You instinctively draw on this experience when you decide that a brief article in a popular magazine is less authoritative than one that appears in an encyclopedia or scholarly journal. You know also that the credentials of the author of a text are important. But to fully evaluate a source, you need to consider more than the credentials of the author and means of publication. You need to gain a sense of the "history" of the conversation that you seek (via your research) to enter. The following guidelines for evaluating print sources will help you achieve this goal.

■ GUIDELINES FOR EVALUATING PRINT SOURCES

1. *Begin by Considering the Traditional Criteria for Evaluating Print Sources.* These criteria are reflected in the following questions:

   ■ Who is the author? Is she or he a recognized expert on the topic? Have other sources referred favorably to this author's work? What biases might the source have?

   ■ Who published this source, and what can the means of publication tell you about the work's authoritativeness? Is this article or book published by a scholarly press? By a general or "trade" publisher? By a special-interest group, business, or industry?

   (continued)

(continued)

- What guarantees the accuracy of the information contained in this source? The reputation of the writer? The prestige of the press publishing it? The source's scholarly apparatus, such as footnotes and works cited? Scholarly or popular reviews? Citations found in other sources? Your own knowledge of the material?

- For whom is the author writing? Is this a work intended for general readers or specialists? What is the relationship between the medium of publication and the intended audience?

- When was this source published? If it was not published within the past five years, is it still current? Or might you have special reasons for wanting to consult an earlier source?

2. *If Your Initial Evaluation Is Positive, Continue to Assess the Source by Exploring It More Thoroughly.* You can accomplish this by reading the preface, foreword, table of contents, and abstract, if provided. You may also want to skim the introduction and conclusion of articles or first and last chapters of books.

3. *To the Fullest Extent Possible, Consider the "History" of the Source You Are Evaluating.* To do so, ask yourself questions like these:

- What seems to be "at stake" in the issue or topic I am researching? Does this issue raise questions of policy? Fact? Value?

- Do those writing on this topic seem motivated primarily by a desire better to understand their subject, or do they seem intent on persuading others to do or believe something? Are those engaged with this topic specialists or generalists — or both? To what extent has the popular press focused attention on this topic?

- Whom do those writing on this topic seem to be addressing? The general public? A specific audience? Multiple audiences?

- Is this a contemporary topic or one with a long history — or both?

- How did I first learn about this topic? In what ways might my own introduction to and understanding of the topic influence my evaluation of my sources?

(continued)

(continued)

4. *When You Locate a Source That Seems Particularly Authoritative and Well Suited to Your Purpose, Use Its Footnotes and Works Cited to Follow a "Paper Trail" That Will Lead You to Other Relevant Sources.* Most researchers have experienced what I have come to think of as the "Eureka" moment — the moment when they find an article or book that is a particularly rich resource for their project. Perhaps the author articulates the issues at stake in ways that you've been trying to express, but haven't quite succeeded in doing. Perhaps the author discusses a body of research that you had not previously been aware of — but that you can immediately see is relevant to your topic. Whatever the particularities of your "Eureka" moment, be sure to take full advantage of your discovery by reading the references in the list of works cited and footnotes with care. They will lead you to many useful sources.

Evaluating Web Sources

The World Wide Web is changing what it means to be a writer, reader, and researcher. Anyone with a computer, modem, and Internet service provider has access to a previously unimagined wealth of resources. Someone recently diagnosed with cancer can locate unprecedented amounts of information on this illness on the Web. The information that this person gains — which can range from advice presented on a personal Web page by someone who has this same illness to notices of trials of new treatments included on government-sponsored Web sites — can literally mean the difference between life and death.

As a student researching an issue or topic, your ability to evaluate Web sources is hardly a life or death matter. But it can make the difference between making a productive, informed use of the Web or wasting your time with endless hours of inefficient surfing. And evaluating information on the Internet and Web can be a challenge. As Janet E. Alexander and Marsha Ann Tate observe in their book *Web Wisdom: How to Evaluate and Create Information Quality on the Web,* "Since the Web is such a new medium, many standards, conventions, and regulations commonly found in traditional media are largely absent" (2). Most television viewers, for instance, can easily distinguish an infomercial for a new cooking appliance — one that the announcer claims will produce tasty food *and* lower blood pressure and cholesterol — from a serious, scientifically grounded documentary on healthy cooking. But on the Web such distinctions can become murkier. While some Web sites, such as that of the Library of Congress, are clearly authoritative, others are much harder to evaluate.

When I searched the Web using the keywords "cancer + treatment," for instance, two of the first sites that appeared were those of the American Cancer Society and an organization called the Cancer Group Institute. You probably recognize the name of the American Cancer Society (ACS). As one of the Web pages linked to the "About the ACS" section of its homepage reminds readers, the ACS is one of the oldest health organizations in the United States. The ACS homepage, reproduced here (Figure 4.1), provides links to a wide variety of resources — from information about various kinds of cancer and their treatment to services provided by the ACS and information about its history and initiatives.

The second Web site mentioned is that of an organization that identifies itself as the Cancer Group Institute (CGI). This Web site, which can be found at <www.cancergroup.com>, announces that it is the "World's Premier Cancer Information Center for Doctors and Lay Persons." The homepage includes a variety of links, including one that states that the Cancer Group Institute is "pleased to announce that The American Cancer Society has granted our site permission to link with this very prestigious organization." Because the CGI homepage is several screens long and is somewhat haphazardly organized, it is harder to navigate than the ACS site. It is also difficult to find information about the status, mission, and history of the CGI. The link to "Press Releases about Our Site" contains no mission statement for or history of the organization. Furthermore, some of the most important links, such as those to information about various kinds of cancer, appear near the end of the homepage. Still, as I scroll through the material, the site looks potentially helpful. In addition to links to discussions of various kinds of cancers, it has links to pages for "parents with children diagnosed with cancer," and links to clubs for survivors of cancer.

But the longer I surf this site, the more questions I have. When I click on a link that says "Press here if you are a Medical Library, Teaching Hospital, or University," I learn that CGI sells reviews about various kinds of cancer research. The fact that CGI is at least in part a money-making venture does not necessarily compromise the quality of the information that it provides — but it does make me skeptical. When I click on one of the cancer-information links, my skepticism increases because I discover that although the page does include recent information on studies of and treatments for various kinds of cancer, the summaries are quite brief. For complete information, I am informed, I will need to order the full review on this topic. The cost is "$25 each for one [review], $22 each for two to four, $20 each for 5 or more, or $220 for the entire set, plus $7.00 post and packing." CGI may indeed provide high-quality information on various forms of cancer — but this information is available only to those who purchase the print reviews.

A few additional minutes of surfing reveals another problem. When I click on the page with testimonials from physicians, I discover that most often they praise the reviews as useful aids for those studying for board exams. This

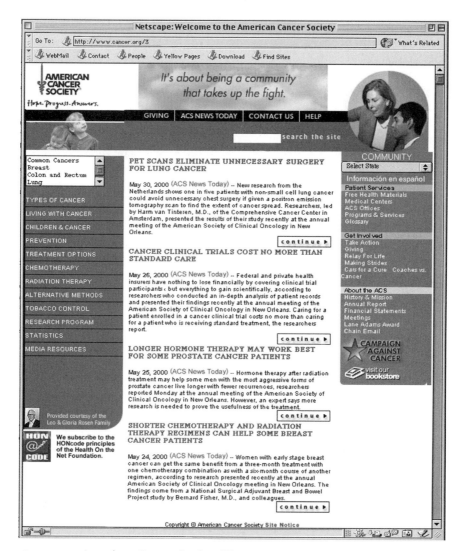

Figure 4.1   American Cancer Society Homepage

relatively specific focus is not suggested by other information presented on the homepage, so I am left with additional questions. To whom is this site directed? People seeking information on cancer and its treatment? Doctors looking for study guides to help them pass medical board examinations? Can one site fulfill both purposes equally well?

As this example indicates, determining whether a Web site provides authoritative information can take a good deal of time. After spending almost an hour surfing the CGI Web site, I learned enough to know that I would not consider the information it presented to be authoritative. But I still feel unable to evaluate the helpfulness of the product that CGI advertises. It may well be that the material provided to those who purchase reviews from CGI is authoritative and objective and that the Web site reflects nothing more than poor design and inadequate information. Much further study would be needed to learn whether this is the case.

Whether you are trying to learn more about potential treatments for a particular kind of cancer or about the problems that beset the steel industry in the United States in the 1970s and early 1980s, you can certainly find a plethora of materials on the Web. But as the previous example illustrates, you will have to evaluate these materials carefully before trusting their authority, objectivity, and accuracy. Many of the questions used to determine the authority of print materials can also be used to evaluate Web texts. But texts presented on the Web require some additional questions. It is important to remember, for instance, that many Web sites mix various kinds of pages.

In *Web Wisdom,* Alexander and Tate identify six different kinds of Web sites — advocacy, business, informational, news, personal, and entertainment — and they argue that each kind of Web site provides different challenges for those who wish to be critical readers and evaluators. Advocacy Web sites, for instance, seek to influence public opinion — to change people's minds and, possibly, encourage them to take action. The site for the Cancer Group Institute included both informational and business pages. You cannot assume that information provided on a Web site's homepage is equally applicable to all pages on the site. This adds to the complexity of evaluating information presented on the Web. The following guidelines provide suggestions you can use to evaluate Web sites and Web pages.

■ GUIDELINES FOR EVALUATING WEB SITES AND WEB PAGES

1. *Establish the Credibility of the Web Site or Page.* The first step in evaluating a Web site or page is to determine what person or organization stands behind the site — and thus takes responsibility for the authority and accuracy of the information presented therein. Sometimes this is easily determined. Even before I consulted the American Cancer Society's Web site, for instance, I knew that the ACS is a highly esteemed and well-established organization known for providing well researched, authoritative information. Had I not already known about the ACS, I could have arrived at the same

(continued)

(continued)

conclusion by reading the "About the ACS" and "History and Mission" sections of the Web site, where the organization explains its history, mission, and procedures. In contrast, it was harder to determine the exact nature of the organization that stands behind the Cancer Group Institute.

In *Web Wisdom,* Alexander and Tate provide a series of questions that can be used to assess the authority of a site and also of a page on a site that contains mixed pages. The authors note that these "questions can also be used by Web authors as a guide to creating pages that can be recognized as originating from a reliable, trustworthy source" (54). Alexander and Tate point out that "the greater the number of 'yes' answers, the greater the likelihood that the quality of the information on the page can be determined" (54). The questions that Alexander and Tate list (pp. 55–57, excerpted here) are important for you to ask of any site you use as a source of information:

Authority of a Site

The following information should be included either on a site's homepage or on a page directly linked to it.

- Is it clear what organization, company, or person is responsible for the contents of the site? This can be indicated by the use of a logo.

- If the site is a subsite of a larger organization, does the site provide the logo or name of the larger organization?

- Is there a way to contact the organization, company, or person responsible for the contents of the site? These contact points can be used to verify the legitimacy of the site. Although a phone number, mailing address, and e-mail address are all possible contact points, a mailing address and phone number provide a more reliable way of verifying legitimacy.

- Are the qualifications of the organization, company, or person responsible for the contents of the site indicated?

- If all the materials on the site are protected by a single copyright holder, is the name of the copyright holder given?

- Does the site list any recommendations or ratings from outside sources?

(continued)

(continued)

Authority of a Page

- Is it clear what organization, company, or person is responsible for the contents of the page? Similarity in page layout and design features can help signify responsibility.

- If the material on the page is written by an individual author,

  Is the author's name clearly indicated?

  Are the author's qualifications for providing the information stated?

  Is there a way of contacting the author? That is, does the person list a phone number, mailing address, and e-mail address?

  Is there a way of verifying the author's qualifications? That is, is there an indication of his or her expertise in the subject area, or a listing of memberships in professional organizations related to the topic?

- If the material on the page is copyright protected, is the name of the copyright holder given?

- Does the page have the official approval of the person, organization, or company responsible for the site?

2. *Evaluate the Quality of the Writing on the Site.* A Web site may be backed by an authoritative and well-established source, but if the quality of the writing is poor or the site is disorganized, the usefulness of the information it presents could be limited. Just as a print text should be free of grammatical, spelling, and other errors, so should a Web site. Web sites and pages should also provide sources for information they present — including information presented in graphs, charts, and tables. Don't assume that a Web site sponsored by an authority (whether an individual, company, or organization) is automatically helpful. That site could have been constructed by a part-time employee with limited knowledge and writing ability.

3. *Determine the Ways in Which Individual, Corporate, or Organizational Biases Influence the Nature and Presentation of Information.* No Web site can be completely objective. In determining what treatments to discuss on its Web site, the American Cancer Society draws on carefully developed and clearly expressed assumptions about what does — and doesn't — count as valid scientific research. As a consequence, the site undoubtedly provides more

(continued)

(continued)

information about treatments that have met established scientific protocols than about newer alternative treatments. Does this mean that the ACS site lacks credibility due to bias? No. The ACS takes care to describe and support its methodology, and it provides considerable support for its recommendations. Furthermore, the ACS has nothing to gain if those who visit the site are persuaded by the information it presents. The ACS is not selling this information or providing a profit-making service. It is a nonprofit organization.

The ACS constructed its Web site, in other words, solely for the purpose of providing helpful information for readers. Its interest is in education and not in promoting sales or services. While it would be a mistake to assume that any educational site automatically provides authoritative and accurate information, the fact that a site exists primarily to educate readers is important. In considering the objectivity of a Web site, then, be sure you understand why the site was constructed and what its goals are.

Does this mean that you should never consult a Web site that reflects a clear bias on a subject? That depends on the purpose of your research. If you are studying current debates on the regulation of tobacco, you may find it helpful to research a variety of position-oriented Web sites, from those of various tobacco company or industry organizations to those constructed by organizations that argue for tighter tobacco regulation. Doing so will help you examine how different parties in an issue represent information. In this case, your research will benefit from position-oriented information.

Whatever information you gather, you will always need to determine the ways in which individual, corporate, or organizational biases influence the nature and presentation of that information. You can use the following questions from *Web Wisdom* to evaluate the objectivity of any Web site or Web page:

Objectivity

- Is the point of view of the individual or organization responsible for providing the information evident?

  If there is an individual author of the material on the page:

  - Is the point of view of the author evident?

  - Is it clear what relationship exists between the author and the person, company, or organization responsible for the site?

(continued)

(continued)

- Is the page free of advertising?

For pages that include advertising:

- Is it clear what relationship exists between the business, organization, or person responsible for the contents of the page and any advertisers represented on the page?

- If there is both advertising and information on the page, is there a clear differentiation between the two?

- Is there an explanation of the site's policy relating to advertising and sponsorship?

For pages that have a nonprofit or corporate sponsor:

- Are the names of any nonprofit or corporate sponsors clearly listed?

- Are links included to the sites of any nonprofit or corporate sponsors so that a user may find out more information about them?

- Is additional information provided about the nature of the sponsorship, such as what type it is (nonrestrictive, educational, etc.)?

4. *Be Sure to Check the Timeliness of the Information Presented on a Web Site.* One of the benefits of conducting research on the Web is that many sites offer up-to-date information. You can't assume, however, that a site that focuses on a timely topic, such as Arab-Israeli relations or the status of gun control legislation, is presenting current information. If a Web master temporarily or permanently stops maintaining a site, it can quickly become dated. For this reason, you should not assume that something found on the Web is up-to-date. When evaluating a Web source, think about whether the timeliness of the information is important for the topic you are researching. If it is, then ask the following questions from *Web Wisdom* to establish when the site you are using was written and how recently it has been updated:

Currency

- Is the date the material was first created in any format included on the page?

- Is the date the material was first placed on the server included on the page?

(continued)

(continued)

- If the contents of the page have been revised, is the date (and time, if appropriate) the material was last revised included on the page?

- To avoid confusion, are all dates in an internationally recognized format? Examples of dates in international format (dd mm yy) are 5 June 1997 and 21 January 1999.

5. *Consider the Information Presented on a Site in the Context of Its Intended Audience, Goals, and Purpose.* What should you do if you locate a Web site that contains technical information that is difficult for you to understand? If you apply Guideline 2 above (p. 112) for evaluating Web site writing, you might determine that the site is unhelpful since it lacks clarity. This could be a mistake. Readers with expertise in the subject area may find that a site with technical vocabulary is useful and informative. Moreover, the quality of the site's information may justify your efforts to understand it. Many Web sites designed for experts include pages with information for those with less knowledge. If you dismiss a site quickly because it appears too technical or complicated, you could miss out on a valuable source of information.

   The focus in this chapter is on providing basic information about evaluating Web sites. If you would like further information about Alexander and Tate's criteria for particular kinds of sites, you may wish to consult *Web Wisdom* or the Web site <http://www2.widener.edu/Wolfgram-Memorial-Library/webeval.htm>.

6. *Recognize the Need to Protect Yourself as a Reader, Researcher, and Navigator of the Web — and to Use the Web Responsibly.* With the advent of the Internet have come a number of new questions and problems regarding your privacy as a Web user. Some sites employ information-gathering technologies such as "cookies," often without your knowledge. Others ask for personal information before allowing you to access their site. And yet other sites may offer to send you information at your email address. This information can be helpful — but it may be passed on to other organizations. Informed users of the Web take care to ensure that their rights to privacy are not violated. They also take care not to violate the rights of those publishing information on the Web by respecting restrictions regarding downloading or other possible uses of material presented at a site. The following questions from *Web Wisdom*

(continued)

(continued)

can help you protect your own right to privacy and respect the rights of those constructing Web sites.

Interaction and Transaction Features

- If any financial transactions occur at the site, does the site indicate what measures have been taken to ensure their security?

- If the business, organization, or person responsible for the page is requesting information from the user, is there a clear indication of how the information will be used?

- If cookies are used at the site, is the user notified? Is there an indication of what the cookies are used for and how long they last?

- Is there a feedback mechanism for users to comment about the site?

- Are any restrictions regarding downloading and other uses of the materials offered on the page clearly stated?

FOR EXPLORATION

Choose an interesting word or phrase, and using one or more search engines search the Web. After reviewing the results of your search, choose two sites that interest you. Using the questions provided by Alexander and Tate, evaluate these sites. Write a paragraph or two for each site summarizing the results of your analysis.

USING SOURCES: QUOTING, PARAPHRASING, AND SUMMARIZING

Earlier in this chapter I said that the scholarly work of the academy is like an ongoing conversation. One writer argues that global warming may be influencing recent climate changes. Others respond to this argument — testing, elaborating, clarifying, questioning. Soon the issues at stake — the questions with which those addressing this subject are concerned — have evolved. The question of whether global warming is occurring becomes less controversial, as evidence accumulates for its existence. In the meantime, other questions become more pressing. How concerned should scientists and the general public be about global warming? Can they do anything about it if, in fact, it is occurring?

As a student engaged in research, you are entering the scholarly (and, depending on your topic, also civic and popular) conversation on your subject. You probably can't participate in this conversation as an expert. But you can't accomplish your purpose simply by presenting one author's views and then another's — like pearls strung on a necklace. Your instructors certainly are interested in your ability to identify and locate information on your topic, but they also are looking at how you make use of that information.

As this chapter has already emphasized, when you conduct research, you have (at least) two purposes. You want to learn something new about your subject by gathering information that helps you understand it. But you also want to understand the history of your subject — by learning what is accepted, what is not, who the experts are, what issues and questions they think are important, and whether you agree with them. The way that you use sources — the way that you integrate sources into your writing — tells readers whether you have accomplished these purposes.

As a writer, you have three options for integrating sources into your writing. You can quote your source's words exactly. You can paraphrase your source's words (by digesting the meaning stated in the source and representing it in your own language). And, finally, you can summarize the information presented in your source (by significantly abbreviating a text, whether a paragraph, a chapter, or even an entire book). How can you determine when to quote, paraphrase, and summarize? The following guidelines suggest criteria you can use to answer this question.

■ GUIDELINES FOR DETERMINING WHEN TO QUOTE, PARAPHRASE, AND SUMMARIZE

1. *Quote Directly from Sources Only When You Have a Specific Purpose for Doing So.* Perhaps the language used in the source is so powerful — so pointed and memorable — that it expresses in a few words what you would take many words to express. Perhaps the author of the source is an authority whose expertise buttresses your own position. Perhaps you disagree with the source and want to play fair with it by allowing the author to speak in his or her own words. These are good reasons for including direct quotations in your writing.

2. *Paraphrase When You Want to Convey the Information in a Passage but Prefer to Represent the Ideas in Your Own Words.* When you paraphrase, you stay close to the meaning expressed in the original

(continued)

(continued)

text, but you recast that language in your own words. You may paraphrase a source, for instance, because the author's words are not particularly memorable or because you do not want to interrupt your discussion with a direct quotation. Paraphrasing may strike you as the most efficient way to convey important information. Whatever your reason, when you paraphrase, it is important that you synthesize the original passage, present it in your own words, and acknowledge the source.

3. *Summarize When You Want to Present the Main Idea of a Text in Your Own Words.* Summaries are useful in many situations. You might be considering two book-length opposing arguments on a topic. If your purpose is to provide a context and not to discuss the arguments in great detail, a brief summary of each argument fulfills your purpose. When you summarize, you want to present the main points of the original text as succinctly as possible.

You may understand why you are quoting, paraphrasing, or summarizing a passage — and yet be unsure about how you should do so. When is a paraphrase just a paraphrase — and not plagiarism, or the inappropriate use of the words and ideas of another? What is the difference between paraphrasing and summarizing? To address questions such as these, I have included some examples from my own use of Janet E. Alexander's and Marsha Ann Tate's *Web Wisdom: How to Evaluate and Create Information Quality on the Web*. In discussing how to evaluate Web sources (pp. 107–16), I drew on Alexander's and Tate's work, for I recognized that their knowledge of and experience with evaluating Web sources was much greater than my own. When did I quote directly, paraphrase, and summarize? What logic guided these decisions?

If you look back at the "Evaluating Web Sources" section of this chapter, you will see that I quoted directly from Alexander and Tate for two general reasons. The first was when I felt that their words were more cogent or memorable than my own might be. This happened, for instance, when I quoted their statement that "since the Web is such a new medium, many standards, conventions, and regulations commonly found in traditional media are largely absent" (2). Here Alexander and Tate succinctly and memorably articulate an important point about the Web. I also quoted them directly when I included their questions for evaluating Web sites. I quoted their questions, rather than paraphrasing them, because I felt that the specific wording that they used was essential to their meaning.

On other occasions I paraphrased Alexander and Tate's wording. On page 58 of *Web Wisdom,* for instance, Alexander and Tate define *advocacy Web pages* as follows: "An advocacy Web page is one with the primary purpose of influencing public opinion. The purpose may be either to influence people's ideas or to encourage activism, and either a single individual or group of people may be responsible for the page." My paraphrase, which appears on p. 110 of this chapter, paraphrases their definition by stating that advocacy Web sites "seek to influence public opinion — to change people's minds and, possibly, encourage them to take action." This paraphrase remains true to the meaning expressed in Alexander and Tate's definition. (Because my purpose was to provide a broad characterization of advocacy sites, I didn't need to mention that advocacy Web sites can be sponsored by either individuals or groups.)

And I also summarized ideas presented at great length in *Web Wisdom.* In Alexander and Tate's book, for instance, the six kinds of Web sites are discussed in six separate chapters. I wanted readers to be aware of these distinctions among Web sites, but I could not go into similar detail. So on p. 110 of this chapter I simply note that the authors of *Web Wisdom* "identify six different kinds of Web sites — advocacy, business, informational, news, personal, and entertainment."

What else do you need to know about using sources? You should recognize that most often sources need to be introduced or contextualized. If you are writing an essay on the history of the concept of the aesthetic for a philosophy class, for instance, and want to include a quotation from Terry Eagleton's *The Ideology of the Aesthetic,* you might introduce this quotation as follows: "As British literary theorist Terry Eagleton observes, ..." It is also important to comment on the significance of quotations. Let's imagine that you want to quote Eagleton's observation that the body is "the enormous blindspot of all traditional philosophy" (234). You might follow this quotation with a sentence such as the following: "In calling attention to traditional philosophy's 'blindspot,' Eagleton challenges readers to place the work of such philosophers as Nietzsche at the center, rather than at the margins, of philosophy." Comments like this demonstrate that you understand the implications of Eagleton's observation and can use it to develop your own analysis.

CONDUCTING FIELD RESEARCH

Thus far, this chapter has focused on locating, evaluating, and using print and online resources. But there are many additional ways to enrich your writing and research. You can find information through interviews, questionnaires, and firsthand observation.

If you are writing an essay on sexual harassment on college campuses, for instance, you will probably find it helpful to do some library research to get a broad perspective on the issue — national trends, the history of the present controversy, incidents on campuses other than your own, and so forth. But it might be especially helpful to interview an adviser or faculty member who is involved in setting or enforcing your own school's policy on the issue, as well as individuals who have publicly opposed that policy. You might distribute a questionnaire to other students designed to measure their opinions on the issue (asking, for instance, how they define sexual harassment; how prevalent they feel it is at your school; what, if any, policy they would like to see enforced; and so on). You might want to spend some hours closely observing the behavior of male and female students in a social setting. Even if these sources of information do not play a major role in your essay, they will enrich your understanding of your subject and help you to consider it from a variety of perspectives.

There are other advantages to this form of research — sometimes known as *field research* because it takes you out of the library or computer lab and puts you directly in the field. Many students find that field research helps them build enthusiasm for and commitment to their subject. Field research allows you to do original work — in effect, *create* new information that no one before you has compiled in quite the same way.

This is not to say that traditional research is unnecessary. Even professional field researchers are careful to keep up with the work of other scholars, to compare their own findings with others', and to place themselves within the ongoing scholarly conversation. Effective mastery of library and Web research skills gives you access to the broadest, most comprehensive perspective on any topic. But depending on the topic you've chosen and the questions you are asking about it, field research can help you arrive at a fascinatingly detailed and particular *local* perspective on a subject.

Interviews

Interviews can often provide information that is unavailable through other kinds of research. Sometimes you may wish to consult an expert on the subject you are studying; on other occasions you may interview individuals to gain local perspectives on your issue, firsthand accounts of relevant experiences, or other information. A good interviewer is first of all a good listener — someone who is able to draw out the person being interviewed. Interviews are more formal and time-pressured than most conversations, so be sure that you do not underestimate the importance of carefully preparing for and conducting them. Here are some suggestions to follow when you interview someone for your writing.

■ GUIDELINES FOR CONDUCTING INTERVIEWS

1. Request an interview in advance. Explain why you want the interview, how long it will take, and what you hope to accomplish.

2. Come prepared with a list of written questions.

3. If you wish to tape the interview, remember to ask permission first.

4. Take notes during the interview, even if you use a tape recorder. Your notes will help refresh your memory later when you don't have time to review the entire tape; they can also help you identify the most important points of discussion.

5. Be flexible. Don't try to make the person you are interviewing answer all your prepared questions if he or she doesn't find some of them appropriate or interesting. If your interviewee focuses on one question or moves to a related issue, just accept this change in plans and return to your list of questions when appropriate.

6. Try a variety of questioning techniques. People are sometimes unable or unwilling to answer direct questions. Suppose that you want to write about your grandmother's experiences during World War II. If you simply ask her what life was like then, she may not respond very fully or specifically. Less direct questions may elicit more detailed answers.

Questionnaires

Distributing a questionnaire can be a good way to gain information about the attitudes, beliefs, and experiences of a large number of people. You might, for instance, question your fellow students on their career plans, their reading habits, or their opinions on your school's policy on hate speech.

A detailed discussion of the design and interpretation of questionnaires is beyond this book's scope. In some disciplines that deal extensively in questionnaire and poll data, such as sociology and political science, these matters are addressed in depth. For an English class, it may be best to use questionnaires as a rough indicator of broad trends and a source of differing perspectives on a topic rather than as a "scientific" measurement of the general population's views. Here are some guidelines for designing and using questionnaires. They assume that you have decided on a topic, determined an appropriate number of representative respondents, devised a way to distribute your questionnaires, and arranged to collect them when completed.

■ GUIDELINES FOR DESIGNING AND USING QUESTIONNAIRES

1. Treat the drafting of your questionnaire as you would any important writing project. In other words, keep your audience in mind, and be prepared to do more than one draft to make sure your questions are clear, easily answerable, and able to solicit the information you seek.

2. Keep in mind that the longer and more difficult a questionnaire is, the fewer completed questionnaires you are likely to have returned. Yes-or-no and multiple-choice questions are the easiest to answer but restrict your respondent's freedom to give complex answers. Open-ended questions yield more nuanced answers but ask more work of your respondent and hence are best kept to a minimum.

3. Show a draft of your questionnaire to some friends before copying and distributing it. Seek feedback on the clarity and "user friendliness" of your questionnaire.

4. Include all appropriate demographic questions in addition to questions about your primary subject. Unless your respondents' names are vital, make clear that they have the option of remaining anonymous. You may want to ask for other personal characteristics, such as sex, income, marital status, age, or education, depending on the questions governing your research. If you are asking about attitudes toward sexual harassment, for instance, you may well want to be able to note differences between the answers given by men and women of various ages. Or if you are gathering opinions about the homeless, your respondents' income levels may be relevant.

5. You should write an explanation on the questionnaire of its purpose and the use you have in mind for it, and ask respondents to check off *yes* or *no* to indicate whether you have permission to quote them.

6. Distribute more copies than you need to have returned. The return rate will be well below 100 percent.

Unless you administer your questionnaire under tightly controlled conditions, you will not generate scientifically verifiable data. Still, there are good reasons for using questionnaires. Responses to questionnaires can prompt you to consider multiple perspectives on an issue; they can also provide illustrative examples and voices to bring into your essay. If, for example, in the course of an essay arguing for more child-care facilities on campus, you quote directly from statements made by single parents who are full-time students, your questionnaire will have contributed a good deal to your essay's persuasiveness.

Observation

Finally, don't overlook the kinds of information available by firsthand observation. Disciplines such as sociology and anthropology have long and rich traditions of case-study research in which "participant-observers" living in and moving among various communities attempt to observe and interpret social customs and patterns of behavior. Scholars using this methodology have gathered research data in twelve-step groups, day-care centers, crack houses, and corporate boardrooms.

Although you will probably not undertake full-scale case-study research, you can generate stimulating questions and gather interesting material for your writing assignments through close observation of various communities. If you are writing a paper on the effectiveness of your college or university's student government, you might interview members of that government (and those who have criticized it) and observe a variety of meetings — from the student senate to various subcommittees and working groups. You may already participate in activities that could contribute to your understanding of an issue. If you work as a restaurant waitperson, you might study the tipping practices of men and women to gain insight into gender differences and their social implications. As with other forms of field research, observation can enrich your understanding by generating questions and exposing you to multiple perspectives on a subject.

DOCUMENTING SOURCES

Whether you are writing a brief essay with three or four sources or a fully developed research paper, when you document your sources, you allow others to participate in an ongoing scholarly conversation. Carefully documented sources allow readers to explore references of interest to them — to gain a fuller understanding of the context in which a passage was presented, for instance, or to check the list of works cited for additional references. To ensure that readers have all the information they need to locate sources, scholarly associations like the Modern Language Association and the American Psychological Association have developed documentation formats or styles that specify both the information to be included in a reference and the format for presenting that information. See the Documentation Guidelines at the back of this book for examples and explanations. MLA guidelines begin on p. 419 and APA guidelines begin on p. 438.

These sections present basic information about MLA and APA documentation styles. Both of these documentation styles use in-text citations with a list of works cited included at the end of the essay. The two documentation styles differ in certain respects, however. When you use MLA style, you will spell out the first name of each author in the list of works cited; when you use APA style, you will use the initial of each author's first name. MLA style places the date of publication at the end of the citation; APA style places it after the name of the author. Other differences exist, so you will want to follow examples given for specific kinds of citations carefully.

SAMPLE RESEARCH ESSAY USING MLA DOCUMENTATION STYLE

Here is an essay by Brenda Shonkwiler, who is a preengineering student at Oregon State University. As a student in Carole Ann Crateau's first-year writing class, Brenda was asked to write a research-based essay on a subject of interest to her. Brenda chose to write about the collapse of the Tacoma Narrows Bridge. As a preengineering student, she was interested in learning more about the causes of the collapse and the steps that were taken to ensure that such a disaster would not recur. Note that, to annotate this essay, we have reproduced it in a narrower format than you will have on a standard (8½" × 11" sheet) of paper.

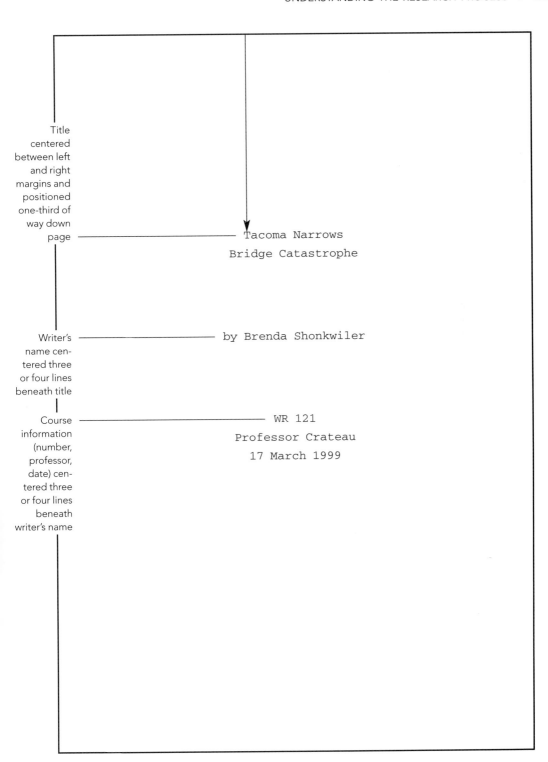

Title centered between left and right margins and positioned one-third of way down page ——————

Tacoma Narrows
Bridge Catastrophe

Writer's name centered three or four lines beneath title ——————

by Brenda Shonkwiler

Course information (number, professor, date) centered three or four lines beneath writer's name ——————

WR 121
Professor Crateau
17 March 1999

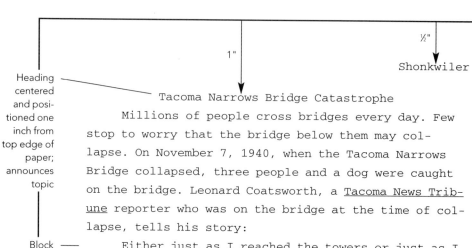

Heading centered and positioned one inch from top edge of paper; announces topic

Block quotation

Shonkwiler 1

Writer's last name , followed by a space and the page number, in upper right corner, positioned one-half inch from top edge of paper

½"

1"

Tacoma Narrows Bridge Catastrophe

Millions of people cross bridges every day. Few stop to worry that the bridge below them may collapse. On November 7, 1940, when the Tacoma Narrows Bridge collapsed, three people and a dog were caught on the bridge. Leonard Coatsworth, a <u>Tacoma News Tribune</u> reporter who was on the bridge at the time of collapse, tells his story:

> Either just as I reached the towers or just as I drove past them, the bridge began to sway violently from side to side. This was something new in my experience with the bridge. Heretofore, the noticeable motion had been up and down and undulating.
>
> Before I realized it, the tilt from side to side became so violent I lost control of the car. [I] thought for a moment it would leap the high curb and plunge across the sidewalk of the bridge and into the railing.
>
> I jammed on the brakes and got out of the car, only to be thrown [. . .] again. Around me I could hear the concrete cracking.
>
> I started back to the car to get the dog, but was thrown before I could reach it. The car itself began to slide from side to side of the roadway. I decided the bridge was breaking up and my only hope was to get back to the shore.
>
> On hands and knees most of the time, I crawled 500 yards or more to the towers. Across the roadway from me I became aware of another man, alternately crawling and then running a few steps in a crouched position.
>
> My breath was coming in gasps, my knees

Shonkwiler 2

were raw and bleeding, my hands bruised and
swollen from gripping the concrete curb. But I
was spurred by the thought that if I could reach
the towers I would be safe. [. . .] Safely back
at the toll plaza, I saw the bridge in its final
collapse and saw my car plunge into the narrows.

Parenthetical citation ——— (Coatsworth 3)

This was a disastrous event that raised many
questions. What factors led to this failure, and how ——— *These questions give readers a clear sense of the major issues that Brenda's essay will address*
could similar failures be prevented?

First-level subhead —— Cause of Failure

The Tacoma Narrows Bridge was built to span
Puget Sound. It was the only fixed roadway connecting
the Washington mainland and the Olympic Peninsula.
At the time of construction, the Narrows Bridge
was praised as the epitome of artistry in bridge
construction. However, the bridge soon earned the
nickname "Galloping Gertie" because of its undulating motion. Many people drove hundreds of miles to
experience the rolling sensation of crossing Gertie's
center span ("Comparison of the Bridges" 1). Despite
the obvious oscillations of the bridge's roadbed
bridge officials had confidence in the structure.
However, only four months after completion, the
bridge collapsed during a windstorm. Wind-induced
vibrations made the oscillating and twisting motions
too extreme for the structure to withstand. (See ——— *Parenthetical reference directs readers to figures*
Figs. 1 through 3.)

Second-level subhead ——— Not Designed for Wind. At the time Galloping
Gertie was built, little was known about the effects
wind had on structures such as bridges. Thus, the
bridge was designed without regard to vertical and
torsional (twisting) motions caused by wind. Design-

Shonkwiler   3

Fig. 1. Twisting of Center Span Just before Failure--Side
View. Source: Rodgers 1.

ers focused on stiffness under the traffic load and
overlooked the role of stiffness in suppressing
oscillations of bridges in wind.

    The Tacoma Narrows Bridge's fundamental weakness
was its extreme flexibility. Several factors led to
this flexibility, including the bridge's narrow deck,
shallow solid girders, and thin support cables that
were spaced far apart. The bridge's narrowness was
based on economic factors and transportation studies,
but the structure was extremely sensitive to torsional motions created by aerodynamic forces.

    Suspension bridges, in general, are more
flexible than other types of bridges. To decrease the
flexibility, suspension bridges are typically sta-
bilized with stiffening trusses. Such stiffening
trusses are frameworks consisting of many intercon-

Figure is
positioned
as soon as
practical
after paren-
thetical ref-
erence;
credit line for
image from
Web source

Fig. 2. Twisting of Center Span as Seen from Bridge Deck.
Source: Rodgers 2.

nected braces that allow wind to flow through them
with relatively little resistance, while diminishing
(dampening) vertical and torsional motions. The
Tacoma Narrows Bridge had been stiffened with solid
girders (horizontal beams) instead of trusses. (See
Fig. 4.) These girders were unusually shallow, only
eight feet deep, in comparison with their length.
This depth-to-span ratio, which was over twice that
of the Golden Gate Bridge, made the Tacoma Narrows
Bridge by far the most flexible bridge of its time
(Koughan 4).

Because the girders were solid, they did not
allow wind to pass through them. This resulted in
higher wind resistance than would be found in bridges
with open stiffening trusses. Charles E. Andrew,
chief engineer in charge of constructing the Tacoma
Narrows Bridge, stated that in his opinion the collapse was due to the solid stiffening girders: "These

Clear and
helpful
identification
of the
credentials of
the person
being
quoted

Fig. 3. Collapse in Progress: 600-foot Section Falling.
Source: Rodgers 3.

caused the bridge to flutter, more or less as a leaf
does in the wind. That set up a vibration that built
up until the failure occurred. [. . .] The Whitestone
Bridge in New York is the only other bridge that has
[. . .] stiffening girders of this type and we understand that it also has undulations in it, similar to
the ones that occurred here [. . .]" ("Big Tacoma
Bridge Crashes" 5). The original plans drawn by
Andrew and fellow engineers called for open trusses,
but another engineer changed the plans.

In addition to these problems, the cables used
to support the bridge were not large enough. Thin
cables are easily stretched. This contributed to the
bridge's inability to resist vertical and torsional

Shonkwiler 6

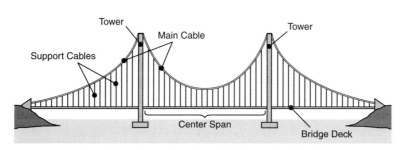

Tower

Main Cable

Tower

Support Cables

Center Span

Bridge Deck

Caption relates figure to text; clip art to which the writer has added her own labels—no credit needed

Fig. 4. Diagram Identifying Major Features of a Suspension Bridge. The bridge deck (roadway) is usually supported by stiffening trusses, but the Tacoma Narrows Bridge used solid girders instead.

motion. All bridges are subject to forces that cause torsion or lateral (side-to-side) lifting of the deck. When suspension bridges are built with ample width and vertical rigidity, such torsional forces are usually of small consequence (Koughan 4).

Second-level subhead

Built for Aesthetics. A trend toward streamlining in the 1930s took suspension bridge design away from the stiff structures that were built in the late nineteenth century and back to the ribbon-like decks of a hundred years earlier. There was a preoccupation with aesthetics that led to a sacrifice of structural integrity. Ever longer, slenderer, and lighter suspension bridges were being conceived and erected. The Tacoma Narrows Bridge was a prime example of this trend. It had been engineered toward a maximum of lightness, grace, and slenderness. Indeed, it was a masterpiece at the time. However, in making the bridge aesthetically pleasing, the designers unintentionally sacrificed much-needed stiffness. Even though the design provided for sufficient strength as dictated by accepted practice at the

Shonkwiler   7

time, the bridge had been made too flexible to withstand certain wind conditions.

Second-level
subhead
Overly Confident.
Noticeable vertical undula-
tions of the bridge were witnessed even in the early
stages of construction. After being built, some
breezes as low as four miles per hour caused vertical
oscillations ("Tacoma Narrows Bridge Failure" 1).
Motorists who crossed the bridge felt that they were
on a giant roller coaster, watching the cars ahead
disappear completely for moments at a time. Clearly,
the Tacoma Narrows Bridge was oscillating more than
was expected.

Although various concerns about the bridge's
stability had been expressed (Klingeman), many people
were confident in the stability of the structure. The
motorists who traveled across the bridge daily were
not fazed by the bridge's motion. In fact, as indicated earlier, some people traveled large distances
just to cross the bridge and experience its rolling
motion. A bank near the Tacoma end of the bridge even
had a billboard advertisement boasting, "Safe as the
Narrows Bridge" (Gotchy 39). Bridge officials were so
confident of the structure they considered canceling
the insurance policies to obtain reduced rates on a
new one ("Galloping Gertie" 2). Many people were
shocked when the bridge collapsed.

First-level
subhead
Prevention

Several things could have been done to prevent
this catastrophe. By looking at past bridge failures
and learning from them, the original plan could have
been designed to account for wind-induced vibrations.
The bridge could have also been strengthened while
being constructed. Finally, after the bridge was

Shonkwiler   8

built, research could have determined the problem and
solutions could have been implemented.

Second-level subhead ——————— Historical Precedent. Burt Farquharson, a professor of civil engineering at the University of
Washington, noted that the failure of the Tacoma Narrows Bridge "came as such a shock to the engineering
profession that it is surprising to most to learn
that the failure under the action of the wind was not
without precedent" (Petroski 157). Had the designers
of the Tacoma Narrows Bridge examined the historical
failures (see Table 1), Galloping Gertie may have

Table positioned as soon as practical after parenthetical reference; table number on one line, table title on next line, both flush left; horizontal dividing lines as needed ——

Table 1
Suspension Bridge Failure Due to Wind

Bridge (location)	Span (ft.)	Failure Date
Dryburgh Abbey (Scotland)	260	1818
Union (England)	449	1821
Nassau (Germany)	245	1834
Brighton Chain Pier (England)	255	1836
Montrose (Scotland)	432	1838
Menai Strait (Wales)	580	1839
Roche-Bernard (France)	641	1852
Wheeling (United States)	1,010	1854
Niagara-Lewiston (USA--Canada)	1,041	1864
Niagara-Clifton (USA--Canada)	1,260	1889
Tacoma Narrows Bridge	2,800	1940

Source: Petroski 160.

Shonkwiler   9

never galloped. In his book <u>Design Paradigms,</u> Petroski explains how historical precedent of failure
could be overlooked:

Block
quotation

It appears to be a trait of human nature to take
repeated success as confirmation that everything
is being done correctly. [. . .] The absence of
dramatic failures can not only make designers
complacent with regard to the genre of which
they are so justifiably proud; a climate of success can also make designers react more slowly
to warning signs that something is wrong. Even
Farquharson, who personally observed the actual
Tacoma Narrows Bridge and studied a model of it
for three months, did not expect the bridge to
fail catastrophically the way it did. (161)

Second-level
subhead

Actions Taken. Several methods were employed to
minimize or eliminate the motions of the Tacoma Narrows Bridge during its short life. Tie-down cables
were attached to the plate girders and anchored to
fifty-ton concrete blocks on the shore. This was use-
less because the cables snapped shortly after being
installed. Inclined cables were also installed. They
connected the main cables to the bridge deck midspan
but did not reduce vibrations. Hydraulic buffers were
installed between the towers and the floor system of
the deck to damp longitudinal motion of the main
span. These were ineffective because the seals were
damaged when the bridge was sandblasted prior to
painting.

In addition, a fifty-foot model was constructed
at the University of Washington. Tests at certain
wind velocities showed that the bridge deck could
rise and fall as much as fifty inches ("A Great
Bridge Falls"). Unfortunately, by the time the bridge

Shonkwiler   10

collapsed, the studies had not progressed far enough
for a permanent stabilizer to be designed.

An effort was made to reduce the oscillations of
the bridge; however, all actions proved to be ineffective. If the problem had been taken more seriously, a greater effort would have been put into
finding a solution. Perhaps the failure could have
been prevented even after construction was complete.

Effects on Bridge Design ————————————————— First-level
subhead

Second-level ———————— Research. The collapse of the Tacoma Narrows
subhead

Bridge initiated research on the aerodynamic stability of bridges. There had been no previous scientific
effort devoted to the dynamic effect of wind passing
over a static structure such as a bridge. After the
bridge failed, a new scale model of Galloping Gertie
was built and tested extensively in a wind tunnel.
Methods and devices necessary to obtain the required
stability were determined. Research on turbulence and
eddies has led to fairly accurate predictions of wind
effects and the ability to control a bridge's reaction to the wind. Many wind tunnels have since been
used to test the behavior and stability of physical
models of proposed bridge designs.

Although there are several competing theories
about the aerodynamic phenomena that caused Galloping
Gertie's catastrophic collapse, research sparked by
the disaster has taught designers to consider such
varied forces as resonance, vortex shedding, and
interactive self-excitation or negative damping
(Koughan, 5-8). Resonance, for instance, is a process
in which an object's natural frequency of oscillation
is amplified by an identical frequency. When resonance occurs, a small input force can produce large
deflections in a bridge (Stetz). In Galloping Ger-

tie's case, the resonant frequency may have been caused by strong wind gusts periodically blowing across the bridge, creating regions of high and low pressure above and below and thereby producing violent oscillations.

Galloping Gertie's oscillations may also be explained by the existence of vortices, or eddies, turbulent flows of air around the bridge structure. Vortices generate alternating high and low pressure regions on the side of the bridge sheltered from the wind and can contribute to resonance. Long-span bridges are especially vulnerable to vortices, resulting in twisting and oscillating motions.

Another phenomenon, called interactive self-excitation, is thought to have contributed to the bridge's violent motion and collapse. The driving force for this type of oscillation is not purely a function of time but rather a function of the bridge's angle during twisting and the rate of change of that angle. The wind supplies the force, but the more the bridge twists and the faster that happens, the greater the effect of the force. Once the bridge starts twisting in high wind, its motion just gets faster and more violent until the bridge finally becomes so unstable it rips apart.

Second-level subhead ———— New Tacoma Narrows Bridge. The research done after Galloping Gertie collapsed enabled engineers to design a more stable Tacoma Narrows Bridge. Built in 1950, the second Tacoma Narrows Bridge replaced Galloping Gertie and still stands today. (See Fig. 5.) This bridge was nicknamed Sturdy Gertie ("Tacoma Narrows Bridge Failure" 1).

Several changes had been made in the design. Open trusses of greater depth replaced the stiffening

Shonkwiler   12

Fig. 5. Current Tacoma Narrows Bridge. Stiffening trusses
are along the sides of the bridge, below the bridge deck.
Source: Stanley 1.

girders of the original bridge that were solid and
too shallow. This added strength to the bridge and
reduced wind resistance. The design of the bridge
deck was also changed. (See Fig. 6.) The new roadway
was almost twice as wide as the old one, 49 feet 10
inches versus 26 feet. This increased the bridge's
resistance to torsion. Open steel grid slots were
installed between each of the four traffic lanes and
both curbs. These open steel gratings function as
vents to relieve oscillations created by passing
wind. Hydraulic energy absorbing and damping devices
at the towers and midspan also helped reduce oscillations by controlling self-excitation.

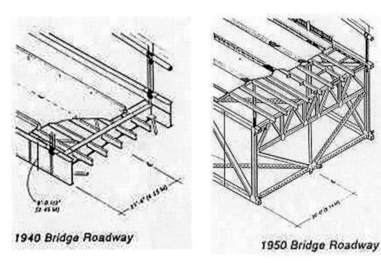

1940 Bridge Roadway   **1950 Bridge Roadway**

Fig. 6. Bridge Deck Comparison. At left, 1940 roadway; at
right, 1950 roadway. Source: "Comparison of the Bridges" 2.

Stability was also increased by strengthening
the supports. The diameter of the main suspension
cable was increased from 17.5 inches to 20.25 inches.
The number of wires in each of the support cables was
also increased. These changes strengthened the
cables. In addition, the weight of each shore anchor
was increased by 13,500 tons, and the weight of each
main tower was increased by 748 tons. These improvements produced a structure of unprecedented function
and stability. The new structure was evidence that
the lessons learned about the collapse of Galloping
Gertie were being rigorously applied to new designs.

Second-level ——————— New Designs. The research initiated by the col-
subhead   lapse of the Tacoma Narrows Bridge provided significant information to suspension bridge engineers around
the world and has had an important effect on all
bridge designs that followed. The need for engineers
to have a complete understanding of nature's inter-

action with their designs has led to new problem-solving techniques. Now, designers still look at static loads but also review the implications of aerodynamic effects on the structures. The control of aerodynamic instabilities can be achieved by an aerodynamically shaped deck, stiffness, mass, and damping of the bridge system (Frandsen 1). After design, models are made and tested. Few bridges are currently constructed without first testing a model in a wind tunnel. Complex computer analyses are used as well. These steps are taken to prevent catastrophes like Galloping Gertie's collapse from occurring again.

Clear summary of the major points made in this research paper ——— Conclusion ——————————————————— First-level subhead

The designers of the Tacoma Narrows Bridge did not anticipate the impact of wind. Historical examples of aerodynamic bridge failure were not well known or taken into account. The Tacoma Narrows Bridge oscillated in certain wind conditions from the start, but confidence in the bridge's stability was too high to invoke serious research. Efforts were taken to limit the oscillations, but proved ineffective. Owing to a combination of factors that is still debated today, only four months after its completion Galloping Gertie's motions became too violent, and the bridge ripped itself apart. The collapse initiated intensive research on bridge aerodynamics, and as a result bridges now are designed to resist wind-induced vibrations.

Today's motorists may grumble about traffic congestion on the Tacoma Narrows Bridge, but their experiences are certainly less harrowing than that of Leonard Coatsworth, who crawled off Galloping Gertie but lost his car and his dog on the fateful morning of November 7, 1940.

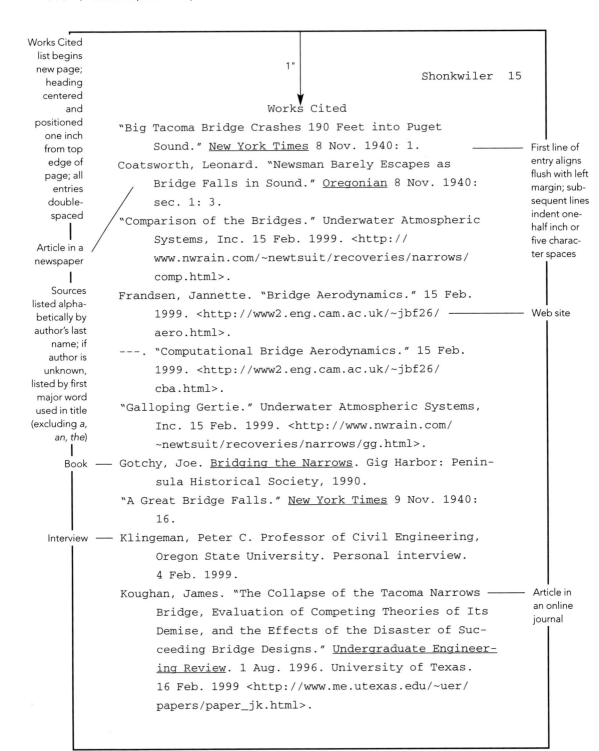

Works Cited list begins new page; heading centered and positioned one inch from top edge of page; all entries double-spaced

Article in a newspaper

Sources listed alphabetically by author's last name; if author is unknown, listed by first major word used in title (excluding *a, an, the*)

Book

Interview

1"

Shonkwiler   15

Works Cited

"Big Tacoma Bridge Crashes 190 Feet into Puget
        Sound." <u>New York Times</u> 8 Nov. 1940: 1.
Coatsworth, Leonard. "Newsman Barely Escapes as
        Bridge Falls in Sound." <u>Oregonian</u> 8 Nov. 1940:
        sec. 1: 3.
"Comparison of the Bridges." Underwater Atmospheric
        Systems, Inc. 15 Feb. 1999. <http://
        www.nwrain.com/~newtsuit/recoveries/narrows/
        comp.html>.
Frandsen, Jannette. "Bridge Aerodynamics." 15 Feb.
        1999. <http://www2.eng.cam.ac.uk/~jbf26/
        aero.html>.
---. "Computational Bridge Aerodynamics." 15 Feb.
        1999. <http://www2.eng.cam.ac.uk/~jbf26/
        cba.html>.
"Galloping Gertie." Underwater Atmospheric Systems,
        Inc. 15 Feb. 1999. <http://www.nwrain.com/
        ~newtsuit/recoveries/narrows/gg.html>.
Gotchy, Joe. <u>Bridging the Narrows</u>. Gig Harbor: Penin-
        sula Historical Society, 1990.
"A Great Bridge Falls." <u>New York Times</u> 9 Nov. 1940:
        16.
Klingeman, Peter C. Professor of Civil Engineering,
        Oregon State University. Personal interview.
        4 Feb. 1999.
Koughan, James. "The Collapse of the Tacoma Narrows
        Bridge, Evaluation of Competing Theories of Its
        Demise, and the Effects of the Disaster of Suc-
        ceeding Bridge Designs." <u>Undergraduate Engineer-
        ing Review</u>. 1 Aug. 1996. University of Texas.
        16 Feb. 1999 <http://www.me.utexas.edu/~uer/
        papers/paper_jk.html>.

First line of entry aligns flush with left margin; subsequent lines indent one-half inch or five character spaces

Web site

Article in an online journal

Shonkwiler   16

Petroski, Henry. <u>Design Paradigms</u>. New York: Cam-
        bridge University Press, 1994.

Rodgers, Kent. "Tacoma Narrows Bridge Disaster."
        16 Feb. 1999. <http://137.142.19.10/NYNEX/
        defaultframe/second/Kent/Kent.html>.

Stanley, Tanja. "Tacoma Narrows Bridge Gallery." 16
        Feb. 1999. <http://www.powerscourt.com/TRS/
        bridge_gallery.htm>.

Stetz, Albert. Professor of Physics, Oregon State
        University. Personal interview. 5 Feb. 1999.

"Tacoma Narrows Bridge Failure." 16 Feb. 1999.
        <http://www.math.uconn.edu/~kmoore/tacoma.html>.

Photograph ——

■ ■ ■

FOR THOUGHT, DISCUSSION, AND WRITING

1. After reviewing this chapter's discussion of paraphrasing and summarizing, select one of the texts included as a reading at the end of Chapter 3, "Understanding the Reading Process." Choose a paragraph from the reading — one that strikes you as particularly interesting, thought-provoking, or informative. After reading this paragraph carefully, first write a paraphrase of it, and then summarize the same passage. Finally, write a paragraph explaining why your paraphrase and summary of this passage are effective.

2. Choose a topic that interests you. Using a Web search engine, do a general search on your topic, noting the number of hits that your search generates. Now develop a list of related terms, and use these to narrow your search. Run a keyword search for at least two items from this list, noting the number of hits for these searches. After reviewing the suggestions for advanced searching provided by your search engine, conduct an advanced search. Take a few minutes to write a paragraph reflecting on this search. What was productive? Unproductive? What would you do differently if you needed to search on this topic again?

3. Select two of the Web sites you located in the previous activity. Using the suggestions for evaluating Web sites provided in this chapter, assess the quality of the information presented on each site. Write one or two paragraphs of evaluation for each site.

PART TWO

RHETORICAL SITUATIONS

Analyzing Rhetorical Situations

Whenever you write — whether you are jotting a note to a friend or working on a lab report — you are writing in the context of a specific situation with its own unique demands and opportunities. A management trainee writing a memo to her supervisor faces different challenges than an investigative journalist working on a story for the *New York Times* or a student writing a research paper for a political science class. Successful writers know that they must consider the situations in which they write; they can't rely on formulas or blind luck when they compose. They know they need to rely on their sensitivity — their understanding of the relationships among writers, readers, and texts — to help them make decisions as they write and revise.

In this section of *Work in Progress* you will learn how to use rhetorical sensitivity to analyze specific writing situations. In this chapter, for instance, you will learn to ask yourself questions about your rhetorical situation — questions that will enable you to determine the most fruitful way of approaching your topic and of responding to the needs and expectations of your readers. In Chapter 6, "Thinking about Communities and Conventions," you will learn how to read the forms and strategies of writing that characterize different communities of language users. This kind of rhetorically sensitive reading is particularly helpful when you are attempting to learn new forms of writing, as happens when students enter college or begin a new job. Finally, Chapter 7, "Negotiating Online Writing Situations," will help you apply what you know to the new challenges — and opportunities — of writing online.

LEARNING TO ANALYZE YOUR RHETORICAL SITUATION

Rhetoric involves three key elements: a writer, a reader, and a text that makes communication possible. When you think about these elements, posing questions about the options available to you as a writer, you are analyzing your rhetorical situation. Such analysis will enable you to make decisions not only about the form and content of your writing but also about the medium of communication.

Imagine, for instance, that you have been meaning to write to a close friend. Now, you decide, is just the time to do so. But should you email or send a handwritten letter? The answer depends on your situation. If you are writing just to say hello and to let your friend know that you're thinking of him, you might choose email as your means of communication, for its ease and informality suit this purpose well. But suppose you are writing because you have just learned of a death in your friend's family. The seriousness of this situation and the more personal nature of a handwritten note might well prompt a letter.

As simple as it might seem, the question of whether to email or to send a handwritten letter is a rhetorical question, one that calls on you to consider all the elements of rhetoric. As a writer you have choices; the more fully you understand your situation, the better choices you can make. Even though people conventionally send handwritten letters of condolence, for instance, your relationship with your friend might in fact make you decide to email him. (You may be, for example, in the habit of emailing each other every few days, even about personal matters.)

■ ■ ■

FOR EXPLORATION

Imagine that you wish to write the following:

An application for an internship in your major

A letter to a friend whose parents have recently decided to divorce

An entry to a radio contest that asks for responses to the prompt "I should be a DJ for a night because . . ."

Keeping the elements of rhetoric in mind, spend a few minutes thinking about how you would approach these different writing situations. Write a brief description of each situation, responding to the following questions:

1. What is your role as writer and your purpose for writing?

2. What image of yourself would you wish to present, and how would you vary your language accordingly?

3. How would the different readers of each text influence the form and content of your writing?

4. What medium of communication, email or print, would be most appropriate?

5. What other factors, such as format, would you need to consider?

Using Your Rhetorical Analysis to Guide Your Writing

As the preceding example shows, writers naturally draw on their common-sense rhetorical sensitivity to determine the most effective ways to communicate with readers. The student deciding whether to email or to write a handwritten letter to his friend did not consciously run through a mental checklist of questions but rather drew on his intuitive understanding of his situation. When you face the challenge of new and more difficult kinds of writing, however, as you do in college, it often helps to analyze your rhetorical situation consciously. Such analysis encourages you to consider each of the elements of rhetoric when you write.

The following guidelines provide questions you can use to analyze your rhetorical situation.

■ GUIDELINES FOR ANALYZING YOUR RHETORICAL SITUATION

Early in any writing project, you can lay a solid foundation by asking yourself the following questions:

Writer

1. Why are you writing?

2. What do you hope your writing will accomplish? Do you want to convey information? Change the reader's mind? Entertain the reader?

3. How might your goals as a writer influence the eventual form and content of your essay?

4. What role does this rhetorical situation invite you as the writer to play? Is your role relatively fixed (as it is when you write an essay exam)? Or is it flexible to some extent?

(continued)

(continued)

5. What image of yourself (*persona*) do you want to convey to your readers? What "voice" do you want readers to "hear" when they read your writing?

Reader

1. Who is your intended audience? How have you envisioned this audience? Is it helpful to think of your readers as members of a specific audience (subscribers to a special-interest magazine, for instance) or as a general audience with a wide range of interests?

2. What role do you intend for readers to adopt as they read your writing? What kinds of cues will you use to signal this role to readers?

3. If you are writing to a specific audience, do those readers have any demographic characteristics that you need to consider — such as age, gender, religion, income, occupation, education, political preference, or something else?

4. How will your writing appeal to your readers' interests? Do you expect your readers already to be interested in the topic, or do you need to create and maintain their interest?

5. How might the needs and expectations of your readers influence the form, content, and style of your writing?

Text

1. If you are writing in response to an assignment, to what degree does the assignment specify or restrict the form and content of your text? How much freedom, in other words, do you as the writer have?

2. What generic or stylistic conventions does your rhetorical situation require you to follow? Are these conventions rigidly defined (as in the case of lab reports) or flexible to some extent?

3. Does the nature of your subject implicitly or explicitly require that you provide certain kinds of evidence or explore certain issues?

4. Could you benefit by looking at models or other examples of the kind of writing your situation requires?

(continued)

(continued)

5. What medium of communication (print, email, hypertext, and so on) seems the most appropriate means of conveying your message to readers?

   As these questions indicate, the process of analyzing your rhetorical situation challenges you to look both within and without. Your intended meaning — what you want to communicate to your readers — is certainly important, as is your purpose for writing. But unless you're writing solely for yourself in your journal or notebook, you can't ignore your readers or other situational factors. Analyzing your rhetorical situation helps you to respond creatively as a writer and yet keeps you aware of limits on your freedom.

Setting Preliminary Goals

Before beginning a major writing project, you may find it helpful to write a brief analysis of your rhetorical situation, or you may simply review these questions mentally. This process of analyzing your rhetorical situation is an opportunity to determine your *preliminary* intentions or goals as a writer. (Your intentions will often shift as you write. That's fine. As you write, you will naturally revise your understanding of your rhetorical situation.) Despite its tentativeness, however, your analysis of your situation will help you begin writing with a sense of direction and purpose.

Here is one student's analysis of her rhetorical situation. The student is Annette Chambers, and her rhetorical analysis is followed by her essay.

> I am writing an essay about my hobby, fantasy role-playing: what it is, why I like it, how it works, how people tend to respond when I tell them about it — and why their responses bother me. I hope that those reading my essay will be entertained by and interested in my topic. But mainly I want them to understand that people who game are not all wild-eyed, psychologically damaged social misfits. I've been really frustrated with the way people respond when they learn that I participate in fantasy role-playing games. Most people make it clear that they think gaming is weird at best; some have gone so far as to ask me if I didn't fear for my soul since I "play" with "demons."
>
> My writing goals require both information and sensitivity to my audience. I need to provide enough information about gaming so people

will understand what it is (and, just as important, what it is *not*) — but not so much that they get bogged down in unnecessary details. I also need to respond to the concerns people have about gaming. I want to show readers that the stereotypes they have about fantasy role-playing are just that: stereotypes. But I've got to be careful not to seem angry or defensive. I'm hoping that humor will help here.

I'm writing this essay for an assignment in my composition class. The assignment is pretty general; it asks us to write an informative essay on a subject that we care about. So I have a fair amount of flexibility. I hope that a wide range of people might find my essay interesting and informative. I am directing this toward a general audience, even though my teacher will be my immediate reader. Though I'm writing this essay for a class, I might submit it for publication to the student or local newspaper or to some magazines that publish brief, general-interest essays, such as airline magazines.

Writer: I've already explained why I'm writing and what I hope this essay will accomplish. Given my goals, I want to present myself as open, conversational, pleasant, and not at all defensive about my hobby. I want readers to see me as a bright, articulate person who likes to make believe but is firmly aware of the difference between reality and fantasy. This is really important to my credibility, since my major goal is to convince readers that game-players are normal people just like them.

Readers: I assume that most readers (especially my teacher!) will have little direct experience with fantasy role-playing, which they probably associate in a vague way with games like Dungeons and Dragons.™ Since some readers will believe the misconceptions about gaming I talk about, I need to be careful not to alienate them by portraying their concerns as stupid or silly. I hope to appeal to my readers by writing a vivid introduction that will draw readers in, and by using lively examples — and humor — to keep them interested. I hope that my use of humor and my general informality will tell readers that they should just sit back and enjoy the essay.

Text: Because my assignment is open-ended, I have quite a lot of freedom as a writer. But that doesn't mean that anything goes. Since I'm hoping to write a personal essay that will appeal to a broad range of readers, I need to make my essay interesting. I've read other personal essays, and we've talked about them in class, so I know that writers need to draw readers in. I can't assume that readers will care about my subject; I have to make them care. And I have to provide the kinds of details that will keep them interested as they read.

"SO, WHAT ARE YOU DOING THIS WEEKEND?"
by Annette Chambers

It's 2:45 in the morning, and I've just spent two and a half hours logged into email pretending to be an elfish woman on another planet. My name is Miri Ravan, and I'm something over 2,000 years old, though (as is the way of elves) I don't look much over 30. At the moment, I'm having an uncomfortable discussion with my lover's daughter, D'versey, about relationships, which is hard because she's half succubus, spent her early life in Hell, and has a unique view of life. For example, she finds it odd that I don't casually become involved with anyone I find attractive, and has recently asked me to explain "just what *is* the difference between acquaintances and friends."

Or it's Saturday night, round 10:00, and I've been sitting in a stuffy little living room with five friends for about eight hours. This is how we've spent most Saturdays for almost ten years. I am Annabelle Jordan, a 30-ish veterinarian with a photographic memory and a knack for "reading" people. I love dogs, hate rap, live in the suburbs of Tacoma, and just happen to hang out with a pack of vampires. Or I might be Maire Clare, an Irish woman living in 12th-century London, who just happens to *be* a vampire. Or Silver, a former "personnel reclamation specialist" (read "kidnapper and sometimes assassin") who now runs the shadows of the mean streets of 21st-century Seattle.

I suppose I shouldn't be surprised that people look at me funny when I tell them about fantasy role-playing. After we get past the "you mean like Dungeons and Dragons™?" stage, their expressions usually range from curious, to wary, to alarmed. There is, I suppose, something odd, something not quite normal, about pretending to be somebody else for hours at a time, especially when that somebody may not even be human. But then, I've never really understood the attraction of staring at a television screen while grown men chase variously shaped balls around a field or court. Anyway, gaming is fun — as relaxing to me as watching sports is to others.

Of course there are other ways to relax that don't make people question your sanity or soul. Rock climbing, for instance. Though rock climbing seems pretty crazy to me, nobody stereotypes climbers as socially inept, psychologically warped, or morally questionable. No one suggests that climbing be banned as harmful to children. And nobody asks climbers if they don't worry about getting "too wrapped up in rock climbing" or wonders, in tones of sincere interest and concern, whether their hobby is "demonic." These are questions I've encountered more than once, and I always find myself pausing while I attempt to frame a reply.

However long the pause, the answer is always "Well, no." I don't worry about getting too involved. I don't spend my days fretting that I identify too strongly with Miri, or that Annabelle is becoming too great an influence on my thinking, or that if I'm not careful I might flip out and start randomly slaughtering innocent bystanders in the mistaken belief that they're monsters. As far as I can tell, no one who knows me well worries about these things either.

Is it possible to get too wrapped up? Yes, certainly; it's possible to take anything too far. It's also possible to fall off a mountain while you're climbing it, but that doesn't mean that all climbers have a death wish. I've been gaming for ten years or so and have encountered exactly one person who I thought allowed himself to get too caught up in the game. But he was like that about other things too. His obsessiveness colored his whole life, not just his role-playing. In some ways the game seemed to serve as a safety valve for him, a way of venting hostility he might otherwise have directed at real people instead of imaginary monsters.

Which brings me to demons. Yes, they do turn up in some of the games I play. So do elves and giants and centaurs and a whole host of other creatures. And, yes, they're powerful and evil and extremely dangerous. Since my group usually plays characters who at least try to be good, demons are popular enemies. But, no, role-playing isn't about summoning, communing with, speaking to, or even believing in demons. Mostly it's a way of being, for a few hours, someone you're not likely to get to be in real life — perhaps even someone you wouldn't want to be. It's a chance for you and some friends to make up imaginary people and see if you can make them work together toward a common goal.

In case you're unfamiliar with fantasy role-playing, here's how it works. Everyone in the group — usually between three and eight players — has a character, and each character has a defined set of skills and physical and mental characteristics, as well as a background including personality, goals, skills, and so forth. There's also a game master (GM) or storyteller who more or less (in my group it's mostly less) controls what's happening by setting up the scenarios to which the player characters respond. The goal is to get as deeply into character as possible, to speak, act, and react as though you are the person you're pretending to be, though the acting is usually limited to gestures and tones of voice.

If I want Annabelle to climb a fifteen-foot rock wall, something she's unlikely to be good at, given the background I've invented and skills I've chosen for her, I do not get up and start scaling the sofa. Instead, I tell the GM what I plan for her to do. Based on a combination of factors including her assigned strength and dexterity, the condition of the wall, and luck, the GM decides whether she manages to scramble over with a few seconds to spare, escapes because one of her companions distracts the werewolves, or falls to her doom.

Now, I don't believe in werewolves any more than I believe in demons, but part of the fun is that Annabelle does. Gaming is a chance to pretend, to play make believe, the way we all do as children. Perhaps it's this similarity to childhood games that makes people uncomfortable. After all, aren't we grown-ups now? Shouldn't we concern ourselves with grown-up things like work and money and having our own children? Well, maybe. But on the other hand, is getting together to play Dragonquest™ or Vampire: The Masquerade™ really so much weirder than getting together to watch football or play poker?

Besides, it's cheap therapy. Everyone in my group has at one time or another arrived looking exhausted, defeated, or just plain irritated, and growled, "I want to kill something." The rest of us sympathize, and then we let him kill something! This may not bring the long-term benefits of therapy, but role-playing is easy and inexpensive, and however much bloodshed our characters may be responsible for, none of us seems to have any trouble maintaining the fantasy–reality distinction. Our families, however irritated we may become with them, are alive and well. None of our coworkers seem worried that just because we spend part of our weekend waving swords or spells at the bad guys we're going to show up on Monday with a gun.

And yes, we do work, and go to school, and have, for the want of a better phrase, "real lives." Most of us have or are working toward college degrees. All of us have or are looking for jobs. Some of us are engaged or living together with another person. We pay our taxes and brush our teeth and can, with allowances for differing personalities and degrees of sociability, hold down our end of a "normal" conversation. Perhaps the real difference between us and rock climbers is that we spend our Saturdays with our feet planted firmly on the ground.

■ ■ ■

FOR EXPLORATION

To what extent does Annette Chambers's essay achieve the goals she established for herself in her analysis of her rhetorical situation? Reread Annette's analysis and essay. Keeping her analysis in mind, list three or four reasons that you believe Annette does or does not achieve her goals, and then find at least one passage in the essay that illustrates each of these statements. Finally, identify at least one way that Annette might strengthen her essay were she to revise.

THINKING ABOUT READERS

If you look again at Annette Chambers's description of her rhetorical situation (on pp. 149–50), you will notice that concerns about her readers influence all aspects of her planning. Annette knows that if she wants to challenge readers' stereotypes about fantasy role-playing, it would hardly make sense to write an angry essay chastising readers for their misconceptions. Her situation invites a light, entertaining, informative approach, one that encourages dialogue and identification. Annette understands as well that the *persona* she projects will help determine how readers respond to her ideas. Consequently, she presents herself as open, pleasant, and friendly (note the role that humor plays in her essay, for instance) — and she invites readers to assume a similar stance. In so doing, she establishes common ground with readers and encourages them to be as open-minded about her hobby as she is about such hobbies as spectator sports and rock climbing.

Annette recognizes that she must do more than establish common ground with readers and project an inviting *persona:* She must respond to readers' misconceptions, and she must provide information they need to understand fantasy role-playing. If she provides too many details, readers may get bogged down; too few, and they will fail to understand how "normal" people could be drawn to her hobby. Annette also understands that she is writing for two potential audiences: for her teacher, who will actually read her essay, and for a more general audience of hypothetical readers. Negotiating this double audience could be tricky, but Annette understands that she can draw on her understanding of personal essay writing to make decisions as she writes. For Annette, the personal essay (an essay grounded in the writer's personal experience) is not an arbitrary form but a means of establishing a particular kind of relationship with readers, one that is conversational and informal. Annette understands that in evaluating her essay her teacher will consider the extent to which Annette has written an interesting, well-organized, personal essay, one that anticipates the needs and interests of a general audience of readers and that comments in significant ways upon its topic.

In a different situation — writing an in-class essay exam, for instance — Annette would adjust her understanding of her reader accordingly. Teachers assign essay exams when they want to determine what students have learned about a subject and how effectively they can express this understanding to others. Given this expectation, a dramatic, attention-getting introduction might irritate, not entertain, her reader. A concise introductory paragraph, one that clearly specifies the writer's main point and indicates how the writer will support this point, would be more appropriate.

Here, for instance, is the introduction to an essay written by Elizabeth Ridlington, a student at Harvard. Elizabeth wrote this essay for an exam in her introductory political science class. The title of Elizabeth's essay is "Political and Economic Power."

> Since the French Revolution, France has believed the state should be composed of citizens who voluntarily joined the nation because of their belief in certain ideals. The United States similarly believes that all citizens

should agree with the principles formed at the time of the Revolutionary War and laid out in the Constitution. Despite this, neither country extends citizenship to everyone who agrees with these ideals and principles. Thus, other factors must influence these nations' understanding of — and laws regarding — citizenship. In this essay I argue that economic and political considerations have been more important in forming either country's understanding of citizenship than have been its founding ideals. Evidence of this can be found in the evolution of the understanding of citizenship, in the forces that initially pulled each nation into a single political unit, and in the outcome of specific crises.

In writing the above introduction to her essay, Elizabeth understood that in this rhetorical situation her reader, her political science teacher, is interested primarily in her understanding of her topic. Whereas Annette's introduction works hard to interest readers and to engage them with her topic, Elizabeth's introduction focuses on establishing a clear position on her topic and on identifying the most important arguments she will use to support this position. This introduction thus serves a dual purpose: It clearly articulates her position and also reassures her professor that the essay will be clearly organized and well supported.

As a writer, your relationship with your readers is always shifting and complex, not fixed and static; this relationship varies with your rhetorical situation. When you consider the expectations and interests of your readers, you naturally think *strategically* and thus build on the rhetorical sensitivity you have already developed as a speaker, listener, reader, and writer.

■ ■ ■

FOR EXPLORATION

Introductions often help signal the relationship the writer intends to establish with readers. The following excerpts introduce two different discussions of stress, both designed for a general audience. The first excerpt is from the introduction to *The Work/Stress Connection: How to Cope with Job Burnout*. The second is from the "Work and Stress" section in *The Columbia University College of Physicians and Surgeons Complete Home Medical Guide*. As you read these excerpts, think about the differing roles that they invite readers to assume.

Sally Swanson, a thirty-eight-year-old mother of four, works as a bank teller in Des Moines, Iowa. Like many women, she feels the pressure of running a home, raising children, managing a job, and carving out leisure time for herself. "I did fine until we got a new supervisor last year," she says with an exhausted sigh. "Within two months I had started to burn out." Sally takes antacid pills several times a day. She worries that she may have an ulcer. "I feel as if he's looking over my shoulder all the time," she says. "He never has a good word to say to anyone. Sometimes the tension at the bank is so thick you could cut it with a knife."

— THE WORK/STRESS CONNECTION:
HOW TO COPE WITH JOB BURNOUT

Particular kinds of work seem to cause special stress, and the effects of health are manifested in an all-too-common pattern: fatigue, insomnia, eating disorders, nervousness, feelings of unhappiness, abuse of alcohol or drugs. Stress is often related to the nature of the job or imposed irregularities. Rotating shift work, in which hours are erratic or inconsistent with the normal sleep cycle, produces both physical and mental stress by constantly upsetting circadian rhythms that control specific hormonal and other responses. Jobs that involve little variation but require constant close attention, for example, assembly-line work or jobs requiring repetitive tasks with dangerous equipment, seem to be particularly stressful. In one study in a sawmill, people who ran the equipment had much higher levels of stress-related hormones than workers who did not come in contact with machinery, even though their jobs also may have been boring and repetitive.

— THE COLUMBIA UNIVERSITY COLLEGE OF PHYSICIANS
AND SURGEONS COMPLETE HOME MEDICAL GUIDE

Now describe the writer-reader relationship established in each of these two introductions. What signals or cues do the authors provide for readers to enable them to recognize and adopt an appropriate role? Cite at least three examples of these signals or cues.

USING ARISTOTLE'S THREE APPEALS

Analyzing your rhetorical situation can provide information that will enable you to make crucial strategic, structural, and stylistic decisions about your writing. In considering how to use the information gained through this process, you may find it helpful to employ what Aristotle (384–322 B.C.) characterized as the three appeals. According to Aristotle, when speakers and writers communicate with others, they draw on these three general appeals:

Logos, the appeal to reason

Pathos, the appeal to emotion

Ethos, the appeal to the credibility of the speaker or writer

As a writer, you appeal to *logos* when you focus on the logical presentation of your subject by providing evidence and examples in support of your ideas. You appeal to *pathos* when you use the resources of language to engage your readers emotionally with your subject or appeal to their values, beliefs, or needs. And you appeal to *ethos* when you create an image of yourself, a *persona,* that encourages readers to accept or act on your ideas.

These three appeals correspond to the three basic elements of rhetoric. In appealing to *ethos,* you focus on the *writer's* character as implied in the text; in appealing to *pathos,* on the interaction of writer and *reader;* and in appealing to *logos,* on the logical statements about the subject made in your particular *text.* In some instances, you may rely predominantly on one of these appeals. A student writing a technical report, for instance, will typically emphasize scientific or technical evidence (*logos*), not emotional or personal appeals. More often, however, you will draw on all three appeals in your effort to create a fully persuasive document. A journalist writing an essay on child abuse might begin her discussion with several examples designed to gain the attention of her readers and to convince them of the importance of this issue (*pathos*). Although she may rely primarily on information about the negative consequences of child abuse (*logos*), she will undoubtedly also endeavor to create an image of herself as a caring, serious person (*ethos*), one whose analysis of a subject like child abuse could be trusted.

In the following examples, Tova Johnson, a biology major at Oregon State University, and Brandon Barrett, a chemistry major at the same university, use Aristotle's three appeals to develop strategies for essays defining their major. Tova and Brandon were students in Carole Ann Crateau's first-year writing class when they wrote these essays. In presenting her assignment, Crateau informed students that their essays should include "information about your major that is new to your readers; in other words, it should not simply repeat the OSU catalog. Rather, it should be your unique perspective, written in clear, descriptive language." Crateau concluded her assignment with this advice: "Have fun with this assignment. Consider your audience (it should be this class unless you specify a different audience). And remember Aristotle's three appeals. How will your essay employ the appeals of *logos, pathos,* and *ethos*? As you write, keep these two questions in mind: What is your purpose? What do you hope to achieve with your audience?"

Following are Tova's and Brandon's essays, preceded by their analyses of their rhetorical situations and of their essays' appeals to *logos, pathos,* and *ethos.*

Tova Johnson's Analysis of Her Rhetorical Situation and of Her Use of Logos, Pathos, *and* Ethos

I am writing this paper for my first-year writing class. My teacher has asked students to present our unique perspective on our academic majors. I see this as an invitation to be creative — to avoid catalog or textbook definitions of our majors and to instead explore our personal understandings. Given this expectation, my goal is to write an essay that conveys what I find exciting about biology and to do so in a way that my readers will find intriguing and accessible. I am not in an "anything goes" situation, however. This is a writing class, so my teacher will expect that my essay will follow the general conventions of English and of personal essay writing. I know from previous writing classes, for instance, that essays are most effective when you use specific examples, so I will try to do that.

Logos: I want readers to see the logical progression that I experienced from playing outdoors as a child to my pursuit of a biology major and to understand the pleasure that I experienced then and now in studying nature. To do this, I need to provide some specific examples that will both show my childhood interest in nature and connect that with the more formal study of biology. I can also help people understand my interest in biology by connecting it with something that most people are familiar with — reading. Perhaps if my readers see biology as connected to something they know, they will become enthused about it, just as I am. Or at least they will better understand why someone might want to major in biology.

Pathos: When I think about *pathos,* I realize that the introduction to my essay will be particularly important, for it's got to hook readers and convince them that this subject is accessible and interesting. Most of us have positive memories of childhood, so my hope is that by beginning with these memories I will connect with readers and encourage them to continue reading. I want readers to understand that there is beauty in biology, so I will need to use vivid details that engage the senses of my readers.

Ethos: For my readers to trust me, I must present myself as knowledgeable about and intimate with my subject. I want to convince my readers that I am genuinely in awe of and fascinated with life in general and biology in specific.

THE TEXTS OF LIFE
by Tova Johnson

I remember warm summer days when my younger sister Kelva and I watched ants that were making their homes in small holes in the cement behind our house. We watched in awe as the little brown scavengers emerged from their dark underground holes to meet the sunlight and to collect bits of grass and leaves that completely covered their backs as they returned to their holes to deposit their newfound treasures. My sister and I wanted desperately to enter their homes with them, to view their magnificent microdens, but our size prevented us. And so, our studies would end at their "doors."

My sister and I also found dried up earthworms, hard as sticks, in our backyard and attempted to hydrate them by putting them into small buckets full of water. Of course, we did not realize that the earthworms were already dead or that once they were dead, they could not be brought back to life. What we had realized, however, was that earthworms need moisture to survive, and we were attempting to satisfy that need for a few unfortunate crawlers. Our experiences with earthworms, along with our experiences with ants and other creatures that roamed the terrain of our yard, was, I believe, my first introduction to biology — the study of life.

Of course, we did not have texts, typically defined as books, but we had texts, nonetheless. The texts were the plants, bugs, worms, and other forms of life that we observed and, although not apparent to us at the time, studied. The life that we observed, that we "read," were our texts. This is the beauty of biology: We can wake up every day and be surrounded by texts waiting to be read, dissected, and engaged into our natural inclinations to attempt to figure out one of life's greatest mysteries — life itself. What life is, what life consists of, what life exists in our universe, and how our own lives are situated in relation to these other forms of life are all issues that we can explore through biology. Indeed, by studying other forms of life, we grow to better understand ourselves.

The more I engage in biology, the more mysteries of life I uncover. And, like a young child looking into an ant hole, the deeper I want to probe. Majoring in biology works for me not just because of the background working knowledge I will gain that will help me should I decide to pursue a career in medicine, but because I satisfy the awe-driven curiosity that began enveloping my being as a child. Majoring in biology works for me because occasionally I find the golden key to one of life's mysteries. I learn more about myself and the world around me in the process, making me a more informed and whole individual.

"Reading" the texts of life that could only have been written with such beauty and perfection by the Divine Creator is a treasure, a gift, an honor, and a privilege. Through biology, I grab hold of this privilege every day.

Occasionally, I will stop once again to watch a little brown ant scouring the landscape for small pieces of grass and leaves to build its home. I will stop to watch a squirrel on the sidewalk flicking its tail like a big flagellum and then suddenly tense up and run up a tree as another squirrel comes along to chase it. I will stop to admire a tree that has fuzzy bell-shaped knobs extending from its branches. Sometimes, I will even stop to watch people like me, running on sneakered feet to make it to the next class, or laughing and teasing each other in the sunshine. I watch, I read, and I study. This is biology.

Brandon Barrett's Analysis of His Rhetorical Situation and of His Use of Logos, Pathos, *and* Ethos

I'm writing this essay to explain how I made the most important decision in my life to date: what to major in while in college. I want to explain this not only to my audience but to myself as well, for bold decisions frequently need to be revisited in light of new evidence. There are those for whom the choice of major isn't much of a choice at all. For them, it's a vocation, in the strict Webster's definition of the word: a summons, a calling. I'm not one of those people, and for me the decision was fraught with anxiety. Do I still believe that I made the right choice? Yes, I do, and I want my essay not only to reflect how serious I feel this issue to be but also to convey the confidence that I finally achieved.

This essay will be read by my professor and the other students in my class. Given this audience, I can speak in more conversational terms than I otherwise might. I can also be sure that all college students can relate to the topic at hand; therefore, the tone can be somewhat looser and less formal.

Logos: This essay is about my own opinions and experiences and therefore contains no statistics and hard facts. What it should contain, though, are legitimate reasons for choosing the major I did. If I seem insincere or uncertain, then my audience may question the honesty of my essay. My choice should be shown as following a set of believable driving forces.

Pathos: Since my audience is composed mostly of college students, I'll want to appeal to their own experiences regarding their choice of major and the sometimes conflicting emotions that accompany such a decision. Specifically, I want to focus on the feelings of confidence and relief that come when you have firmly made up your mind. My audience will be able to relate to these feelings, and it will make the essay more relevant and real to them.

Ethos: The inherent danger in writing an essay about my desire to be a chemistry major is that I may be instantly labeled as boring or snooty. I want to dispel this image as quickly as possible in my essay, and humor is always a good way to counter such stereotypes. On the other hand, this is a serious subject, and the infusion of too much humor will portray me as somebody who hasn't given this too much thought. I want to strike a balance between being earnest and being human.

THE ALL-PURPOSE ANSWER
by Brandon Barrett

When I was a small child, I would ask my parents, as children are apt to do, questions concerning the important things in my life. "Why is the sky blue?" "Why do my Cocoa Puffs turn the milk in my cereal bowl brown?" If I asked my father questions such as these, he always attempted to provide detailed technical answers that left me solemnly nodding my head in complete confusion. But if I asked my mother, she would simply shrug her shoulders and reply, "Something to do with chemistry, I guess." Needless to say, I grew up with a healthy respect for the apparently boundless powers of chemistry. Its responsibilities seemed staggeringly wide-ranging, and I figured that if there was a God he was probably not an omnipotent deity but actually the Original Chemist.

In my early years, I regarded chemistry as nothing less than magic at work. So what is chemistry, if not magic — or a parent's response to a curious child's persistent questions? Chemistry is the study of the elements, how those elements combine, how they interact with one another, and how all this affects Joe Average down the street. Chemists, then, study not magic but microscopic bits of matter all busily doing their thing. When all those bits of matter can be coerced into doing something that humans find useful or interesting — like giving off massive quantities of energy, providing lighting for our homes, or making Uncle Henry smell a little better — then the chemists who produced the desired effect can pat themselves on the back and maybe even feel just a little bit like God.

Chemists solve problems, whether the problem is a need for a new medicine or a stronger plastic bowl to pour our Wheaties into. They develop new materials and study existing ones through a variety of techniques that have been refined over the decades. Chemists also struggle to keep the powers of chemistry in check by finding ways to reduce pollution that can be a by-product of chemical processes, to curb the dangers of nuclear waste, and to recycle used materials.

Chemistry is a dynamic field, constantly experiencing new discoveries and applications — heady stuff, to be sure, but heady stuff with a purpose. Chemistry isn't a static, sleepy field of dusty textbooks, nor does it — forgive me, geologists — revolve around issues of questionable importance, such as deviations in the slope of rock strata. Those who know little about chemistry sometimes view it as dull, but I am proud to say that I plan to earn my B.S. in chemistry. And from there, who knows? That's part of the beauty of chemistry. After graduating from college, I could do any number of things, from research to medical school. The study of chemistry is useful in its own right, but it is also great preparation for advanced study in other fields since it encourages the development of logical thought and reasoning. In one sense, logical thought (not to mention research and medical school) may seem a giant step away from a child's idle questions. But as chemistry demonstrates, perhaps those questions weren't so childish after all.

■ ■ ■

FOR EXPLORATION

In what ways do Tova Johnson's and Brandon Barrett's essays draw on Aristotle's three appeals? Write one or two paragraphs responding to this question. Be sure to include at least two or three examples in your analysis.

The strategies described in this chapter — analyzing your rhetorical situation and employing Aristotle's three appeals — are grounded in commonsense principles of communication, principles that date back at least to the time of Plato and Aristotle. Understanding these principles and knowing how to apply them will enable you to respond effectively in a variety of writing situations.

■ ■ ■

FOR THOUGHT, DISCUSSION, AND WRITING

1. The following letter from the U.S. Committee for UNICEF is typical of many letters requesting charitable contributions for worthwhile causes. Using this letter as evidence or data, try to determine the assumptions the writer or writers made about this rhetorical situation. (Though Hugh Downs, a popular television personality, signed this letter, he may not have actually composed it.) After you have listed

these assumptions, indicate ways in which these assumptions may have influenced the form or content of the letter. What assumptions about the readers, for example, may have led the writer to introduce the letter as he or she did?

> Dear Friend:
> In the ten seconds it took you to open and begin to read this letter, three children died from the effects of malnutrition somewhere in the world.
>
> No statistic can express what it's like to see even one child die that way . . . to see a mother sitting hour after hour, leaning her child's body against her own . . . to watch the small feeble head movements that expend all the energy a youngster has left . . . to see the panic in a dying tot's innocent eyes . . . and then to know in a moment that life is gone.
>
> But I'm not writing this letter simply to describe an all-too-common tragedy.
>
> I'm writing because, after decades of hard work, *UNICEF* — The United Nations Children's Fund — *has identified four simple, low-cost techniques which, if applied, have the potential to cut the yearly child mortality rate in half.*
>
> These methods don't depend on solving large-scale problems like increasing food supply or cleaning up contaminated water. They can be put into effect before a single additional bushel of wheat is grown, or before a single new well is dug.
>
> They do depend on *what you decide to do* by the time you finish reading this letter. You see, putting these simple techniques to work requires the support of UNICEF's projects by people around the world. In our country, it means helping the U.S. Committee for UNICEF contribute to that vital work.
>
> With your help, millions of children will be given the chance of a lifetime — the chance to live — to grow up healthy and strong. Without your help, more children will continue to die painfully, slowly and needlessly — children like the nine who have died in the past 30 seconds.
>
> The first method is called *"oral rehydration."* Most children who die of malnutrition don't starve to death — they die because their body weight has been severely lowered by germs that cause diarrhea.
>
> Simple medicines can stop such illness in our own country. But in the developing countries, there are no such medicines — and children may develop a new infection every six weeks. Until recently, there was no easy way of stopping the symptom and saving their lives.
>
> But now, it's known that a mixture of sugar, salt and water in the right proportions will stop the critical loss of fluids and salts that

leads to death. The cost of this "miracle" cure — less than ten cents a dose. But for want of that simple mixture, five million children die each year.

With your help, the U.S. Committee for UNICEF can assist UNICEF's projects to provide "oral rehydration salts" to mothers in developing countries around the world — and to teach families how to make the mixture on their own, to save the lives of children.

The second breakthrough method of saving children is to provide *worldwide immunization* against six childhood diseases: measles, polio, TB, tetanus, whooping cough and diphtheria. Together, these diseases kill three and a half million children each year in developing countries — the vast majority of them are malnourished youngsters with little resistance to disease.

It used to be hard to keep vaccines stable in their long journeys from laboratories to remote, often tropical places where children needed them most. But within the last year and a half, a measles vaccine has been developed that does not require refrigeration. The result: measles can now join smallpox on the list of child-killing diseases that have been wiped out — permanently.

The cost of this new measles vaccine is less than ten cents a dose. With it, *the lives of one and a half million children can be saved this year alone.* But without it, they will continue to die — like the child who has died of measles in the past 30 seconds.

With your help, the U.S. Committee for UNICEF can assist in UNICEF's work to deliver the new measles vaccine — and vaccines to fight the five other major child-killers — to youngsters who need them so badly in the developing world.

The third and fourth breakthrough methods of saving children's lives are even simpler. They require no medication at all. But they do require a worldwide education campaign — to promote *breast-feeding* among mothers, instead of the tragic trend toward bottle-feeding in developing lands, and to provide mothers with simple *paper growth charts* to detect the "hidden malnutrition" that can leave a child irreparably retarded in mind and body.

With your help, the U.S. Committee for UNICEF can assist UNICEF in mounting the massive educational campaign needed to teach parents these basic ways of preventing malnutrition — and can save the lives of children for years to come.

There you have it: four easy ways of saving the lives of millions of children for years to come.

Now it's time for you to decide what you're going to do about it.

I know you receive appeals for many good causes. But I can't think of a single cause more important than the life of a child. And in a very real sense, the life of a child somewhere in the world can be drastically changed by what you decide to do right now. You see, UNICEF's good work is supported entirely by voluntary contributions. That means your help does make a critical difference.

That's why I'm asking you to take a moment now to send a gift of $20, $50, $100, $500 — as much as you possibly can — to the U.S. Committee for UNICEF in the enclosed reply envelope.

Your gift is tax deductible to the extent allowed by law. And by the time you fill out next year's tax returns, there will be one or more healthy, living children in the world as a result of the gift you send today. You will have given those kids the chance of a lifetime. And I hope that will make you feel very proud, indeed.

We're counting on your help. My personal thanks and best wishes.

Sincerely,
Hugh Downs

2. Annette Chambers, Tova Johnson, and Brandon Barrett did a good job, you'll probably agree, in anticipating the expectations and interests of their readers. In writing their essays, they focused not just on content (what they wanted to say) but also on strategy (how they might convey their ideas to their readers). Not all interactions between writer and reader are as successful. You may have read textbooks that seemed more concerned with the subject matter than with readers' needs and expectations. Or you may have received direct mail advertising or other business communications that irritated or offended you. Find an example of writing that in your view fails to anticipate the expectations and needs of the reader and write one or two paragraphs explaining your reasons. Your teacher may ask you to bring your example and written explanation to class to share with your classmates.

3. Analyze the ways in which the following three advertisements draw on Aristotle's three appeals: *logos, pathos,* and *ethos.*

Which man looks guilty? If you picked the man on the right, you're wrong. Wrong for judging people based on the color of their skin. Because if you look closely, you'll see they're the same man. Unfortunately, racial stereotyping like this happens every day. On America's highways, police stop drivers based on their skin color rather than for the way they are driving. For example, in Florida 80% of those stopped and searched were black and Hispanic, while they constituted only 5% of all drivers. These humiliating and illegal searches are violations of the Constitution and must be fought. Help us defend your rights. Support the ACLU. www.aclu.org **american civil liberties union**

In some public schools, it's a science textbook. What's taught in Sunday school shouldn't be taught in Monday through Friday school. But that's exactly what's happening. School officials that impose their religious beliefs on your children are in direct violation of the First Amendment. Help us defend your rights. Support the ACLU. www.aclu.org **american civil liberties union**

On February 4th, 1999, the NYPD gave Amadou Diallo the right to remain silent. And they did it without ever saying a word. Firing 41 bullets in 8 seconds, the police killed an unarmed, innocent man. Also wounded that night was the constitutional right of every American to due process of law. Help us defend your rights. Support the ACLU. www.aclu.org **american civil liberties union**

CHAPTER 6

Thinking about Communities and Conventions

Whenever you analyze a rhetorical situation, you ask yourself a number of commonsense questions about your writing purpose and situation. As you do so, you naturally draw on your previous experiences as a writer and reader and as a speaker and listener. No one had to teach you, for instance, that you would approach a letter of condolence to a friend whose mother had recently died differently than you would approach an email asking a friend to drop by for pizza. Your general social and cultural understanding of the seriousness of the former situation would cause you automatically to write a formal, respectful letter. As Chapter 3, "Understanding the Reading Process," pointed out, readers often make similar rhetorical judgments. Though you may not think consciously about it, when you glance through your mail, tossing ads aside while eagerly searching for a letter from a friend, your actions are the result of a rhetorical judgment about the nature and value of these texts. You may see a letter from a friend as an invitation to settle into a chair for welcome news. A sales brochure brings quite different expectations.

Whether you are reading or writing, you draw on your previous experiences to make a number of judgments about a text's purpose, subject matter, and form. When you are writing or reading familiar kinds of texts, these judgments occur almost automatically. In less familiar situations, you may have to work to understand the form and purpose of a text. I recently received a letter from a former student, Monica Molina, who now works at a community health center, where one of her responsibilities is to write grant proposals. In her letter, she commented:

> It took quite a while before I could feel comfortable even thinking about trying to write my first grant proposal. Most of the ones at our center run 50 to 100 pages and seem so intimidating — full of strange subheadings, technical language, complicated explanations. I had to force myself to calm down and get into them. First I read some recent proposals, trying to figure out how they worked. Luckily, my boss is friendly and supportive, so she sat down with me and talked about her experiences writing proposals. We looked at some proposals together, and she told me about

how proposals are reviewed by agencies. Now we're working together on my first proposal. I'm still nervous, but I'm beginning to feel more comfortable. When I feel stressed out about it, I try to tell myself that "firsts" are always difficult.

Most writers sooner or later face the challenge of writing (and reading) unfamiliar kinds of texts. Students entering a new discipline may find themselves puzzled by unfamiliar language or writing styles. And like Monica, those entering new professions often must learn new forms of writing.

Writers who wish to participate in a new community must strive to understand its reading and writing practices — to learn how to enter its conversations, as the rhetorician Kenneth Burke might say. For the forms and strategies of writing that characterize different communities are not arbitrary but rather reflect important shared assumptions and practices. These shared assumptions and practices — sometimes referred to as *textual conventions* — represent agreements between writers and readers about how to construct and interpret texts. As such, they are an important component of any rhetorical situation.

ANALYZING TEXTUAL CONVENTIONS

The notion of *textual convention* may be new to you, but you can understand it easily if you think about other uses of the word *convention*. For example, *social* conventions are implicit agreements among the members of a community or culture about how to act in particular situations. At one time in the United States, for example, it was acceptable for persons who chewed tobacco to use spittoons in such public places as restaurants and hotel lobbies. Now this behavior is no longer acceptable; this particular social convention has changed over time.

If social conventions represent agreements among individuals about how to act, textual conventions represent similar agreements about how to write and read texts. Just as we tend to take our own social conventions for granted, so too do we take for granted those textual conventions most familiar to us as readers and writers. When we begin a letter to our parents by writing "Dear Mom and Dad," for instance, we don't stop to wonder if this greeting is appropriate; we know from our experience as writers and readers that it is. When we read a text from another time or culture, we can sometimes see more clearly than in our own writing the extent to which such texts depend on shared understandings. During the Middle Ages, salutations (such as "Dear Mom and Dad") were much more formal and elaborate than contemporary greetings. Here are two suggested salutations for teachers and pupils from *The Principles of Letter Writing,* a medieval guide for writers:

The Salutation of a Teacher to a Pupil

N —— , promoter of the scholastic profession, wishes N —— , his most dear friend and companion, to acquire the teachings of all literature, to possess fully all the diligence of the philosophical profession, to pursue not folly but the wisdom of Socrates and Plato.

The Salutation of a Pupil to a Teacher

To N —— , by divine grace resplendent in Ciceronian charm, N —— , inferior to his devoted learning, expresses the servitude of a sincere heart.*

The Principles of Letter Writing includes fourteen additional categories of salutations, including "Salutations of Close Friends or Associates," "Salutations of Subjects to Their Secular Lords," and "Salutations of Lords to Blamable and Offending Subordinates." The textual conventions governing these greetings reflect this period's attentiveness to differences in rank and station. Over time, such elaborate, ritualized salutations have been replaced by much simpler forms of address — thus, "Dear Mom and Dad."

Textual conventions are dynamic, changing over time as the assumptions, values, and practices of writers and readers change. Consider some of the textual conventions of email and other online writing. Emoticons, for instance — symbols such as **:-)** to indicate happiness, **:-(** to indicate sadness, or **:-O** to indicate shock or surprise — were developed by online writers who wished to express the kind of emotion often conveyed in face-to-face communication by such elements as voice, gesture, and facial expression. Not all who use email use emoticons, and those who do use them recognize that they may be more appropriate in some situations than others. But as a textual convention, emoticons clearly respond to the needs of some email users, writers, and readers.

■ ■ ■

FOR EXPLORATION

The transition from print to electronic writing technologies represents a significant change in the situation of writers and readers. If you have some experience in online writing situations, freewrite for five or ten minutes about the extent to which the textual conventions of online writing differ

---

*These salutations are excerpted from James J. Murphy, ed., *Three Medieval Rhetorical Arts* (Berkeley: U California P, 1971), 14–15. (The letter "N ——" in these salutations stands for "name.")

from those of traditional print communications. If you have little or no experience with online writing, take this opportunity to reflect on the questions and concerns you bring to this new writing situation.

Making Appropriate Decisions about Your Writing

Whether you are entering a community of online writers or a new academic or professional community, analyzing your rhetorical situation will enable you to communicate effectively with others. Because they play such a critical role in making communication between writers and readers possible, textual conventions are an important component of the rhetorical situation. When you think about the kind of writing that you are being asked to do, for instance, you are thinking in part about the textual conventions that may limit your options as a writer in a specific situation. Textual conventions bring constraints, but they also increase the likelihood that readers will respond appropriately to a writer's ideas.

Some textual conventions are quite specific. Personal letters always begin with a greeting and end with a signature. Sonnets have fourteen rhymed lines, usually consisting of an octave (eight lines) and sextet (six lines) or three four-line quatrains with a closing couplet. Similarly, lab reports usually include the following elements: title page, abstract, introduction, experimental design and methods, results, discussion, and references. Someone writing a sonnet or a lab report can deviate from these textual conventions, but doing so runs the risk of confusing or irritating readers.

Other textual conventions are much more general. Consider, for instance, the conventions of an academic essay:

Characteristics of an Effective Academic Essay

1. An effective essay is well organized and well developed. It establishes its subject or main idea in the introduction, develops that idea in a coherent manner in the body, and summarizes or completes the discussion in the conclusion.

2. An effective essay is logical. It supports its main points with well-chosen evidence, illustrations, and details.

3. An effective essay is clear and readable. It uses words, sentences, and paragraphs that are carefully crafted, appropriate for the writer's purpose and subject, and free of errors of usage, grammar, and punctuation.

These statements summarize some of the most general conventions that govern academic essays. But because these statements are so general and apply to so many different kinds of writing, you may not know just what they mean in specific situations and in your own writing.

Seeing Textual Conventions in Use

To see how general textual conventions operate and to illustrate how you can analyze textual conventions, let's consider just one of the conventions of an "effective essay" — that it establishes its subject or main idea in an introduction. This particular textual convention is learned early, for even young children introduce stories, if only (in Western cultures, at least) with the words *Once upon a time.* Most writers and readers can easily understand why an essay needs an introduction. No one likes to be thrown into the middle of a discussion without any idea of the subject. Still, writers are not always certain about what constitutes the best introduction for a specific essay.

Let's look at three articles by psychologist John H. Flavell to see how one writer tackled this problem. All three articles were written by Dr. Flavell, although the third was coauthored with two colleagues. Each article discusses research conducted by Flavell and his colleagues on the ability of young children to distinguish between appearance and reality.

The first article, "Really and Truly" (pp. 174–75), was published in *Psychology Today,* a popular magazine designed for members of the general public who are interested in learning about and applying principles of psychology in their own lives. The second article, "The Development of Children's Knowledge about the Appearance–Reality Distinction" (pp. 176–77), was published in *American Psychologist,* an academic journal of the American Psychological Association, whose members include psychologists and other behavioral and social scientists. The third article, "Development of the Appearance–Reality Distinction" (pp. 178–79), was published in *Cognitive Psychology,* a specialized academic journal for researchers in that field. As you read each article's introduction, think about the impact that the different publications and intended audiences may have had on the form and content of each essay. Pay attention also to the format used to present each article.

■ ■ ■

FOR EXPLORATION

Read the introductions to Flavell's three articles, and write one paragraph characterizing the approach of each article. How would you describe the tone of each article and the kind of language used? What can you learn from your paragraphs about the differences among these articles?

Comparing and Contrasting Textual Conventions

You need only glance at the first pages of Flavell's three articles to notice some striking differences. The first two pages of "Really and Truly," the *Psychology Today* article, have a great deal of white space and several large illustrations.

Really and Truly

*UNTIL THEY ARE 4 OR 5, CHILDREN
DON'T UNDERSTAND THE DISTINCTION BETWEEN
APPEARANCE AND REALITY;
WHAT YOU SEE IS NOT ALWAYS WHAT YOU GET.*

BY *JOHN H. FLAVELL*

I t looks like a nice, solid piece of granite, but as soon as you squeeze it you know it's really a joke-store sponge made to look like a rock. If I ask what it appears to be, you say, "It looks just like a rock." If I ask what it really is, you say, "It's a sponge, of course." A 3-year-old probably wouldn't be so sure. Children at this age often aren't quite able to grasp the idea that what you see is not always what you get.

By the time they are 6 or 7 years

old, however, most children have a fair grasp of the appearance-reality distinction that assumes so many forms in our everyday lives. Misperceptions, misexpectations, misunderstandings, false beliefs, deception, play and fantasy—these and other examples of that distinction are a preoccupation of philosophers, scientists, artists, politicians and other public performers and of the rest of us who try to evaluate what they all say and do.

For the past half dozen years, my colleagues and I have been asking children questions about sponge rocks and using other methods to find out what children of different ages know about the difference between appearances and reality. First we give the children a brief lesson on the meaning of the appearance-reality distinction by showing them, for example, a Charlie Brown puppet inside a ghost costume. We explain and demonstrate that Charlie Brown "looks like a ghost to your eyes right now" but is "really and truly Charlie Brown," and that "sometimes things look like one thing

Continued on Page 42

It looks like a rock, it feels like a sponge, but to a 3-year-old the distinction between appearance and reality can be quite confusing.

1985 APA Award Addresses

The Development of Children's Knowledge About the Appearance–Reality Distinction

John H. Flavell   *Stanford University*

ABSTRACT: *Recent research on the acquisition of knowledge about the important and pervasive appearance–reality distinction suggests the following course of development. Many 3-year-olds seem to possess little or no understanding of the distinction. They fail very easy-looking tests of this understanding and are unresponsive to training. At this age level, skill in solving simple appearance-reality tasks is highly correlated with skill in solving simple visual perspective-taking tasks. This and other findings are consistent with the hypothesis that what helps children finally grasp the distinction is an increased cognizance of the fact that people are sentient subjects who have mental representations of objects and events. It does so by allowing them to understand that the selfsame stimulus can be mentally represented in two different, seemingly contradictory ways: (a) in the appearance–reality case, how it appears to the self versus how it really is; and (b) in the perspective-taking case, how it presently appears to self versus other. In contrast to young preschoolers, children of 6 to 7 years manage simple appearance-reality tasks with ease. However, they have great difficulty reflecting on and talking about such appearance-reality notions as "looks like," "really and truly," and especially, "looks different from the way it really and truly is." Finally, children of 11 to 12 years, and to an even greater degree college students, give evidence of possessing a substantial body of rich, readily available, and explicit knowledge in this area.*

Suppose someone shows a three-year-old and a six-year-old a red toy car covered by a green filter that makes the car look black, hands the car to the children to inspect, puts it behind the filter again, and asks, "What color is this car? Is it red or is it black?" (Flavell, Green, & Flavell, 1985; cf. Braine & Shanks, 1965a, 1965b). The three-year-old is likely to say "black," the six-year-old, "red." The questioner is also apt to get the same answers even if he or she first carefully explains and demonstrates the intended difference in meaning, for illusory displays, between "looks like to your eyes right now" and "really and truly is," and then asks what color it *"really and truly is."* At issue in such simple tasks is the distinction between how things presently appear to the senses and how or

what they really and enduringly are, that is, the familiar distinction between appearance and reality. The six-year-old is clearly in possession of some knowledge about this distinction and quickly senses what the task is about. The three-year-old, who is much less knowledgeable about the distinction, does not.

For the past half-dozen years my co-workers and I have been using these and other methods to chart the developmental course of knowledge acquisition in this area. That is, we have been trying to find out what children of different ages do and do not know about the appearance–reality distinction and related phenomena. In this article I summarize what we have done and what we think we have learned (Flavell, Flavell, & Green, 1983; Flavell et al., 1985; Flavell, Zhang, Zou, Dong, & Qi, 1983; Taylor & Flavell, 1984). The summary is organized around the main questions that have guided our thinking and research in this area.

Why Is This Development Important To Study?

First, the distinction between appearance and reality is ecologically significant. It assumes many forms, arises in many situations, and can have serious consequences for our lives. The relation between appearance and reality figures importantly in everyday perceptual, conceptual, emotional, and social activity—in misperceptions, misexpectations, misunderstandings, false beliefs, deception, play, fantasy, and so forth. It is also a major preoccupation of philosophers, scientists, and other scholars; of artists, politicians, and other public performers; and of the thinking public that tries to evaluate what they say and do. It is, in sum, "the distinction which probably provides the intellectual basis for the fundamental epistemological construct common to science, 'folk' philosophy, religion, and myth, of a real world 'underlying' and 'explaining' the phenomenal one" (Braine & Shanks, 1965a, pp. 241–242).

Second, the acquisition of at least some explicit knowledge about the appearance–reality distinction is probably a universal developmental outcome in our species. This knowledge seems so necessary to everyday intellectual and social life that one can hardly imagine a society in which normal people would not acquire it. To

April 1986 • American Psychologist
Copyright 1986 by the American Psychological Association, Inc. 0003-066X/86/$00.75
Vol. 41, No. 4, 418–425

cite an example that has actually been researched, a number of investigators have been interested in the child's command of the distinction as a possible developmental prerequisite for, and perhaps even mediator of, Piagetian conservations (e.g., Braine & Shanks, 1965a, 1965b; Murray, 1968).

Third, knowledge about the distinction seems to presuppose the explicit knowledge that human beings are sentient, cognizing *subjects* (cf. Chandler & Boyce, 1982; Selman, 1980) whose mental representations of objects and events can differ, both within the same person and between persons. In the within-person case, for example, I may be aware both that something appears to be A and that it really is B. I could also be aware that it might appear to be C under special viewing conditions, or that I pretended or fantasized that it was D yesterday. I may know that these are all possible ways that I can *represent* the very same thing (i.e., perceive it, encode it, know it, interpret it, construe it, or think about it—although inadequate, the term "represent" will have to do). In the between-persons case, I may be aware that you might represent the same thing differently than I do, because our perceptual, conceptual, or affective perspectives on it might differ. If this analysis is correct, knowledge about the appearance–reality distinction is but one instance of our more general knowledge that the selfsame object or event can be represented (apprehended, experienced, etc.) in different ways by the same person and by different people. In this analysis, then, its development is worth studying because it is part of the larger development of our conscious knowledge about our own and other minds and, thus, of metacognition (e.g., Brown, Bransford, Ferrara, & Campione, 1983; Flavell, 1985; Wellman, 1985) and of social cognition (e.g., Flavell, 1985; Shantz, 1983). I will return to this line of reasoning in another section of the article.

How Can Young Children's Knowledge About the Appearance–Reality Distinction Be Tested?

The development of appearance–reality knowledge in preschool children has been investigated by Braine and

---

Editor's note. This article is based on a Distinguished Scientific Contribution Award address presented at the meeting of the American Psychological Association, Los Angeles, California, August 1985.

Award addresses, submitted by award recipients, are published as received except for minor editorial changes designed to maintain *American Psychologist* format. This reflects a policy of recognizing distinguished award recipients by eliminating the usual editorial review process to provide a forum consistent with that employed in delivering the award address.

Author's note. The work described in this article was supported by National Institute for Child Health and Human Development (NICHD) Grant HD 09814. I am very grateful to my research collaborators, Eleanor Flavell and Frances Green, and to Carole Beal, Gary Bonitatibus, Susan Carey, Sophia Cohen, Rochel Gelman, Suzanne Lovett, Eleanor Maccoby, Ellen Markman, Bradford Pillow, Qian Man-jun, Marjorie Taylor, Zhang Xiao-dong, and other colleagues and students for their invaluable help with this research.

Correspondence concerning this article should be addressed to John H. Flavell, Department of Psychology, Jordan Hall, Building 420, Stanford University, Stanford, CA 94305.

Shanks (1965a, 1965b), Daehler (1970), DeVries (1969), Elkind (1966), King (1971), Langer and Strauss (1972), Murray (1965, 1968), Tronick and Hershenson (1979) and, most recently and systematically, by our research group. In most of our studies we have used variations of the following procedure to assess young children's ability to think about appearance and reality (Flavell, Flavell, & Green, 1983). First, we pretrain the children briefly on the meaning of the distinction and associated terminology by showing them (for example) a Charlie Brown puppet inside a ghost costume. We explain and demonstrate that Charlie Brown "*looks like* a ghost to your eyes right now" but is "*really and truly* Charlie Brown," and that "sometimes things look like one thing to your eyes when they are really and truly something else." We then present a variety of illusory stimuli in a nondeceptive fashion and ask about their appearance and their reality. For instance, we first show the children a very realistic looking fake rock made out of a soft sponge-like material and then let them discover its identity by manipulating it. We next ask, in random order: (a) "What is this *really* and *truly?* Is it *really* and *truly* a sponge or is it *really* and *truly* a rock?" (b) "When you look at this with your eyes right now, does it *look like* a rock or does it *look like* a sponge?" Or we show the children a white stimulus, move it behind a blue filter, and similarly ask about its real and apparent color. (Of course its "real color" is now blue, but only people who know something about color perception realize this.) Similar procedures are used to assess sensitivity to the distinction between real and apparent size, shape, events, and object presence.

How Do Young Children Perform on Simple Appearance–Reality Tasks?

Our studies have consistently shown that three- to four-year-old children presented with tasks of this sort usually either answer both questions correctly, suggesting some ability to differentiate appearance and reality representations, or else give the same answer (reporting either the appearance or the reality) to both questions, suggesting some conceptual difficulty with the distinction. Incorrect answers to both questions occur only infrequently, suggesting that even the children who err are not responding randomly. There is a marked improvement with age during early childhood in the ability to solve these appearance–reality tasks: Only a few three-year-olds get them right consistently, whereas almost all six- to seven-year-olds do (Flavell et al., 1985).

Some illusory stimuli tend to elicit appearance answers to both questions (called a *phenomenism* error pattern), whereas others tend to elicit reality answers to both (*intellectual realism* pattern). The intellectual realism pattern is the more surprising one, because it contradicts the widely held view that young children respond only to what is most striking and noticeable in their immediate perceptual field (Flavell, 1977, pp. 79–80; for a review of other research on intellectual realism, see Pillow & Flavell, 1985). If the task is to distinguish between the real and apparent properties of color, size, and shape, phenomen-

Development of the Appearance–Reality Distinction

JOHN H. FLAVELL, ELEANOR R. FLAVELL, AND FRANCES L. GREEN
Stanford University

Young children can express conceptual difficulties with the appearance–reality distinction in two different ways: (1) by incorrectly reporting appearance when asked to report reality ("phenomenism"); (2) by incorrectly reporting reality when asked to report appearance ("intellectual realism"). Although both phenomenism errors and intellectual realism errors have been observed in previous studies of young children's cognition, the two have not been seen as conceptually related and only the former errors have been taken as a symptom of difficulties with the appearance–reality distinction. Three experiments investigated 3- to 5-year-old children's ability to distinguish between and correctly identify real versus apparent object properties (color, size, and shape), object identities, object presence–absence, and action identities. Even the 3-year-olds appeared to have some ability to make correct appearance–reality discriminations and this ability increased with age. Errors were frequent, however, and almost all children who erred made both kinds. Phenomenism errors predominated on tasks where the appearance versus reality of the three object properties were in question; intellectual realism errors predominated on the other three types of tasks. Possible reasons for this curious error pattern were advanced. It was also suggested that young children's problems with the appearance–reality distinction may be partly due to a specific metacognitive limitation, namely, a difficulty in analyzing the nature and source of their own mental representations.

The acquisition of knowledge about the distinction between appearance and reality is a very important developmental problem for at least two reasons.

1. The distinction arises in a very large number and variety of ecologically significant cognitive situations. In many of these situations, the information available to us is insufficient or misleading, causing us to accept an apparent state of affairs (appearance) that differs from the true state of affairs (reality). We are variously misled or deceived by the information we receive from or concerning people, objects, actions, events, and experiences. The deceit may be deliberately engineered by another person; the person intentionally misleads us—through the use of lies, facades, dis-

This research was supported by NICHD Grant HD 09814. We are most grateful to the children, teachers, and parents whose cooperation made these studies possible. We are also much indebted to Ellen Markman, Marjorie Taylor, Carole Beal, and numerous other colleagues and students for their useful suggestions over the course of this project. Finally, we thank Rochel Gelman and two anonymous reviewers for their helpful critiques of this article. Please send requests for reprints to Dr. John H. Flavell, Department of Psychology, Stanford University, Stanford, CA 94305.

guises, and other artifices. Very often, however, there is no intention to deceive. The time or distance seemed longer to us than it really was; the sun looks like it moves around the earth but it really does not; it appeared that S–R theory could explain language development but the reality turned out (appeared?) otherwise. The last two examples make it clear that all systematic pursuit of knowledge presupposes at least some awareness of the appearance–reality distinction (Carey, in press): "the distinction which probably provides the intellectual basis for the fundamental epistemological construct common to science, "folk" philosophy, religion, and myth, of a real world "underlying" and "explaining" the phenomenal one" (Braine & Shanks, 1965a, pp. 241–242). Although we may not know that appearances have in fact deceived us in any specific cognitive situation, we do know as a general fact that such deception is always possible. That is, although always susceptible to being deceived by appearances, we have acquired the metacognitive knowledge that appearance–reality differences are always among life's possibilities. There are also many situations in which we are aware of an existing appearance–reality discrepancy. In the above examples, for instance, we may subsequently discover the discrepancy of which we were initially unaware. Dreams constitute a frequent case in point: the events seem real during the dream; we know they were apparent rather than real when we wake up. We also deliberately create or seek out appearance–reality differences as well as discover them. Examples are as diverse as pretense and other forms of play, fantasy, the creation of imaginary or possible worlds (by philosophers, scientists, other adults, and children), magic, tricks, costume parties, jokes, tall tales, metaphor, and the arts (e.g., drama). Some differences between appearance and reality are unwanted and painful; for instance, the apparently "sure-fire" investment (financial or emotional) that really is not. Others, however, are sought after and pleasureful; good magic shows and well-crafted "whodunits" are two examples.

2. The development of knowledge about the distinction between appearance and reality is probably a universal development in human beings. The distinction seems so necessary for everyday adaptations to the human world that one can scarcely imagine a society in which normal children would not acquire it. Developments that are both ecologically significant and universal within the species seem particularly worthy of scientific investigation.

How might young children think and act if, as seems likely, their knowledge about the appearance–reality distinction were not as fully developed as our own? In situations where appearance and reality differ they might not consistently attend to both and keep the difference between them clearly in mind, even when evidence is available to indicate

The title doesn't actually state what the essay is about, but it does pique the reader's curiosity. The article begins informally with an attention-getting image: "It looks like a nice, solid piece of granite, but as soon as you squeeze it you know it's really a joke-store sponge made to look like a rock." Addressing readers directly, the writer quickly establishes the contradiction that the article will explore: "If I ask what it appears to be, you say, 'It looks just like a rock.' If I ask what it really is, you say, 'It's a sponge, of course.' A 3-year-old probably wouldn't be so sure." The final sentence of the first paragraph clearly indicates the main subject that the essay will explore, but its revision of a popular saying — "what you see is not always what you get" — ensures that the reader's interest will be maintained.

The second article, from *American Psychologist,* is visually dense, with little white space and no illustrations. It states prominently that this essay is an APA Award Address; readers of this journal would recognize the importance of this award. The title is straightforward and easy to understand. The article begins not with an attention-getting introduction but with an abstract, which summarizes the findings of the research reported in the article. The first paragraph of the article opens with a concrete incident but quickly moves to a more theoretical discussion: "At issue in such simple tasks is the distinction between how things presently appear to the senses and how or what they really and enduringly are, that is, the familiar distinction between appearance and reality."

The third article, which appeared in *Cognitive Psychology,* the most specialized of these publications, presents the most cramped and least inviting first page. The title is abbreviated. As with the *American Psychologist* article, an abstract summarizes the article. The article itself begins abruptly with a general statement: "The acquisition of knowledge about the distinction between appearance and reality is a very important developmental problem for at least two reasons." The numbered paragraphs that follow this statement are dense; the authors use a number of technical terms, such as *ecologically significant cognitive situations* and *S-R theory,* without defining them.

Analyzing these first few pages supplies important clues about these three publications and the expectations of their writers and readers. One fact is clear from these introductory pages: The less specialized the publication, the greater the expectation that the writer will attempt to interest readers in the article. More attention will also be paid to the effective use of visual images and such design elements as white space. People who subscribe to *Psychology Today,* the most general and popular of these journals, often don't have a clear purpose when they read; they're broadly interested in psychology, but they may read only the articles that pique their curiosity. A writer who hopes to be read will consequently attempt to gain the attention of these readers.

Readers of *American Psychologist* are, like Flavell, professionals in that field. Because psychology is such a broad field with so many subdisciplines,

Flavell can't assume that everyone who subscribes to the journal will be interested in his essay. Not even all the readers who subscribe to *Cognitive Psychology*, a more specialized journal that publishes only research in Flavell's area, will read the article by Flavell and his colleagues, though proportionately more are likely to do so.

Why then doesn't Flavell do more to gain the interest of readers in the introductions to these more specialized journals, as he does in his *Psychology Today* article? Readers of *American Psychologist* and *Cognitive Psychology* read with different purposes and in different ways than readers of *Psychology Today*. They read these journals not so much for pleasure or curiosity but because they want to keep up with advances in their field. The readers of these two journals probably subscribe to many professional publications. They don't have the time to read every article in these journals, so they skim the tables of contents, noting articles that directly affect their own research or have broad significance for their field. Reviewing an article's abstract helps these psychologists determine not only if but also *how* they will read an article. Some will read only an article's conclusion, for instance; others will be more interested in how an experiment was designed and conducted.

These psychologists would find an engaging introduction like that of the *Psychology Today* article a waste of time. Instead, they want a straightforward, to-the-point approach. Their needs are best met by an abstract that allows them to judge for themselves if they should read an article. Furthermore, whereas readers of *Psychology Today* may discard issues after reading them, readers of *American Psychologist* and *Cognitive Psychology* probably save theirs. They know that an essay that seems unimportant today may need to be read later. They don't read articles in these journals just once, as readers of popular magazines like *Psychology Today* probably do. They may reread important articles a number of times as they work on similar studies or experiments. Because they are reading primarily for content, they do not mind if the text is cramped and visually uninteresting. They value clear, specific headings over inviting images.

Although these three articles report the same research, they differ dramatically in structure, tone, language, and approach to readers. Textual conventions play an important role in these differences. As shared agreements about the construction and interpretation of texts, textual conventions enable readers and writers to communicate successfully in different rhetorical situations.

■ ■ ■

FOR EXPLORATION

Answer the following questions about the three Flavell introductions to analyze further the differences and similarities among them:

1. What kinds of examples are used in each excerpt? What function do they serve?

2. What relationship is established in each article between the writer and the reader? What cues help signal each relationship?

3. How do the abstracts of the *American Psychologist* and *Cognitive Psychology* articles differ? How do you account for these differences?

4. How would you characterize the styles of these three excerpts? Point to specific features that characterize each style. What is the effect of these stylistic differences?

5. What assumptions does Flavell make in each article about what readers already know? Point out specific instances that reflect these assumptions.

6. How would you describe the *persona*, or image of the writer, in each article? What specific factors contribute to the development and coherence of this *persona*?

UNDERSTANDING THE CONVENTIONS OF ACADEMIC WRITING

Some textual conventions are easy to identify. After reading just a few lab reports, for example, you recognize that this form of writing adheres to a set format. Other textual conventions are less easy to discern and to understand. When you first read the introductions to Flavell's three essays, for instance, you probably noticed that the introduction to the *Psychology Today* essay differed considerably from the introductions to the other two, which were published in scholarly journals. You may not, however, have noted the differences between the latter two introductions.

To recognize and understand these differences, you need some knowledge of the journals in which the essays were published and also of the readers of these journals. The authors' decision to use technical terms, such as *phenomenism* and *S-R theory*, in the introduction to the *Cognitive Psychology* article reflects their assumption that readers would not only understand these terms but would expect them. Furthermore, using such terms subtly tells readers that the writers are insiders, privy to the terminology used by those in this field.

As this example indicates, recognizing and understanding textual conventions requires considerable knowledge not only of the forms of writing but also of the *situations* of writers and readers. When you join a new community of writers and readers, as you do when you enter college, you need to understand the demands of the writing you are expected to complete. Look again, for instance, at the characteristics of an effective essay on p. 172. When you first read these characteristics, they probably made sense to you. Of course, essays should be well organized, well developed, and logical.

When you begin work on an essay for history, sociology, or economics, however, you may find it difficult to determine how to embody these characteristics in your own writing. Just what will make your analysis of the economic impact of divorce on the modern family logical or illogical, you might ask yourself. What do economists consider to be appropriate evidence, illustrations, and details? And does your economics teacher value the same kind of logic, evidence, and details as your American literature teacher?

■ ■ ■

FOR EXPLORATION

Freewrite for five or ten minutes about your experience thus far with academic writing. What do you find productive and satisfying about such writing? What seems difficult and frustrating? Does your ability to respond to the demands of academic writing vary depending on the discipline? Do you find writing essays about literature easier, for instance, than writing lab reports and case studies? What do you think makes some kinds of academic writing harder or easier for you?

Using Textual Conventions

You already know enough about rhetoric and the rhetorical situation to realize that there can be no one-size-fits-all approach to every academic writing situation. To respond successfully to the challenge of academic writing, you must explore rhetorical situations; you must also draw on the rhetorical sensitivity you have gained as a reader, writer, speaker, and listener.

A rhetorical approach to writing suggests a number of commonsense strategies that you can use when writing in an academic context. For writing to be successful, rhetoric emphasizes, you must have something to say, something to communicate with others. There is thus no substitute for direct critical engagement with the subject matter of your courses. Your teachers share an intellectual commitment first of all to education as inquiry and then to their own discipline. When teachers read your writing, they are looking for evidence that you have *learned* (not simply memorized) something.

Becoming critically engaged with a subject and communicating that engagement with others are not necessarily the same thing, however. What can you do when you are unfamiliar with the textual conventions of academic writing in general or of a particular discipline? A rhetorical approach to writing suggests that one important way to learn about textual conventions is to read examples of the kind of writing you wish to do. Discussing these models with an insider — your teacher, perhaps, or an advanced student in the field — can help you understand why these conventions work for these readers and writers. Forming a study group with others in your class or meeting with a writing assistant at a writing center can also help you increase your rhetorical sensitivity to the expectations of your teachers and the conventions of academic writing.

Finally, a rhetorical approach to writing encourages you to think *strategically* about writing — whether personal, professional, or academic — and to respond creatively to the challenges of each situation. As a writer, you have much to consider: your own goals as a writer, the nature of your subject and writing task, the expectations of your readers, the textual conventions your particular situation requires or allows. The rhetorical sensitivity you have already developed can help you make appropriate choices in response to these and other concerns. But you can also draw on other resources — textual examples; discussions with teachers, writing assistants, and other students — as you work on a variety of writing tasks. As a writer, you are not alone. By reaching out to other writers, in person or by reading their work, you can become a fully participating member of the academic community.

■ ■ ■

FOR EXPLORATION

Interview a teacher in another course you are taking this term, preferably one in which you have done some writing, so that you can learn more about your teacher's expectations of student writing. You may wish to ask some or all of the following questions:

1. What do you look for when you read students' writing? How would you characterize effective student writing in your discipline?

2. In your discipline, what is the difference between an A and a C student essay (or lab report or case study)?

3. What are the major weaknesses or limitations of the writing produced by your students?

4. What advice would you give to students who want to understand how to write more effectively in introductory classes in your field?

5. Do you think your discipline values particular qualities in student writing not necessarily shared by other fields, or is good writing good writing no matter what the discipline?

6. Could you suggest some examples I could read that would help me understand the conventions of effective writing in your discipline?

7. How would you characterize the differences between effective student writing and effective professional writing in your field?

8. What role do you see yourself playing when you read student writing?

9. Is there anything else you can tell me that would help me better understand the kind of student writing valued in your discipline?

After your interview, write a summary of your teacher's responses. Then write at least two paragraphs reflecting on what this interview has taught you about academic writing.

FOR GROUP WORK

Once you have completed the preceding Exploration activity, meet with a group of students. Begin by reading your summaries out loud. Working together (be sure to appoint a recorder), answer these questions:

- Can you find three statements or beliefs shared by all the people interviewed?

- What were some major points of disagreement? Did some faculty members feel, for instance, that good student writing is good student writing whatever the discipline, while others believed that their discipline valued particular qualities in student writing?

- What surprised you in the interviews? Briefly explain why you were surprised.

- What did these interviews help you understand about academic writing? Include at least three statements that reflect your group's discussion of your interviews.

Be prepared to share your findings with the rest of the class.

FOR THOUGHT, DISCUSSION, AND WRITING

1. From a newspaper or a magazine, choose an essay, an editorial, or a column that you think succeeds in its purpose. Now turn back to the guidelines for analyzing your rhetorical situation on pp. 147–49, and answer the questions *as if you were the writer*. To answer the questions, look for evidence of the writer's intentions in the writing itself. (To determine what image or *persona* the writer wanted to portray, for instance, look at the kind of language the writer uses. Is it formal or conversational? Full of interesting images and vivid details or serious examples and statistics?) Answer each of the questions suggested by the

guidelines. Then write a paragraph or more reflecting on what you have learned from this analysis.

2. Writers can follow appropriate textual conventions and still not be successful. Most textbooks follow certain conventions, such as having headings and subheadings, yet undoubtedly you have found some textbooks helpful and interesting, while others have seemed unhelpful and boring. Choose two textbooks — one that you like and one that you dislike — and make a list of at least four reasons that the former is successful and the latter is not.

3. Working with a group of students, write an essay that summarizes and reflects on what you have learned about academic writing as a result of completing the Exploration on pp. 184–85 and the group activity on p. 185.

Negotiating Online Writing Situations

As Chapter 6 emphasized, textual conventions are dynamic, changing over time as the values and situations of the writers and readers employing them change. Many factors played a role in the development of modern textual conventions. As medieval monarchies in Europe evolved into nations, and as these nations established democratic governmental and social structures, writers and readers moved away from the elaborate, status-conscious greetings typical of medieval salutations. As the daily lives of Europeans became less governed by rigid social and cultural hierarchies, so too did the texts they read and wrote change.

Significant cultural changes bring new opportunities and new challenges for writers. One of the most significant developments in North American culture in the last thirty years has been the evolution of electronic technologies. From the development of the microprocessor in 1971 to the growth of the Internet, electronic technologies are providing new opportunities for writers to express their ideas.

There is considerable debate about the consequences of these technologies. Some commentators argue that electronic technologies will enable people to lead more flexible, productive lives. A businessman needing to care for a sick child, for instance, can email coworkers from home if he has a computer with a modem. Many believe that electronic technologies represent a positive force for global understanding, enabling people in vastly different locations and situations to communicate with one another. Some commentators even see these technologies as catalyzing a revolution, making it possible for ordinary citizens who have previously lacked access to the media to publish or broadcast their ideas via a variety of electronic forums.

Others challenge this optimistic vision. Some parents and educators fear that rather than using electronic technologies to improve their communication skills and increase their understanding of the world, many online writers and readers use the Internet to engage in mind-numbing chat-room conversations. Another concern involves the unequal distribution of electronic technologies: Not everyone can pay the toll necessary to enter the information superhighway. Currently, in comparison with North America and western Europe, Africa, India, and Latin America have minimal access to the Internet.

Clearly, the development of electronic technologies raises a number of important social, political, cultural, and economic questions — and the way our society addresses these questions will significantly impact your personal and professional life. Nevertheless, as a student you may find yourself more immediately preoccupied with a number of practical concerns. How can you make the most productive use of the online technologies available to you? If you have little or no online experience, how can you learn the conventions appropriate for such new forms of texts as email and the World Wide Web? And what about such real-time forms of communication as chat rooms, MOOs, and MUDs. What conventions govern these new forms of online communication?

It would be foolhardy even to attempt to provide definitive answers to such questions, for electronic technologies are evolving too rapidly to permit once-and-for-all responses. Nevertheless, there is a good deal you can do to understand the special demands of online writing. As we saw in Chapter 6, you can learn a great deal about textual conventions by reading examples of forms you wish to compose. Before developing your own Web site, for instance, you would want to spend considerable time exploring the Web as well as learning how to write and design a Web page. But you can also learn appropriate conventions for online writing situations by drawing on your commonsense understanding of how language works. Such a rhetorically grounded understanding will enable you to recognize that although email communications are generally much less formal than traditional print communications, you still need to consider your rhetorical situation. Though an email message to your supervisor at work might be less formal than a conventional print business memo, it should probably not be as informal and chatty as email to your friends or family. You would be naive not to recognize that since your supervisor has a printer as well as a computer, your message could well be printed out and become as permanent as any paper document. In the brave new world of electronic technologies, as in the world of print, you can and should draw on your rhetorical sensitivity to determine the best way to respond to specific online writing tasks.

■ ■ ■

FOR EXPLORATION

Take five or ten minutes to freewrite about your own experiences with online writing situations. What uses, if any, have you made of such electronic technologies as email and the World Wide Web? What excites you about these technologies — and what questions or reservations about them do you have?

UNDERSTANDING WHAT'S AT STAKE
IN THE TRANSITION FROM SCRIPT TO PRINT
AND ONLINE TECHNOLOGIES

A rhetorical perspective on communication encourages you to consider the particular situation in which you are writing. One aspect of this situation involves the *medium* you are using to convey your thoughts to readers. Throughout the centuries, people have relied on a variety of media — from stone, clay tablets, and papyrus to parchment, paper, and now electronic communications technologies — to capture their words and ideas. Each of these media brings advantages and disadvantages. In comparison with the clay tablets used by the Sumerians in the fourth century B.C., even high-quality paper is shockingly fragile. But thanks to printing and photocopying, paper holds significant advantages over clay tablets when one considers the ease of mass producing texts.

From carved symbols to movable type to email, what difference does it make to writers how and under what conditions they compose and reproduce their texts? To begin to answer this question, consider the following two messages to parents written by students living away from home. The first was written with a quill pen on parchment in the twelfth century in France; the second was composed online on October 28, 1999, by Matthew Johnston, a student at the University of Oregon. You'll see other examples of Matthew's online writing later in this chapter.

A Letter to Parents: France, the Twelfth Century

> To their very dear and respected parents M. Martre, knight, and Mme. his wife, M. and N., their sons, send greetings and filial obedience. This is to inform you that, by divine mercy, we are living in good health in the city of Orléans and are devoting ourselves wholly to study, mindful of the words of Cato, "To know anything is praiseworthy," etc. We occupy a good and comely dwelling, next door but one to the schools and marketplace, so that we can go to school every day without wetting our feet. We have also good companions in the house with us, well advanced in their studies and of excellent habits — an advantage which we as well appreciate, for as the Psalmist says, "with an upright man thou wilt show thyself upright," etc. Wherefore lest production cease from lack of material, we beg your paternity to send us by the bearer, B., money for buying parchment, ink, a desk, and the other things we need, in sufficient amount that we may suffer no want on your account (God forbid!) but finish our studies and return home with honor. The bearer will also take charge of the shoes and stockings which you have to send us, and any news as well.

An Email to Mom: Oregon, 1999

```
From matt2518@gladstone.uoregon.edu Fri Oct 29 16:54:59
1999
Date: Fri, 29 Oct 1999 16:54:59 -0700 (PDT)
From: Matt Johnston <matt2518@gladstone.uoregon.edu>
To: Jim Johnston <jim4075@home.com>
Subject: Re: Money . . .
In-Reply-To:
<001201bf2267$1a1c4760$78880718@potlnd1.or.home.com>
Message-ID: <Pine.GSO.3.96.991029165255.22098B-
100000@gladstone.uoregon.edu>
MIME-Version: 1.0
Content-Type: TEXT/PLAIN; charset=US-ASCII
Status: RO
X-Status:


Mom,

The money situation is fine. Thanks. ^_^

School's going well -- I have 3 midterms next week. I hope
to come back home next weekend (first weekend in Novem-
ber) to see Devin on Saturday.

Work isn't too bad. I have good shifts and only one
really late-night one now. Well, just thought I'd let you
know. Thanks again!

Love,
-- Matt


-----------------------------------------------------------------
    "I love to go to art museums and name the untitled
        paintings . . . 'Boy With Pail' . . . 'Kitten On
                Fire' . . . " -- Steven Wright
              -------------------------------------
 The Cafe Pierrot: Quality Original and Series-Based Anime
                         Fanfiction
           http://gladstone.uoregon.edu/~matt2518/
  Last Updated on Oct. 18th  Next Scheduled Update: Oct. 28
-----------------------------------------------------------------
```

Although these messages share some features — both include greetings to their parents, for instance, and both attempt to give them some sense of the students' daily life away from home — they differ in striking ways. The letter written in twelfth-century France uses formal diction and sentence structure.

The brothers' frequent citation of ancient authorities, like their deferential salutation, reflects the textual conventions of their time, conventions that reflect that culture's veneration of authority. In contrast, Matthew Johnston's email message is quite informal. Matthew uses an emoticon to express emotion. And he has an elaborate signature line (or "sig") that includes a favorite quotation from comedian Steven Wright as well as the URL that was then current for "The Café Pierrot," a Web fanfiction site that he has created. Its tone is chatty and relaxed — almost as if the writer were speaking to his mother rather than writing to her.

Some of the differences between these two messages reflect broad cultural shifts that have occurred over the centuries. Today's family and social structures are much less hierarchical than those of medieval times, and this change has certainly influenced the ways in which modern writers address readers. But what role might differences in the written medium have played in the evolution of these textual conventions? What significance might such factors as the ease or difficulty, and the financial cost, of composing and reproducing texts hold for writers?

Consider the situation of the brothers in Orléans. To write to their parents, they had to purchase parchment and ink — expensive luxuries that the small percentage of the population who could read and write used only for important messages. When they did put pen to paper, medieval writers worked slowly and carefully, fearful of making an error and ruining their materials. Making even a single copy of an important document was time-consuming and costly. Since there was no regular postal service in medieval Europe, letter writers either had to convey letters themselves or pay a courier to do so; conveying a letter from sender to receiver could take as long as several months. The decision to compose and send a letter was thus not made lightly; once received, letters were considered important documents and were often retained indefinitely.

Matthew Johnston is writing at a time when reading and writing are common practices. Like many who have access to computers, Matthew has found email to be a particularly user-friendly means of written communication. Thanks to his school Internet account and the availability of computer labs on his campus, Matthew pays no fee to use email, as he would with a long-distance phone call. He can email friends or family whenever a lab is open, and he knows that barring a system failure the message will be delivered almost immediately. Best of all, his email correspondents don't expect him to write the kind of formal prose he associates with school assignments and conventional personal letters. After all, many messages are deleted immediately after they are read.

As these examples indicate, the medium that writers use to communicate their ideas can make a big difference in how they approach and experience the act of writing. Because of the high cost of materials, the labor involved with handwriting, and the difficulty of transporting their letter once written, the brothers writing in twelfth-century France took the act of writing a letter very seriously indeed. The nature of the written medium thus reinforced their culture's preference for elaborate and formal written communication. Because so many social and textual conventions have changed over the centuries, even if Matthew Johnston were handwriting a letter to his mother, he would surely write much less formally than the brothers. But email's immediacy and ease — as well as the repertoire of abbreviations and symbols that have developed along with this medium — encourage a particularly chatty and informal message.

Clearly, the new electronic technologies are providing exciting opportunities for communication. As anyone who has been flamed (verbally attacked online) knows, however, these technologies open the door to *mis*communication and *mis*understanding as well. Consequently, experienced writers understand that they must draw on their rhetorical sensitivity when composing online. Even though email communications are generally less formal than written communications, for instance, writers must still consider their audience. If Matthew Johnston were writing to his employer to explain why he could not attend a meeting, he would undoubtedly take a more formal tone than he did with his mother. Similarly, some of Matthew's emails are even looser and less formal than his already informal email to his mother. Here, for instance, is an email that Matthew sent to an electronic discussion group for people interested in the progressive rock group Dream Theater. Notice how in this email Matthew chooses not to follow a number of conventions of standard written English, such as putting quotation marks around song titles ("Through Her Eyes") or using correct spelling ("Does this album seem to [instead of too] short to some of you?"). The voice here is of one fan speaking to another about very specific aspects of the music — such as a certain technique that appears "at the 2:08 mark of track 10."

```
From matt2518@gladstone.uoregon.edu Sat Oct 30 14:20:50
1999
Date: Sat, 30 Oct 1999 14:20:50 -0700 (PDT)
From: Matt Johnston <matt2518@gladstone.uoregon.edu>
To: ytsejam@torchsong.com
Subject: Myung Slap (that just sounds nasty . . . )
Message-ID: <Pine.GSO.3.96.991030141831.20480A-
100000@gladstone.uoregon.edu>
MIME-Version: 1.0
Content-Type: TEXT/PLAIN; charset=US-ASCII
Status: O
X-Status:

Little tidbit I liked (besides the fretless work in
Through Her Eyes, which gives me shivers . . . ooh!) from
Mr. Myung and his Magic Bass:
```

```
Slap-happy technique at the 2:08 mark of track 10.
Nice . . . clean . . . Myungy goodness!

Does this album seem to short to some of you? I have a
tendency to treat it like a movie . . . ^_^

-- Matt


-----------------------------------------------------------------
    "I like to go to art museums and name the untitled
       paintings . . . 'Boy With Pail' . . . 'Kitten On
              Fire' . . . " -- Steven Wright
              ---------------------------------------
 The Cafe Pierrot: Quality Original and Series-Based Anime
                      Fanfiction
           http://gladstone.uoregon.edu/~matt2518/
 Last Updated on Oct. 30th  Next Scheduled Update: Nov. 20
-----------------------------------------------------------------
```

When writing online, you can often draw on what you've learned from previous experiences with oral and written communication. But if you want to take full advantage of such new media as email and Web pages, you must understand the opportunities — and the constraints — they present to writers. The best way to become familiar with the new electronic technologies is, of course, to experience them. Many colleges and universities make electronic technologies available to their students at little to no extra cost. If that is the case for you, take advantage of this opportunity to explore these technologies if you have not already done so. Although the following discussion is no substitute for participation on a listserv or for surfing the Web (activities described later in this chapter), it can alert you to some of the issues writers face when they go online.

CONSIDERING COMMON ONLINE WRITING SITUATIONS

Online technologies are providing new opportunities for communication — ones that have already influenced many reading and writing practices. Many writers have already experienced the benefits of email. Such electronic forums as mailing lists (sometimes also called listservs or discussion lists, where email is routed through a server program to subscribers) and *newsgroups* (electronic discussion groups anyone may visit) have brought new opportunities for communicating.

These and other online forums represent potentially — but not necessarily — radical innovations in the means of communication. All offer different opportunities and constraints.

Email

Email is sometimes characterized, for instance, as a medium that mediates between speech and writing. The ease and speed with which writers can compose, send, and receive email messages are remarkable. Yet depending on the situation, email can be as permanent as the most traditional printed text — and can have similar long-term consequences. Many in business, government, and industry regularly print important email messages, retaining them as written evidence they may rely on later. In these situations, email functions primarily as a fast and inexpensive means of producing printed text.

Electronic Discussion Groups

As was the case with Matthew Johnston's email to his mother, many email messages are person-to-person. But the Internet supports software programs that enable emails from individuals to be transmitted to many other people. It is impossible to know for certain how many electronic discussion groups exist on the Internet, but estimates run as high as 15,000 to 20,000. These discussion groups serve a variety of purposes. I have already mentioned newsgroups, which are topic-specific forums on the Internet that include personal postings on a particular subject as well as traditional kinds of information, such as that gathered from wire services like the Associated Press. You can log on to most newsgroups whenever you wish and take part in the electronic conversation. Mailing lists maintain lists of subscribers interested in discussing a specific topic. Once you subscribe to the list, you are automatically sent all the messages posted there. Some enthusiasts refer to these forums as the "Cafés of the Global Village," for they enable anyone who has access to the Internet — whether they live in Los Angeles or in an isolated outpost in Tonga — to converse with others who share their interest, whether <alt.exotic-music> or <misc.activism.progressive>. Matthew Johnston, for instance, subscribes to three mailing lists. The first, <emulab@lists.uoregon.edu>, is for students who work at a computer lab in the student union at the University of Oregon, while <blazers@interscapes.com> is, according to Matthew, a "mailing list for the Portland Trail Blazers and was set up as an alternative to the rah-rah attitudes of the newsgroup." The third, <ytsejam@torchsong.com>, is a mailing list for the music group Dream Theater. Matthew also sends emails to a related newsgroup for fans of Dream Theater, <alt.music.dream-theater>.

Not all those who subscribe to newsgroups or email lists participate actively in the electronic dialogue, however. Some "lurk" online, silently reading postings much as they read their newspaper. A number occasionally send messages — and others spend hours each day in online conferences. Whether just lurking or actively posting messages, those who participate in online discussion enjoy a freedom to exchange ideas that is generally not available in print. For though some online discussion groups are moderated (and thus do not accept all messages), most are open to anyone who wishes to log on or subscribe. Given the economic realities of such print media as newspapers, magazines, and books — almost all of which are controlled by corporations — this represents a considerable expansion of individuals' ability to publish their ideas to a broad audience.

Clearly, online forums have expanded the opportunity to exchange ideas. A posting to a newsgroup such as <alt.culture.somalia> could result in an enormous range of responders — a U.N. employee who is an expert on this African country, a student from Somalia studying in the United States, or an uninformed thirteen-year-old. And therein, of course, lies a potential limitation of electronic discussion groups as sources of information. The same openness, freedom, and anonymity that characterize electronic discussion groups create potential difficulties for those who wish to use — and thus need to evaluate — information obtained online. (See Chapter 4 for help evaluating online sources.)

Real-Time Communication

Internet chat rooms (provided by some commercial services) and IRCs (Internet relay chat) provide even greater openness and freedom. These applications enable writers to meet with others online at a given time and to "talk" with each other with almost the same ease and rapidity as if they were speaking over the phone. If you have not participated in an IRC, you might imagine them as the Internet equivalent of a conference phone call.

Like newsgroups and email discussion groups, chat rooms and IRCs enable people who share an interest — or who just want to chat with others who happened to be logged on to their computers at that moment — to engage in real-time discussions. Often, those participating in these discussions choose to or are required to communicate under pseudonyms, or assumed nicknames. Some participants take advantage of the anonymity of the Internet to conceal or change such individual characteristics as age and gender. Many people find the opportunity to converse online with others who share their interests exciting; others find chat-room and IRC conversations repetitive, superficial, and even offensive — for those talking online will sometimes write things that they would never say in face-to-face conversations. Particularly when many people are participating in a single conversation, discussions or "chats" can be hard to follow. Only those with well-developed keyboarding skills can keep up with such conversations.

In case you haven't experienced chat-room conversation, here is a transcript of the first part of a conversation Matthew Johnston had with two friends. As is often the case in chat rooms, Matthew and his friends have chosen pseudonyms. Since all three are fans of Japanese anime — animated figures, like those of Pokemon characters — their names draw on that culture.

```
Tanakahibiki Chat 10pm

You have just entered room "tanakahibiki Chat60."
MIzumi2 has entered the room.
Karigari Marie has entered the room.
MIzumi2:          HiHi
tanakahibiki:     'ello!
Karigari Marie:     Meow! =^.^=
tanakahibiki:     <blink blink>
Karigari Marie:       hehe
tanakahibiki:     You're feeling cute today, ne?
Karigari Marie:       too much caffiene . . .
tanakahibiki:     Any particular (Emily) Reason (EK)?
tanakahibiki:     Mr. Subliminal strikes again . . . ^_^
Karigari Marie:     Emily? Dun know any Emily . . . EK on
   the other hand . . . ^^;;;
tanakahibiki:     I thought that was her first name. My bad.
Karigari Marie:       Elizabeth. ^_^
tanakahibiki:     D'oh. I basically had a one in three
   chance, and I knew it wasn't Erin.
tanakahibiki:     ^_^
Karigari Marie:       hehe
tanakahibiki:     Strikeout!
Karigari Marie:       You on the Braves?
tanakahibiki:     I hate the Braves . . .
Karigari Marie:       ^^;;
Karigari Marie:       Exactly.
Karigari Marie:       Doesn't everyone?
tanakahibiki:     Yep.
Karigari Marie:       I dub this channel, the Braves
   Haters . . .
tanakahibiki:     Aye!
Karigari Marie:       I was hoping the Mets would beat the
   Braves and go to the Series . . . Mets vs. Yankees . . .
   woulda sucked to be in NY . . . ^^;;
tanakahibiki:     It woulda started a war.
tanakahibiki:     But it could have been classic.
Karigari Marie:       yup
MIzumi2:          Back! Told you the Yanks won, Rich!
Karigari Marie:       oro?
MIzumi2:          Yankees.
```

```
MIzumi2:          4-0!
Karigari Marie:     I didn't say the Yankees lost . . .
    only that they were losing in the 6th inning . . .
MIzumi2:          Ah, ok.
Karigari Marie:     And that was game 3 . . .
tanakahibiki:     hehehe . . .
tanakahibiki:     My how time flies.
Karigari Marie:     and lonly a 4 run deficit . . .
Karigari Marie:     Clean your ears Alex . . .  ^^;;
MIzumi2:          Speaking of 3's . . .  ^_^
tanakahibiki:     oh?
MIzumi2:          I noticed that your typo hasn't returned,
    Matt. ^^
```

MUDS and MOOS are electronic spaces for real-time conversations — where participants can create text-based virtual environments. Some college teachers use MUDS (multiuser domains) to create virtual classrooms. Those logged into a MUD use commands to create or manipulate objects, enter or leave "rooms," comment on others' ideas, and so on. The first MUD was developed in 1979 to enable British students to play Dungeons & Dragons™ by computer.* MOOS (object-oriented MUDS) give participants the ability to create and manipulate their own virtual objects. There are hundreds of MUDS and MOOS in cyberspace. Some are designed entirely for play, as is the case with many fantasy and science-fiction MUDS. Others enable writers to engage in virtual scholarly conferences or similarly serious activities.

The World Wide Web

One of the most popular Internet applications is the World Wide Web, commonly known as the Web. Developed in the early 1990s at CERN, the European Particle Physics Laboratory in Geneva, the Web is based on hypertext, a system that links electronic texts. Unlike print texts, which are written to be read in a specific sequence, one page after another, hypertexts have links that allow readers to chart their own pathways through documents, clicking on "hotlinks" to jump from one document to another. Those constructing Web sites can use hypertext links to connect documents they have created with other documents on the Web. A student interested in politics, for instance, might provide a link to the site of the United States Congress, where readers can learn about current legislation.

Web pages include words — but they may also include such hypermedia as images, sound, and video. Imagine writing a paper on the role of music in

---

*Ellen Germain, "In the Jungle of MUD," *Time*, 13 September 1993, 61.

Shakespeare's dramas. On the World Wide Web you could include recordings of the music, pictures of the instruments, and photos from several productions showing the musicians on stage. Anyone who has access to the Internet and the technological know-how can create a site on the Web.

When viewers connect to a Web site, the first thing they usually see is a homepage that establishes the site's identity and incorporates highlighted words or images that link to other locations of information. (If, for any reason, viewers don't reach a Web site's homepage first, they nevertheless expect to be able to find it easily.) For an example of the type of information typically found on a homepage, see p. 199. If you were visiting this site, which is sponsored by Oregon State University, you might click on to "Colleges, Departments, and Programs" to learn about a possible major area of study, consult campus maps, or gather information about courses currently being offered.

Because the Web combines the powers of hypertext, hypermedia, and the Internet, it represents a powerful new way of organizing and conveying information — and a powerful new invitation to writers and readers. In the few years since its development, the Web has experienced phenomenal growth: One recent discussion of the World Wide Web claims, for instance, that "today, there are more Web pages than people on the planet. In less than a decade, the Web . . . [has become] the most powerful publishing technology ever, surpassing not only the number of words that are printed every day but even the volume of spoken words on telephone traffic."*

And yet as those who have spent a good deal of time surfing the Web point out, the quality of the communications available on the Web varies considerably. The Web has enabled thousands of people around the world to make their ideas available to others — with inevitably mixed results. Some people constructing Web pages work hard to present accurate, helpful information, to take full advantage of the Web's hypertext and hypermedia capabilities, and to attend to the needs and interests of possible users. Others indulge themselves in quirky, eccentric presentations. And still others fail to take full advantage of the capabilities of this medium. Just as writers can take more or less advantage of the potential of such conventional print forms as the essay, so too can those constructing Web sites take more or less advantage of this medium. Some Web sites take full advantage of the Web's ability to interconnect words, sounds, and images and offer valuable links to other sites, whereas others may use links as mere footnotes or glosses, doing little that couldn't be done on a printed page.

As even a brief discussion such as this one indicates, the brave new world of electronic technologies offers numerous opportunities for self-expression and communication with others. Just as the invention of the printing press helped to change the culture of fifteenth-century Europe — encouraging the development of new forms of writing, such as the novel — so too are elec-

---

*Lester Faigley and Jack Selzer, *Good Reasons* (Boston: Allyn and Bacon, 2000), 237.

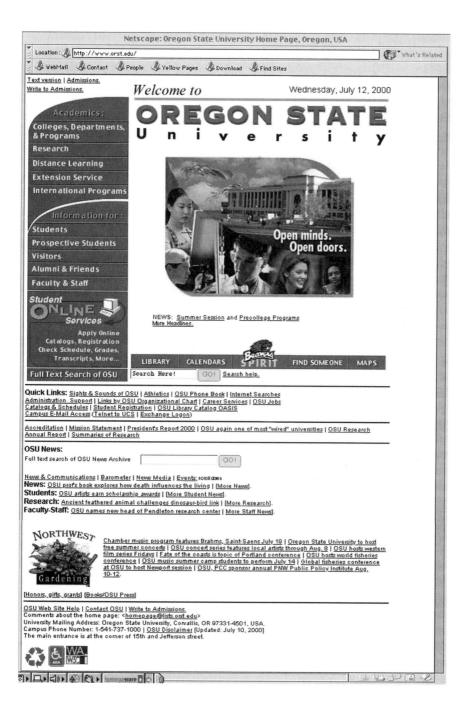

tronic technologies changing both our world and its possibilities for written communication.

■ ■ ■

FOR GROUP WORK

Meet with a group of students to discuss the advantages and disadvantages of online writing situations. Begin your discussion by having group members read their responses to the Exploration on p. 188. (If your group is typical, some members will have little or no experience in this regard, while others will have spent a good deal of time online.) Then respond to the following questions:

1. What personal, social, cultural, and economic factors have encouraged some of you to experiment with electronic technologies, while others have not?

2. To what extent do those who are online use these technologies to fulfill personal needs and interests? For academic assignments?

3. What advantages do these technologies offer? What disadvantages?

4. Looking beyond your own experiences, what larger ramifications do electronic technologies hold for our society? Consider, for instance, the unequal distribution of access to online resources. What other concerns do you all have about the ways that electronic technologies are influencing our society — and the world?

USING RHETORICAL SENSITIVITY IN ONLINE SITUATIONS

An example may help clarify how writers can use rhetorical sensitivity in online writing situations. A few years ago, WCENTER, an email discussion group for those who work at or are interested in writing centers, posted an interesting "thread" of related messages that demonstrates how such an analysis might proceed. The discussion addressed the question of why subscribers sometimes become irritated by "off-task" messages such as jokes and yet respond patiently when a new subscriber — generally a new writing center director — asks for the hundredth time how others keep writing-center records. Such a question might well prompt impatient or even angry responses, given the high volume of email messages that many subscribers to this list receive and the existence of a number of readily available print sources that address this and related questions. One subscriber, Carol Haviland, speculated that subscribers' differing responses had to do in part with the nature of WCENTER's email forum: "Email is virtually a different kind of text than either speech or book/journal print, but we tend to write it like the former and treat [or read] it like the latter."* Here is the response of another email discussion group subscriber, Sara Kimball:

```
I agree, it's a medium in between speech and writing, and
we sometimes write online like speech but react to it
like writing -- and this can cause problems. Take, for
example, the disputes we've occasionally had on this list
when some people get a little playful and others get
annoyed at "off-topic" threads. Quite a bit of f2f [face-
to-face] conversation is . . . [talk] that establishes or
maintains human relationships rather than conveying
information. . . . Think of how much workplace talk is . . .
chit-chat, joking, ritual greetings. For example, I'm
currently in the midst of serving a two-year sentence on
the English Department's Executive Committee. Most of our
meetings begin with a few minutes of joking around and
teasing each other. I've known playful speech to work
wonders in bringing together people who are otherwise at
odds with each other, at least to the point where we can
work together. Mostly we're not aware of . . . [this kind
of talk] until it's gone on for awhile, because it's
ephemeral. I think one of the reasons this list works so
well, normally, is that we do establish relationships
with each other and with the list. Jokes about Harleys or
crawfish and rounds of congratulations on births, promo-
tions, new jobs, etc. are some of the ties that bind.
*But* . . . . What might be play if it were speech becomes
work if it's writing, something that might get tiresome
to deal with if you're tired, distracted, or have a low
message quota.

BTW [by the way] Congratulations on the new babies!†
```

Sara Kimball's comment demonstrates that when faced with a question about online writing situations you can often draw on your general understanding of

---

*Haviland, Carol. <cph@wiley.csasb.edu> "Re: Repeating." 20 August 1996. <wcenter@ttacs.ttu.edu> (20 August 1996).
†Kimball, Sara. <skimball@uts.CC.utexas.edu> "Re: Repeating." 21 August 1996. <wcenter@ttacs. ttu.edu> (21 August 1996).

human communication. In this instance, Kimball draws on her own work experience. In some situations — appropriate moments at work, parties — we all enjoy such ephemeral language play as chitchat and joking. In other situations, such conversation not only violates decorum but may even intrude on or interrupt our work or personal time.

In the case of WCENTER, those who subscribe to this email discussion group do so to interact with and learn from others who share their professional commitment. They are willing to go the extra mile when new subscribers ask questions that have been addressed many times in the past because they are aware of the demanding nature of writing-center work. Even though they enjoy the email discussion group's collegiality — as demonstrated in Sara Kimball's congratulations to the new parents — some may become irritated when the tenth or twentieth motorcycle joke appears onscreen.

Because WCENTER is a relatively small email discussion group, and because many on the list know one another personally through professional meetings, subscribers avoid flames or angry withdrawals from the list. When one or more posts elicit irritated responses, subscribers usually take time to reflect on the incident so that future postings can remain cordial. Subscribers to larger, more diverse email discussion groups might accept a more rough-and-ready atmosphere, where those who violate conventions are speedily flamed.

Whether you are emailing your supervisor or friend, posting a message to an electronic forum, or constructing a Web site, you can employ your rhetorical sensitivity to make appropriate decisions about online writing tasks. The following guidelines present general considerations to keep in mind as you navigate the multiple pathways of cyberspace.

■ GUIDELINES FOR WRITING EMAIL

1. *Consider Your Online Rhetorical Situation.* Some online rhetorical situations are more consequential than others. If you are "playing around" in an unmoderated chat room, the most serious consequence you face if you make a false step is wasting your time or being flamed. But if you are emailing someone important to you or are participating in a newsgroup or email discussion group discussion, you have more at stake. The following questions can help you to assess what's at stake in a given online situation:

   ■ What is your purpose in wanting to send or post this message? Relatively trivial? Serious?

(continued)

(continued)

- If you are emailing one or more individuals, what is your relationship to this person or persons, and how might that influence the consequences of your message?

- If you are posting a message to an online forum, what are the nature and purpose of this forum? To what extent does the discussion typically focus on a single topic? How long are most messages? Does the discussion emphasize the sharing of information, freewheeling debate, personal expression, or some combination thereof?

- Who typically participates in this online forum? A diverse, continually shifting group of individuals? A focused group of continuing subscribers?

- Have you taken advantage of opportunities to learn more about this forum? You can learn a good deal simply by lurking or listening online to electronic conversations. Most newsgroups and email discussion groups provide a list of FAQs (frequently asked questions) for new subscribers. Be sure to study the responses to these questions, if available, and to save them for future reference.

2. *Recognize That Electronic Messages May Circulate in Unintended Ways — and Have Unanticipated Consequences.* Due to the ease, speed, and apparent transience of email, writers sometimes forget that email messages are public, not private, in nature. As mentioned earlier, email messages are often printed and saved. Businesses, nonprofit organizations, and government agencies sometimes monitor email, and email messages (which many systems automatically archive) have been used as evidence in legal proceedings. When composing an email message to a friend, family member, or coworker, it's easy to imagine that your communication is private. Before you hit the SEND key, however, imagine that your message will appear in your daily newspaper or be forwarded to the worst possible person. If you have any hesitation, rewrite.

Be aware that inattentiveness to the address of a forwarded communication has caused many an online writer considerable embarrassment. If a coworker forwards a message from your supervisor to you and you accidentally respond by the REPLY command, rather than initiating a new message using your friend's

(continued)

(continued)

email address, your message will go to your supervisor, not to your friend. A humorous or critical comment intended for your friend but received by your supervisor could have unintended — and quite negative — consequences.

You should also consider your own ethical responsibilities before forwarding a message to another. Did the writer intend this communication to be private? Might forwarding this message embarrass or cause problems for the writer? Even if the answer to these questions is no, you should check with the writer before forwarding a message you have received.

3. *Consider the Needs of Your Readers and the Constraints of Online Communication.* What difference does it make whether a person reads text onscreen or on a page? According to research on this subject, quite a lot. Recent studies have found that those reading text onscreen often find it difficult to keep a message's "big picture" clearly in mind. As a consequence, those composing email messages need to pay particular attention to such matters as the length and structure of their message, the placement of important points, and the use of headings. The following suggestions — all of which assume that you are composing an important posting and not just "playing around" on the Internet — address these constraints.

   ■ *Be as concise as possible.* The relatively small size of most computer screens makes it difficult for readers to comprehend lengthy messages. Whereas someone reading a book can easily glance back to earlier sections, online readers must scroll through previous text — a more difficult and even disorienting process. If possible, try to limit your messages to two to three screens of text. If your purpose does require considerable development of ideas, break your text into brief paragraphs, and double the space between paragraphs. The appropriate use of space can also aid comprehension. Rather than string together a long list of items within a paragraph, for instance, put items on separate lines, using the * symbol or dashes (—) at the beginning of each item to create a bulleted list.

   ■ *Provide cues for your readers.* If you are emailing someone that you do not know personally, begin your message with a brief introduction and statement of purpose. A simple "Dear Dr.

(continued)

(continued)

Smith, I am a student in your history of Western civilization lecture class, and I would like to ask you about next week's assignment" should suffice. If you are posting to an online forum, a similar contextualizing introduction will encourage readers to take you seriously.

If you find it necessary to post a lengthy message, be sure to use headings and numbered items to help your readers keep track of your ideas. If you desire a response to your message, you may find it helpful to place your most important point or request at the end of your message.

Pay attention, as well, to the relationship of the subject line of your message and its text. Many writers simply reuse subject lines as they appear in the reply when a new heading might better reflect the purpose and content of their message. Subscribers to email discussion groups sometimes become irritated when a message under a thread's subject line has nothing to do with the thread. It takes just a moment to tab through your options to the subject line and revise it to fit your purpose; doing so tells readers that you care enough about your message — and about their response to it — to do so.

- *Use shortened spellings, abbreviations, email jargon, and emoticons only in informal messages to individuals you know well or for electronic forums that regularly employ these devices.* It's fine for Matthew Johnston to use email jargon when writing to his mother. Many subscribers to electronic forums also employ these devices: By "listening in" to the conversation a while before posting a message, you can learn what's appropriate. But rhetorical common sense should tell you that in some situations, such as an important work-related message, you would do well to use more formal language and style.

- *Use conventional capitalization and punctuation.* Don't make your readers go to extra trouble just to decipher your message. Sometimes online writers compose and send their messages so hurriedly that they type all words entirely lower case or entirely upper case. Some writers even omit all but the most essential punctuation marks. Given the challenges that onscreen reading already poses, time-saving practices such as these place extra burdens on readers, who may press their DELETE key rather

(continued)

(continued)

than struggle to decipher your text. You should be aware, as well, that some online readers experience the use of all uppercase letters as SHOUTING.

- *When appropriate, include parts of the message to which you are responding.* Many email users have had the disconcerting experience of logging on to their computer after a weekend or a brief vacation and discovering a message such as this: "Great idea! Let's meet next Friday to discuss it." If they're lucky, their email program will enable them to retrieve previously sent messages, so they'll be able to discover just which "great idea" their correspondent is referring to. But how much easier it would have been if the person composing the message had included the relevant section from the previous message.

Most email programs have an option that allows you to include the message to which you are responding in your response. Particularly when the message to which you are responding is lengthy, or when you suspect the person to whom you are sending it may not open his or her email immediately, it can be both a courtesy and an aid to communication to include relevant portions of the original message. Doing so can help ensure that you get a speedy and positive response. When you are responding to lengthy messages, be sure to include only those parts of the message that pertain to your response. Here, for instance, is an email that Matthew Johnston sent me in response to an emailed query.

```
On Thu, 23 Dec 1999 Lede@orst.edu wrote:

>Hi Matt,
>If you don't mind, I'd like to ask you about the
>fanfiction on your Web site. How did you get
>interested in Japanese anime? And when you write
>fanfiction, are you basically extending an
>already developed plot and characters, or are
>you starting from scratch?

I learned about anime through a friend who was in
an anime club in Portland. Through him, I saw a
number of titles in Japanese, and that got my
```

(continued)

(continued)

```
interests going. College age students are more
likely than not to have at least a cursory knowl-
edge of anime (through Pokemon), though those of
us who use computers are more likely to know
more. All the labbies in the computer lab here at
the U of O know a little. Also, interest in anime
seems to be gender marked. Something like 80% of
anime fans (don't quote me on that) are male.
```

By including the section of my email to which he was responding, Matthew helped ensure that I would have the fullest — and quickest — understanding of the context for his response.

- *Recognize that what you see onscreen as you type may not be what readers will receive.* Your word-processing program undoubtedly has a number of features, such as "block" or "indent," that enable you to take helpful shortcuts when composing at the computer. Some email programs have similar features. It's tempting to use these features because they can save time; unfortunately, only those readers who use the same email software that you do will receive the message as sent. Others may receive a confusing, weirdly indented mess. Since most people on email post messages to a variety of individuals and electronic forums, the best practice is to avoid using special formatting. That way you can ensure that all your readers will receive your text as written.

- *Avoid elaborate sigs.* Many email programs enable users to develop a sig, or signature file, that automatically appears at the bottom of every email message. In some cases it's possible to develop quite elaborate sigs — including ones with visuals, mottos, or other individually devised features. But should you do so? Many users of email say no and suggest that sigs be kept to a maximum of five lines. Because of the limitations of reading onscreen text, an overly elaborate sig can actually detract from your message.

4. *Avoid "Flaming" — and Know How to Respond If You Are Flamed.* Email communications sometimes generate strong emotions, possibly because relationship cues (such as tone of voice) that might moderate hostility or suspicion are absent. In situations such as

(continued)

(continued)

these, the ease and speed of responding to email can be a liability, rather than an asset, for an irate message composed in haste may be one you come to regret. If you get a message that angers you, count to ten, and ask yourself how many ways you might have misunderstood this message — or the person writing the message might have misunderstood you. Give yourself the time and distance needed to reflect on your situation and to ensure that you've read the message carefully.

Be aware, too, that writers can unintentionally post messages that elicit flames. It can be particularly difficult to convey irony or wit online. Writers who post a message that they intend to be humorous or ironic are sometimes surprised to discover that readers interpret their post quite differently — and respond with a flame, rather than with appreciation. If you are flamed, resist the urge to counterattack. Depending on the nature of the flame, you might respond with a simple explanation or with silence.

The preceding guidelines should help you participate effectively in a variety of email writing situations. It is important to acknowledge, however, that the textual conventions governing email, newsgroups, and email discussion groups are still in flux and that many acceptable variations exist. The preceding guidelines offer a practical, conservative approach. After all, if you are at a social event and a person you don't know well makes a comment that may — or may not — be meant as a joke, you probably take the cautious step of waiting a moment to gather further information before responding. If you are in an unfamiliar online writing situation, similar caution may be justified. It takes only a minute to consider your audience or to tame an ironically barbed sentence; doing so may encourage a reader who might otherwise ignore — or flame — you to respond helpfully instead.

Look at the two email messages on p. 209. The first follows the guidelines suggested above. Thanks to the use of spacing and lists, the email is clearly organized and visually pleasing. And the writer cues his reader by including a relevant passage from the message that prompted his email. The second message is much more cluttered and difficult to read. The elaborate "sig" is distracting, while the eccentric spelling, punctuation, and formatting suggest little regard for the reader. Which message would you prefer to receive?

```
Date:     Wed 8 June 92 10:45 MST
From:     Bill Diaz <wt_diaz@hs.idacrk.idaho.edu>
To:       Jim Allen <jtallen@jrhs.lkside.wash.edu>
CC:       Susan Allen <sallen@hs.idacrk.idaho.edu>
Subject: Prospecting in Ponderosa Canyon? You Bet!

Jim,

I'm *delighted* to hear you're visiting this summer! You wrote:

> When I'm there, do you think that geology teacher Bill Diaz
> could take me prospecting again in the mountains?

You bet, I'd be glad to have you come along! I've planned a trip
from July 24-27, if that fits with your plans. Here's a few things
to get ahold of before you visit:

            a geological hammer, and plastic sunglasses
            a good field guide for rocks and minerals
            a *light* sleeping bag (remember how HOT you were in
               that down bag last summer? :-)
            a sturdy pair of hiking boots

If you need advice, feel free to contact me! Take care,

Bill
```

```
Date:     Wed 8 June 92 10:45 MST
From:     wt_diaz@hs.idacrk.idaho.edu
To:       jallen@jrhs.lkside.wash.edu
i'm delEted to hear that you're visiting us in idaho creek again
this
i'd be happy to have you come prosepcting. i've already planned
a m july 24-27. here's some things you should probely bring
along:
^Z logical hammer, a g   od field guide f   rocks and minerals, a
light sleep if  king boots, and      sunglasses with plastic
boots would be     Free to MAil ba    ser-id. Here's my sig!/-
 ^   ^          /  \    /\      /\ \  |  / / 'tis a gift to be sim
     ^ _       /----\  /  \    /  \ \ | / / 'tis a gift to be free
   / \     /      \/----\  /----\ \ / / +-------------------
   /   \  /"home is \    \ /     \ ° / |__   o   |         |
  /     \/ where the \    \      \ / / | \ |    |         |
 /         \heart is" \            |_/ _|_   _|_     _|_
tel: (208) 999-1234 (home) 999-4321 (woodshed) 999-3456 (car fax)
user-ids: wt_diaz@hs.idacrk.idaho.eud (INTERNET) wt_diaz@idacrkh
```

---

*These examples appear in Jonathan Kochmer's *Internet Passport: NorthWestNet's Guide to Our World Online* (Bellevue, Wash.: NorthWestNet and Northwest Academic Computing Consortium, 1993), 48–49.

CONSTRUCTING PAGES ON THE WORLD WIDE WEB

Though more people currently browse the Web than compose Web pages of their own, that situation is rapidly changing. With the development of browsers such as Internet Explorer and Netscape Communicator, interest in the Web has spread far beyond the scientific community for which it was first developed. You may only surf the Web now — but next year or next month you might wish or be asked to build a Web site.

In publishing your own pages on the World Wide Web, as with other forms of communication, you will do well to consider your rhetorical situation. Why do you wish to create a site on the Web? Is it an educational site, one designed to inform your audience about a particular topic? A personal site meant to reflect your interests and experiences? A professional or institutional site? Whom do you wish to visit your site? People seeking specific information about a topic or casual browsers? What kind of experience do you want your readers or "visitors" to have?

■ ■ ■

FOR EXPLORATION

Earlier in this chapter you saw the homepage for Oregon State University (p. 199). On p. 211 is the homepage for Matthew Johnston's Web site. Matthew uses his Web site to "publish" his Japanese anime fanfiction. When I asked Matthew about the name of his site, he replied that "the name is a reference to the Boku No Marie anime, which my first fanfic was based on. The characters in Boku No Marie sometimes gather at the Café Pierrot. Pierrot is also the name of the animation studio, Studio Pierrot, which did the bulk of the animation for the show."

Compare the two homepages. What differences do you observe in format and content? Spend five minutes writing about these differences. Now spend another five minutes writing about possible reasons for these differences. In doing so, consider such rhetorical issues as the purpose and audience for the two Web sites.

Writers constructing Web sites also need to consider the current constraints of Web technologies. At the present time, for instance, pages with many images can take a long time to download. Additionally, some browsers may not be able to access pages that include such graphic options as tables, frames, and image maps. How can you present innovative and interesting pages and also accommodate readers using a variety of browsers? How can you achieve the best balance between visual interest and textual information? All of these questions are *rhetorical* questions, for they require you to consider your own purpose in constructing a Web site, the audience for this site, and the most appropriate

Netscape: The Cafe Pierrot -- Fanfiction of Matthew Johnston

Location: http://www.cafe-pierrot.net/   What's Related

WebMail   Contact   People   Yellow Pages   Download   Find Sites

Welcome to
The Cafe Pierrot
Quality Anime
Fanfiction

WELCOME TO THE

Cafe Pierrot

QUALITY ANIME FANFICTION

Please choose one of the following:

What do you do when your mind rebels against itself? What does a young girl from Hiroshi's past have to do with Marie's new-found malfunction? Can Hiroshi finally confess to his crush and the model for his creation, the ever-beautiful tennis starlet Mari? And why does Tanaka order a White Russian?! Find all this out and more in "Boku No Marie: Music-Box Angel."

There's simply nothing worse for a writer than writer's block. And Kenji Terada will do *anything* to get rid of it. But when his teacher offered him a technique, he forgot to tell Kenji just what the side-effects would be, especially when his muse wakes up next to him! For an original series in the spirit of "Oh My Goddess!" and "Video Girl Ai," try "It's A Rainy Day, Sunshine Girl."

Coming Soon! Satoru knew he would miss Kaori when she left for school in America. What he didn't expect was the phone call that came months early: Kaori was back, but things had changed, and they may *never* return to normal... "Okaeri, Kaori-chan!" is an original drama with an anime twist.

The quality of a waking dream permeates the anime "Serial Experiments Lain", something slightly unsettled. Thus affected, and armed with a couple synthesizers, I recorded a 32-minute musical experiment: "Bootlegged Self-Image," taking dialogue samples from Lain, as well as key phrases transposed to musical notation, to create what may be the first album of anime fan-music available in America, or perhaps the world!

A number of small code errors have been fixed.

Last Updated on July 4, 2000
Next Scheduled Update: July 24, 2000

E-mail me at: caravan@cafe-pierrot.net

3 1 9 1

People have stopped for coffee since February 16, 2000.
(counter courtesy of WebCounter.)

Open the web page editor

means (which in this case goes beyond words to include images, sounds, and video) of communicating with your intended audience.

It is beyond the scope of this chapter to provide detailed instructions for Web publishing — and even if it weren't, developments in scripting languages and Web browsers would quickly render such suggestions obsolete. Here are some general considerations to keep in mind when constructing a Web site.

■ GUIDELINES FOR CONSTRUCTING A WEB SITE

1. *Just as Writers Develop Plans for Essays and Architects Draw Up Blueprints for Homes, so Too Should You Establish a Plan for Your Web Site.* In planning your Web site, remember that readers access your site as a series of pages. How you organize these pages — the ways you relate them to each other both conceptually and through hyperlinks — can make your site an inviting, interesting, educational experience for readers, or a confusing, irritating one. The most effective Web sites have an easily grasped organization that readers can move through easily. They also use a combination of links and menu bars to facilitate navigation within the site.

2. *As in Any Other Effort to Communicate with Readers, Consider Your Audience.* When considering the audience for a Web site, online writers face a rhetorical challenge — for in many cases their audience is both known and unknown. A collaborative team developing a site for a university theater program, for instance, would do well to keep its specific audience in mind. Reflecting on this audience will enable team members to make important decisions about the purpose, design, and structure of their Web pages:

   What should the University Theater Web site do? Hmmm . . . let's see. The immediate audiences will be students, faculty, alums, and people in our college's community. They'll want to know about this year's productions, current students and faculty, and ticket availability, box office times, and seating. There should be a link to the academic theater programs, and probably to other theater programs in the region. It would be nice to include some history of the program and a page of photos from past productions. How about some music from last summer's Gilbert and Sullivan operetta? And there should be a couple of email links to faculty and students — and a suggestion box as well.

   Based on their own experiences on the Web, these team members would recognize that many unanticipated readers might be inter-

(continued)

(continued)

ested in accessing the site. Even if the theater program chose not to publicize its Web address, search engines such as Infoseek or AltaVista might bring readers to the site. Accordingly, the team will attempt to construct a Web site that helps diverse readers with a variety of interests navigate its pages with ease.

If you are constructing a personal page, one designed primarily to present yourself to others, you may or may not have a specific audience of readers in mind. If you have a passionate interest in several specific subjects (rock climbing? environmental politics? something else?) you would certainly want to highlight these interests by including links to other sites so that others can easily access more information on them. If you simply want to construct a Web site that expresses your individuality, a multidimensional presentation of yourself is likely to attract the broadest range of readers.

3. *As with Other Internet Applications, Consider the Needs of Your Readers by Working within the Constraints of Current Web Technologies.* In the years since the World Wide Web's inception, technologies have developed rapidly. Several years ago, those wishing to publish Web pages needed to learn HTML (hypertext markup language); now several commercial products make it possible to construct Web pages without knowing a lot about HTML. Because the Web has drawn such interest from the public and from commercial software developers, the conventions of Web publishing are very much in flux.

As you plan your Web site, remember that the presence of such features as sophisticated graphics will make a difference in the length of time it takes for pages to load on readers' screens. So you'll want to balance your desire for a sophisticated, image-enhanced Web site with readers' varying hardware and software capabilities. After all, you don't want people to decide that loading your site takes so much time that they'll just keep surfing.

4. *Recognize the Importance of an Inviting, Well-Organized Homepage.* In a recent issue of *The New Yorker,* writer John Seabrook posed the question "What exactly is a homepage?" Here is his response:

In the simplest terms, it is like an E-mail address, a place on the Net where people can find you; but whereas an E-mail address is just a mailbox, a home page is a reception area. . . . a way to meet people. You want

(continued)

(continued)

guests to have a good time when they visit your home page, and you hope they will take away a favorable impression of you. You can link your home page to the home pages of friends or family, or to your employer's Web site, or to any other site you like, creating a kind of neighborhood for yourself. And you can design your page in any way you wish, and furnish it with anything that can be digitized — your ideas, your voice, your causes, pictures of your scars or your pets or your ancestors.*

As Seabrook emphasizes, your homepage serves an important rhetorical purpose, for it determines whether readers will "take away a favorable impression of you." Depending on your purpose, your homepage may be relatively serious or humorous, complex or simple. But it should be suited to your intended audience.

5. *Remember That Basic Design Principles Apply to the Web as Well as to Print Materials.* In *The Non-Designer's Web Book,* Robin Williams and John Tollett remind readers that certain fundamental design principles are essential — whether you're writing a newsletter for a civic group or a Web page for that same organization. They define these principles as alignment, proximity, repetition, and contrast.

A Web page is *aligned* if the items on the page are lined up either flush left, flush right, or centered. Williams and Tollett argue that "lack of alignment is the single most prevalent problem on web pages." Their advice to those constructing Web pages: "Don't mix alignments" (106).

A Web page makes effective use of the design principle of *proximity* when the relationships between headings and subheadings, and between items in a list and other textual elements, are clear. An easy way to evaluate your Web page's use of proximity is to squint your eyes and see how your Web page looks. Does your eye move logically from one part of the page to another? If not, you will want to work on the internal relationships of items in your Web page.

Repetition in Web design can involve elements that are visual, verbal, or both. Repetition is an important factor in tying your site together.

---

*John Seabrook, "Home on the Net." *The New Yorker,* 16 October 1995, 66–76. (You may have noticed that while this chapter had used the spelling "email" and "homepage," Seabrook prefers "E-mail" and "home page." Here, as in other instances, conventions for online writing are still evolving.)

(continued)

(continued)

A Web page effectively employs *contrast* when the design attracts your eye to the page and draws you in: "Contrasting elements guide your eyes around the page, create a hierarchy of information, and enable you to skim through the vast array of information . . . [to] pick out the information you need" (118). Focal points play an important role in establishing contrast. A focal point — a point that the eye travels to first — may be an image or a logo. But it helps organize and orient readers' interactions with your Web site.

6. *Establish a Meaningful Visual Identity for Your Site.* Those surfing the Web have a particularly strong need to know where they are, where they came from, and where they are going. Establishing a clear and consistent visual theme for your site can help readers keep themselves on track as they navigate your site. There are other reasons for establishing a visual theme. Whether you are constructing a personal or institutional site, a visual theme — achieved through the use of photographs, images, and other aspects of design — creates an overall impression that will persuade readers that your site is (or isn't) worth visiting. It can also increase the rhetorical persuasiveness of your site.

7. *Keep the Demands of Online Reading in Mind as You Organize the Text on Your Site.* Most online readers find long stretches of unbroken text difficult to read at best. Often, those surfing the Web will simply move to another site rather than go to the trouble of reading large blocks of text. After all, most are reading on relatively small monitors. Furthermore, as the Web has developed, it has strongly emphasized visual as well as verbal content. Sophisticated readers of the Web expect sites to be constructed with online readers in mind. For these reasons, you will want to attend as closely to how you present the text you write as to the text itself. Chunking texts into small groupings, using bulleted lists, leaving plenty of white space, coordinating texts with relevant images: Through these and other means you can create a site that will make the process of reading online easy and enjoyable.

8. *Use Color to Increase Your Site's Visual Impact, but Be Sure to Keep Online Readers' Needs in Mind as You Do So.* Writers and designers have always understood that the effective use of color can significantly enhance a text's appeal. But the use of color in traditional

(continued)

(continued)

print publications can be expensive; moreover, the range of colors that can be achieved in print is limited. Those constructing Web sites have many more colors available to them. Surf the Web, and you'll discover that color is an important element of most Web sites. This does not mean, however, that just any use of color on the Web will enliven your site. Use too dark a background, for instance, and viewers will have difficulty reading your text. (This will be especially true if you use all caps or italics for your text.) Including too many colors can result in a page that feels "busy" and disorganized. Remember the basic principle of *contrast*: Readers looking at a Web page need a strong overall impression and pattern of movement to guide their eyes and help them understand how best to navigate your site. Too much color — used too many different ways — can make navigation difficult.

9. *Remember That Web Sites Are Always Works in Progress.* Those navigating the Web are almost by definition looking for timely information about a subject of interest to them. Whether they are interested in learning more about the situation in South Africa or the best places to mountain bike in Moab, Utah, those surfing the Web expect the information they locate to be timely and accurate. So those publishing Web pages should feel a particular obligation to keep their pages up-to-date. And because the Web itself is in continual flux — because Web sites constantly appear and disappear — conscientious Web publishers regularly update their pages and list the date on which they've most recently done so.

FOR EXPLORATION

Here are two Web sites. The first is for The American Society for the Prevention of Cruelty to Animals (ASPCA); the second, for the National Aeronautics and Space Agency (NASA). Study these Web sites carefully, and then analyze them according to the guidelines for Web sites presented earlier in this chapter. (To see the use of color on these sites or to navigate them yourself, you may want to visit them online. The URL for the ASPCA is <http://www.aspca.org>; the URL for the NASA site is <http://www.nasa.gov>.) To what extent do these sites model good Web design? Are

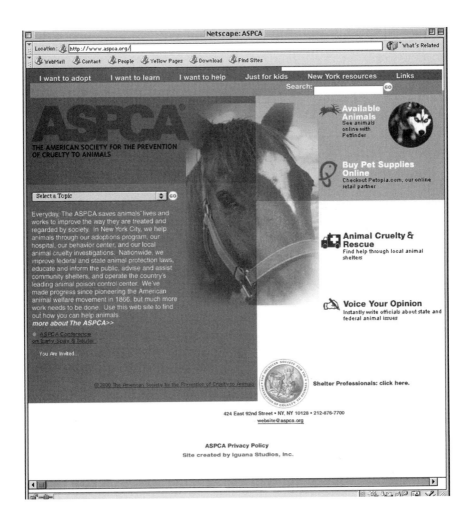

there ways in which they might be improved? Write at least two paragraphs of analysis for each Web site.

FOR GROUP WORK

Meet with a group of peers to discuss your responses to the previous Exploration. Appoint a recorder to take notes about your discussion and to share the results of your analysis with the class. Be sure to consider the following questions. To what extent did group members agree in your analysis of each Web site? If there was disagreement, what points were

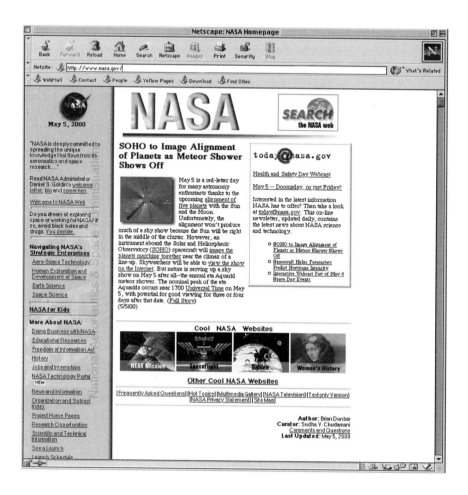

most often sources of controversy? Did group members raise questions about these Web sites that were not covered in the preceding guidelines? What did your group learn about writing for the Web as a result of this analysis?

As with the guidelines presented earlier in this chapter for sending email to individuals, email discussion groups, or newsgroups, these guidelines represent a conservative approach to the Web. Depending on your own purpose and intended audience, you might reasonably choose to disregard one or more of these suggestions. Just as those writing essays can make appropriate decisions by considering such rhetorical considerations as their purpose, audience, and situation, so too should those writing for an online audience ask similar questions that will guide their writing.

■ ■ ■

FOR THOUGHT, DISCUSSION, AND WRITING

1. If you have access to the Internet, subscribe for at least a week to an email discussion group of interest to you. (Web sites such as <http://www.liszt.com> provide information about a number of email discussion groups; your teacher or a college librarian may also have information about these forums.) After "listening in" on this electronic conversation — and perhaps participating as well — write an analysis of this email discussion group. Be sure to consider the questions in Guideline 1 on pp. 202–3.

2. While listening in on an email discussion group's electronic conversation, identify at least five posts that you find particularly effective and five that seem ineffective. Save and print these posts, and write a brief explanation of why they are effective or ineffective, referring to the guidelines presented on pp. 202–8. Be prepared to discuss your conclusions with your classmates.

3. You have already seen several examples of Web pages. If you have access to the Web, spend at least an hour exploring as many sites (institutional, commercial, personal) as possible. Download several examples of sites you find particularly successful or unsuccessful. Drawing on this chapter's discussion of the Web and on your own experience, identify three or four characteristics that successful sites share.

4. Chapter 5 includes three advertisements for the American Civil Liberties Union (ACLU) for analysis (p. 166). On p. 220 is the downloaded Web page for this same organization. After reviewing the print ads presented earlier, compare them with the downloaded Web page. In what ways are the ads and Web page similar? Dissimilar? What factors account for the similarities and differences? Spend five to ten minutes writing in response to these questions.

5. Write an essay considering one or more of the possible implications of the rapidly developing electronic technologies. As part of your research for this topic, you may wish to read the selections on this subject at the end of Chapter 3. You may also wish to consult a number of relevant online and library resources.

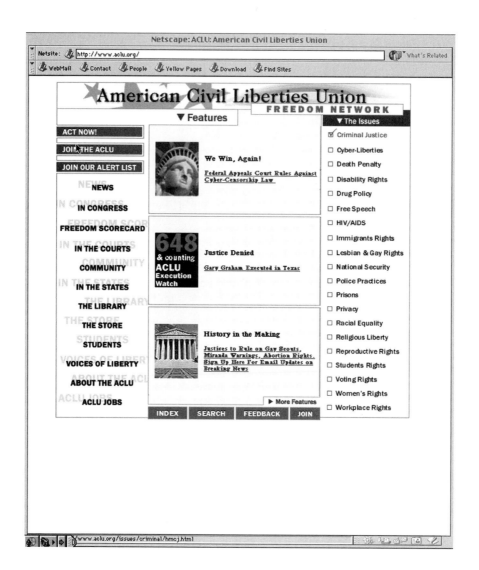

PART THREE

PRACTICAL STRATEGIES
FOR WRITING

Strategies for Invention

Writing is a complex, dynamic process, one that challenges you to draw on all your resources as you compose. As a writer, you don't need to wait in frustration at your desk or computer for inspiration to strike. By analyzing your rhetorical situation and by reflecting on your previous writing experiences, you can respond effectively and efficiently to the demands of writing.

Experienced writers are pragmatists. Understanding that different writing tasks call for different approaches, they develop a repertoire of strategies they can employ depending on the situation. They also tend to be flexible, recognizing that their writing may take unpredictable twists and turns. They know they may have to work their way through moments of frustration or difficulty to achieve the insights that make writing worthwhile. And they know, too, that they needn't work alone. Both informally and formally — from conversations with friends to collaboration with classmates, writing assistants, and teachers — successful writers benefit from the support and insights of others.

Like thinking, writing is too complex and situated a process to be reduced to rules or formulas. But even if writing can't be reduced to a set of directions, it does involve activities that you can understand, practice, and improve. In general, the writing process involves planning, drafting, and revising. Successful writers follow a variety of strategies as they work on these activities. Part Three presents a number of these strategies.

Read the chapters in Part Three with a writer's eye. Which of these strategies do you already use? Which ones could you use more effectively? What other strategies might extend your range or strengthen your writing abilities? As you read about and experiment with these strategies, remember to assess their usefulness based on your needs and preferences as a writer and your particular writing situation.

UNDERSTANDING HOW INVENTION WORKS

Like many writers, you may feel that discovering ideas to write about is the most mysterious part of the writing process. Where do ideas come from? How can you draw a blank one minute and suddenly know just the right way to support your argument or describe your experience the next? Is it possible to increase your ability to think and write creatively?

Writers and speakers have been concerned with questions such as these for centuries. The classical rhetoricians, in fact, were among the first to investigate this process of discovering and exploring ideas. The Roman rhetoricians called it *inventio,* for "invention" or "discovery." Contemporary writers, drawing on this Latin term, often refer to this process as *invention.* This chapter focuses on discovering and exploring ideas as part of the writing process.

In practice, invention usually involves both individual inquiry and dialogue with others. In writing this textbook, for instance, I spent a great deal of time thinking and working alone. I even experienced a few moments of what might be described as inspiration. As the acknowledgments in the note to instructors at the start of this book indicates, however, I could not have written *Work in Progress* without the help of many other people. In the earliest stages of this project I spoke with textbook editors and with other textbook authors. They helped me understand the intricacies of writing a textbook and the rhetorical situation to which a textbook generally responds. Once the project was under way, I spent many hours talking with both students and fellow composition instructors. By reading articles and books on the teaching of writing, I expanded these conversations. My silent dialogues with these writers were just as important as face-to-face conversations in helping me develop my ideas.

Most people don't write textbooks. But most writers generate and explore ideas by sitting quietly and thinking, brainstorming at the computer, reading, conducting research, and exchanging ideas with friends and colleagues. The following strategies aim to help you to invent successfully, whether you're working alone or with classmates or friends.

USING INFORMAL METHODS OF DISCOVERING AND EXPLORING IDEAS

You probably already use several informal methods of discovering and exploring ideas. You don't need extensive training to learn to brainstorm or cluster, for instance. Yet these methods can help you discover what you know — and don't know — about a subject. They can also enable you to explore your own ideas and to formulate productive questions that can guide you as you plan, draft, and revise your writing.

Most writers find that some of the following methods work better for them than others. That's fine, but be sure you give each method a fair chance. You may surprise yourself, as did Joanne Novak, a composition student in Professor Robert Inkster's composition class at St. Cloud State University. The following entry from her journal describes how her experience with informal invention methods taught her something new about writing.

> I began the process of using the informal methods thinking it was a waste of time because I just simply was not in the mood to write. I intended to try each of the informal methods to prove that they didn't work for me. I chose a topic I'd been thinking of writing about and tried freewriting. It was a jumbled mess. At that point I had trouble looping because I was embarrassed by the unorganized words that appeared on the paper, but I finally did come up with a shallow summarizing sentence. It sounded good, but it wasn't from the heart. It was something I knew I *should* feel. From the summarizing sentence I used the brainstorming method and came up blank.
>
> Feeling confident that my theory was correct and the text was wrong, I decided to prove it by clustering. As suggested, I put my topic in the center of the page and just drew in whatever came to mind around the outside. I saw some organization to this method. That started ideas coming faster than I could write. I jotted down a few words so I could remember the main idea, and before I knew it I was writing so small I could hardly form the letters as I was running out of space.
>
> I returned to brainstorming, which worked this time, and I ended up with a long list of things to write about. It was amazing. I reread my freewriting and found a few more ideas. I was shocked. I've always believed that I had to be in the mood to write or I couldn't come up with ideas. Now I see that that belief has in fact inhibited my writing.
>
> — JOANNE NOVAK

Like Joanne Novak, you too may find informal methods of invention to be a productive means of discovering and exploring ideas.

Freewriting

Freewriting is the practice of writing as freely as possible without stopping. It is a simple but powerful strategy for exploring important issues and problems. Freewriting may at first seem *too* simple to achieve very powerful results — the only requirement is that you write continuously without stopping — but in fact it can help you discover ideas that you couldn't reach through more conscious and logical means. Because you generate a great deal of material when you freewrite, freewriting is also an excellent antidote for the nervousness many writers feel at the start of a project. (Freewriting can, by the way, be done quite effectively on the computer.) Finally, freewriting also encourages you to improve your fluency; this is especially beneficial if your first language is not English.

Freewriting is potentially powerful in a variety of writing situations. See how one student used freewriting as a means of exploring and focusing her ideas for a political science paper on low voter turnout.

> I just don't get it. As soon as I could register I did — it felt like a really important day. I'd watched my mother vote and my sisters vote and now it was my turn. But why do I vote; guess I should ask myself that question — and why don't other people? Do I feel that my vote makes a difference? There have been some close elections but not all that many, so my vote doesn't literally count, doesn't decide if we pay a new tax or elect a new senator. Part of it's the feeling I get. When I go to vote I know the people at the polling booth; they're my neighbors. I know the people who are running for office in local elections, and for state and national elections — well, I just feel that I should. But the statistics on voter turnout tell me I'm unusual. In this paper I want to go beyond statistics. I want to understand *why* people don't vote. Seems like I need to look not only at research in political science, but also maybe in sociology. (Check journals in economics too?) I wonder if it'd be okay for me to interview some students, maybe some staff and faculty, about voting — better check. But wait a minute; this is a small college in a small town, like the town I'm from. I wonder if people in cities would feel differently — they might. Maybe what I need to look at in my paper is rural/small town versus urban voting patterns.

This student's freewriting not only helped her explore her ideas but also identified a possible question to answer in her paper and sources she could draw on as she worked on her project.

Freewriting can also help you explore your personal experience, enabling you to gain access to images, events, and emotions that you have forgotten or suppressed. If you were writing an essay about your sense of family — how you developed this sense, what it is, and what it means to you now — freewriting could help you recall details and images that would lend a rich specificity to your essay. Here, for example, is my own freewriting about my sense of family. (You may understand this freewriting more easily if you know that I grew up in a family of twelve children, two of whom died in infancy.)

> Family. Family. So strong. So many children. Ten. But really twelve. Brian and Anthony dead, both babies. The youngest kids don't even remember — they know but don't remember. Odd. Our own family so enormous, but so little extended family. Mom's parents dead — I do remember Nana, though — one sister. Dad's parents dead too, one sister. Some of my brothers and sisters don't remember any grandparents. Older kids spread out. Leni and Robin in Florida. Sara in Virginia. Andy in Mass. Younger kids closer: Laurie, Shelley, Jeff, Robbie, Julie — all in

Ohio, close to Mom and Dad. Me in Oregon, the farthest. Have I forgotten anyone? The list, run down the list. (Memory: amazing friends with how quickly I could say the names, but only in order.) Leni, Lisa, Andy, Sara, Jeff, Robin, Michelle, Laurie, Julie, Robbie. The photo from last summer's reunion: thirty people, Mom and Dad, brothers, sisters, spouses, children. Could be a photo of a company's annual picnic — but it isn't. Families like this just don't exist anymore. When did it change? People used to smile at us when we all went out and ask how many. Now a friend with four children tells me people are shocked at the size of her family. I have no children, but I have family. Family — an invisible web that connects.

My brief freewrite did more than generate concrete images and details; it gave me a new insight into my own sense of family. Rereading my freewriting, I am surprised at the strong sense of loss that appears as I comment on my infant brothers' deaths and those of my grandparents. I also notice a potential contradiction between my strong sense of family and my recent experience of living a great distance from my family.

Looping

Looping, an extended or directed form of freewriting, alternates freewriting with analysis and reflection. Begin looping by first establishing a theme or topic for your freewriting; then freewrite for five or ten minutes. This is your first loop. After you have done so, reread what you have written. In rereading your freewriting, look for the center of gravity or "heart" of your ideas — the image, detail, issue, or problem that seems richest or most intriguing, compelling, or productive. Write a sentence that summarizes this understanding; this sentence will become the starting point of your second loop. In looking back at my previous freewriting, I can locate several potential starting points for an additional loop. I might, for instance, use the following question to begin another freewriting session:

What does it mean that my family includes a number of people — my brothers and grandparents — that my younger brothers and sisters never knew, can't remember?

When you loop, you don't know where your freewriting and reflection will take you; you don't worry about the final product. My final essay on my sense of family might not even discuss the question generated by my freewriting. That's fine; the goal in freewriting and looping is not to produce a draft of an essay but to explore your own ideas and to discover ideas, images, and sometimes even words, phrases, and sentences that you can use in your writing.

■ ■ ■

FOR EXPLORATION

Freewrite for five minutes, beginning with the word *family*. (If you would prefer to write about another subject, simply choose a single word to begin your freewrite — sports, music, college, whatever — and continue this activity.) Then stop and reread your freewriting. What comments most interest or surprise you? Now write a statement that best expresses your freewriting's center of gravity or "heart." Use this comment to begin a second loop by freewriting for five minutes more.

After completing this second freewriting, stop and reread both passages. What did you learn from your freewriting? Does your freewriting suggest possible ideas for an essay? Finally, reflect on the process itself. Did you find the experience of looping helpful? Would you use freewriting and looping in the future as a means of generating and exploring your experiences and ideas?

Brainstorming

Like freewriting and looping, brainstorming is a simple but productive invention strategy. When you brainstorm, you list as quickly as possible all the thoughts about a subject that occur to you without censoring or stopping to reflect on your ideas. A student assigned to write an essay on child abuse for a sociology class would brainstorm by listing everything that comes to mind on this subject, from facts to images, memories, fragments of conversations, and other general impressions and responses. Later, the student would review this brainstorming list to identify ideas that seem most promising or helpful.

To brainstorm effectively, take a few moments at the start to formulate your goal, purpose, or problem. Then simply list your ideas as quickly as you can. You are the only one who needs to be able to decipher what you've written, so your brainstorming list can be as messy or as neat as you like. You can also brainstorm at the computer.

Brainstorming can enable you to discover and explore a number of ideas in a short time. Not all of them will be worth using in a piece of writing, of course. The premise of brainstorming is that the more ideas you can generate, the better your chances of coming up with good ones. Suppose that after freewriting about my family, I decided to explore the possibility of writing an essay about the potential contradiction between my sense that family is "an invisible web that connects" and the fact that I live so far away from my family. In the five minutes after I wrote that last sentence, I used brainstorming to generate the following list of ideas:

Think about role of place (geography) and family.

The house on Main St. — home since the 4th grade

Mom's letters: so important in keeping us all in touch!

Laurie, Shelley, and Sara all with new babies at Julie's wedding

Andy pulling the same joke on me for 30 years

The old house on Corey St. Why do I always remember the kitchen?

My sadness at missing Robin's, Shelley's, and Laurie's weddings because we were in Oregon

The wonderful, friendly, comfortable chaos at our reunion (the grandkids getting confused by all the aunts and uncles)

Am I fooling myself? Is the tie I feel with my family as strong as I think it is? Greeting-card sentiments versus reality?

Special family times: birthdays, Christmas, cooking and baking together. How to evoke these without making it all seem sentimental and cliché?

Maybe it's the difficult times that keep families together. The hard times that (especially when you're a teenager) you think you'll never get beyond.

Families change over time. So does your sense of family. How has mine changed?

I certainly would have a long way to go before I could write an essay about my sense of family, but this brief brainstorming list of ideas and questions has raised important issues I'd want to consider.

■ ■ ■

FOR EXPLORATION

Reread the freewriting you did about your sense of family (or about another topic of your choice), and then choose one issue or question you'd like to explore further. Write a single sentence summarizing this issue or question, and then brainstorm for five to ten minutes. After brainstorming, return to your list. Put an asterisk (*) beside those ideas or images that hadn't appeared in your earlier freewriting. How do these ideas or images add to your understanding of your sense of family?

Clustering

Like freewriting, looping, and brainstorming, clustering emphasizes spontaneity. The goal of all four strategies is to generate as many ideas as possible to discover what you know and what you might explore further. Clustering differs, however, in that it uses visual means to generate ideas. Some writers find that it enables them to explore their ideas more deeply and creatively.

Start with a single word or phrase. If you are responding to an assigned topic, choose the word that best summarizes or evokes that topic. Write this word in the center of a page of blank paper, and circle it. Now fill in the page by expanding on or developing ideas connected with this word. Don't censor your ideas or force your cluster to assume a certain shape. Simply circle your key ideas, and connect them either to the first word or to other related ideas. Your goal is to be as spontaneous as possible.

Figure 8.1 presents a cluster that I created shortly after freewriting and brainstorming about my sense of family. Notice that even though I wrote this only a short time later, the cluster reveals new details and images. After clustering you must distance yourself from the material you've generated so that you can evaluate it. In doing so, try to find the cluster's center of gravity — the idea or image that seems richest and most compelling.

■ ■ ■

FOR EXPLORATION

Choose a word to use as the center of a cluster. Without planning or worrying about form, fill in your cluster by branching out from this central word. Just include whatever comes to mind.

FOR GROUP WORK

Meet with a group of classmates to discuss informal methods of discovering and exploring ideas. Begin by having group members briefly describe the advantages and disadvantages they experienced with these methods. (Appoint a recorder to summarize each person's statements.) Then, as a group, discuss your responses to these questions: (1) How might different students' preferences for one or more of these strategies be connected to different learning, composing, and cultural preferences? (2) What influence might such situational factors as the nature of the assignment or the amount of time available for working on an essay have on the decision to

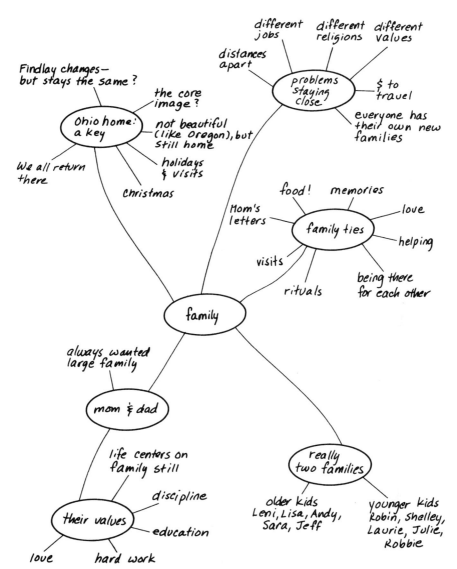

Figure 8.1   **Cluster Diagram about "Family."**

use one or more of these strategies? Be prepared to discuss your conclusions with your classmates.

USING FORMAL METHODS OF DISCOVERING AND EXPLORING IDEAS

The informal methods of discovering and exploring ideas have a number of advantages. They are easy to employ, and they can help you generate a reassuringly large volume of material when you're just beginning to work on a paper. These strategies also help you become interested in and committed to your work in progress. Sometimes, however, you may find more formal and systematic methods of discovering and exploring ideas helpful.

You are already familiar with one formal method of discovering and exploring your ideas: analyzing your rhetorical situation. The activities discussed in this section — the journalist's questions, tagmemics, and the topical questions — provide a variety of strategies you can use to explore a topic, consider it from diverse perspectives, and generate ideas about it. Because they *systematically* probe a topic, these strategies can help you discover not just what you know about a topic but also what you *don't* know and thus alert you to the need for additional reading and research.

The Journalist's Questions

The journalist's questions — *who, what, when, where, why,* and *how* — are perhaps the easiest of the formal methods to understand and apply. If you have taken a journalism class or written for a newspaper, you know that journalists are taught to answer these six questions in articles they write. By answering these questions, journalists can be sure that they have provided the most important information about an event, issue, or problem for their readers.

You may find these questions particularly useful when you are describing an event or writing an informative essay. Suppose that your political science instructor has assigned an essay on political conflict in the Middle East. Using the journalist's questions as headings, you could begin working on this assignment by asking yourself the following questions:

- *Who* is involved in this conflict?

- *What* issues most clearly divide those engaged in this dispute?

- *When* did the troubles in the Middle East begin, and how have they developed over time?

- *Where* does the conflict seem most heated or violent?

- *Why* have those living in this area found it so difficult to resolve the situation?

- *How* might this conflict be resolved?

Although you might discover much the same information by simply brainstorming, using the journalist's questions ensures that you have covered all these major points. Furthermore, using the journalist's questions as headings automatically organizes information as you generate it, whereas a brainstorming list would need to be analyzed and reorganized.

Tagmemics

The basic principle underlying tagmemics can be easily stated: an object, experience, or idea can be viewed as a particle (a static unit), a wave (a dynamic unit changing over time), or a field (a unit seen in the context of a larger network of relationships). Each of these perspectives encourages you to ask different kinds of questions about your subject (represented here as X).*

- *Particle perspective:*   What is X?
- *Wave perspective:*   How has X changed over time?
- *Field perspective:*   How does X relate to Y or Z?

If you view something as a *particle,* you focus on it as a *static* entity. For example, if you were exploring ideas for a sociology paper on the transformation of the American nuclear family, you could use a particle perspective to ask questions like the following:

What does the term *nuclear family* mean?

Who formulated the term *nuclear family* ?

What features characterize the nuclear family?

If you look at a subject from the *wave* perspective, you view it as *dynamic* or *changing over time.* The wave perspective would encourage you to ask the following questions:

How long has the nuclear family characterized family structure in America?

When did the nuclear family begin to change?

---

*This discussion is adapted from the work of Richard E. Young, Alton L. Becker, and Kenneth L. Pyke, *Rhetoric: Discovery and Change* (New York: Harcourt, Brace and World, 1970).

What factors have caused the nuclear family to change?

How might these factors affect the American family in the future?

Finally, if you look at a subject from the *field* perspective, you ask questions about the way that the subject functions as *part of a larger network of relationships.* This perspective would encourage you to ask questions like these:

How are changes in the structure of the American family related to other changes, such as those in the work force, organized religion, the educational system, and divorce rates?

What are the consequences of changes in the nuclear family for American life in general? For politics? For social services? For education?

Tagmemics is a formal method of discovering or exploring ideas because its three perspectives of particle, wave, and field encourage you to examine your subject *systematically.* Don't be intimidated by the formality of tagmemics; adapt this method to meet *your* needs. Sometimes, for instance, you may use the three perspectives of tagmemics to determine how you might best approach or limit a general subject or problem, such as the transformation of the nuclear family. In other cases, you may use tagmemics to generate a long list of details, examples, and ideas in support of a clearly defined thesis.

■ ■ ■

FOR EXPLORATION

Using the journalist's questions and tagmemics, systematically explore the subject you have investigated in preceding Explorations in this chapter. (If you feel that you have exhausted this subject, feel free to choose a different topic.)

Once you have employed each of these methods, take a few moments to reflect on this experience. To what extent did each strategy help you organize and systematically review what you already know, and to what extent did each define what you still need to find out?

The Topical Questions

The last formal method of discovering and exploring ideas is based on the topics of classical rhetoric. In his *Rhetoric,* Aristotle describes the topics as potential lines of argument or places (*topos* in Greek means "place") where speakers and writers can find evidence or arguments. Aristotle defined twenty-eight topics, but the list is generally abbreviated to five: *definition, comparison, relationship, circumstance,* and *testimony.*

The classical topics represent natural ways of thinking about ideas. When confronted by an intellectual problem, we all ask such questions as these:

- What is it? (definition)

- What is it like or unlike? (comparison)

- What caused it? (relationship)

- What is possible or impossible? (circumstance)

- What have others said about it? (testimony)

Aristotle's topics build on these natural mental habits.

You may use these questions to discover and explore ideas about a subject. To do so, simply pose each question in turn about your subject, writing down as many responses as possible. You may also find helpful the following list of topical questions.*

Questions about Physical Objects

1. What are the physical characteristics of the object (shape, dimensions, materials, etc.)?

2. What sort of structure does it have?

3. What other object is it similar to?

4. How does it differ from things that resemble it?

5. Who or what produced it?

6. Who uses it? For what?

Questions about Events

1. Exactly what happened? (who? what? when? where? why? how?)

2. What were its causes?

3. What were its consequences?

4. How was the event like or unlike similar events?

---

*These questions appear in Edward P. J. Corbett, *The Little Rhetoric and Handbook* (Glenview, Ill: Scott, Foresman, 1982), 38–39.

5. To what other events was it connected?

6. How might the event have been changed or avoided?

Questions about Abstract Concepts (e.g., democracy, justice)

1. How has the term been defined by others?

2. How do you define the term?

3. What other concepts have been associated with it?

4. What counterarguments must be confronted and refuted?

5. What are the practical consequences of the proposition?

Questions about Propositions (statements to be proved or disproved)

1. What must be established before the reader will believe it?

2. What are the meanings of key words in the proposition?

3. By what kind of evidence or argument can the proposition be proved or disproved?

4. What counterarguments must be confronted and refuted?

5. What are the practical consequences of the proposition?

Like the other formal methods for discovering and exploring ideas, the topical questions can help you pinpoint alternative approaches to the subject or probe one subject systematically, organizing what you know already and identifying gaps that you need to fill.

■ ■ ■

FOR EXPLORATION

Use the topical questions to continue your investigation of the subject that you explored with the journalist's questions and tagmemics. What new information or ideas do the topical questions generate? How would you compare this method to the other two formal strategies?

INVENTING WITH OTHERS

Invention can be done collaboratively, in dialogue with others. Much of this dialogue occurs naturally as you go about your daily affairs. While riding the bus home after class, you might talk over a writing assignment with a friend, for example, or you might brainstorm about an essay topic with your spouse over dinner. The ideas you gain through such exchanges can contribute a great deal to your understanding of your subject.

This section presents two strategies you can use to learn with and from others as you write — group brainstorming and group troubleshooting — that build on the informal exchanges you already have with friends, classmates, and family members.

Group Brainstorming

You have already experimented with brainstorming alone, so you are aware of its basic procedures and benefits. You can also brainstorm as part of a group. In fact, Alex Osborn, the person generally credited with naming this technique, originally envisioned brainstorming as a group, not an individual, activity. Osborn believed that the enthusiasm generated by the group helped spark ideas. You will not be surprised to learn, then, that those who regularly write with teams or groups cite increased intellectual stimulation and improved quality of ideas as major benefits of collaboration.

Group brainstorming can be used for a variety of purposes. If your class has just been assigned a broad topic, for instance, your group could brainstorm a list of ways to approach or limit this topic. Or your group could generate possible arguments in support of or in opposition to a specific thesis.

Because more than one person is involved, group brainstorming is more complicated than brainstorming alone. But it can be quite rewarding, as Johanna Wills, a student at Florida State University, indicates here: "I do like brainstorming alone, but group brainstorming is a terrific outlet for support as I face the challenges of writing."

■ GUIDELINES FOR GROUP BRAINSTORMING

1. Carefully define the problem or issue to be addressed at the start of your group session.

2. Appoint someone to act as a recorder. This person can write down everyone's ideas, to be reproduced and distributed later.

3. Encourage group members to contribute freely and spontaneously to the discussion. Don't stop to discuss or evaluate ideas; your goal is to generate as many ideas as possible.

Group Troubleshooting

Group troubleshooting is a simple but often productive means of helping group members identify and resolve writing problems by discussing work in progress with peers who respond with questions and advice. To troubleshoot effectively, follow this procedure:

■ GUIDELINES FOR GROUP TROUBLESHOOTING

1. Decide how much time to spend on each person's writing; appoint a timekeeper to enforce these limits.

2. Begin by having the writer describe the issue or problem he or she would like discussed. The writer also should try to identify particular questions for group response. These questions may be very general ("This is what I'm planning to do in my essay; can you think of any problems I might run into?" "Do you have any suggestions about how I might develop my thesis?") or quite specific ("I've only been able to think of two potential objections to my thesis; can you think of others?" "I like these four ideas, but I don't think they fit together very well. What could I do?").

3. Let the writer facilitate the resulting discussion. If the writer needs a moment to write an idea down, for example, he or she should ask the group to pause briefly. The writer should feel free to ask group members to clarify or elaborate on suggestions.

4. Try to respond to each writer's request for assistance as carefully and fully as possible.

You will probably find group troubleshooting most productive in the early stages of writing when you are still working out your ideas and determining your approach to your subject.

■ ■ ■

FOR THOUGHT, DISCUSSION, AND WRITING

1. Early in this chapter you used freewriting, looping, brainstorming, and clustering to investigate your sense of family. Continue your exploration of this topic by drawing on the formal methods of invention.

Then write an essay in which you explore just what the word *family* means to you.

2. Observe a group of your classmates brainstorming, and make notes about what you see. You may find it helpful to record how often each member of the group participates in the discussion, for example. Pay attention, too, to group dynamics. Is the group working effectively? Why or why not? What could group members do to interact more effectively? Summarize the results of your observations in a report addressed to the group. Be sure to suggest several ways the group could work more effectively in the future.

3. Choose one of the strategies discussed in this chapter that you have not used in the past, and try it out on your current writing assignment. If there is time, discuss this experiment with some classmates. Then write a brief analysis of why this strategy did or did not work well.

Strategies for Planning, Drafting, and Document Design

Planning is an important part of the writing process. As the discussion of differing composing styles in Chapter 2 indicated, people plan in different ways: Some develop detailed written plans; others rely primarily on mental plans; others might plan by freewriting a draft and then determining their goals by rereading and reflecting on their own written text. Many other factors can affect the process of planning, from the time available to the complexity of the writing task. Nevertheless, planning always involves the following activities:

- Analyzing your rhetorical situation

- Discovering and exploring ideas

- Establishing a controlling purpose

- Developing a workable plan

Earlier chapters have already discussed strategies you can use to analyze your rhetorical situation and to discover and explore ideas. This chapter focuses on the remaining two activities in the list: establishing a controlling purpose and developing a workable plan. It also presents a number of strategies for effective drafting and document design.

UNDERSTANDING THE PROCESS OF PLANNING

It may be helpful to think of planning as involving waves of "play" and "work." When you are discovering and exploring ideas, for example, you are in a sense playing. When you freewrite, loop, brainstorm, cluster, or engage in other creative blockbusting activities, your major goal is to be creative — to push your ideas as far as you can without worrying about how useful they may turn out to be later. Even more formal methods of invention, such as tagmemics or the topical questions, encourage mental play and exploration.

Most people can't write an essay based on a brainstorming list or thirty minutes of freewriting, however. At some point, they need to settle down to work, considering questions like the ones presented in the following guidelines.

■ GUIDELINES FOR PLANNING AN ESSAY

1. What main point do you want to make in this essay? How does this main point relate to your purpose — to what you want this essay to *do* for readers?

2. Who might be interested in reading this essay?

3. How might readers' expectations influence the form and content of this essay?

4. How can you structure your essay to communicate your ideas most effectively to readers?

5. What kinds of examples and details will best support your main point? What kind of evidence will your readers find most persuasive?

6. What textual conventions might you need or want to follow?

7. What elements of document design should you consider as you envision your essay?

Questions such as these require you to determine what point you want to make and *can* make in your essay, to decide if you have all the information you need to support your assertions, and to consider the most effective way to present your ideas to readers. These planning activities generally require more discipline than the informal or formal play of invention. Because much of the crafting of your essay occurs as a result of these activities, however, this work can be intensely rewarding.

■ ■ ■

FOR EXPLORATION

How do you typically plan when you are working on a writing project? Do you rely on written plans, or do you use other means to determine goals and strategies for your writing? How might you make your process of planning more efficient and productive? Freewrite for five or ten minutes in response to these questions.

ESTABLISHING A CONTROLLING PURPOSE

The planning strategies discussed in this chapter are *goal-oriented*. You can't establish a controlling purpose or a workable plan for your essay without having at least a tentative sense of the goals you hope to achieve by writing. These goals may change as you work on your essay, but they represent an important starting point or preliminary set of assumptions for guiding your work in progress.

How can you determine appropriate goals for your writing? Whether you are writing a brief memo to your supervisor, a term paper for your history class, or an application for your first job, you can best understand and establish goals for writing by analyzing your rhetorical situation. This process, described in Chapter 5, encourages you to ask questions about the elements of rhetoric: writer, reader, and text. Once you have analyzed your rhetorical situation, you should have a clearer understanding of both your reasons for writing and also the most appropriate means to communicate your ideas to your readers.

Your *controlling purpose* reflects your essay's topic but differs from it in important ways. Unlike your topic, your controlling purpose is both action- and content-oriented. Your controlling purpose reveals not just what you want to write about, but also the point you wish to make and the effect you wish to have on your readers. It is an *operational statement of your intentions*.

Suppose that you are writing a guest editorial for your campus newspaper. "What are you going to write about?" a friend asks. "Library hours," you reply. You have just stated your topic — the subject you're going to write about — but this statement doesn't satisfy your friend. "What about library hours? What's your point?" "Oh," you say, "I'm going to argue that students should petition the vice president for academic affairs to extend the library hours. Current hours just aren't adequate." This second statement, which specifies the point you want to make and its desired effect on readers, is a good example of a clearly defined controlling purpose.

If you and your friend had time for a longer conversation, you could elaborate on the rhetorical situation for your editorial. You could discuss your own intentions as the writer more clearly, and you could note how you intend to anticipate and respond to readers' needs and interests. Your friend might be able to give you good advice about how your text should reflect one of the most important textual conventions of editorials — brevity. Your friend may be too busy for such extended conversation, however; luckily, your controlling-purpose statement briefly and succinctly summarizes your goals.

An effective controlling purpose limits the topic and helps you clarify and organize your ideas. Once you have established a controlling purpose, you should be able to develop a number of questions that can guide you as you work on your writing. Here are some of the questions you might consider in response to the controlling purpose in the library editorial.

- What arguments will most effectively support my position?

- How can I focus my discussion so that I can make my point in the limited space typically given to editorials?

- Do I know enough about the reasons why current library hours are limited? Should I interview the director of the library or the vice president for academic affairs and ask them this question?

- Am I correct in assuming that other students find current hours a problem? Should I talk with some students to get their reactions to this problem? Should I develop a brief questionnaire that I could send to various campus Usenet and listserv groups?

- Should I find out how our library's hours compare with those at similar schools?

- Assuming that current library hours are a problem — and I'm convinced they are — how can I persuade students to sign a petition?

- Given my rhetorical situation, how formal should my language be? What image of myself should I try to create in my editorial?

As this example indicates, establishing a controlling purpose encourages you to be pragmatic and action-oriented. You may revise your controlling purpose as you work on your essay. In the meantime, you can use the insights gained by formulating and analyzing your controlling purpose to set preliminary goals for writing.

Once you have established a preliminary controlling purpose, you can test its effectiveness by asking yourself the questions listed in the following guidelines. (Or you may wish to discuss these questions with classmates.) If you can't answer one or more of these questions, you may not have analyzed your rhetorical situation carefully enough or spent adequate time discovering and exploring ideas.

■ GUIDELINES FOR EVALUATING YOUR CONTROLLING PURPOSE

1. How clearly does your controlling purpose indicate what you want this essay to do or to accomplish? Is your controlling purpose an operational statement of your intentions and not just a description of your topic?

(continued)

(continued)

2. How realistic are these intentions, given your rhetorical situation, the nature of the assignment, and your time and length limitations?

3. How might you accomplish this controlling purpose? Should you do additional reading? Talk with others? Spend more time discovering and exploring ideas?

4. In what ways does your controlling purpose respond to your understanding of your rhetorical situation, particularly the needs and expectations of your readers?

5. What questions, like those listed on p. 243, does your analysis of your controlling purpose indicate that you need to consider as you work on your writing?

FOR EXPLORATION

For an essay you are writing for this or another course, use the questions listed here to evaluate your current controlling purpose. Then write a paragraph evaluating the effectiveness of your controlling purpose and suggesting ways to improve it. Finally, list the questions your evaluation indicates you need to consider as you work on this essay.

In some cases, you may be able to establish a controlling purpose early in your writing process. In many other instances, however, you will first have to think about your rhetorical situation and use informal and formal methods of invention. You will, in other words, think and write your way into understanding what you want to say. You may even decide that the best way to determine your controlling purpose is to write a rough draft of your essay and see, in effect, what you think about your topic. This strategy, which is sometimes called discovery drafting, can work well as long as you recognize that your rough draft may need extensive analysis and revision.

You should always view any controlling purpose as preliminary or tentative, subject to revision. After you have worked on an essay for a while, your controlling purpose may evolve to reflect the understanding you have gained through further planning and drafting. You may even discover that your controlling purpose isn't feasible. In either case, the time you spend thinking about your preliminary controlling purpose is not wasted, for it enables you to begin the process of organizing and testing your ideas.

FORMULATING A WORKABLE PLAN

A written plan enables you to explore and organize your ideas and establish goals for your writing. Plans can take many forms. Some writers develop carefully structured, detailed plans. Others find that quick notes and diagrams are equally effective. The form that a plan takes should reflect your own needs, preferences, and situation.

As mentioned earlier, writers don't always make written plans. A very brief writing project or one that follows clearly defined textual conventions (such as a routine inventory update for a business) may not require a written plan. Nevertheless, as a college student, you will often find written plans helpful. Plans are efficient ways to try out your ideas. Developing a plan — whether a jotted list of notes or a formal outline — is also a good way to engage your unconscious mind in your writing process. Finally, many students find that by articulating their goals, by putting them on paper or onscreen, they can more effectively critique their own ideas, an important but often difficult part of the writing process.

There is no such thing as an ideal one-size-fits-all plan. An effective plan is a workable plan — one that works for you. Plans are utilitarian, meant to be used — and revised. In working on an essay, you may draw up a general plan only to revise this plan as you write. Nevertheless, if it helps you begin drafting, your first plan will fulfill its function well.

You may better understand how plans work by examining three students' actual plans. These plans vary significantly, yet each fulfilled the author's needs. The first plan is by Lisa DeArmand, a freshman majoring in business. It is a plan for a brief essay reviewing three popular pizza parlors near campus. As you can see, Lisa's plan, which consists of little more than a few notes about each pizza parlor, is brief and simple. But it was all that Lisa needed. Lisa had already analyzed her rhetorical situation and recognized that the most effective way to organize her essay would be to compare the three restaurants. She also had detailed notes about these restaurants, including interviews with students, which she planned to use in her essay. Because Lisa had such a clear mental image of what she wanted to say and how she wanted to say it, she didn't need a complex or highly detailed written plan.

Lisa DeArmand's Plan

BOBBIE'S PIZZA	PIZZA-IN-A-HURRY	PIZZA ROMA
$8.00	$8.55	$9.10
close	coupons	best pizza!
limited hours	crust thin and soggy	unusual sauce
delivery charge	tastes like frozen pizza	two kinds of
pizza OK but not great		crust
little variety		more toppings

Now look at the plan (below) by Dodie Forrest, a junior English major, for a take-home midterm in an American drama class. This plan is much more complex than the one for the pizza parlor review. It includes two diagrams that helped Dodie visualize how the essay might be organized, several quotes from the play that Dodie thought were important, reminders to herself, definitions of terms, and many general comments about the play. Dodie's task was more complex than Lisa's, so her plan needed to be more complex. Her task was also more open-ended. The question that Dodie was required to answer was this: "Explain why it is necessary for Arthur Miller to create wide sympathy for his character Willy Loman in *Death of a Salesman*. Does he create sympathy for

Dodie Forrest's Plan

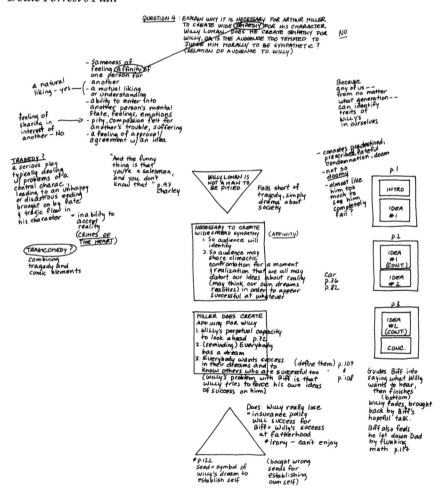

Willy, or is the audience too tempted to judge him morally to be sympathetic?" Dodie used her plan to help explore her ideas and to determine the best organization for her essay. Although probably no one but Dodie could develop an essay from the various diagrams and notes she created, the plan fulfilled Dodie's needs — and that's what counts.

Here is a third plan, by Dave Ross, a returning student intending to major in natural resource economics. Dave began by writing about the "feel" he wanted his essay to have and then developed a detailed plan.

Dave Ross's Plan

This will be a personal essay about my experiences working at Urban Ore, a business that sells salvaged building materials. I want the reader to share my pleasure at working among all that great recyclable junk. The interesting "finds," the colorful characters, my own satisfaction at organizing the chaos. The essay should feel <u>crowded</u> with odds and ends, just like the salvage yard is: strange bits of description, stories, humorous observations. I guess "funky" is the word.

I. Description of the yard

Among one-family underclass homes, rusting railroad tracks, corrugated sheet metal auto body shops: a weedy, dusty scrapyard surrounded by eight-foot cyclone fence, filled with doors, windows, kitchen cabinets, lamps, toilets, sinks, bathtubs, faucets, pipes, bricks, stoves, coils of wire.

A real business: this junk generates nearly $200,000 a year in sales to construction workers, contractors, or just weekend fixer-uppers.

II. People working there

Joe, the owner: Urban Studies Ph.D., abstract painter, two-time candidate for mayor.

Webb, looks like Jerry Garcia but with a rhino's strength.

Charles, lives on brown rice and has a passion for snakes.

Vagrant cats and a German shepherd named Ripthroat who melts when you scratch his butt.

III. Me working there

My first big job, organizing the windows and doors. First big rush of satisfaction: being able to tell a customer <u>exactly</u> where to find the bottom half of a double hung window, 36" by 28".

First Law of Urban Ore: "The more organized we are, the more we sell." But that's not the only reason I liked doing it. Bringing order out of chaos. An artist of the junkyard.

IV. Treasure island

Found among the weeds and blackberry brambles: Art Deco bathroom tiles, mint-condition platform heels, bottles of all shapes and colors, a Three Stooges coffee mug (think of more).

V. Not all fun

No electricity, heat, running water or toilet. Only one shack, crowded when it rains.

Winter: cold, stiff hands, wet gloves. Summer: pounding sun, dust.

rusty nails, metal or glass edges

hauling cast-iron bathtubs, six-burner ranges: hernia city!

VI. Conclusion

Honest, constructive work and creative in its way. Great when a customer found just what he/she wanted — or something they'd never dreamed of.

One evening, local skid-row types formed a band with stuff they'd found lying around. Played "Working on the Chain Gang" — sounded pretty bad, but a lot of spirit. A certain strange beauty amid the disorder — sums up Urban Ore for me.

Dave's plan is more detailed than Lisa's and more clearly organized than Dodie's. His approach to planning probably reflects his preference for detailed, well-organized plans. It also reflects the nature of the essay he had envisioned: He wanted to include such a profusion of material that a detailed plan would help ensure a coherent structure. Dave probably couldn't have worked efficiently from a freer, less clearly organized plan, like Dodie's — and Dodie might find Dave's approach equally difficult.

Plans play an important role in writing. They help you explore, organize, and try out your ideas; they also enable you to set goals for your writing. You might think of plans as notes, reminders, or directions that you write to yourself. No one else needs to be able to understand your plans, just as no one else needs to be able to shop from your grocery list. Through experimentation, you should be able to arrive at a style of planning that works for you.

■ ■ ■

FOR EXPLORATION

What kinds of plans do you typically draw up? Do you formulate detailed, carefully structured plans, or do you prefer to develop less structured ones? Do you use diagrams or other visual elements in planning? Can you think of one or more suggestions that might enable you to develop more useful plans?

Use these questions to think about your plans. Then spend ten minutes writing down your most helpful observations about them.

FOR GROUP WORK

Meeting with a group of classmates, take turns reading your responses to the previous Exploration. After each person has read, work together to answer these questions. (Be sure to appoint a recorder.)

1. What planning strategies do the members of the group most often employ?

2. How often do you all develop written plans? What kinds of plans do you most often develop? How formal and detailed are your plans? Does anyone often use diagrams or other visual plans?

3. Did anyone suggest planning strategies that other members thought they might like to experiment with? If so, briefly describe these strategies and explain why they seem useful.

4. List three conclusions about planning with which all group members can agree. Make another list of at least three suggestions of ways to plan more efficiently and productively.

Be prepared to share the results of your discussion with your classmates.

DEVELOPING EFFECTIVE STRATEGIES FOR DRAFTING

Drafting is the point in the process when you actually write words on paper or online. You actually begin writing, of course, with your first freewriting or brainstorming in response to an assignment. Revision, too, often occurs before you complete a rough draft: If you make a list of possible titles for an essay, cross out two, and circle one as your best current choice, you have revised. Drafting is nevertheless an important component of the writing process, for it is through drafting that you create a text that embodies your preliminary intentions.

Overcoming Resistance to Drafting

When you first sit down at your desk or computer to begin drafting, it can be hard to imagine the satisfaction of completing a rough draft. Indeed, just picking up pen or pencil or beginning to type can seem daunting, leading you to think of a hundred things you'd rather do. All writers experience some resistance to drafting; productive writers, however, have developed ways to overcome this resistance.

Many writers rely on rituals, such as those described on pp. 36–38, to help them deal with what Tom Grenier calls the "prewrite jitters." There are other strategies you can use to overcome resistance to drafting. If you've already spent time discovering and exploring ideas and making one or more tentative plans, you will have the reassuring knowledge that you're not starting from scratch. Reading through early notes and plans is an effective way to begin a drafting session. You may find yourself turning hasty notes and fragments into full sentences or grouping them into paragraphs — drafting before you know it.

Another way to motivate yourself to start drafting is simply to remind yourself that you're only working on a draft; it doesn't have to be perfect. When you begin drafting, your initial goal should simply be to *get the words down.* If you can't think of a way to open your essay, for instance, don't try to do so; simply begin writing whatever section you are ready to write. As you reread what you've written, you'll eventually discover an introduction that works.

Managing the Drafting Process

Once you pass the initial hurdle of getting started, you'll probably experience the drafting process as a series of ebbs and flows. You may write intensely for a short period, stop and spend time reviewing what you've written, make a few notes about how you might best proceed, and then draft again more slowly, pausing now and then to reread what you've written. The process of rereading your text as it develops is an important part of the drafting process. Research shows that experienced writers reread their writing often while drafting —

and that they reread with an eye toward such major concerns as the extent to which their draft responds to the needs and expectations of readers. Chapter 11 presents a number of strategies that will help you read work in progress. Here are some suggestions that should help make the process of drafting efficient and productive.

■ GUIDELINES FOR DRAFTING AN ESSAY

1. *Don't Try to Correct — or Perfect — Your Writing as You Draft.* When you are drafting, your goal should be to put enough words on paper so that you can reflect on and revise your writing. The easiest way to produce a rough draft is to work at an even pace so the momentum of drafting can help you move steadily toward your goal. Stopping to worry whether a word is spelled correctly or to fiddle with a sentence can interrupt your momentum and throw you off balance. Furthermore, most writers find that it's easier to delete unnecessary or repetitive material when they revise than to add new material. When drafting, your goal should be to get words written, not to make decisions about revising. If you can't quite articulate an argument or formulate an example, write yourself a note and keep drafting. When you return to your draft, you can fill in these gaps and omissions.

2. *Try to Keep in Touch with Your "Felt Sense" — Your Awareness of What Your Writing Is Doing — as You Draft.* You attend to many things when you draft. You stop and reread the words on the page; you reflect about your topic and assignment; you think about your readers. If you are an effective writer, you look at what you have written not just to see what is on the page but also what *might be* there. Some writers call this kind of attention "keeping in touch with their *felt sense* as writers."*

You might think of felt sense as inspiration — and it is, in the sense that many writers would find it difficult to articulate why they are writing a particular sentence or paragraph. The ability to

---

*Professor Sondra Perl discusses the concept of felt sense in "Understanding Composition," *College Composition and Communication* 31 (1980): 363–69.

(continued)

(continued)

develop felt sense does not require magical or mysterious gifts, however. Writers develop felt sense when they are deeply immersed in their writing.

To develop and maintain a felt sense, you need to draft for long enough periods so that you can become immersed in your writing — an hour, minimally, but longer if possible. And as you write words, sentences, and paragraphs, you need to keep one eye on such global issues as the appropriateness of your organization. Reflecting on concerns such as these and jotting down notes about your current thoughts are good ways to keep in touch with your felt sense.

3. *Take Advantage of the Capabilities of Word Processing Programs.* Most writers find that computers make composing less frustrating and more productive. But if you are using a computer only to enter and change text, you are not taking advantage of its full range of options. One useful word processing feature allows you to write notes that appear onscreen but not on your printed text. If you are drafting quickly and wish to maintain your momentum but also remember a question or an idea, you can insert comments as you write and return to them in a later drafting session. Another common word processing feature, the split-screen or windows option, enables you to work with two texts at the same time. You might place a freewrite, outline, or plan in one window and write your draft in the other. Or you might keep your introduction in view as you write later sections.

You can employ your program's BLOCK and MOVE (or CUT and PASTE) options to move text from one file to another; this option enables you, for instance, to transfer sections of freewriting directly into your draft. You can also use this option to move paragraphs or sections within a file to see the effect of changes that you might wish to make. If you do so, however, save and copy the file that you are working on, making changes only on the copy. Be sure to title your files so you can follow your essay's development; you might title various drafts of an argument "arg1," "arg2," "arg3," and so on. Do not delete any of these files until you are sure that your essay is complete.

Using your word processing program to advantage while drafting might also mean resisting the temptation to spend time playing

(continued)

(continued)

with formatting options such as font changes, varied line spacing, and the like.

Always remember to protect your work by saving frequently, making backup copies of your drafts, and printing hard copies in case disk or computer problems occur.

4. *Develop a Repertoire of Blockbusting Strategies.* All writers experience moments when the words just won't come. Experienced writers don't just sit and bemoan their fate when this occurs. Instead, they draw on a repertoire of blockbusting strategies, including the following:

- Lower your standards. If you can't find the right words to express your ideas, get them down in any form you can. Write enough to remind yourself of the point you want to make; then keep going.

- Stop trying to draft, and instead spend ten minutes freewriting or brainstorming.

- Switch to some writing task that you can do. If you can't determine how best to organize the body of your essay, for instance, spend some time revising your introduction or reviewing some background material on your subject. Or switch to another project you need to complete.

- Change strategies. If you've been trying to develop a written plan for your essay, try diagramming, clustering, or doodling instead.

- Talk out your ideas. Find a friend to talk with, or talk into a tape recorder. Begin by saying, "I've been trying to work on my essay, but I'm blocked. What I want to do is . . . "

- Take a few minutes to describe the difficulty you're experiencing; then take a break from writing to do something that will give you satisfaction — exercising, cooking, whatever.

5. *Learn When — and How — to Stop Drafting.* Ideally, you will come to a natural stopping point, a moment when you feel you've solved a problem you've been wrestling with or concluded the section of your essay you've been working on. At this point it's a very good

(continued)

(continued)

idea to take a few moments to jot down notes about what you think you've accomplished in that drafting session as well as about what you need to do when you return to your writing. You may also wish to ask yourself a few questions: "What's the best transition here?" "Which examples should I use next?" If you're like many writers, your subconscious mind will reflect on these questions and present appropriate answers to you when you next sit down to draft.

6. *Benefit from the Process of Incubation.* Sometimes it helps to *stop* thinking consciously about your ideas and just let them develop in your mind while you relax, sleep, or occupy yourself with other projects. After this period of incubation, you will often spontaneously recognize how to resolve a problem or answer a question.

You can't draw on your mind's subconscious powers, however, if you don't build in time for incubation. And don't confuse incubation with procrastination. Procrastination means avoiding the writing process; incubation means recognizing and using the fluctuations of the process to advantage.

FOR EXPLORATION

How do you typically draft an essay? How long do your drafting sessions usually last? What do you do when you run into problems while drafting? Could one or more of the suggestions presented here enable you to draft more productively? How might you best implement these suggestions? Spend five or ten minutes freewriting in response to these questions.

FOR GROUP WORK

Meeting with a group of classmates, take turns reading your responses to the preceding Exploration. After each person has read, work together to answer these questions. (Be sure to appoint a recorder.)

1. What drafting strategies do the members of your group most often employ?

2. How do group members overcome resistance to drafting? How long do drafting sessions typically last? How do you keep in touch with your felt sense while drafting?

3. Did anyone suggest drafting strategies that others think they might like to try? Briefly describe any such strategies, and explain why you believe they might be useful.

4. List three conclusions about drafting with which all group members can agree. Make another list of at least three suggestions on how you can draft more efficiently and productively.

Be prepared to share the results of your discussion with your classmates.

ORGANIZING AND DEVELOPING YOUR IDEAS

The British writer E. M. Forster once asked, "How can I know what I think until I see what I say?" By working through drafts of your work in progress, you gradually learn what you think about your subject. As you move from drafting to revising — a process that proceeds differently with each writing project — you also become increasingly engaged with issues of style and structure. "What do I think about this subject?" becomes less important than "How can I best present my ideas to my readers?"

This section presents guidelines for responding to the second question. These guidelines are only suggestions; your responses to these suggestions should be based on your understanding of your assignment, purpose, and rhetorical situation.

■ GUIDELINES FOR ORGANIZING
AND DEVELOPING YOUR IDEAS

1. *Check for Any "Code" Words That Mean Something to You but Not to Your Readers.* If you've spent time employing various invention strategies, begin your drafting session by reviewing the material you've already generated, looking for ideas and details you can use in your draft as well as for ones that need to be more fully developed. Often in rereading these explorations and early drafts, writers realize that they've relied on what Professor Linda Flower calls "code words," words that convey meaning to the writer but not necessarily to readers.* Learning to recognize and expand or

---

*Linda Flower, *Problem-Solving Strategies for Writing in Colleges and Communities,* 5th ed. (Fort Worth, Tex.: Harcourt Brace, 1996), 139.

(continued)

(continued)

"unpack" code words in your writing can help you develop your ideas so that their significance is clear to readers.

Here is a paragraph one student did when freewriting about what the word *family* meant to her. Rereading the freewriting at the start of her drafting session, she recognized a number of code words, which she underlined.

When I think of the good things about my family, Christmas comes most quickly to mind. Our house was filled with such <u>warmth and joy</u>. Mom was busy, but she was <u>happy</u>. Dad seemed less absorbed in his work. In the weeks before Christmas he almost never worked late at the office, and he often arrived with brightly wrapped presents that he would tantalizingly show us — before whisking them off to their hiding place. And at night we <u>did fun things together</u> to prepare for the big day.

Words like *warmth* and *joy* undoubtedly evoke many strong connotations for the writer; most readers, however, would find these terms vague. By looking for code words in her freewriting, this writer realized that in drafting she would have to provide readers with plenty of concrete, specific details to enable them to visualize what she means.

2. *Share Your Controlling Purpose with Your Readers.* One way to help organize a draft is to share your controlling purpose with your readers. How to do so most effectively depends on a number of factors. If you are working on a take-home essay examination for your history class, for example, you may wish to include a *thesis statement,* a single sentence that states the main idea of your essay, in your introduction. You may also preview the main lines of argument you will use to support your position so that your instructor doesn't have to hunt for your main point.

In other situations, including a specific thesis statement in the first paragraph of your essay may not be necessary or even desirable. If you are writing an essay about what the word *family* means to you, you might decide that you don't want to reveal the main point of your essay at the start. Instead, you might begin with a specific example that will create interest in your essay and show, rather than tell, what *family* means to you.

(continued)

(continued)

Readers quickly become irritated if they feel they're reading unorganized, disconnected prose or if their expectations about how a certain kind of writing should be organized are violated. For these reasons, sharing your intentions with readers and providing cues about how you will achieve them is essential. By analyzing your rhetorical situation and by studying how others engaged in similar writing tasks have fulfilled this obligation to readers, you can determine strategies to use to keep in touch with your readers.

3. *Take Advantage of Appropriate Methods of Organizing Information.* When you begin drafting, you don't have to come up with an organizational structure from scratch. Instead, you can draw on conventional methods of organization, methods that reflect common ways of analyzing and explaining information. Suppose that you are writing an essay about political and economic changes in Eastern Europe in the 1990s. Perhaps in your reading you were struck by the different responses of Russian and Czech citizens to economic privatization. You could draw on conventional methods of *comparing and contrasting* to organize your analysis. Or perhaps you wish to discuss the impact that severe industrial pollution in Russia could have on the development of a Western-style economy. After *classifying* the most prevalent forms of industrial pollution, you could discuss the consequences of this pollution for Russia's economy.

As these examples indicate, your subject may naturally lend itself to certain methods of organization. In some cases, you may be able to use a single method of organization — such as *comparison, definition, cause and effect,* or *problem-solution* — to organize your entire essay. More often, however, you will draw on several methods of organization to present your ideas. In considering how you can best draw on conventional methods of organizing information, remember that you should not impose these methods formulaically. Begin thinking about how to organize your writing by reflecting on your goals as a writer and your rhetorical situation. If your analysis suggests that one or more methods of organizing information represent commonsensical, logical ways of approaching your subject, use them in drafting. But remember, form should grow out of meaning and not be imposed on it.

DESIGNING EFFECTIVE DOCUMENTS

During the twentieth century, the situations of readers and writers changed in significant ways. The development of electronic and digital technologies in recent years is an example of such a change. As you are already aware, these technologies require communicators to make many more decisions about texts than in the past. Someone who wants to share her passion for black Labrador retrievers, for instance, could write a research paper or article about this popular breed of dogs or create a Web site or video dedicated to this subject. Whether creating a research paper, an article, a Web site, or a video, she would have to be as concerned with the visual as with the verbal, for in all of these media the verbal and visual are interdependent.

Electronic and digital technologies are part of a larger historical trend that has increased the role of visual elements in communication. Over the course of the twentieth century, the dramatic proliferation of advertising has led to situations in which consumers read hundreds of messages every week that attempt to persuade them to purchase products and services. Whether these messages take the form of magazine, television, or Web advertisements, visual elements play a critical role in their success. Television, video games, and movies have also created an appetite for visually sophisticated texts and images, and newspapers and magazines increasingly include sophisticated graphics and enhanced color in their articles and advertisements.

Until recently, relatively few writers concerned themselves with the visual look of a text. Design was considered by those composing advertising copy, editing magazines and newspapers, and writing business and technical texts (where issues of format have long played an important role). After all, just twenty years ago most writers composed either in longhand or at the typewriter. Students writing essays for college classes did have to use appropriate paper, margins, and (in the case of long, research-based essays) headings. And they were often required to follow particular formats that specified the location of their name, course number, title of the essay, and so on. But these were the only visual elements that they needed to include in their papers.

The development of personal computers and word processing programs opened up a new world of options for writers, who can now easily vary text formats, print with color and multiple fonts, and develop sophisticated charts and graphs. Thanks to their large-capacity hard drives and fast processors, many personal computers can now handle software programs with powerful graphics capabilities. Writers with access to the World Wide Web can easily (if not always legally) download texts, images, and even audio clips and integrate them into their own writing. It is increasingly common for students to develop texts that take full advantage of these options.

In this brave new world of visual and textual media, document design takes on increasing importance. And this is true whether you are deciding how to present an essay for a class or developing a Web site. In word processing a document, for instance, writers need to consider such questions as these:

- What margins, spacing, and font should I use?

- Would my writing benefit from the use of special formats such as columns, bulleted lists, and text boxes?

- Should I use headings and subheadings to help organize my ideas?

- Would visual elements (such as a border, graph, chart, or some created or imported image) add to the effectiveness of my text?

- Would color make illustrations easier to interpret? Would color add to the overall effectiveness of my text?

■ ■ ■

FOR EXPLORATION

How attuned are you to the visual? Take a few moments to think about the wide range of reading that you do — from magazines, newspapers, and advertisements to Web sites, college textbooks, and letters. How conscious are you of the ways that various design elements and images influence your response to and understanding of a text? (How does a magazine intended for twenty-somethings, for instance, use visual elements to differentiate itself from one intended for a different readership?) Do you have strong preferences about such visual features as type font, color, and images? Take five minutes to freewrite in response to these questions.

Looking at Document Design from a Rhetorical Perspective

Questions about word processing formats cannot be determined on a once-and-for-all basis. They are, in fact, rhetorical questions — questions that depend on your rhetorical situation. Just as you can analyze a rhetorical situation to make decisions about your writing (see Chapter 5, pp. 147–49, for questions you can use to analyze your rhetorical situation), so too can you analyze your situation to make decisions about document design and other visual elements of communication.

Imagine two students working on projects for a class. One student is taking an art history class: he is writing a twenty-page seminar paper on the nineteenth-century British artists who called themselves the Pre-Raphaelite

Brotherhood. The second student, who is in an English class, is writing a four-page analysis of a poem by the contemporary American poet Mary Oliver. How should these students use visual elements in their writing? Both have access to computers and online technologies that allow them to import images (such as reproductions of paintings by various Pre-Raphaelites or photographs of Mary Oliver). But should they?

A rhetorical response to these questions would consider the students' particular situations. Though these two students are writing different kinds of essays for different classes, one aspect of their situation is shared. Both are writing academic essays, so both need to understand that any visual elements they use should reflect the seriousness and formality that generally characterize academic writing. Ideas are central in academic writing, so any image, chart, or other visual element that is used in a class assignment should be essential to the overall intellectual richness and impact of the writing.

As you have perhaps already realized, given the particularities of his situation, it makes good sense for the student writing about the Pre-Raphaelites to both attend to and employ visual elements. This student is writing a long paper, so the use of headings could help orient readers to critical divisions within the writing. Even more important in this case, however, is the role that reproductions of art by the Pre-Raphaelites could play in this student's analysis. Reproductions would enable those reading the essay to understand and evaluate the student's analysis of various paintings without reference to other sources. The art history student might also choose to include photographs of the Pre-Raphaelites — though only if he is sure that the photos will enrich his analysis. Such would be the case if the student is discussing the historical, cultural, or social role that this movement played in nineteenth-century England.

The student writing on Oliver would also need to attend to visual elements. She would want to consider such visual issues as the use of white space, fonts, and headings, for instance, which are important for anyone writing an essay. And she would also need to recognize that the availability of word processing has raised the standards for the visual look of a text. Twenty years ago some professors may have accepted messy, hand-corrected essays. Now most professors would be unwilling to receive such papers. But unless some aspect of the analysis *requires* visual support or clarification, the student writing about Oliver would probably not include photographs or other visual images. These images would add little to the development of her ideas and might even distract readers.

As these examples suggest, document design may play a critical — or minimal — role in your writing process, depending on your situation. The student writing about the Oliver poem needs to follow the conventions her professor requires for basic essay format (margins, line spacing, titles, and so on). Concerns about document design would, however, play a relatively minor role in her writing process. The student writing about Pre-Raphaelites, on the other hand, needs to attend to document-design issues from the very start. He needs to select early on, for instance, the paintings by the Pre-Raphaelites that he will discuss at length. In making this decision, the student needs to focus on reproductions that are most relevant to his analysis, easily available, and legally reproducible.

■ ■ ■

FOR EXPLORATION

Chapter 15, "Putting It all Together: Writing Academic Arguments," concludes with a collection (or miscellany) of examples of student writing. This miscellany appears on pp. 391–414 of Chapter 15. Skim these essays, taking quick notes about each document's design and its effectiveness. When you look at the documents, note minor as well as major features. Monica Molina's essay, for instance (p. 402), uses asterisks to break her essay into three sections. This is not as obvious or strong a feature as the headings that Tara Gupta uses in her application for a summer fellowship (p. 397) — but it is still significant. Then based on your notes, write two or three paragraphs about what you learned from this analysis.

FOR GROUP WORK

Bring your analysis to class, and meet with a group of students. Appoint someone to serve as recorder or reporter. Then have each student read his or her analysis. To what extent did group members agree and disagree about the effectiveness of the document designs used in the essays? Conclude by articulating two things you have learned as a result of this activity. Be prepared to share the results of your discussion with classmates.

Making Effective Decisions about Document Design

New technologies for communication bring new opportunities — and new choices and demands. Consider cell phones. Is it courteous to hold a lengthy cell-phone conversation in a restaurant? In what situations is it safe to drive while talking on a cell phone? Reasonable people might well answer these questions differently. Conversations over a cell phone are transitory and ephemeral; they cannot be evaluated and reproduced — at least not easily. But written communications can. An anthropology teacher reading a student's report on a recent archaeological dig may expect that this paper will include downloaded photographs from a digital camera and elaborate charts or graphs presenting the dig's findings. A teacher in a different discipline might prefer that students follow the traditional conventions for academic document design that subordinate the visual to the verbal. And another might specify the most important elements of document design. This was the case when Brenda

Shonkwiler, whose research paper on the collapse of the Tacoma Narrows Bridge is presented in Chapter 4, "Understanding the Research Process," wrote a proposal for this project for her first-year writing teacher, Carole Ann Crateau. Ms. Crateau instructed students to write their proposals in memo form and specified the headings that each proposal needed to use. Here is Brenda Shonkwiler's proposal for her research project. Note that Brenda chose to develop a chart to represent her work schedule for the project.

THE COLLAPSE OF TACOMA NARROWS BRIDGE : PROJECT PROPOSAL

February 10, 1999

To: Carole Ann Crateau

From: Brenda Shonkwiler

Subject: The Collapse of Tacoma Narrows Bridge

One of the largest suspension bridges in the world, the Tacoma Narrows Bridge, spans 2,800 feet across the Tacoma Narrows of Puget Sound. It is the only fixed roadway link crossing the Puget Sound. The bridge is currently overburdened with traffic, which has led to many accidents and injuries. However, this bridge is much safer than its predecessor, "Galloping Gertie." Almost sixty years ago, the first Tacoma Narrows Bridge collapsed due to wind-induced vibrations.

The first Tacoma Narrows Bridge earned its nickname "Galloping Gertie" because of its rolling, undulating motion. This bridge depended on plate suspension girders that caught the wind, rather than allowing it to pass through. Motorists who crossed the bridge felt as though they were on a giant roller coaster. On the eventful day in 1940, the wind speed reached forty miles per hour. As the wind increased, so did Gertie's rolling, corkscrewing motion until it finally ripped the bridge apart. When the twisting motion was at its maximum, the sidewalk on one side was 28 feet higher than the sidewalk on the other side. Then a 600-foot section broke out of the suspension span and crashed into Puget Sound. Gertie had collapsed only a few months after it was built.

THE ISSUE

Failures are a part of life. However, the goal in engineering is to anticipate failures and to prevent such catastrophes from occurring. When the first

Tacoma Narrows Bridge was designed, the effects of wind and resonance had not been adequately considered. After the first bridge collapsed, its problems were analyzed. What factors led to this failure, and how could it be prevented in future designs? And what did engineers learn as a result of subsequent aerodynamic testing, which is now a standard procedure in suspension span structural analysis? These are the two major questions I hope to address in my project.

THE AUDIENCE

My target audience is the general public. Most people in the northwest have heard of the Tacoma Narrows Bridge failure; however, few know the details. I plan to explain what happened, what was learned from the failure, and how the information gained has been applied to current bridge design methods. I want my audience to understand how failures such as the Tacoma Narrows Bridge collapse can lead to better engineering designs.

THE INTERVIEWS

To get a better understanding of the role resonance had on the collapse of the Tacoma Narrows Bridge, I will interview Albert Stetz, a physics professor at OSU. I will also conduct an interview with a professor in the civil engineering department. This will give me a better grasp of Gertie's structural problems and subsequent improvements in bridge design, testing, and construction.

WORKING BIBLIOGRAPHY

Billah, K. Yusuf, and Robert H. Scanlan. "Resonance, Tacoma Narrows Bridge Failure, and Undergraduate Physics Textbooks." *American Journal of Physics* Feb. 1991: 118–24.

Gotchy, Joe. *Bridging the Narrows.* Gig Harbor: Peninsula Historical Society, 1990.

Janney, Jack R. *Guide to Investigation of Structural Failures.* Washington: Federal Highway Administration, 1980.

Myer, Donald Beekman. *Bridges and the City of Washington.* Washington: U.S. Commission of Fine Arts, 1974.

Petroski, Henry. "Still Twisting." *American Scientist* Sept.–Oct. 1991: 398–401.

Petroski, Henry. *To Engineer Is Human.* New York: Vintage Books, 1992.

264 | PRACTICAL STRATEGIES FOR WRITING

"Proposed Alternatives." Solve 16. <http://www.wsdot.wa.gov/solve16/designs.html>.

"Tacoma Narrows Bridge." Washington Online Highways. <http://www.ohwy.com/wa/t/tacnarbr.html>.

WORK SCHEDULE

Week	Task
3	Research and identify sources
	Draft of proposal due
4	Proposal due
	Arrange interviews
5	In-depth research
	Conduct interviews
	Draft of interview report due
6, 7	Write final report
8	Revise and edit report
	Prepare for presentation
9	Deliver oral presentation
10	Complete final report
11	Final report due! (Monday!)

CALL TO ACTION

Throughout history, there have been numerous engineering failures. The Tacoma Narrows Bridge collapse is one that stands out because of the severity of the oscillations that led to the bridge's collapse. Although it is impossible to prevent all failures, much can be learned from these events to prevent such problems from occurring in the future. The Tacoma Narrows Bridge is an excellent illustration of how the causes of a catastrophe can be analyzed and used to improve future designs, making structures safer for public use.

■ ■ ■

As a student, how can you make effective decisions about document design at a time when expectations and conventions are in transition? One teacher requires a certain document design, another expects but does not specify essential features of this design — and yet another assumes that students will follow traditional academic formats. The following guidelines provide suggestions you can use to address this increasingly important question.

■ GUIDELINES FOR EFFECTIVE DOCUMENT DESIGN

1. *When Considering Issues of Document Design, Think Rhetorically.* As noted earlier, a rhetorical approach to document design encourages you to ask questions about your audience, your text, and yourself. Let's consider several different situations.

   The Audience   If you are word processing a take-home midterm for a political science class, your audience — your teacher — does not expect and probably does not want a visually complicated text to read. In a situation like this, you should follow traditional conventions of document design, which downplay the visual elements of communication. But suppose you are a college senior writing an honors thesis, your subject cries out for illustration, and your audience is a committee of faculty members who are willing to discuss various visual elements with you. If you're writing about the therapeutic value of improvisational dance, for instance, or about the recent development of new techniques for ground-water purification, you might well decide to include illustrations, charts, and graphs in your thesis. Because you have worked intimately with your professors on this project, you can talk about these issues with them. You will of course have to meet the honors thesis format requirements, but anything else is up for negotiation with committee members.

   The Text   Textual conventions play a role in your design decision making. For instance, Brenda Shonkwiler's teacher informed her students that they should write memos about their proposed research projects, and thereby defined a number of aspects of the design of their documents. Memos are formatted in certain ways, and they often include headings. (As noted earlier, Brenda's teacher also provided the headings that students should use to organize and present their thoughts.) Conventions about designing (and especially formatting) texts already exist in many of the sciences; an example of such conventions would be the headings used in lab reports and grant proposals.

   The Writer   When you approach a writing assignment, you need to consider a number of issues and options. Perhaps the most important are the following: How much authority do you have in this particular situation? How knowledgeable are you about the textual conventions that inform the kind of writing you are

(continued)

(continued)

undertaking? How much knowledge do you have of various technologies of writing that might visually enhance your text? And how much time do you have to take advantage of this knowledge?

As noted earlier, if you are writing a take-home midterm, the brief amount of time available to you and the emphasis on evaluation suggest a fairly traditional approach to document design. A neatly presented and correctly formatted essay is essential. In determining whether to include complex visual elements, your knowledge (or lack thereof) of the conventions of various disciplines comes into play. You may know that in some disciplines, such as geosciences, tables and figures are commonly used. In traditionally text-based disciplines such as English and philosophy, tables and figures are rarely included. If you are unsure of what is appropriate for a particular discipline, take a conservative approach — or ask your teacher.

2. *Remember the Importance of Basic Design Principles.* Some basic principles of visual design — alignment, proximity, repetition, and contrast — are discussed in Chapter 7 (pp. 214–15) of this textbook, "Negotiating Online Writing Situations." If a text is *aligned*, items on the page are consistently placed on the page. Lines of text and the edges of illustrations are usually aligned on the left side; less frequently lines align on the right side or are centered. When the relationships between textual elements (such as headings and subheadings and items in a list) and between textual and visual elements (such as captions and photos) is clear, a page makes effective use of *proximity*. If *repetition* is used appropriately, it gives a page coherence. One obvious example of repetition is the practice of indenting paragraphs.

And finally, when graphic designers emphasize the importance of white space for visual and verbal texts, they are recognizing the need for *contrast*. The white spaces around text — created by margins and double-spacing, for instance — frame the text and lead the reader's eyes easily through it. To test yourself about this, read a single-spaced text with narrow margins, and then read a double-spaced text with ample margins. It is much more tiring to read a cramped text, whether that text includes only words or words and visuals.

(continued)

(continued)

3. *Use Visuals That Are Appropriate to Your Situation and Purpose.* Different visuals achieve different purposes. Tables, for instance, are excellent for communicating numerical information. Maps concisely and graphically convey information about locations. Charts and graphs help explain relationships among data. Photographs provide a you-are-there realism, as well as visual information, about a subject. And illustrations — whether drawings, diagrams, or cartoons — help clarify and emphasize information provided in the text.

   Typically, when you use visuals, you should number and title them. You should also refer to the visual in the text and explain the reason why it is included. A student writing on the number of casualties during the Vietnam War might introduce significant information by noting, "As Table 1 illustrates, many more Vietnamese than American soldiers lost their lives during this war."

4. *Be a Responsible User of Visuals Created by Others.* Whether you are using print- or Web-based visuals, take care to follow the conventions of copyright law. These laws are constantly being refined and revised — especially in the case of the Web — but in general the concept of "fair use" allows students to use brief excerpts of copyrighted material if they are using the material for a class and are not publishing or in some other way profiting from it. If you are downloading visuals from the Web, be sure to look for copyright notices and information about fair use. You will find that many sites allow you to download information without requesting permission. If there is no such statement on a site, you should email the site's Webmaster for permission. Of course, whenever you use visuals created by others, you should credit your source fully.

5. *Avoid Using Visuals as Decorative Devices.* The primary reason for using visuals in academic writing is to enhance the quality of your writing. Clip art, elaborate (but generally unnecessary) borders, and other decorative elements interfere with, rather than enhance, the expression of your ideas. Stick to a common and easily readable font. A standard 10- or 12-point type is used for academic writing.

(continued)

(continued)

6. *Recognize That the Unexpected Can (and Often Will) Happen Whenever You Use a Technology.* Don't wait until your project is nearly due to discover whether your printer can actually do the work you expect of it. If it can't, you will have to build in time to locate one that will. Plan the placement of visuals in the earliest stages of your writing, and when you print drafts for revision (or for peer response), include the visuals if at all possible. You need to know whether an important graph, chart, photograph, or other visual is strategically placed. Finally, if you are counting on downloading something from the Web, do it sooner rather than later. Web pages are constantly being revised, with some links being deleted while others are added.

FOR THOUGHT, DISCUSSION, AND WRITING

1. Think of a time when you simply couldn't get your writing going. What did you do to move beyond this block? How well did your efforts work — and why? After reflecting on your experience, write an essay, humorous or serious, about how you cope with writer's block.

2. Choose a writing assignment that you have just begun. After reflecting on your ideas, develop and write a workable plan. While drafting, keep a record of your activities. How helpful was your plan? Was it realistic? Did you revise your plan as you wrote? What can you learn about your writing process from this experience? Be prepared to discuss this experience with your class.

3. Interview someone working in the field you hope to enter after graduation to discover how he or she plans and drafts on-the-job writing. What kinds of plans does he or she typically construct? In what ways have electronic or other technologies (such as the tape recorder) influenced that person's planning and drafting strategies? Does he or she experience writing blocks? If yes, what blockbusting strategies does he or she rely on? How does this person's profession and work schedule influence his or her preferred methods of planning and drafting? How often does he or she write alone or as a member of a group or team? What advice about writing would he or she give to a student, such as yourself, who hopes to enter this field? Write an essay summarizing the results of your interview.

4. Turn back to the introductions to the two articles by John H. Flavell and the article by Flavell and two coauthors presented in Chapter 6, "Thinking about Communities and Conventions" on pp. 174–79. The Chapter 6 discussion of these three introductions touched on issues of document design, noting, for instance, that the article introduction intended for the broadest audience takes advantage of several visual opportunities to interest readers in Flavell's topic. But it did not discuss these visuals in depth. Drawing on the guidelines presented in this chapter, analyze the visual design of these documents and relate the elements of each design to the intended audience.

Strategies for Managing the Revision Process

In the broadest sense, revision occurs throughout the writing process. If you write a tentative first sentence, decide that it doesn't work, and cross it out, you have revised. Although revision can occur at any time, you will probably revise most intensively after you have completed a rough draft. At this point, you will have managed to articulate at least a preliminary statement of your ideas. Revision challenges you to look at your work from a dual perspective: to read your work with your own intentions in mind and also to try to consider your readers' perspectives.

Reading thus plays a crucial role in revision. When you read over your work, you attempt to discover strengths to build on and weaknesses to remedy. Consequently, you must think about not just what is actually in your text but also what is *not* there and what *could be* there. You must read the part (the introduction, say, or several paragraphs) while still keeping in mind the whole.

As a writer, you should have a healthy respect for the demands of revision, but you should not be overwhelmed by it. By studying both your own writing process and the products of that process (the essays and other papers that you write), you can develop an awareness of your strengths and weaknesses that will enable you to revise effectively and efficiently. As you write and revise, and as you read and respond to the work of others, you'll discover that revising can be the most rewarding part of the writing process. For when you revise, you have the satisfaction of bringing your ideas to completion in an appropriate form.

Here is how the popular columnist Ellen Goodman describes the satisfaction of revising.

> What makes me happy is rewriting. In the first draft you get your ideas and your theme clear, if you are using some kind of metaphor you get that established, and certainly you have to know where you're coming out. But the next time through it's like cleaning house, getting rid of all the junk, getting things in the right order, tightening things up.

— ELLEN GOODMAN

Christine Hoekstra, a junior English major, describes her experience of revision in very similar terms.

> Revision is an extremely important part of the writing process for me. It's really the part of writing where I feel the bulk of the work gets done — where the story takes shape, the essay is created. I couldn't imagine writing without revising.
>
> — CHRISTINE HOEKSTRA

For writers like Ellen Goodman and Christine Hoekstra, revision is the heart of the writing process.

Chapters 10 and 11 aim to help you experience the satisfaction of successful revision. Chapter 10 focuses on revision as a process, an activity. It answers questions like the following:

- What is revision? How does revision differ from proofreading, or correcting mistakes?

- How can you use responses to work in progress to help establish priorities for revision?

- How can you learn to read work in progress more objectively so that you can recognize strengths and weaknesses?

- How can you develop strategies that will help you revise more effectively and efficiently?

Chapter 11 discusses ways to improve your essay's structure and style. Together, Chapters 10 and 11 should help you understand why writers like Ellen Goodman and Christine Hoekstra can't imagine writing without revising.

REVISING THROUGH RE-VISION

You can learn a great deal about revision just by considering the word itself. *Revision* combines the root word *vision* with the prefix *re-*, meaning "again." When you revise, you "see again": You develop a new vision of your essay's shape or of the most emphatic way to improve the flow of a paragraph to help readers understand your point.

Revision is very different from editing, an activity that generally occurs at the end of the writing process. When you edit, you are concerned mainly with correctness. Does your essay have any errors of grammar, punctuation, or usage? Are your words spelled correctly? Do you need to fix any obvious problems of word choice or sentence structure? Editing is the tidying up that concludes the writing process.

■ ■ ■

FOR EXPLORATION

Using the preceding distinction between revision and editing, think back to some of your own writing experiences. When, and for what reasons, have you revised your work rather than just edited it? How would you characterize these revision experiences? Were they satisfying? Frustrating? Why? Freewrite for five or ten minutes about these revision experiences.

Unlike editing, revision is most typically a process of discovery where much more than correctness is at stake. Because it generates growth and change, revision sometimes requires you to take risks. Often these risks are minor. If you spend three or four minutes attempting to find just the right words to clarify an idea, for instance, you've lost only a little time if you're unsuccessful. Sometimes, however, when you revise, you make large-scale or global decisions with potentially more significant consequences.

After writing the first draft of an essay, for instance, Matt Brown, a first-year student planning to major in physics, met with members of his writing group to talk about his draft. He was unhappy with his essay, which argued that newspaper carriers work too hard and are paid too little, given the difficulty of their work. The members of his group were sympathetic to Matt's problems, but they couldn't help teasing him a bit. After all, how serious are a newspaper carrier's problems in the overall scheme of things?

Gradually, Matt recognized that he needed to take a different approach to his material. He realized that he could more effectively encourage his readers to empathize with carriers by taking a humorous approach, pointing out the problems carriers face in a lighthearted manner. Once he made this decision to revise his approach to his topic, Matt found that he was able to write and revise more quickly with much less frustration. In his case, taking the risk of trying a new approach paid off.

BENEFITING FROM RESPONSES TO WORK IN PROGRESS

As Matt Brown's experience indicates, you can draw on the responses of others to help you resee your writing. Talking with others can also provide crucial support. You may write alone a good deal of the time, but writing needn't be a lonely process.

When you ask others to respond to your writing, you are asking for feedback. Sometimes students confuse feedback with criticism. When you give writers feedback, you are attempting to help them see their writing in fresh and different ways. Providing feedback is thus not a negative process, and its goal is not to criticize but to help writers gain additional perspectives on their writing. Responses to work in progress can take a number of forms.

Eliciting Descriptive Responses   Sometimes you may find it helpful to ask others to describe your writing for you. Professors Peter Elbow and Pat Belanoff suggest a number of questions you can ask readers to elicit descriptive responses to work in progress:*

> *Sayback*   "Say back to me in your own words what you hear me getting at in my writing."
>
> *Pointing*   "Which words or phrases stick in your mind? Which passages or features did you like best? Don't explain why."
>
> *Summarizing*   "What do you hear as my main point or idea (or event or feeling)? And the subsidiary ones?"
>
> *What's almost said or implied*   "What's *almost* said, implied, hovering around the edges? What would you like to hear more about?"
>
> *Center of gravity*   "What do you sense as the source of energy, the focal point, the seedbed, the generative center for this piece?"

Eliciting Analytical Responses   On other occasions, you may find more analytical responses helpful. You might ask readers to comment on the organization of your essay or the extent to which it responds to the needs and interests of readers. Or you might ask readers to play what Elbow and Belanoff call "believing and doubting."

> *Believing*   Simply ask readers to *believe* everything you have written — and then tell you what that makes them notice. Even if they disagree strongly with what you have written, their job is to *pretend* to agree.
>
> *Doubting*   Now ask readers to pretend that everything is false, to find as many reasons as they can why you are wrong in what you say (or why your story doesn't make sense).

Eliciting Responses to Your Essay's Structure and Logic   Finally, if you are writing an argumentative essay, you might ask readers to respond to a series of questions designed to uncover potential weaknesses in your essay's structure or logic. The following "Skeleton Feedback" questions focus on three central issues:

---

*Peter Elbow and Pat Belanoff, *A Community of Writers: A Workshop Course in Writing*, 3d. ed. (Boston: McGraw-Hill, 2000). Excerpted from the appendix "Sharing and Responding."

1. Reasons and Support

   What is the main point/claim/assertion of the whole paper?

   What are the main reasons or subsidiary points?

   Taking each reason in turn, answer these questions: What support, backing, or argument is given for it? What support *could* be given?

   What counterarguments could be made against this reason?

2. Assumptions

   What assumptions does the paper seem to make? What does the paper seem to take for granted?

3. Readers or Audience

   Who is the implied audience? Who is being addressed by the writer?

   Looking at the reasons, arguments, and assumptions, tell what kind of readers would tend to accept which ones (and what kind of readers would reject them).

   How does the writer *treat* the audience? As enemies? Friends? Equals? Children? What's the stance toward the audience?

To determine what kind of feedback is most helpful to you, think commonsensically about your writing. Where are you in your composing process? How do you feel about your draft and the kind of writing you are working on? If you have just completed a rough draft of an argument, for instance, you might find descriptive feedback most helpful. After you have worked longer on the essay, you might invite more analytical responses.

As a student, you can turn to many people for feedback. Some of these individuals, such as your instructor and classmates, can approach your writing as insiders. They know the assignment you are working on and the standards for evaluation. Others, such as your writing assistant, friends, or family members, must approach your writing as outsiders. The differences in the situations of these potential respondents will influence how they respond; these differences should also influence how you use their responses. No matter who your respondent is, you must ultimately decide how to interpret and apply his or her comments and criticisms.

Responses from Friends and Family Members

You can certainly ask friends and family members to read and respond to your writing, but you should understand the strengths and weaknesses they bring as readers. One important strength is that you trust them — otherwise, you wouldn't ask them to read your writing. Unless you spend time filling them in, however, friends and family members won't understand the nature of your assignment or your instructor's standards for evaluation. This lack of knowledge, as well as their natural desire to see you do well, may cause them to be less critical of your work than other readers might be. Still, friends and family members can provide useful responses to work in progress. When you are considering getting such responses, here are some suggestions to keep in mind.

■ GUIDELINES FOR GETTING RESPONSES FROM FRIENDS AND FAMILY

- Choose your respondents carefully. Is this person a competent writer? Have you benefited from his or her response in the past?

- Recognize that friends and family members can't fully understand the assignment or situation, even if you take some time to explain it. Take this lack of knowledge into consideration when evaluating their comments.

- Draw on their strengths as outsiders. Rather than asking them to respond in detail to your essay, for instance, ask them to give a general impression or a descriptive response. You might also ask them to tell you what they think is the main idea or controlling purpose of your essay. If they can't identify one, or if their understanding differs substantially from your own, you've gained very useful information about your essay.

- Try asking them to read your work aloud to you *without having first read it silently themselves.* When you read your own work, you unconsciously compensate to reflect your intentions. Listening to someone else read your work can help you hear problems that you might not otherwise detect yourself. If your reader falters over a phrase or has to read a sentence several times before it makes sense, that may indicate a problem of style or logic.

- Don't rely solely on the response of friends or family members. Try to get at least one other informed response to your work.

Responses from Classmates

If you have been getting responses to your writing from fellow students, you know how helpful their reactions and advice can be. Here is a comment by education major Karen Boaz about her experience with peer response:

At first, I was wary of peer response to my writing. I was afraid of criticism and of exposing something as personal as writing to my classmates. Peer response turned out to be one of the most valuable aspects of my writing class. The members of my writing group were genuinely interested in my ideas, and they gave responses and suggestions I could really use.

Because your classmates know your instructor and the assignment as insiders, they can provide particularly effective responses to your writing. Students participating in writing groups typically form strong bonds; they genuinely want group members to do well, to develop as writers. Yet group members can often read work in progress more objectively than family members and friends can. When student writing groups function well, they provide a helpful balance of support and constructive criticism. To ensure that your writing group works well, follow these guidelines.

■ GUIDELINES FOR GETTING RESPONSES FROM A WRITING GROUP

Advice for Writers

- Learn to distinguish between your writing and yourself. Try not to respond defensively to suggestions for improvement, and don't argue with readers' responses. Instead, use their responses to gain insight into your writing.

- Prepare for group meetings by carefully formulating the questions about your work that you most need to have answered.

- Always bring a legible draft to class.

- Be sure to bring a working draft, not a jumble of brainstorming ideas, freewriting, and notes.

- Provide information that will enable readers to understand your rhetorical situation. If you are addressing your essay to a specific audience — members of a certain organization, for example, or readers of a particular magazine — be sure classmates know.

- Remember that your fellow students' responses are just that: responses. Treat these comments seriously, for they are a potentially powerful indication of the strengths and weaknesses of your draft. But maintain your own authority as the writer. Your read-

(continued)

(continued)

ers' responses may be useful evidence about the effectiveness of your essay, but you must always decide how to interpret these responses — what to accept and what to reject.

Advice for Readers

- Remember the golden rule: Respond to the writing of others as you would like them to respond to your work.

- Don't attempt to "play teacher." Your job is not to evaluate or grade your classmates' writing but to respond to it.

- Take your cue from the writer. If he or she asks you to summarize an essay's main point, don't launch into an analysis of its tone or organization.

- Remember that the more specific and concrete your response is, the more helpful it will be.

You don't need to be an expert to provide helpful responses to work in progress. You simply need to be an attentive, honest, supportive reader.

FOR GROUP WORK

Take five minutes to think about responses to your work that you have received from classmates. Freewrite for five or ten minutes about these experiences, and then draw up a list of statements describing the kinds of responses that you have found most helpful.

Meet with a group of your classmates. Begin by having each group member read his or her list. Then, working together, list all the suggestions for peer response. Have one student record all the suggestions, and distribute them to everyone in the group for future use.

Responses from Writing Assistants

Many colleges and universities have writing centers staffed by undergraduate and graduate writing assistants or tutors. Sometimes students misunderstand the writing assistant's role. They may regard writing assistants as editors trained to correct their writing. Or they may think they're faculty aides standing in for "real" instructors, who are unavailable or too busy to meet with students. Neither view is accurate.

Writing assistants are simply good writers who have been trained to respond to peers' work. Like your classmates, a writing assistant's main job is to *respond* to your writing, not to analyze or critique it extensively. But unlike your classmates, a writing assistant has been formally trained in peer response methods. Because writing assistants work with many students, they are likely to have experience reading and responding to a broad range of writing. The following guidelines will enable you to make the most productive use of the time you spend with a writing assistant.

■ GUIDELINES FOR MEETING WITH A WRITING ASSISTANT

- Before meeting with your writing assistant, reread your writing and identify your major goals. Would you benefit most from a discussion of your essay's organization, an examination of a section of your draft, or some other activity?

- Begin your conference by sharing these goals with your writing assistant. You might also find it helpful to give the writing assistant some sense of where you are in your process — in the early stages of drafting, for instance, or in the process of final editing.

- Be realistic about what you can accomplish in the time available to you. Recognize, as well, that the writing assistant's job is to respond and advise, not to correct or rewrite your draft.

Responses from Your Instructor

Because your instructor is such an important reader for your written assignments, you want to be certain that you make good use of any written comments he or she provides. Use the following suggestions to help yourself benefit fully from an instructor's comments.

■ GUIDELINES FOR USING YOUR INSTRUCTOR'S RESPONSES

- Read your instructor's written comments carefully. They are the clearest, most specific indication you have of the degree to which you have fulfilled the assignment.

(continued)

(continued)

- Read your instructor's comments *more than once.* When you first read them, you will be reading mainly to understand his or her general response to your writing. That's a useful reading, but it does little to help you set goals for revision. Later, read the comments again several times, looking to establish priorities for revision.

- Recognize the difference between your instructor's local and global comments. Local comments indicate specific questions, problems, or errors. For example, *awkward sentence* is a local comment indicating some stylistic or structural problem with a specific sentence. Global comments address broader issues, such as organization or the effectiveness of your evidence. The global comments in particular can help you set large-scale goals for revision.

- Meet with your instructor if you don't understand his or her comments. Even if you do understand the comments, you may wish to meet to discuss your plans for revision.

Friends, family members, classmates, writing assistants, instructors: All can provide helpful responses to work in progress. None of these responses should take the place of your own judgment, however. Nor should you automatically accept responses, whether criticism or praise. Your job as the writer is to *interpret* and *evaluate* these responses, using them along with your own assessment of your rough draft to establish goals for revising.

BUILDING OBJECTIVITY TOWARD WORK IN PROGRESS

As the one who must finally evaluate your own writing as well as interpret the responses of others, you will need to develop strategies for objectively viewing your own work in progress. Building such objectivity enables you to achieve the distance necessary to make the hard decisions that revision sometimes requires. The following suggestions should help you develop this objectivity.

■ GUIDELINES FOR REVISING OBJECTIVELY

1. *Plan at Least a Short Break between Writing and Revising.* It's difficult to critique your rough draft if you've only just finished composing it. Your own intentions are still too fresh for you to be able to read your words as they are, not as you intended them to be. Read what one student, Audrey Meier, wrote in her journal about the importance of letting work in progress "sit a while":

   > I can only do so much good thinking and writing at any one time. I need to work as hard as I can for a reasonable amount of time — say, two to three hours. But then I need to let go, shift gears. I call this the "baking" part of my writing process — it's when I put papers in my mental oven for a while. The result is almost always a better paper.

2. *Prepare Mentally for a Revising Session.* Taking a break from your writing before revising can help you gain distance from work in progress. But you also need to consider how you can best prepare for — and begin — revising. You may find it helpful to review your assignment and your analysis of your rhetorical situation before you reread your draft. As you do so, ask yourself the following questions:

   - To what extent does your draft respond to the assignment?

   - To what extent does your draft respond to your rhetorical situation as you have analyzed it and to the goals and objectives you established?

   - What state is your draft in — how rough or near completion?

   - What goals should you establish for this revising session, and how can you fulfill them? What should you work on first?

   By preparing mentally before you begin revising, you will make the most efficient and most productive use of your time.

3. *Revise Work in Progress from Typed or Printed Copy.* We all grow used to our own handwriting, no matter how awkward or homely our scrawl. Even the letters on a computer screen can become overfamiliar after staring at them for hours. Perhaps for this reason, you may find that you're less critical of handwritten or electronically displayed texts than you are of typed or printed drafts. To counteract this tendency, you may find it helpful to type or

   (continued)

(continued)

print your essays out as you write and revise. Once your words appear in print, you can often see problems that were invisible before. Revising from typed or printed copy can help you detect local stylistic problems and also help you recognize global problems of organization and development.

4. *Use Descriptive Outlines to Help You "X-Ray" Your Draft.* Familiarity can make it difficult for you to evaluate your writing objectively. To gain distance from work in progress, you may find it helpful to "X-ray" your draft by developing what Professor Kenneth Bruffee calls a "descriptive outline."* To construct a descriptive outline, indicate the content and purpose of each paragraph in your essay — in other words, what each paragraph in your essay *says and does* for readers. To illustrate how you might use descriptive outlining when you revise, here is an essay by Rosie Rogel exploring what the word *family* means to her. She wrote this essay in response to the first activity on p. 228.

---

*Kenneth A. Bruffee, *A Short Course in Writing: Composition, Collaborative Learning, and Constructive Reading*, 4th ed. (New York: HarperCollins, 1993), 51.

MEMORIES
by Rosie Rogel

My earliest memories are in Spanish. This seems a bit odd to me because I no longer think in Spanish; English has long since prevailed in that department. But, nonetheless, scattered images of my family replay themselves word for word in my first language. It's always been soothing for me to hear my parents speak Spanish — those soft rolling R's can calm me even today. These early childhood flashbacks have acted as a basis for what my concept of a family truly is.

The word *family* causes my mind to flood with emotions and sensations straight out of my childhood. Images of my mother, the matriarch of the small kingdom she and my father chose to create, fill my mind. My mother's approval and support have always been very important to my sisters and me. When we were small and contemplating behaving poorly, one stern glance in our direction was (usually) enough to temper the three-girl storm threatening to break. I recall somersaulting down the grassy hill behind our home with my sisters, dizzy with delight at the incredible feeling of freshly cut grass against our skin. I remember warm summer mornings when I'd brush my grandmother's hair in the early morning sun. I'd stand on a chair, on the tips of my daintily painted pink toes. How I loved to brush those thick locks. Before the brush reached the ends of her hair, I'd pull it up and into the sun to admire the shimmering fan of black strands, lightly threaded with silver, that I had created. I remember my daddy trying to get me excited about my first day of kindergarten and how his strong, calloused hand knitted softly in mine miraculously seemed to transfer his courage to me. These memories emerge from some sweet corner of my mind, whispering to me just what the word *family* means. It means comfort, security, warmth, and happiness.

When I was small, my family was my entire world. As in most families, the threads of our lives are entwined together. I learned everything I know about relationships with other human beings from them. My interaction with them has been the foundation for my ability to relate to the rest of the world — whether I saw the world as good or bad largely depended on how my parents taught me to view it. Thanks to my parents, I saw the world as a beautiful garden with hundreds of flowers just waiting to be admired and examined — each one different and each one equally important.

My definition of the word *family* stretches much farther than simply those people one lives with who are related (or not). As I got older, my family stretched to include close friends. To me, a family member is someone who loves me unconditionally. It makes almost no difference to me whether he or she is a blood relation. My definition of the word *family* also includes the human race as a whole. We are family because we are here, together. I believe our humanity makes us family.

The word *family,* in every sense, is extremely important to me because of the huge impact our family (or lack of family) has on who it is we become. What we learn from the people who gave birth to us and raised us is something we'll carry with us always. Unfortunately, not everyone is lucky enough to be born among stable, loving families. There are those who are not, and entire communities are suffering because of it. This is where my far-stretching sense of the word *family* comes in.

The concept of the family unit has, of late, been furiously discussed in the media and in politics. The traditional, "typical" American family doesn't really exist anymore. To me, whether a family has one mother or one father (or two mothers, for that matter) doesn't matter. If there is love, acceptance, and trust swirling around, then it qualifies as a family. With these basic human needs met, a child can grow up, perhaps remembering somersaulting sisters, black-silver strands shimmering in the sun, or a reassuring hand-hold, to make a family of his or her own.

When Rosie Rogel asked members of her writing group to respond to this essay, they praised its vivid and moving examples, but they also indicated that the essay seemed to shift gears midway and that it covered quite a number of issues. To get a clearer sense of how her essay worked, Rosie decided to construct a descriptive outline. As she did so, she wrote comments she could use to establish priorities for revision; these appear in parentheses following her analysis of each paragraph.

Paragraph 1

What it says: This paragraph describes the importance of Spanish and of my earliest memories to my concept of family.

What it does for readers: This paragraph provides information readers need to know to understand my experience of family, and it emphasizes the importance of my early childhood experiences.
(I like the way this paragraph emphasizes the importance of my heritage, but I wonder if the last sentence could be stronger.)

Paragraph 2

What it says: This paragraph presents a number of images and examples of my family life.

What it does for readers: By presenting vivid and concrete images, this paragraph will, I hope, create interest in my family and give readers a sense of what my family was like when I was growing up.
(I like this paragraph; my writing group also said this was one of the strongest paragraphs in the essay.)

Paragraph 3

What it says: This paragraph discusses several issues, such as the importance of my family to my development as a person and what I learned from my family.

What it does for readers: This paragraph continues to give readers information about what family means to me.
(This paragraph could be more focused. Also, I had a hard time determining what this paragraph does for readers.)

Paragraph 4

What it says: This paragraph presents my definition of family.

What it does for readers: This paragraph presents a new element in my understanding of family. Since most readers are likely to think of family as including their parents, sisters, brothers, etc., this paragraph asks readers to expand their understanding of family.

(I can see that this is quite a jump from the earlier paragraphs; this must be one of the places where my writing group started to feel I was switching gears. The early part of my essay is personal and concrete; this almost feels like it's from a different essay.)

Paragraph 5

What it says: This paragraph develops my argument that it's important to think of family as more than simply the people who are directly related to us. But it also goes back to the earlier topic of how much impact my immediate family had on me.

What it does for readers: ??
(I wanted this paragraph to bring together the early part of my essay, which focuses on my own experiences, and the expanded idea of family that I introduce in paragraph 4, but I'm not sure it really does this.)

Paragraph 6

What it says: This paragraph argues that the traditional American family doesn't exist.

What it does for readers: This paragraph raises a new issue and asks readers to agree with my position about this issue.
(Now that I'm summarizing each paragraph, I can see that this paragraph, like paragraphs 4 and 5, raises another new topic. Although the last sentence tries to remind readers of the first part of the essay, this paragraph doesn't really draw the essay together.)

After developing her descriptive outline, Rosie was able to see the kinds of shifts in purpose and tone that had concerned her readers. She also recognized that her draft attempted to cover too many issues; she couldn't both develop a rich and vivid portrait of her family and support several arguments about the nature and role of family in society today. By summarizing not only what each paragraph in her essay said but also what it did for readers, Rosie was able to establish priorities for revision.

■ ■ ■

FOR EXPLORATION

Choose an essay that you are currently working on, and develop a descriptive outline for each paragraph. Once you have done so, exchange essays with a classmate, and construct a similar outline for your classmate's essay. After you have completed this activity, compare the outlines of your essays. To what extent do your outlines coincide? To what extent do they differ? Did this exchange enable you to better understand the strengths and weaknesses of your essay? If so, in what ways?

REVISION IN ACTION: A CASE STUDY

What kinds of changes do writers make as they revise? The following case study, which chronicles the development of an essay by Kira Wennstrom, a first-year biology major, should give you a clearer, more concrete understanding of how revision works.

Kira's assignment was relatively broad and open-ended: to write an essay describing some personal experience and explaining the significance of that experience. Kira had few problems coming up with a topic. During the previous summer she had cared for two children while their mother was in the hospital. The experience had taught her a great deal about herself and about the bond between parents and children. She wanted to explore her experience further and to share with others what she had learned.

Kira describes herself as a heavy planner, and her self-assessment seems accurate. She did much of the planning for this essay in her head rather than on paper. She thought for several days about her experience, and she also discussed it with friends and classmates. By the time she sat down to write the first draft, reproduced below, she had thought through her ideas so carefully that she was able to write using only a brief list of major ideas as a guide.

Kira's first draft is reprinted here. Its paragraphs are numbered for ease of reference. Also included are some of the written comments that members of Kira's writing group made in response to her draft.

Kira Wennstrom's First Draft

(1)   While my friends swam and tanned at the lake, I ran a household with two incredibly rambunctious and mildly accident-prone children. However, I think in the long run my time was better spent than that of my peers.

Can you do more to draw readers in?

(2)   When Josh and Timmy's mother had to go into theee hospital, she asked me if I would be willing to stay with the boys until she could come home. I quickly accepted. However, the few days I had planned on became two weeks, and there was work and trouble and responsibility I never imagined.

Do you really want to emphasize these negative factors so strongly?

(3)   Since the children were only five and eight, I couldn't leave them alone in the house; I had to be there or be with them 24 hours a day. In addition to the normal precautions of

Nice concrete details in these, but do you need them all?

making sure I knew where they were, I also had to worry about their father. He and the boys' mother had divorced several years ago, and there were still problems with custody.

The sentence structure flows smoothly here & during the rest of the essay, too

(4)   I spent my days as a housewife: planning meals, doing laundry, cleaning house. I handled all the typical minor emergencies. There were scraped knees to be washed and bandaged, fights to be settled, Kool-Aid to be cleaned out of the carpet, and once or twice I had to rescue pots and pans from the sandbox to cook dinner.

(5)   My evenings were spent preparing meals and dishes and settling disputes as to who was going to bed when and whose turn it was to choose the TV channel. After things settled down and the kids were in their rooms, I was finally left alone to read or watch the <u>Tonight Show</u> before I hit my own pillow, exhausted. However, my nights were seldom complete without being awakened to check out at least one scary noise or to deny a request for a midnight snack.

(6)   I had agreed to care for the kids knowing that it wouldn't be <u>all</u> fun, but I never dreamed the amount of laundry two active children can go through. I did a load of wash almost every other day and was just barely keeping up. I was also amazed by the complexities of working out a simple dinner schedule. There was no single entree that both boys liked. They would sooner have starved, I think, than eat anything that didn't come in a wrapper, a can, or a box. Gradually, as the days

Whew — this feels abrupt!

passed, however, I began to realize what it is about parenting that makes my mother's eyes bug out at the end of the day. I <u>loved</u> those children terribly.

(7)   I discovered that perhaps the hardest part of parenting is the loss of privacy. I never had a moment to myself, completely to myself, when I could just let my mind catch up to the rest of me. Having always been used to spending hours alone and enjoying my own company, I found it incredibly difficult sometimes to force a smile when one of the boys interrupted a quiet minute with yet another demand on my

time. I learned to treasure the ten or so minutes of silent darkness between the time I shut off the light and the time I went to sleep.

Now that I've read your essay twice, Kira, I can see that you want to balance the work of caring for Josh & Timothy with your love of them. Develop more fully?

(8)   My own mother, whom I telephoned with great regularity, seemed to find enormous delight in the fact that I was going through the same thing that she had been trying (and failing) to explain for seventeen-odd years. She gave me marvelous advice and brilliant suggestions on how to cope with the whole mess and then, I am sure, hung up the phone and laughed her socks off in utter vindictiveness. But I can forgive her this because although I didn't realize it then, what I was experiencing would prove invaluable.

(9)   I look at mothers, especially mine, with better understanding now, with less scorn. I look at children with a little more appreciation. I use my time alone more carefully now; I spend it wisely, now that I know how crucial it is. Most of all, I value my freedom more highly than ever because I know what it is to lose that freedom. As much as I cared about those children, it's not time yet to give up my claim to my life. I understand now how important it is to live for yourself before you live for anyone else.

Nice sentence structure

Your conclusion might have more impact if you helped readers understand how much you came to love Josh & Timmy.

Kira was fortunate when she began revising. Her first draft had many strengths, which members of her writing group had acknowledged. But they had suggestions for improvement as well. A number of them commented in their closing notes that her abrupt shift in paragraph 6 to a strong statement of her love for Josh and Timmy confused them since it conflicted with her previous emphasis on all the "work and trouble" involved in caring for the two boys. This potential contradiction also made it difficult for Kira's readers to grasp the significance of her final paragraph; several commented that they weren't sure, finally, what point she was trying to make in this paragraph.

After Kira thought about her readers' responses to her draft, she met with a tutor and established the following priorities for revision:

To work on her introduction

To try to show more clearly why Josh and Timmy meant so much to her, despite all the work

To see if she could cut any of the housekeeping detail

To play with style a bit

Kira nicely identifies several ways that she could improve the focus, organization, and content of her essay. It's not possible to show all the stages that Kira's draft went through, for this process involved many scribbles, inserts, and crumpled papers. But the final draft (below) demonstrates that Kira's analysis enabled her truly to revise her essay, to "see again" how she could most effectively make her point. Here is Kira's revised essay with comments in the margin pointing out some of her most important changes.

THE BOYS OF SUMMER
by Kira Wennstrom

New intro-
duction gets
the reader's
attention.

(1)   Few teenagers get the chance to be parents, and for those who do, it's usually too
late to change their minds. One summer, though,
I was given the opportunity to become a
mother -- without the lifetime commitment.

(2)   When Josh and Timmy's mother had to go
into the hospital, she asked me if I would be
willing to stay with them until she could come
home. I quickly accepted, envisioning a few
days of playing "mommy" to the kids whose
babysitter I had been for about two years. However, my visions of happy homemaking paled when
the few days became two weeks and the trouble
and responsibility of being a parent began to
hit home.

Revised
paragraph
consolidates
details about
her situation
from three
draft para-
graphs.

(3)   Since the children were only five and
eight, I couldn't leave them alone in the house;
I had to be with them twenty-four hours a day.
While my friends swam and tanned at the lake, I
spent my days as a housewife: planning meals,
doing laundry, cleaning house. I handled all
the minor emergencies that seem to follow little boys around like shadows. There were fights
to be settled, Kool-Aid to be cleaned out of
the carpet, and once or twice pots and pans to
be rescued from the sandbox to cook dinner.

(4)   My days were whittled away with meals, dishes, and mountains of laundry. I did a load of wash almost every other day and just barely kept up. I was also amazed by the complexities of working out a simple dinner schedule. There was no single entree that both boys approved of, and it was like walking hot coals to try to serve anything new. They would sooner have starved, I think, than eat anything that didn't come out of a wrapper, box, or can. Most of all, though, I missed my privacy. Because the children were so dependent on me, I never had a moment to myself. I sometimes found it very difficult to force a smile when one of the boys interrupted a quiet moment with yet another demand on my time.

> Concise and balanced paragraph combines details on routine work from three draft paragraphs.

(5)   As the days passed and I became more proficient at running my little household, I began to realize a very surprising thing. Despite the trouble they caused, despite the demands they made, my two charges were becoming very special people to me -- people who needed me.

> Paragraph prepares readers for the shift from responsibilities to emotions.

(6)   I remember taking the boys to the beach one afternoon and buying them a corn-dog-and-soda lunch with Gummi worms for dessert. Josh, who was older than Timmy, loved the lake and delighted in swimming out just past the dock where the water was especially cool. Timmy was afraid to follow his brother and sat beside me on the sand, sucking on his last Gummi worm and looking wistfully out to where Josh was laughing and diving. After half an hour of this, Timmy touched me on the arm and said, "Take me to Josh, Kira."

> New dramatic scene *shows* readers Kira's deep feelings for the boys.

(7)   "Are you sure, Timmy?"

(8)   "Mm-hm. But hold on tight to me."

(9)   So I held on tight to him, and we waded into Rainy Lake's cool green water. When we got out past the point where Timmy could touch bottom, he locked his arms around my neck and pressed his face against my shoulder, but he didn't ask me to take him back. As we neared the spot where Josh was playing, I called, and he swam over to us. We splashed each other and

giggled, and Timmy clutched me with one hand and Josh with the other. Their bodies were slick like seals, warm against me in the chill lake water. Together we swam out to where none of us could touch bottom, and they held on to me to keep afloat. They trusted me to keep them safe, and I would have drowned before I broke that trust. I loved them.

(10)   Because I loved them, the children had a hold on me like nothing else I know. Simply by going out to play each day, they gave me more hours of worry than I like to admit. Every time one of them was late coming home, I imagined all the dreadful things that might be happening -- an angry dog, a child molester, a car accident -- until he walked through the door, perfectly safe and wanting supper. When one of them was angry or hurt, I hurt. They were children, and it's so hard to be a child sometimes -- almost as hard as being a mother.

Paragraph adds detail that helps clarify Kira's feelings.

(11)   My own mother, whom I telephoned with great regularity, seemed to find enormous delight in the fact that I was going through the same things she had been trying (and failing) to explain to me for seventeen-odd years. She gave me marvelous suggestions on how to cope with the demands of my new family and then, I am sure, hung up the phone and laughed her socks off in utter vindictiveness. But I can forgive her this because, although I didn't know it then, what I was experiencing was invaluable.

Mother is an effective new transition that connects paragraphs.

(12)   I look at mothers, especially my own, with better understanding now, with less scorn. I look at children with a little more appreciation. I use my time alone more carefully now; I spend it wisely, now that I know how crucial it is. Most of all, I value my freedom more highly than ever because I know what it is to give up that freedom. As much as I cared about those children, it's not time yet to let others make such claims on my life. I understand now how important it is to live for yourself before you live for anyone else.

Conclusion now has greater impact and complexity.

Kira's revision is successful, I'm sure you'll agree. She combined and deemphasized the details about how hard she worked — details that misdirected some of her readers and were also somewhat repetitive. She added paragraph 10 to explain her feelings for Josh and Timmy. And the scene at the beach, another important addition, gave concreteness and immediacy to these feelings. The resulting essay is a penetrating exploration of the rewards, and the demands, of caring for children.

■ ■ ■

FOR THOUGHT, DISCUSSION, AND WRITING

1. To study your own revision process, number and save all your plans, drafts, and revisions for a paper you're currently writing or have written recently. After you have completed the paper, review these materials, paying particular attention to the revisions you made. Can you describe the revision strategies that you followed and identify ways to improve the effectiveness of this process? Your instructor may ask you to write an essay discussing what you have learned as a result of this analysis.

2. Ellen Goodman said that for her, revision is "like cleaning house." Take ten or fifteen minutes to make your own list of possible analogies for revision. Is revision for you like tuning a motor? Pruning a plant? Later, return to this list, and decide which analogy best expresses your process of revising. Develop this analogy in one or two paragraphs.

3. Interview two students in your class about their revision strategies. How do their revision strategies reflect their preferred composing styles? How are their strategies similar to and different from your own? How do these students feel about revising, and how do their feelings compare with your own? Can you apply any of the strategies they use in your own writing? What can you learn from these interviews about how revising works and about how you can improve your own revising process? Your instructor may ask you to write an essay summarizing the results of your interviews.

4. Here is a rough draft of an essay by Audrey Meier, a first-year writing student. Audrey's assignment was to write an essay about an experience that was important to her; she was asked both to describe the experience and to comment on its significance.

PINK LUNCH TICKETS
by Audrey Meier

Growing up on welfare has had lasting effects on me and how I've developed as a person. I grew up with a lot of shame, which turned to anger and eventually became a chip on my shoulder. More important, however, living in poverty has given me a different perspective on life.

In elementary school I had pink lunch tickets instead of yellow. Pink lunch tickets were for free lunches; yellow were for kids whose parents paid for them. I knew that my pink lunch tickets meant that I was different, or bad, so I'd hold the pink ticket in my fist until my sweat made the perforated edges soft and fuzzy. I'd drop it in the bowl as fast as possible and not look back. My mom always said not to let anyone know we were getting public assistance, but in a town of 711 people gossip flies. I was ashamed to use a medical card to get my teeth cleaned. I was afraid that someone might learn our secret.

As I got older, the shame twisted in me and left a sizable chip on my shoulder. I wondered why, when it was my turn to bring treats to Girl Scout meetings, it was a burden on our food budget. Why didn't I get school pictures like my friends, and get stuck holding the chalk-board instead? Why couldn't I have piano lessons and voice lessons and hate practicing like my friend Jessica?

The bitterness really sunk in when I learned that to get anywhere I had to have money. Not just the leftover coins from food stamps, but disposable income. Even now when I hear piano music, I think that could have been me playing a concerto. But because my parents couldn't afford lessons, I'll never know what I could have become.

This summer I rented a piano for two months and took five lessons — which was all I could afford. Even though I have residual bitterness toward people who have it easier, I'd like to think I appreciated those five lessons more than if they were just handed to me. Besides, there were *always* people worse off than I was. Most of the time I hated being on welfare, but at least I was well fed and cared for.

Now as a college student I find that coming from a low-income family has its benefits — full financial aid. I'm working hard at my education: I don't want my children to live through the shame and bitterness I experienced. I want to raise them with everything I couldn't have, but I don't want them to take their advantages for granted. I want them to have something money can't buy: perspective.

Now that you have read Audrey's essay, turn back to pp. 273–74 in this chapter, which describe descriptive and analytical responses to work in progress. Using the prompts on p. 273, first write brief descriptive responses to this essay. Then turn to the discussion of analytical response on pp. 273–74. Using the prompts for "believing and doubting" and the questions for "Skeleton Feedback," analyze Meier's essay. (Alternatively, you could construct a descriptive outline of this essay, following the directions presented on p. 281.)

5. Bring your descriptive and analytical responses to "Pink Lunch Tickets" to class. Working with a group of students, first discuss your responses to this essay, addressing each of the prompts in turn. As you do so, pay particular attention to similarities and differences in group members' responses. Next, make a list of the three major points of agreement in your responses to Meier's essay and then of three major points of disagreement. Finally, discuss the process of providing descriptive and analytical responses to this essay. Did the essay seem to lend itself better to one kind of response or another? How about group members' preferences? Did group members find one kind of response more comfortable or productive than another? Finally, agree on one or two things you have learned about responding to work in progress as a result of this experience.

Strategies for Revising Structure and Style

Revision is a demanding but rewarding process. Chapter 10 presented suggestions for managing the process of revision effectively and efficiently. Chapter 11 provides strategies for revising structure and style. These strategies are designed to help you evaluate and revise your work.

As you read this chapter, remember that decisions about structure and style, even about a single word, always require that you consider *context*. To decide whether a sentence is awkwardly written, for instance, you must look not just at that sentence but also at the surrounding paragraph.

From the moment you begin thinking about a writing project until you make your last revision, you must be an analyst and decision maker. Even though some decisions may seem minor, together they determine the character and the effectiveness of your writing.

ASKING THE BIG QUESTIONS: REVISING FOR FOCUS, CONTENT, AND ORGANIZATION

When you revise a draft, begin by asking yourself the big, important questions — questions about your essay's focus, content, and organization. These questions are big because they challenge you to consider the degree to which your essay has fulfilled its most significant goals. If you discover — as writers often do — that your essay has not achieved its original purpose or that your purpose evolved as you wrote, you will make major changes in your draft, changes that will significantly affect the meaning of your essay.

Asking the big questions first is a practical approach to revising. You will only waste your time if you spend half an hour revising a paragraph that you will eventually delete because it doesn't contribute to your essay's main point. Furthermore, once you are confident that the overall focus, content, and organization of your essay are satisfactory, you will be better able to recognize less significant, but still important, stylistic problems.

Use the questions in the following guidelines to assess the effectiveness of your draft's focus, content, and organization.

■ GUIDELINES FOR EVALUATING FOCUS, CONTENT, AND ORGANIZATION

Focus

- What do you hope to accomplish in this essay? How clearly have you defined — and communicated — your controlling purpose?

- How does your essay represent an appropriate response to your rhetorical situation? If it is an academic essay, how does it fulfill the requirements of the assignment?

- Have you tried to do too much in this essay? Or are your goals too limited and inconsequential?

- How does your essay respond to the needs, interests, and expectations of your readers?

Content

- How does your essay develop or support your controlling purpose? How does it fulfill the commitment stated or implied by your controlling purpose?

- What supporting details or evidence have you provided for your most important generalizations? Are these supporting details and evidence adequate? Do they relate clearly to your controlling purpose and to each other?

- What additional details, evidence, or counterarguments might strengthen your essay?

- Have you included any material that is irrelevant to your purpose?

Organization

- What overall organizational strategy does your essay follow?

- Have you tested the effectiveness of this strategy by outlining or summarizing your essay?

- What is the relationship between the organization of your essay and your controlling purpose?

(continued)

(continued)

- Is this relationship clear to readers? How? What cues have you provided to make the organization clear and easy to follow?

- Does your essay follow the general conventions appropriate for this kind of writing?

- How could your introduction and conclusion be made more effective?

Here is how one student, Todd Carpenter, used these questions to establish goals for revision. Todd was responding to the following assignment: "Write a two- to three-page argumentative essay on a subject of your own choice. Consider your instructor and your classmates the primary readers of your essay." Todd described his rhetorical situation in these terms:

> I am writing an argumentative essay for my composition class. I want to convince my readers — my instructor and my classmates — that our government should institute a national bottle law. Oregon is one of the nine states that currently have bottle laws, so most students in the class may already agree with me about this law's importance. (Since Oregon has had a bottle bill for more than twenty years, students may not realize how important it is.) But because this is an essay for my writing class, I've got to present an unbiased view. Even if my instructor agrees that there should be a national bottle law, she won't give me a good grade unless I write an effective argument. In class, my instructor has stressed the importance of looking at both sides of the issue and presenting evidence for my views, so I'll try to do that here.

Todd Carpenter's First Draft

WHY ISN'T THERE A NATIONAL BOTTLE LAW?

```
(1)      Our country faces an important problem,
     yet it's one that few people take seriously --
     what to do with the bottles and cans we use
     daily. When thrown away, bottles and cans cause
     pollution, increase the volume of solid wastes,
     waste energy, and use up natural resources. To
     control these problems only nine states have
     adopted bottle laws. What a shame.
```

(2)   If you're like me, you're tired of walking
down streets and seeing fast-food wrappers,
bottles, and cans. Last week I went to the
coast and found a beautiful isolated beach. It
was great until I came upon some hamburger
boxes and beer bottles. This happened with a
bottle law. Think how much worse things would
be if Oregon didn't have a bottle law.

(3)   Bottle laws are important because they
require recycling, and recycling reduces pollution and solid waste. Recycling aluminum
reduces air emissions associated with aluminum
production by 96 percent. Solid waste would
reduce as aluminum and glass are eliminated
from landfills. Also, a large percentage of the
pollution on and around streets and highways is
bottles and cans. If these cans and bottles
were worth some money, people would be less
likely to throw them away.

(4)   Extracting aluminum ore requires twenty
times as much electricity as recycling the
metal. Therefore, if we recycled more aluminum,
then less aluminum would have to be extracted.
This would save enough energy to provide electrical power for at least two million people
annually.

(5)   Bottle laws are currently effective in
Oregon, Vermont, Maine, Michigan, Iowa, Connecticut, Delaware, Massachusetts, and New
York. These laws work largely because of the
legislation's support by the people. Of the
Americans polled, 73 percent would support such
bottle laws. Some people are getting tired of
the environment being polluted and abused and
now realize that this planet and its resources
are finite. Aluminum is a natural resource and
without recycling we will eventually run out.

(6)   With all the people in favor and the obvious environmental reasons supporting it, one
would think that a national bottle law would
have started long ago. But some people just
don't want to bother with saving their containers, and it is a lot easier to just throw them
away, despite the fact that they're worth five

cents each. Steel and aluminum companies
unfairly attack bottle bill laws -- and so do
supermarkets. These biased efforts must be
stopped now.

(7)   Although 54 percent of the aluminum beverage cans made and used in the U.S. are recycled
at more than twenty-five hundred recycling centers, this could be increased to as much as 90
percent by requiring a national bottle law.
Instead of considering unions' and companies'
losses for a basis of decision on the bottle
law, we should consider the ecological gains.
In the future, a few dollars saved will mean
nothing compared to a polluted and destroyed
environment society will face without recycling.

Using the questions about focus, content, and organization earlier in this chapter, Todd analyzed his draft. His analysis revealed that his essay would be more effective if he made several important changes. Here is Todd's analysis of his essay.

Focus: My essay needs to be focused on a single subject, and I think it is, but I don't indicate my controlling purpose clearly enough at the start of my essay. I can also see that paragraph 2 gets off track because it talks about litter in general, not just the need for a bottle law. I should revise or drop this paragraph. I also may need to drop the last sentence of paragraph 6. It may get off track, too.

I tried to emphasize evidence in writing this draft, but I think I need to provide more. I need to talk more about the reasons why some companies and supermarkets attack bottle bills, and I should try to present their side of the issue also.

Content: The focus questions already helped me see that I need to revise paragraph 2 and add more evidence. I also don't describe how bottle laws work — and I should.

Organization: I think the basic organization of my essay is OK. I don't think that I have to make big changes in the structure of my essay. I just have to provide more information and take out some details that don't fit.

I'm not sure about my introduction and conclusion — maybe they could be better. I'll work on the rest of the essay and decide later.

By using the questions about focus, content, and organization to analyze his rough draft, Todd was able to set the following priorities for revising:

Stating his controlling purpose early in his essay

Cutting unnecessary material

Adding evidence in support of his position

Explaining how bottle laws work

Checking to be sure he's considered both sides of the argument

In analyzing his essay, Todd also realized that his introduction and conclusion might be made more effective. Given the importance of the other changes he needed to make, however, Todd put off working on the opening and closing paragraphs. Once he made the major changes his analysis called for, he could look again at his introduction and conclusion.

■ ■ ■

FOR EXPLORATION

Here is the revised version of Todd Carpenter's essay. Read the essay carefully, noting the major changes that Todd made as he revised. Write down the two or three most important changes. Finally, reread the essay with an eye for ways this essay could be improved further. Write down one or two suggestions for further revision.

WHY ISN'T THERE A NATIONAL BOTTLE LAW?
by Todd Carpenter

What do you do with your empty cans and bottles? There are two choices, throwing them away or recycling. Throwing away an aluminum beverage container wastes as much energy as filling a can with gasoline and pouring half out. Besides wasting energy, throwing away bottles and cans causes pollution, increases the volume of solid wastes, and uses up natural resources. To control these problems, only nine states have adopted bottle laws. The United States government should require every state to have a bottle law or institute a national bottle law.

To understand how a bottle law can help, you must know how it works. When consumers buy canned or bottled beverages at the store, they pay deposits. This deposit can range from five to twenty cents per bottle or can. In order to get this deposit back, the bottles and cans must be returned to a supermarket after they are emptied. The supermarkets then return the bottles and cans to their manufacturers for either reuse or recycling.

Recycling plays a significant role in reducing pollution and solid waste. Recycling aluminum reduces air emissions associated with aluminum production by 96 percent. Solid waste is also reduced as aluminum and glass are eliminated from landfills. Finally, a large percentage of the pollution on and around the streets and highways is bottles and cans. If these could be returned to supermarkets for cash, people would be less likely to throw them away.

Extracting aluminum ore requires twenty times as much electricity as recycling the metal. Therefore, if we recycled more aluminum, less aluminum ore would have to be extracted. This could save enough energy to provide electrical power for at least two million people annually.

Bottle laws are currently in effect in Oregon, Vermont, Maine, Michigan, Iowa, Connecticut, Delaware, Massachusetts, and New York. These laws work largely because the general public supports them. A recent poll of Americans revealed that 73 percent support bottle laws. This support undoubtedly results from people's concern about pollution and our planet's limited resources.

Given the large number of people in favor of bottle laws, you might expect that we would already have a national bottle law. But a vocal minority of people don't want to bother with saving their containers, so they oppose such legislation. Some supermarket chains also lobby against bottle laws; they don't want to have to deal with all the cans that people would bring to them. I understand these individuals' concerns. Recycling bottles and cans does require extra effort from consumers and distributors. The larger economic and ecological issues indicate that this extra effort is worthwhile.

Finally, steel and aluminum companies and metal workers' unions oppose bottle laws because they fear they would cause cuts in their production and therefore affect jobs and wages. EPA and General Accounting studies estimate, however, that a national bottle law would produce a net increase of eighty thousand to one hundred thousand jobs, so these fears are misplaced.

Although 54 percent of the aluminum beverage cans made and used in the U.S. are currently recycled at more than twenty-five hundred recycling centers, we could increase this to as much as 90 percent by requiring a national bottle law. Instead of worrying about the inconvenience and possible economic consequences of instituting a national bottle law, we should consider the ecological gains. In the future, a little time saved will mean nothing compared to a polluted and destroyed environment.

■ ■ ■

FOR EXPLORATION

Use the guidelines for evaluating your focus, content, and organization to evaluate the draft of an essay you are currently working on. Respond as specifically and as concretely as possible, and then take a few moments to reflect on what you have learned about your draft. Finally, make a list of goals for revising.

KEEPING YOUR READERS ON TRACK: REVISING FOR COHERENCE

Most writers are aware that paragraphs and essays need to be unified — that they should focus on a single topic. You know, for instance, that if you interrupt a paragraph on the benefits of walking as a form of exercise with a sentence praising your favorite walking shoes, your readers will be confused and irritated. You may not be aware, however, that a paragraph or an essay can be unified and yet still present difficulties for readers. These difficulties arise when a paragraph or essay lacks coherence.

Writing is *coherent* when readers can move easily from word to word, sentence to sentence, and paragraph to paragraph. When writing is coherent, readers are often unaware that writers are giving them signals or cues that enable them to stay on track when they read; the writing just seems to flow. Writers have various means of achieving coherence. Some methods, such as *repeating key words and sentence structures* and using *pronouns* to refer to antecedent nouns, reinforce or emphasize the logical development of ideas. Another method is to use *transitional words*. Words like *but, although,* and *because* function as directions for readers; they tell readers what to do as they read. A sentence beginning with "For example" tells readers that this sentence will substantiate or exemplify a preceding point, not introduce a new idea or concept.

The following introduction to "Home Town," an essay by Ian Frazier, uses all of these methods to help keep readers on track. The most important means of achieving coherence are italicized. (As you read this paragraph, notice the unusual sentence structure that Frazier employs in the long fifth sentence, which describes the melting of a glacier. What stylistic reason might Frazier have had for constructing this sentence in this manner?)

> *When glaciers* covered much of northern Ohio, the land around Hudson, the town where I grew up, lay under one. *Glaciers* came and went several times, the most recent departing about 14,000 years ago. *When* we studied *glaciers* in an Ohio-history class in grade school, I imagined our *glac-*

ier receding smoothly, like a sheet pulled off a new car. *Actually, glaciers can move forward but they don't back up — they melt in place. Most likely the glacier* above Hudson softened, *and* began to trickle underneath; rocks on its surface absorbed sunlight and melted tunnels into *it; it* rotted, *it* dwindled, *it* dripped, *it* ticked; *then it* dropped a pile of the sand and rocks *it* had been carrying around for centuries onto the ground in a heap. Hudson's landscape was hundreds of these little heaps — hills rarely big enough to sled down, a random arrangement made by gravity and smoothed by weather and time.

— IAN FRAZIER, "HOME TOWN"

Most writers concern themselves with coherence *after* writing a rough draft and determining that the essay's focus, content, and organization are effective. At this point, the writer can attend to fine tuning, making changes that enable readers to move through the writing easily and enjoyably.

When you read work in progress to determine how you can strengthen its coherence, use your common sense. Your writing is coherent if readers know where they have been and where they are going as they read. Don't assume that your writing will be more coherent if you sprinkle transitions liberally throughout your prose. The logic of your discussion may not require numerous transitions; in such a case, adding them will only clutter up your writing. For example, the following introduction to an article published in *Yo! Youth Outlook,* a journal by and for youth in the San Francisco Bay Area, has relatively few explicit transitions. Rather, the author (who uses the pen name Atom) relies on logical relationships to keep the reader on track.

The guy on the billboard looks like me: twentysomething; clad in baggy cut-offs, a T-shirt and tennies; scraggly hair hanging in his face. But he's not me. I'm a former bike messenger who's held onto the look but is trying to avoid the profession, due to its life-endangering aspects. He's a fashion model in a Calvin Klein ad, projecting a studied hip indifference while marketing upscale versions of my clothes that I couldn't possibly afford.

Maybe Calvin and his peers in the fashion industry have noticed that a large percentage of young people today have jobs, not careers, and are sporting comfy, utilitarian togs in our pursuit of service sector nirvana. Or maybe the fashion industry is just moving on to the next slack thing, now that grunge is dead and flannel has been reclaimed by its traditional champions in agriculture and marketing.

But marketing thrift-store clothes as high-priced high fashion is something of a paradox. Young folks who aren't proceeding directly to the boardroom don inexpensive apparel out of necessity rather than trendiness. Fifteen bucks for a white T-shirt that'll probably be stained with bike grease and spilled coffee within an hour? Calvin's gotta be kidding.

Fifteen dollars is two or three hours' work for the average bicycle delivery specialist or espresso jockey.

— Atom, "The Bike Messenger Look Goes High Fashion"

The logic of this essay's introduction is so clear that readers need relatively few explicit transitions: The first paragraph contrasts the "guy on the billboard" with the author of the essay; the second paragraph speculates on reasons why the bike messenger look has suddenly become fashionable; the third paragraph explores the paradox that most young people cannot afford to purchase the high-fashion versions of their own preferred dress. Such transitions as *but, or,* and *now* provide all the cues that readers need to keep on track.

Revision for coherence proceeds more effectively if you look first at large-scale issues, such as the relationship among your essay's introduction, body, and conclusion, before considering smaller concerns. When you revise for coherence, follow these steps.

■ GUIDELINES FOR REVISING FOR COHERENCE

- Read your draft quickly to determine if it flows smoothly. Pay particular attention to the movement from introduction to body and conclusion. How could you tighten or strengthen these connections?

- Now read slowly, paying close attention to the movement from paragraph to paragraph. How do new paragraphs build on or connect with previous paragraphs? Would more explicit connections, such as transitions, help readers better understand your ideas?

- Finally, read each paragraph separately. How do your word choice and sentence structure help readers progress from sentence to sentence? Would repeating key words or using pronouns or adding transitions increase a paragraph's coherence?

EXPLORING STYLISTIC OPTIONS

"Proper words in proper places" — that is how the eighteenth-century writer Jonathan Swift defined style. Swift's definition, though intentionally abstract, is accurate. Writing style reflects all of the choices that a writer makes, from global questions of approach and organization to the smallest details about punctuation and grammar. In this sense, *all* of the decisions that you make as a writer are stylistic decisions.

As Swift's definition indicates, style is an elusive yet essential feature of texts. It is difficult to articulate — or consciously to control — all the decisions that influence a writer's style. When proper words *are* in proper places, readers are able to follow the writer's ideas with understanding and interest. In addition, they probably have some sense of the person behind the words, the writer's presence.

We often associate style with the personal, referring, for instance, to a person's style of dress or style of interacting with others. And a writer's style does reflect his or her individual taste and sensibility. But just as people dress differently for different occasions, so too do writers vary their style, depending on their rhetorical situation. Just as you may choose to dress conservatively for a job interview, for instance, so too may you decide that certain rhetorical situations call for a writing style that does not call great attention to itself. When you are writing an essay examination, for instance, you know that your instructor is primarily interested in your ability to write intelligently about a subject. A style that calls attention to itself might interfere with, not promote, communication.

Effective writers vary their style to suit their rhetorical situation. As they do so, they are particularly attentive to the *persona,* or voice, they convey through their writing. Sometimes writers present strong and distinctive voices. Here, for instance, is the beginning of an essay by the novelist Ken Kesey on the Pendleton Round-Up, a Northwest rodeo.

> My father took me up the Gorge and over the hills to my first one thirty-five years ago. It was on my fourteenth birthday. I had to miss a couple of days' school plus the possibility of suiting up for the varsity game that Friday night. Gives you some idea of the importance Daddy placed on this event.
>
> For this is more than just a world-class rodeo. It is a week-long shindig, a yearly rendezvous dating back beyond the first white trappers, a traditional powwow ground for the Indian nations of the Northwest for nobody knows how many centuries.
>
> — KEN KESEY, "THE BLUE-RIBBON AMERICAN BEAUTY ROSE OF RODEO"

Kesey's word choice and sentence structure help create an image of the writer as folksy, relaxed, and yet also forceful — just the right insider to write about a famous rodeo.

In other situations, writers don't wish to present a distinctive personal voice, as in the following introduction to an article in *Sky & Telescope* that explores a cooperative effort being undertaken by software vendors.

> Not all astronomical software is created equal. Some have features that others do not. Consequently, much as a carless commuter may have to make multiple transfers with public transportation to arrive at a destina-

tion, performing all the actions desired for a night's observing may require several programs. Make your finder chart with one program, point the telescope with another, take some CCD images with a third, and process them with yet a fourth. Imagine how much more productive you could be if such steps could be performed in a seamless flow.

— JEFF MEDKEFF, "THE ASCOM REVOLUTION"

■ ■ ■

FOR EXPLORATION

From a newspaper, magazine, or book that you are currently reading, choose one passage that presents a distinctive personal voice. Choose another passage that presents a more anonymous public voice. Then answer these questions in writing:

1. How would you describe the voice evoked by each passage?

2. How does the author of each passage succeed in creating this voice? (Cite specific examples to support your analysis.)

3. Write several sentences explaining how you respond personally to each of these passages.

If you think rhetorically, always asking yourself questions about your rhetorical situation, you will naturally consider such major stylistic issues as the voice you wish your writing to convey to readers. Look again at the guidelines for analyzing a rhetorical situation on p. 147. These guidelines pose questions that can help you determine the appropriate style for specific situations. You may also find it helpful to review the discussion of Aristotle's three appeals — *logos, pathos,* and *ethos* on p. 156. Considering the degree to which you wish to draw on appeals to reason *(logos),* emotion *(pathos),* and your own credibility as writer *(ethos)* will help you consider your own voice and your relationship with readers.

REVISING FOR EFFECTIVE PROSE STYLE

In addition to considering such major stylistic issues as the voice you wish to convey to readers, you will also need to make a number of smaller but no less important stylistic decisions. Some of these decisions you will make consciously. When you study several sentences to determine which provides the most effective transition from one paragraph to the next, you are consciously considering an aspect of style. Other decisions are only partly conscious. When you write a word, strike it out, and write another, you are making a stylistic choice — even if you are only partly aware of the reasons why you prefer the latter word over the former.

The choices you make as you draft and revise reflect not only your understanding of your rhetorical situation but also your awareness of general principles of effective prose style, principles that apply to much academic and professional writing. Perhaps the easiest way to understand these principles is to analyze a passage that illustrates effective prose style in action.

Here are two paragraphs from the first chapter of a psycholinguistics textbook. As you read these paragraphs, imagine that you have been assigned to read them for a course in psycholinguistics, an interdisciplinary field that studies linguistic behavior and the psychological mechanisms that make verbal communication possible.

(1) Language stands at the center of human affairs, from the most prosaic to the most profound. (2) It is used for haggling with store clerks, telling off umpires, and gossiping with friends as well as for negotiating contracts, discussing ethics, and explaining religious beliefs. (3) It is the medium through which the manners, morals, and mythology of a society are passed on to the next generation. (4) Indeed, it is a basic ingredient in virtually every social situation. (5) The thread that runs through all these activities is communication, people trying to put their ideas over to others. (6) As the main vehicle of human communication, language is indispensable.

(7) Communication with language is carried out through two basic human activities: speaking and listening. (8) These are of particular importance to psychologists, for they are mental activities that hold clues to the very nature of the human mind. (9) In speaking, people put ideas into words, talking about perceptions, feelings, and intentions they want other people to grasp. (10) In listening, they turn words into ideas, trying to reconstruct the perceptions, feelings, and intentions they were meant to grasp. (11) Speaking and listening, then, ought to reveal something fundamental about the mind and how it deals with perceptions, feelings, and intentions. (12) Speaking and listening, however, are more than that. (13) They are the tools people use in more global activities. (14) People talk in order to convey facts, ask for favors, and make promises, and others listen in order to receive this information. (15) These actions in turn are the pieces out of which casual conversations, negotiations, and other social exchanges are formed. (16) So speaking and listening ought to tell us a great deal about social and cultural activities too.

— HERBERT H. CLARK AND EVE V. CLARK, *PSYCHOLOGY AND LANGUAGE*

These two paragraphs, you would probably agree, do embody effective prose style. They are clearly organized. Each paragraph begins with a topic sentence, which the rest of the paragraph explains. The paragraphs are also coherent, with pronouns, key words, and sentence patterns helping readers proceed. But what most distinguishes these two paragraphs, what makes them so effective, is the authors' use of concrete, precise, economical language and carefully crafted sentences.

Suppose that the first paragraph were revised as follows. What would be lost?

> (1) Language stands at the center of human affairs, from the most prosaic to the most profound. (2) It is a means of human communication. (3) It is a means of cultural change and regeneration. (4) It is found in every social situation. (5) The element that characterizes all these activities is communication. (6) As the main vehicle of human communication, language is indispensable.

This revision communicates roughly the same ideas as the original paragraph, but it lacks that paragraph's liveliness and interest. Instead of presenting vivid examples — "haggling with store clerks, telling off umpires, and gossiping with friends" — sentences 2, 3, 4, and 5 state only vague generalities. Moreover, these sentences are short and monotonous. Also lost in the revision is any sense of the authors' personalities, as revealed in their writing. The original examples not only describe how language is used but also convey to readers a sense of the authors' character and interests.

As this example demonstrates, effective prose style doesn't have to be flashy or call attention to itself. The focus in the original passage is on the *ideas* being discussed. The authors don't want readers to stop and think, "My, what a lovely sentence." But they do want their readers — students required to read their book for a course — to become interested in and engaged with their ideas. So they use strong verbs and vivid, concrete examples whenever possible. They pay careful attention to sentence structure, alternating sequences of sentences with parallel structures (sentences 2, 3, and 4 as well as sentences 9 and 10) with other, more varied sentences. They take care that the relationships among ideas are clear. In both paragraphs, for example, the first and last sentences (which readers are most likely to remember) articulate the most important ideas. As a result of these and other choices, these two paragraphs succeed in being both economical and emphatic.

Exploring your stylistic options — developing a style that reflects your understanding of yourself and the world and your feel for language — is one of the pleasures of writing. The following guidelines will help you revise your own writing for structure and style.

■ GUIDELINES FOR REVISING STRUCTURE
AND STYLE

1. *Vary the Length and Structure of Your Sentences.* If you look again
at the paragraphs from the psycholinguistics textbook (p. 306),
you will notice that the authors vary the length and structure of
their sentences. In the first paragraph, for instance, the initial sentence is followed by a much longer sentence with multiple examples of the ways in which language "stands at the center of human
affairs." The third and fourth sentences, while briefer than the second, are linked to it by their repetition of "it is" at the start of each
sentence. Such repetition is helpful, for these sentences serve primarily to expand on the idea presented at the start of the paragraph. The authors are careful, however, to vary the structure of
the fifth and sixth sentences, which emphasize the extent to which
"language is indispensable."

Now contrast this paragraph with the following excerpt from
an essay urging students to use coupons when they shop:

(1) Almost everywhere you look, there are coupons. (2) Daily newspapers are probably the best sources for coupons. (3) The *Oregonian* and
the *Barometer* have coupons every day. (4) The *Gazette-Times* has
coupons too. (5) The Sunday *Oregonian* is loaded with coupons.
(6) Some of the sources that are not so obvious may be coupon trader
bins in groceries and flyers handed out in dorms. (7) The backs of store
receipts and coupons on boxes or other items you have previously pur-
chased are also common.

The sentences in this paragraph lack variety. Sentences 2, 3, and
4 are all roughly the same length; they also follow the same subject-
verb-object structure. (All also employ either "be" or "have" verbs.)
Because the information they express is so obvious — each simply
indicates a possible source of coupons — these sentences seem repetitive. The final two sentences break this pattern, but they are
awkward and hard to follow.

See how this paragraph could be revised to be much more effective:

(1) You may be surprised by how easy it is to find coupons. (2) Daily
newspapers, such as the *Oregonian*, the *Gazette-Times*, and the *Barometer,* are probably the best sources for coupons. (3) If you don't want to
purchase a daily paper, the Sunday *Oregonian*, which is loaded with

(continued)

(continued)

coupons, may be the next best choice. (4) Don't just look for coupons in newspapers, however. (5) You can also watch for special coupon bins in grocery stores and for flyers used to distribute coupons in dorms. (6) You can even discover coupons on the backs of store receipts or on the boxes or packages from other purchases.

You may have noticed that the revised paragraph changes more than sentence length and structure. The wording of the first sentence is now more emphatic. The final two sentences are more direct because they begin with *you,* the subject of the action. Finally, added transitions clarify the relationships among ideas in the paragraph. As this revision shows, even though you may be revising with a particular purpose in mind (in this case to vary the sentences), revision usually involves a multitude of changes.

When you revise, you generally want to achieve an appropriate variety of sentence lengths and structures, one that carries readers forward with a clear yet unobtrusive rhythm. The following paragraph from a student essay on salmon fishing illustrates this accomplishment.

Picture yourself in a scenic river setting. The fall colors are at their peak, and shades of burnt red and copper gold brighten up the shoreline. The crisp, clean smell of fall is in the air, and a gentle breeze blows lightly against your face. Off in the distance you hear the sound of swift white water thundering over massive boulders until it gradually tames into slower-moving pools of crystal green. As you look out across the river, the smooth glassy surface is momentarily interrupted as a large salmon leaps free of its natural element.

You may at times want to use more dramatic sentence structures to emphasize a point. Here, for instance, is the first paragraph of Ian Frazier's book-length exploration of the heartland of America:

Away to the Great Plains of America, to that immense Western short-grass prairie now mostly plowed under! Away to the still-empty land beyond newsstands and malls and velvet restaurant ropes! Away to the headwaters of the Missouri, now quelled by many impoundment dams, and to the headwaters of the Platte, and to the almost invisible head-waters of the slurped-up Arkansas! Away to the land where TV used to set its most popular dramas, but not anymore! Away to the land beyond the hundredth meridian of longitude, where sometimes it rains and sometimes it doesn't, where agriculture stops and does a double take!

(continued)

(continued)

Away to the skies of sparrow hawks sitting on telephone wires, thinking of mice and flaring their tail feathers suddenly, like a card trick! Away to the air shaft of the continent, where weather fronts from two hemispheres meet, and the wind blows almost all the time! Away to the fields of wheat and milo and sudan grass and flax and alfalfa and nothing! Away to parts of Montana and North Dakota and South Dakota and Wyoming and Nebraska and Kansas and Colorado and New Mexico and Oklahoma and Texas! Away to the high plains rolling in waves to the rising final chord of the Rocky Mountains!

— IAN FRAZIER, *GREAT PLAINS*

This dramatic paragraph encourages readers to abandon their conventional understandings of the Great Plains and reconsider this expansive region through Frazier's eyes. The contrast between Frazier's diction (which speaks of such mundane realities as "fields of wheat and milo and sudan grass") and his sentence structure, which is almost poetic in its intensity, establishes a tension that the rest of the book will explore.

Readers can hardly sustain such a dramatic and feverish pace, however, so just a few pages later Frazier's style shifts considerably:

The Great Plains are about 2,500 miles long, and about 600 miles across at their widest point. The area they cover roughly parallels the Rocky Mountains, which mark their western boundary. Although they extend from the Southwestern United States well into Canada, no single state or province lies entirely within them.

— IAN FRAZIER, *GREAT PLAINS*

This plainer, more conventional style is appropriate to Frazier's purpose, which is to provide readers with basic information about his subject.

2. *Use Language Appropriate to Your Purpose and Situation.* Look again at the two paragraphs from the psycholinguistics textbook on p. 306. One of the strengths of these two paragraphs is the *specific, concrete words* and examples. Rather than writing that language "is a means of human communication," the authors say that language "is used for haggling with store clerks, telling off umpires, and gossiping with friends as well as for negotiating contracts, discussing

(continued)

(continued)

ethics, and explaining religious beliefs." This sentence doesn't merely interest readers; it challenges them to pause and think about just how many ways they use language to communicate.

Specific, concrete words can give your writing power and depth. Such language isn't always appropriate, however. Sometimes you need to use *abstract* or *general terms* to convey your meaning. Abstract words — like *patriotism, love,* and *duty* — refer to ideas, beliefs, relationships, conditions, and acts that you can't perceive with your senses. General words designate a group. The word *computer* is general; the words *Macintosh iMac* identify a specific machine within that group.

Effective writing usually interweaves the specific and the concrete with the abstract and the general. The sentences in the paragraphs on psycholinguistics, for example, move back and forth from specific and concrete to general and abstract words and statements. After specifying and describing various ways people use language to communicate, the writers close the first paragraph with a much broader statement: "As the main vehicle of human communication, language is indispensable." Good writers use general and abstract language when appropriate — and for writing about intellectual problems or ideas or emotions, such language often is appropriate — but they balance abstract generalities with concrete, specific words and examples that give their ideas force and vigor.

Some writers overuse abstract, general words, perhaps assuming such words sound more intellectual, formal, or official. Here, for instance, is a paragraph from an essay analyzing *Sports Illustrated* (notice how vague much of the language is):

Sports Illustrated's articles are informative because its writers try to get information which nobody else knows. The articles explain how the subject is unique and how the subject became popular and successful. Articles are rarely negative. Most are positive and explain the good things in sports rather than emphasizing the negative aspects, such as drugs.

This paragraph leaves readers with more questions than answers. What does this writer mean when he calls articles "informative"? What kind of information that "nobody else knows" are writers for *Sports Illustrated* able to get? Just what kinds of subjects does the

(continued)

(continued)

publication cover? (Many magazines feature articles about subjects that are "unique," "popular," and "successful.") Does the magazine emphasize the human drama of competition, for example, or strategy, techniques, and statistics? Readers familiar with *Sports Illustrated* can probably use their prior knowledge to interpret this paragraph; others can only guess at the writer's intentions.

3. *Reduce Wordiness.* Readers can be impatient. They are reading for a reason — their reason, not yours — and they may well become irritated by unnecessary words or flabby sentences. Experienced writers read their work carefully when revising to determine if they can prune unnecessary words and sentences.

    In revising to eliminate wordiness, your goal is not necessarily to eliminate every possible word. Rather, your goal should be to ensure that *every word serves a purpose.* Words that are not strictly necessary can serve purposes of emphasis, rhythm, flow, or tone; the degree to which these are important to your writing is a question that can only be answered by considering your rhetorical situation and purpose.

    Words and phrases that add unnecessary length to your sentences without serving any rhetorical purpose are known as *deadwood,* and deadwood turns up in the drafts of even the most experienced writers. The revision phase is the time to concentrate on finding deadwood and clearing it out.

    While rereading an early draft of the second chapter of this book, for instance, I noticed the following sentence:

Rather than *attempting to determine a sequence of activities that you always follow when you write,* you should develop a range of strategies that you can employ at any point in the writing process.

The deadwood is italicized; see now how I revised the sentence:

Rather than following a rigid sequence of activities, you should develop a range of strategies that you can employ at any point in the writing process.

This revised sentence communicates the same idea as the original but uses significantly fewer words (twenty-six rather than thirty-

(continued)

(continued)

four). Like me, you will often discover wordy sentences when you reread your drafts. Don't be surprised at such discoveries. When you're struggling to express ideas, you can't expect to worry about being concise at the same time. Knowing this, however, you should be particularly alert for deadwood — words that clutter up your sentences and lessen their impact — when you revise.

Sometimes you can eliminate deadwood by deleting unnecessary words; in other cases, you may need to revise your sentence structure. The following examples of sentences clogged with deadwood are from early drafts of this textbook; I have italicized the unnecessary words. My revisions follow below the original sentence.

As you *work to improve your* writing, you can *benefit a great deal from* drawing on your *own* commonsense understanding of how people in our culture use language.

As you write, you can draw on your commonsense understanding of how people in our culture use language.

Your discussion with your instructor will be most profitable (for both of you) if you *have already done a fair amount of preparation before* the conference.

Your discussion with your instructor will be most profitable (for both of you) if you prepare for the conference.

One traditional way of viewing these disciplines is to see them as falling into one of the following *major* categories: sciences, humanities, and social sciences.

Most academic disciplines fall into one of the following categories: sciences, humanities, or social sciences.

These examples from my own writing emphasize that even experienced writers need to revise their writing to achieve an effective prose style. Placing "proper words in proper places" does require patience and commitment, but it is also one of the most rewarding parts of the writing process, for it ensures effective communication between writer and reader.

FOR THOUGHT, DISCUSSION, AND WRITING

1. From an essay you are currently working on, find a paragraph that lacks adequate coherence. Determine the main reasons why the paragraph lacks coherence. Then use the strategies discussed in this chapter to revise your paragraph.

2. From the same essay, choose two or three paragraphs that you suspect could be more stylistically effective. Using this chapter's discussion of style as a guide, revise these paragraphs.

3. Here is an essay written by Ian Frazier, whose introduction to *Great Plains* you read earlier in this chapter. This essay was published in *The New Yorker* magazine. Read the essay, and then answer the questions that follow it.

TO MR. WINSLOW
by Ian Frazier

On June first, in the afternoon, four teen-agers approached a forty-two-year-old drama teacher named Allyn Winslow on Quaker Hill, in Brooklyn's Prospect Park, and tried to steal his new mountain bike. When he resisted and rode away, they shot him four times with a .22-calibre pistol. He rode down the hill to the cobbled path leading to the Picnic House, fell off his bike, and died. The TV news that evening showed the bike on the grass, and his body, covered by a sheet, next to it. I recognized the spot where he lay. I take my daughter to the pond nearby to throw bread to the ducks. She and I had sat there, or near there.

I walked by the spot the next day. It was marked by a wad of discarded surgical tape and an inside-out surgical glove. The day after, when I went by there I saw a Timberland shoebox with a bouquet of flowers in it, and a glass wine carafe with more flowers. In the shoebox was a piece of lined paper on which someone had written in blue ink: "To the biker Mr. Winslow, May you be in a better place with angels on a cloud." These words echoed in the media as reporters quoted and misquoted them. Men and women were carrying microphones and TV cameras in the vicinity, and if you weren't careful they would interview you. About a week later, an American flag had been stuck into the ground next to the shoebox. There was a bunch of papers in a clear-plastic envelope, and the one on top said, "AVENGE THIS ACT OF COWARDICE." In and around the shoebox were notes addressed to Mr. Winslow and his wife and their two children; a blue-and-white striped ribbon; a ceramic pipe; a bike rider's reflector badge in the image of a peace sign; a red-and-white bandanna; a flyer from the Guardian Angels organization; and an announcement of an upcoming service to be held in his memory.

The following week, the accumulation around the shoebox had grown. The flowers in it and in the wine carafe were fresh — roses, peonies, yellow freesias. Someone had arranged many pinecones and sprigs of oak leaves in a circle on the perimeter. In the ground by the flag was a cross made of wood, bound with red ribbon and draped with a string of purple glass beads, and, near the cross, a photocopy of a newspaper photograph of Allyn Winslow. A Dover edition of Shakespeare's "Complete Sonnets" rested on a pedestal made of a cross-section of a branch from a London Plane tree. There were also several anti-N.R.A. stickers, a blue candle in a plastic cup, and a five of spades from a pack of Bicycle playing cards. Chunks of paving stones held down a poster showing the number of people killed in 1990 by handguns in various countries: thirteen in Sweden, ninety-one in Switzerland, eighty-seven in Japan, sixty-eight in Canada, ten thousand five hundred and sixty-seven in the United States. A girl visiting the park on a class picnic asked another girl, "Is he buried here?"

A week or two later, many of the items had vanished. Someone had burned the flag, but the charred flagpole remained. The cross, broken off at the base, lay on the ground. The plastic cup with the candle was cracked. The grass around the spot was worn down in a circle and littered with dried flower stems. The carafe had a big chip out of the top. The shoebox had begun to sag. The papers were gone, except for a rain-stained sign saying, "To Honor, To Mourn Allyn Winslow," and a pamphlet, "Verses of Comfort, Assurance and Salvation."

By mid-July, the shoebox was in pieces. There were a few rocks, two small forked branches stuck in the ground, the ashes of a small fire, and a "You gotta have Park!" button. By mid-August, the tramped-down grass had begun to grow back. I noticed a piece of red-and-white string and a scrap from the shoebox. By September, so little of the memorial remained that the spot was hard to find. A closer look revealed the burned patch, some red-and-white string now faded to pink, and flower stems so scattered and broken you'd have to know what they were to recognize them.

Just now — a bright, chilly fall day — I went by the place again. Color in the park's trees had reached its peak. In a grove of buckskin-brown oaks, yellow shot up the fountain of a ginkgo tree. A flock of pigeons rose all at once and glided to a new part of the Long Meadow, circling once before landing, like a dog before it lies down. A police car slipped around the corner of the Picnic House, a one-man police scooter rode down the path, a police helicopter flew by just above the trees. At first, I could find no trace of the memorial at all: grass and clover have reclaimed the bared dirt. I got down on one knee, muddying my pants. Finally, I found a wooden stake broken off about half an inch above the ground: the base of the memorial cross, probably — the only sign of the unmeasured sorrows that converge here.

- How would you describe the general style of this essay? Write three or four sentences describing its style.

- How would you describe the *persona* or voice conveyed by this essay? List at least three specific characteristics of the writer's voice, and then indicate several passages that you think particularly exemplify these characteristics.

- Find three passages from this essay that you believe demonstrate the principles of effective prose style as discussed in this chapter. Indicate the reasons why you believe each passage is stylistically effective.

- What additional comments could you make about the structure and style of this essay? Did anything about the style of this essay surprise you? Formulate at least one additional comment about the essay's structure and style.

4. Ian Frazier's essays are published in a variety of magazines, from *The New Yorker* to *The Atlantic Monthly* to *Audubon*. As has already been discussed, Frazier's style varies considerably depending on his topic, purpose, and rhetorical situation. Here, for instance, are the first two paragraphs of a humorous essay Frazier published in *The Atlantic Monthly* titled "Laws Concerning Food and Drink; Household Principles; Lamentations of the Father":

Of the beasts of the field, and of the fishes of the sea, and of all foods that are acceptable in my sight you may eat, but not in the living room. Of the hoofed animals, broiled or ground into burgers, you may eat, but not in the living room. Of the cloven-hoofed animal, plain or with cheese, you may eat, but not in the living room. Of the cereal grains, of the corn and of the wheat and of the oats, and of all the cereals that are of bright color and unknown provenance you may eat, but not in the living room. Of the quiescently frozen dessert and of all frozen after-meal treats you may eat, but absolutely not in the living room. Of the juices and other beverages, yes, even of those in sippy-cups, you may drink, but not in the living room, neither may you carry such therein. Indeed, when you reach the place where the living room carpet begins, of any food or beverage there you may not eat, neither may you drink.

But if you are sick, and are lying down and watching something, then may you eat in the living room.*

Spend a few minutes reflecting on the stylistic differences between this introduction and Frazier's "To Mr. Winslow." Then write several paragraphs explaining why the shift in style in this essay is appropriate.

5. You can learn a great deal about the effective use of style by reading a variety of works by the same author. Here are references for several additional essays by Ian Frazier, including the essay whose introduction you read for the preceding activity:

> Frazier, Ian. "Home Town." *The Atlantic Monthly.* Oct. 1994: 96+.
>
> ———. "Laws Concerning Food and Drink; Household Principles; Lamentations of the Father." *The Atlantic Monthly.* Feb. 1997: 89–90.
>
> ———. "Making Marks." *Audubon.* Nov.–Dec. 1996: 34+.
>
> ———. "The Positive Negative." *The Atlantic Monthly.* June 1997: 24+.
>
> ———. "Your Face or Mine." *The New Yorker.* 29 May 1995: 96.

Locate copies of these essays in the library, and read them with care. Once you have done so, write an essay discussing the relationship of style and content in Frazier's writing. In what ways does Frazier vary his style depending on the content of his article and his situation? What aspects of his style remain consistent?

6. Find a brief article or essay that you think adheres to the principles of style discussed in this chapter. Bring a copy of this selection to class for discussion. Also bring a list of five specific reasons why you think the essay or article is well written.

---

*Subsequent sections of this essay include "Laws When at Table," "Laws Pertaining to Dessert," "On Screaming," "Concerning Face and Hands," "Various Other Laws, Statutes, and Ordinances," and "Complaints and Lamentations."

Strategies for Successful Collaboration

> Writing together has taught us a great deal. It has taught us how to read each other's illegible scrawls; how to be patient and flexible; how to listen to and criticize a draft; how to smile, not cry, when one of us announces that something the other has just written is not quite right. Most important, perhaps, it has taught us something we know as writers but can easily forget: that there is no simple, single, static writing process. Rather, there are writing processes — repertoires of strategies and habits that writers can learn, and change, if they have a strong enough motive for communicating.*

When Professor Andrea Lunsford and I wrote this statement in 1988, we had been writing regularly as coauthors for a number of years — and we had been studying collaborative writing practices for almost as long. In the mid-1980s, we surveyed fourteen hundred members of seven professional associations, including engineers, city planners, chemists, and psychologists.** Of the seven hundred professionals who responded to our survey, 87 percent indicated that they regularly wrote as members of a team or group. Since 98 percent of these same individuals also rated writing as important or very important to the successful execution of their jobs, it is safe to say that the writing they do as members of groups or teams matters a great deal to them. Later surveys and interviews with members of each organization only confirmed and enriched our understanding of the essential role that collaborative writing plays in these professionals' lives.

UNDERSTANDING COLLABORATIVE WRITING: INSIGHTS FROM THE WORLD OF WORK

The individuals Professor Lunsford and I studied are pragmatic, task-oriented writers: They engage in collaborative writing activities primarily because their

---

*Andrea A. Lunsford and Lisa Ede, "Collaboration and Compromise: The Fine Art of Writing with a Friend," *Writers on Writing,* Vol. 2, edited by Tom Waldrep (New York: Random House, 1988), 127.
**Lisa Ede and Andrea A. Lunsford, *Singular Texts/Plural Authors: Perspectives on Collaborative Writing* (Carbondale: Southern Illinois UP, 1990).

work requires them to do so. Sometimes the complexity and ambition of their project necessitates collaboration. This was certainly the case with Bill Qualls, a city planner working in a consulting engineering firm in the south, who heads a team responsible for designing and building large military installations. Albert Bernstein, a clinical psychologist in private practice in the northwest, gave other reasons, describing a collaborative effort to draft an informational brochure for a statewide organization. Although the brochure was a brief document, its development involved a time-consuming series of complex negotiations. Despite these difficulties, Bernstein characterized this and most other collaborations as effective — and as personally rewarding: "[When I write with others,] I do a much better job than I would have done alone. I extend myself further and I have a clearer idea of what we are trying to do."

People have many reasons for writing collaboratively — and an equally diverse number of ways for effectively negotiating the complex processes that such an effort involves. When you write with others, as when you write alone, there is no simple, single, static writing process that you can follow. You must consider each writing task you work on by analyzing your rhetorical situation and determining the most appropriate strategies to employ in a particular case.

Whether writing on the job or at school, writers face a number of challenges. Collaborative projects generally require more explicit planning, coordination, and monitoring of efforts than do individual projects. Melding a uniform style from the efforts of individual writers can require patience and a willingness to negotiate. Finally, collaborative writing efforts can engender the same kinds of difficulties that occur whenever human beings (with all our complexities and foibles) attempt to work together. Poor interpersonal communication, ineffective group dynamics, or inequitable sharing of responsibilities can turn a potentially productive group effort into a frustrating, time-consuming tug-of-war.

Collaborative writing does require sensitivity, patience, flexibility, and commitment. But the rewards of writing collaboratively with others can be substantial. Writers working collaboratively can, most obviously, take on projects that they would be unable to complete alone. If you're part of a group that wishes to study a complex issue or problem, such as the adequacy of your campus's computer services, you *have* to work together. Only by sharing responsibilities can you hope to do justice to your topic in the time available to you. Just as important, when you collaborate with others you can draw on group members' diverse interests, experiences, and capabilities. Group members will undoubtedly have had diverse experiences with your school's computer services, for example. These and other differences enable your group to examine all the issues at stake and thus can improve both your process of inquiry and the essay or report that will result from this process.

Collaboration can also bring individual satisfaction. Many of those Professor Lunsford and I interviewed commented on the ways in which working collaboratively with others on writing enabled them to "learn the ropes" and gain confidence. A number also emphasized that collaborative writing can bring personal rewards: When a collaboration works well, it becomes — as one city planner indicated — "as much a support group as a professional team."

RECOGNIZING THE DEMANDS OF ACADEMIC COLLABORATIVE WRITING PROJECTS

Like those in business and industry, many students find collaborative writing projects to be productive and personally rewarding. Here, for instance, is a journal entry by Latisha Armstrong, a sociology major, about one of her collaborative experiences:

> I was worried when I found out that the major project for my sociology class, an evaluation of a local social service agency, was a group project. My life is pretty complicated already — I didn't know how I'd find the time to meet. I wondered how we'd get along, divide up the work, keep track of who's doing what. Also, I'm really sweating it to do well in school, but not all students care. What if my grade suffered, or if I had to do most of the work to get the project done right? My group did have some rough moments, but we really pulled together. We were able to do a lot of library work *and* interview almost everyone at the agency. Sean did some fancy statistical stuff that really helped us analyze our data. And Sharon's final edit really worked out the kinks. Especially at the end of our project, when we were talking through our conclusions, I felt that I wasn't just studying sociology; I was doing it!

Latisha's comments suggest many of the rewards of collaborating on academic writing assignments. But they also call attention to some potential difficulties — difficulties that, while hardly unique to student collaborations, can prove troublesome: managing logistical and pragmatic matters, developing a shared commitment to the project and an equitable distribution of tasks, and negotiating interpersonal and group issues.

Those working collaboratively in business and industry also face these difficulties, of course, but they are often provided with support systems and incentives unavailable to students. A group of managers working on a report for their company often have the advantage of such in-house services as networked computers with shareware designed specifically for collaborative writing, photocopying services, conference rooms, and secretarial help. In addition, these managers may well have worked together on previous projects, so they will have had opportunities to get to know one another. Finally, teams in business and industry know that performance evaluations, as well as such incentives as salary increases, are directly tied to the success of their endeavor. Given this orientation, these managers are likely to understand the importance of subordinating their own interests or inclinations to the job at hand.

As you are aware, students lack a number of the advantages that I have just detailed. Students cannot count on the kind of support services available to those in business and industry. Most often, students writing collaboratively have not worked together previously. Finally, even though students may be assigned a group grade for a project, they receive an individual grade at the end of the term. Unfortunately, the individualistic, competitive nature of academic grading can work against the development of a strong identification with a team and its collaborative project.

The rest of this chapter suggests steps you can take to address these and other potential difficulties inherent in collaboration. Collaborative writing does pose special challenges for students, but as Latisha Armstrong's journal entry indicates, it can also provide significant personal and academic rewards — not the least of which is the opportunity to learn the skills necessary for much work-related writing.

■ ■ ■

FOR EXPLORATION

Think back to experiences you've had writing with others, whether in school, at work, or elsewhere. Recall one specific experience that you felt was particularly successful, and take five to ten minutes to freewrite or brainstorm a list of factors that made for a productive, satisfying collaboration. Now think of a less successful experience that involved collaboration on writing. Once again, freewrite or brainstorm a list of factors that played a role in the outcome of this collaboration. (If you haven't written collaboratively with others, recall experiences where you worked closely with others on extramural, civic, or similar projects.)

FOR EXPLORATION

Reread what you wrote in the previous Exploration. What has this Exploration helped you to understand about collaborative writing? Write two or three paragraphs detailing this understanding.

Developing Effective Interpersonal and Group Skills

The potential problems described in the previous section are just that — potential but not inevitable problems. As a later section of this chapter will discuss, you can avoid some of the logistical and pragmatic difficulties of collaborative writing by making the fullest possible use of the electronic technologies available to you.

What makes or breaks a group collaboration is the ability to develop effective interpersonal and group skills. If your group wastes time bickering over trivial matters or allows one or two members to dominate (or withdraw from) the project, you will not be able to take advantage of one of the major benefits of collaboration: the enriched understandings that develop when individuals with diverse experiences and skills jointly investigate a subject. In situations like this, morale falters and resentment grows. Your group should place a high priority on establishing a good working relationship. The following guidelines provide suggestions group members can use to ensure an efficient, congenial, and productive working relationship.

■ GUIDELINES FOR EFFECTIVE INTERPERSONAL AND GROUP SKILLS

---

1. *Understand the Importance of Attending to the Task and to the Group.* Whenever people work together, they are following at least two agendas: the explicit agenda of completing a designated project and the implicit and perhaps hidden agenda of developing a productive and rewarding working relationship with members of the group. To fulfill both agendas, group members need to adopt what Professors Linda Flower and John Ackerman refer to as task-conscious and interactive roles.* You are being task-conscious when you set deadlines, negotiate responsibilities, or argue for a particular approach or position. You are playing an interactive role when you encourage reserved group members to share their ideas, use humor to reduce a moment of tension, or praise a group member for a job well done. In effective groups, members know intuitively when they need to take on "task-conscious" and "interactive" roles; they also share responsibility for these roles so that all members can contribute as fully as possible to the group's effort.

---

*The concepts of task-conscious and interactive roles are explained in Linda Flower and John Ackerman, *Writers at Work: Strategies for Communicating in Business and Professional Settings* (Fort Worth, Tex.: Harcourt Brace, 1994).

(continued)

(continued)

2. *Find Ways to Acknowledge and Value Individual, Cultural, and Other Differences.* To succeed in any collaborative project, you need the good will and good work of every member of the group. And yet sometimes differences among group members can result in feelings of exclusion. Reserved students or those whose first language is not English may need more time to formulate and express their ideas. Students who in some way differ from the majority of group members — whether culturally, racially, or because of age or other differences — may wonder if other group members will understand and value their opinions. Effective groups find ways to demonstrate their respect for, and desire to learn from, all members. A simple request for additional perspectives ("Matt has made a good point here, but I wonder if others have different ideas") can encourage reluctant or uncertain members.

3. *Develop Your Active Listening Skills.* Many interpersonal and group problems can be avoided if participants regularly practice active listening. Active listening involves more than focusing on what others are saying; it includes being willing fully to engage with and credit their ideas — even (and especially) when you disagree with them. Active listeners are also attentive to body language and other cues that reveal what participants are thinking and feeling. Imagine that your group is discussing an important aspect of a project and that one person begins to articulate an idea that strikes you as wrongheaded. An active listener resists the temptation to interrupt or discredit the speaker but instead concentrates with particular care on the ideas being expressed. If on reflection the ideas still seem problematic or confusing, an active listener paraphrases or "mirrors" the speaker's comments, perhaps saying something like "What I think I hear you suggesting is . . . " or "Am I right in thinking that you believe we should . . . ?" Rather than attacking ideas with which they disagree, active listeners ask questions that invite speakers to clarify or elaborate on their ideas. Many apparent disagreements turn out to be misunderstandings that are resolved in further discussion. Even where disagreements continue, active listening and "mirroring" enable you to demonstrate your respect for other group members.

(continued)

(continued)

4. *Recognize That How Your Group Handles Meetings Can Make or Break Your Collaborative Effort.* One question Professor Lunsford and I asked in our survey of collaborative-writing practices was this: "In your experience, what are the three greatest *disadvantages* of group writing in your profession?" One response aptly represented the views of many: "Time. Time. Time." Collaboration does take time — and when that time seems wasted, irritation and dissension can quickly develop. Here are some suggestions for planning, conducting, and evaluating group sessions that will help you make the most of your time:

   ■ *Spend your first meeting exploring your assignment, establishing basic ground rules, and encouraging the development of interpersonal trust and group identity.* No matter how elaborate and detailed an assignment is, students need to "read between the lines" to determine the processes and resources they should use to complete the assignment. When a group of students is working collaboratively on a major project, the need to talk explicitly and in detail about the assignment increases, for unless you develop a shared vision of its demands, the group is likely to waste time and effort. At the initial meeting, then, group members should spend a good deal of time discussing the assignment. Be sure to talk about both what the assignment requires and what processes and tasks are necessary to fulfill it. By the end of the meeting, you should have a preliminary or working consensus about how to proceed. This consensus may well include a number of alternate plans that you want to keep on the table; it might also include a list of questions for further discussion.

   You should also reserve time at your initial meeting to get to know one another — and to establish some ground rules for your collaborative effort. How will your group negotiate responsibilities? What will you do if a member is consistently late to meetings or does not follow through with tasks? How will you resolve conflicts or impasses? It's tempting to avoid questions such as these in the hope that your group will not need to address them. But discussing such issues up front is the best way to forestall later problems.

(continued)

(continued)

If your meeting is effective, the process of discussing the assignment and agreeing on ground rules should have already laid the foundation for an effective group process, for your discussion will have demonstrated not only that group members respect each other but also that two or more heads are indeed better than one when it comes to generating ideas and analyzing options. Nevertheless, you may find it helpful to conclude your meeting by encouraging members to discuss how they feel they can best contribute to the group effort and to raise any questions or reservations they have about the collaborative process.

■ *Use an agenda to organize your meetings.* Once your project is under way, the structure of individual meetings may vary considerably depending on the goals for each meeting. Whatever your purpose in meeting, however, you will find it helpful to follow an explicit — and written — agenda. This agenda need not be elaborate, but it should include specific goals to be accomplished and a plan for carrying them out. Conclude each meeting by reviewing the agenda, summarizing what you have accomplished, and assigning responsibilities for your next meeting. Save agendas from all meetings, so you can consult them if necessary.

■ *Supplement individual and group memory with written records.* When your group is engaged in an intensive, task-oriented discussion, it can seem tedious to make written notes summarizing your meeting. And yet both individual and group memory can be surprisingly brief — and varied. To ensure that all group members have the same understanding of group decisions, take turns keeping notes during your meetings. Conclude each meeting by reviewing (and, if necessary, revising) these notes, which should then be reproduced and distributed to all members of the group.

To facilitate communication among everyone in the group, you may find it useful to share regular progress reports. Members can also use such written reports to raise questions about current research or writing and to note issues for group discussion. At several points during your project, you may even find it

(continued)

(continued)

helpful to devote all or part of a group meeting to generating a group progress report that summarizes what you have accomplished and lists tasks that still need to be completed.

5. *Develop Nonthreatening Ways to Deal with Problems.* All groups experience moments of difficulty. A brief flash of irritation between two group members may not merit attention, but significant interpersonal or group problems will worsen if not promptly addressed. Difficult as it can be, groups need to respond to such problems when they occur, and they need to do so in a way that encourages rather than diminishes group solidarity and effectiveness. But how? Whenever possible, avoid identifying problems with specific individuals. Even if you feel that a single group member has failed to carry out responsibilities, try to avoid directly accusing this person. You might suggest that it's an appropriate time for the group to review what tasks have been completed, by whom, and when — with an eye to future assignments. Another strategy that is helpful when you wish to make a point but avoid conflict is to substitute "I" statements for "you" statements. Rather than saying to another student that "your ideas don't make sense," for instance, say "I'm having trouble following your point." By locating a problem in your understanding rather than in your group member's ideas, you avoid unnecessary conflict and encourage the clarification of ideas rather than anger.

6. *Know When You Should — and Shouldn't — Strive for Consensus.* The preceding suggestions aim to encourage cooperative, flexible, respectful working relationships. Placing too high a value on cooperation, however, can actually limit a group's effectiveness. Sometimes conflict can be productive. In a study of student collaborative writing groups, Professor Rebecca E. Burnett discovered that productive conflicts encourage groups to "re-examine opinions, share diverse ideas, and discover creative solutions."* A group cannot discover the most efficient way to divide responsibilities or to organize a group report without fully exploring all options. As a group, you should strive to avoid conflicts that interfere with your

---

*Rebecca E. Burnett, "Substantive Conflict in a Cooperative Context: A Way to Improve the Collaborative Planning of Workplace Documents," *Technical Communication* 38 (1991): 535.

(continued)

(continued)

group's effectiveness, but you should encourage the free play of ideas. Premature consensus on such issues as the approach you should take to your topic or the most effective way to introduce your essay can work against decision-making.

7. *Build in Regular "Reality Checks" to Resolve Any Difficulties.* Even if you feel that your group is working well, it's helpful to schedule regular "reality checks." To do so, reserve time in meetings to discuss your collaborative process in a friendly, nonevaluative manner. You might conclude meetings, for instance, by freewriting about your group effort or about that particular meeting. Or you could respond to specific questions, such as the following:

> What in our group process is working well?
>
> How might we improve the productivity and efficiency of our collaborative effort?
>
> What about our group effort do we each find personally satisfying?
>
> What changes might make the group process more satisfying for me?
>
> Are there any issues, such as workload or deadlines, that we need to discuss or renegotiate?

If you regularly take time to raise questions such as these, your group should be better prepared to identify and resolve interpersonal or group problems.

8. *Expect the Unexpected.* Even with the best planning, most groups find that their work doesn't go quite as expected. One person's research may prove more time-consuming than anticipated, or it may uncover information that requires the group to rethink its approach to the topic. Illness or a family emergency may prevent another from completing work on time. As you organize and schedule your tasks, build in time for unexpected delays and problems. Recognize, too, that the group may need to redefine its goals or renegotiate the division of labor as you progress.

As these guidelines suggest, when groups are working well, members share responsibilities, engage in an ongoing effort to analyze the group's effort, and make any needed modifications in process and product. As an example of such an analysis, here is an essay written by Merlla McLaughlin after she was involved in a collaborative writing project. Merlla and her classmates completed an investigative report on parking services at Oregon State University. After completing the collaborative report, they wrote individual essays analyzing their small-group dynamics. In her essay, Merlla refers to a personality assessment that she and other group members took in class. This assessment identified students as reds, blues, yellows, or whites. According to Merlla's instructor, Babette Bushnell, the significance of these colors was as follows: "Blues" are people-oriented and attend closely to interpersonal relations, "reds" are organizers and "take-charge" individuals, "whites" dislike conflict and thus often serve as peacemakers, and "yellows" are "fun" people who enjoy having a good time.

SMALL-GROUP DYNAMICS IN A CLASS PROJECT
by Merlla McLaughlin

College lectures provide learners with volumes of information. However, there are many experiences that cannot be understood well simply by *learning about* them in a classroom. Instead, these experiences can only be understood by *living* them. So it is with the workings of a small, task-focused group. What observations about small-group dynamics would I make after working with a group of peers on a class project? And what have I learned personally as a result of my involvement with our collaborative project?

LEADERSHIP EXPECTATIONS AND EMERGENCE
Our six group members were selected by our instructor; half were male and half female. Because we had performed personality assessments in class — and because these assessments identified most of us as "blues," concerned with intimacy and caring — I had expected that Nate, our only "red," might become our leader. (Kaari, the only "white," seemed poised to become the peacekeeper if need be.) However, after Nate missed the first two meetings, it seemed that Pat might emerge as leader. Pat had contributed often during our first three real meetings. More important, he has strong communications skills — and he is a tall male (and thus a commanding presence). Pat is also rhetorically sensitive. I was somewhat surprised, then, when our group developed a distributive type of leadership. The longer we worked together, however, the more convinced I became that this approach to leadership was best for our group.

ROLES PLAYED
Thanks in part to the distributed leadership that our group developed, the strengths of group members increasingly became apparent. While early in our process Pat had been the key initiator and Nate had acted largely as

information seeker, all group members eventually took on these task functions. We took turns serving as recorders, and we all gathered information and worked on our questionnaire. McKenzie, Kaari, Pat, and I all coordinated the group's work at some point. Joe was especially good at catching important details the rest of us were apt to miss. An example of this ability occurred at our second meeting when he asked us all to come to the third meeting with prepared questions. Later, he pointed out that parking problems on campus could affect surrounding businesses and that interviewing business owners and employees could be informative. Joe, McKenzie, Kaari, and I frequently clarified and elaborated information. Pat, Kaari, and Nate were particularly good at contributing ideas during brainstorming sessions. Nate and McKenzie kept humor in the group and in the project, with tension-relieving jokes.

Gender did seem to influence group members' approach to our project. For example, the women all seemed to take a holistic approach to the project and to make intuitive leaps in ways that the men generally did not. The men preferred a more systematic process. But our differing preferences complemented each other well and enabled us to conduct research effectively, organize the information we gathered logically, and prepare for, practice, and give a successful presentation.

DECISION-MAKING METHODS

Our decision to do an investigative report on Parking Services was not the result of a majority vote but was achieved instead through negotiated consensus. Nate was absent on the day that we made our decision, but we felt that we needed to move from brainstorming — which we had already done — to action. Several of us argued that a presentation on Parking Services at OSU would interest most students, and after discussion the others agreed. At our next meeting, Nate seemed happy to go along with our collaborative decision.

We spent a good deal of time negotiating the topic for our presentation. Once we did this, other, smaller decisions came naturally. At one point, for instance, we considered producing a videotape for part of our presentation. But after we discussed whether we had the resources and skills to shoot, edit, and produce a videotape, we quickly realized that it was not feasible. Pat and Nate did slides instead. We used the slides to tie the whole presentation together through visual images.

SOCIAL ENVIRONMENT: HAPPY, HARMONIZING INTIMACY-SEEKERS

As previously noted, our group primarily consisted of blues, and at least three of the four blues had white as their secondary color. (The other secondary color was yellow.) This partly explains why our group had little confrontation and conflict. Nate, the red, was most likely to be blunt in his speech, but everyone was rhetorically sensitive and self-monitoring during group interactions. The one time that Nate seemed put off, at the third meeting, it was not his words but his body language that expressed his discomfort. Nate sat on the far end of the group, leaned back in his chair, arms crossed, legs stretched out, ankles crossed. By contrast, everyone else in the group had scooted in close together. This was an awkward moment, but a rare one given our group's generally positive handling of conflict. This was not, I think, the result of groupthink, or of a fear of conflict. Instead, obstacles were treated not as one person's problems but rather as a group problem. As a consequence, we approached problems from a united position instead of forming "camps" and opposing each other.

LOOKING TOWARD THE FUTURE

Perhaps my most important personal understanding as a result of this project has to do with conflict. Although I personally find conflict difficult, I have found that some kinds of conflict are essential for increasing understanding between group members and creating an effective collaborative product. It was essential, for instance, that our group explore everyone's (well, everyone's but Nate's) ideas about possible topics for our presentation — and this inevitably required some conflict as one person suggested an idea and another said "But what about. . . . " Conflict (in the sense of discussion of multiple possibilities) is essential to the full exploration of ideas. When groups handle conflict positively, they increase the group's cohesiveness. I think all the members of our group felt, for instance, that their ideas about possible topics for our presentation were considered. Once we negotiated a topic, everyone could fully commit to it.

I think that as a result of this project I have a better sense of when conflict is — and isn't — productive. My group used conflict productively when we thrashed out our ideas, and we avoided the kind of conflict that creates morale problems and wastes time. Each group operates somewhat differently, but with the grounding this class has provided I feel more prepared to understand and participate in future small-group projects.

■ ■ ■

FOR GROUP WORK

The two Explorations on p. 321 encouraged you to reflect on previous collaborative writing experiences. Meet with the members of your writing group (or with other members of your class) to share your responses to these activities. What common factors did group members cite as leading to productive or unproductive collaborations? After listing these factors, look with particular care at those that led to unsatisfying, unproductive collaborations. To what extent do the guidelines on pp. 322–27 provide suggestions you can use to address these problems? Did your group identify problems not discussed in the guidelines? If so, make a list of these problems and of ways your group might anticipate or avoid them.

Planning, Drafting, and Revising Collaboratively

There's a reason why many in business and industry emphasize teamwork: They know that when groups work well, they can produce better ideas — and better written products — than people working individually. To achieve this productivity, however, groups must learn how to maximize the benefits inherent in collaboration. Sometimes this involves taking the fullest possible advantage of group members' diverse experiences, interests, and ideas. Sometimes it involves finding effective and efficient ways to manage the collaborative process. If you're writing an essay alone, for instance, it doesn't matter if your plan is a jumbled, indecipherable mass of notes. As long as the plan makes sense to you, that's fine. When you write collaboratively, the development and maintenance of group "memory" requires more explicit, organized planning. The following guidelines provide suggestions for planning, drafting, and revising a collaborative work.

■ GUIDELINES FOR COLLABORATIVE PLANNING, DRAFTING, AND REVISING

PLANNING

1. *Take Advantage of Multiple Roles and Perspectives in the Planning Process.* When you plan collaboratively, you naturally draw on group members' varied experiences and perspectives. Researchers have identified several strategies that can maximize the effectiveness of this process. After studying student groups engaged in collaborative planning, for instance, Professor Rebecca E. Burnett discovered that students in the most effective groups regularly assumed a variety of roles. Sometimes they initiated ideas; in other instances they served as questioners, clarifiers, or recorders. As they worked together, they demonstrated a task-oriented, problem-solving approach to planning.

(continued)

(continued)

Good questions are the heart of the collaborative planning process. To encourage her students to ask productive questions — questions that challenge them to look at their topic from multiple perspectives — Professor Burnett developed the following questions for collaborative planning.*

QUESTIONS FOR COLLABORATIVE PLANNING

Content Questions

What more can we say about _____?

What additional information might we include?

Have you considered including (excluding) _____?

Don't you think we should include (exclude) _____?

Purpose/Key Point Questions

What do we see as our main point (purpose)?

What did you mean by _____? Could you clarify the point about _____?

I can't quite see why you've decided to _____. Could you explain why?

I see a conflict between _____ and _____. How will we deal with it?

Audience Questions

Who is our intended audience? Why is this the appropriate audience?

What does the reader expect to read (learn, do)?

How will our reader react to _____? Connect _____ to _____?

---

*Rebecca E. Burnett, "Benefits of Collaborative Planning in the Business Communication Classroom," Bulletin of the Association for Business Communication 53.2 (1990): 12.

(continued)

(continued)

What problems (conflicts, inconsistencies, gaps) might our reader see?

Questions Relating to Conventions
of Organization and Development

How can we explain _____?

How will we organize (develop, explain) this?

What support (or evidence) could we use? What examples could we use?

How does this (convention) let us deal with _____?

Questions Relating to Conventions of Design

Have you considered using _____? How do you think it would work?

Couldn't we also try _____?

How does this (convention) let us deal with _____?

Why do you like _____ better than _____ as a way to present this information?

Synthesis/Consolidation Questions

How does _____ relate to (develop, clarify) _____?

Given our purpose and audience, should we use _____?

Is there a conflict between using _____ and _____?

Why do you think _____ is a good way to explain our key point to this audience?

2. *Use Visual Representations to Develop and Clarify Your Group's Ideas.* When you're in an intense discussion, it can be easy to lose track of your ideas. Many collaborative writers have found that using such aids as chalkboards, large notepads of paper, or computers to record ideas can do a great deal to organize discussion — and also

(continued)

(continued)

to clarify and stimulate ideas. It's much easier to determine how to organize a report, for instance, if the entire group can actually look at two or three possible organizational patterns, rather than trying to keep them in mind. Working with visual representations of ideas helps keep everyone on the same mental page; it also encourages group, rather than individual, ownership of ideas. Recording ideas will help your group stay organized and on task.

3. *Be Prepared to Shift Gears as Work Progresses.* As a group moves from exploring ideas to planning and drafting, its understanding of the assignment and of the best ways to fulfill it may well change. Your group might begin a project assuming that you will present a strong argument for or against a specific issue, for instance, only to discover through reading and discussion that your arguments are in fact more complex. Be prepared to recognize — and act on — such shifts in position.

DRAFTING

4. *Take Time to Nurture a Collective "Felt Sense" of Your Writing.* Writers composing alone are often able to draw on their "felt sense" to make decisions as they write. While working on an essay for a women's studies class, for instance, you may suddenly realize that your introduction is too formal and may "see" how a more personal introduction would work better. Collaborative writers need to nurture a collective "felt sense." There are several strategies your group can use to do so. You might begin some of your group meetings, for instance, by having each member freewrite for five minutes in response to questions such as these: What are we trying to achieve in this essay or report? What is working well in our current draft? What seems rough or awkward? Or you might each respond in writing to the "Guidelines for Analyzing Your Rhetorical Situation" on pp. 147–49. Discussing group members' responses should enable you to articulate — and, if necessary, negotiate — a collective "felt sense" of your evolving text.

As your writing develops, you may occasionally find it useful to have one group member read the text aloud while others listen and make notes. The person reading should read the entire text without stopping; others should take notes quietly. Each group

(continued)

(continued)

member should read his or her comments before you begin a general discussion of your responses. This activity can help you develop a holistic grasp of your text as it evolves and can generate responses you can use as you write and revise.

5. *Avoid a "Cut-and-Paste" Approach to Drafting.* Collaborative writers often find it efficient to take responsibility for drafting different sections of the text. This approach can work well — as long as you avoid a cut-and-paste approach to drafting. Such an approach assumes that once you have developed an outline or organization for your writing, individual members will work only on those portions of the text for which they are responsible. This approach has several negative consequences. For one thing, a cut-and-paste approach to drafting makes it difficult for group members to develop any felt sense about their work. Also, group members may develop such strong individual ownership of their writing that they resist changes to their drafts. Cut-and-paste approaches to drafting also make it difficult for group members to notice redundant sections.

   Even if group members initially assume responsibility for different sections of the text, you should begin exchanging and revising one another's drafts as soon as possible. (Be sure to keep a clear paper trail of all changes made, in case you ever wish to return to an earlier version.) The exchange of drafts will encourage group ownership of the text and make the process of developing a coherent and unified style much easier. It will also give you a head start on revising the final draft of your essay or report.

REVISING

6. *Maximize Your Group's Resources by Drawing on a Variety of Revision Strategies.* Collaborative revision presents a number of advantages over solitary revision. A group can draw on members' diverse perspectives to develop a richer, more detailed vision of its text's strengths and weaknesses. When your group meets to discuss alternative ways of organizing your essay, for instance, you can consider more options — and evaluate them more fully — than when you write alone. Group members can also function as a sample audience and as a peer response and support group. And once you articulate a shared understanding of the changes that need to be made, you can distribute tasks according to individuals' strengths

(continued)

(continued)

and interests. One group member might agree to revise your essay's transitions so that they are more consistent and fluid, for example, while another rewrites the conclusion, and a third checks all references to be sure they are accurate and in the correct form.

As your group revises its text, choose strategies appropriate for your situation and purpose. In some instances, it may be most efficient for members to trade drafts and revise one another's writing. At other times you may choose to work together in group revision sessions. To do so, have one group member function as secretary while others suggest changes. As your deadline nears, one or two members may take responsibility for a final revision to ensure consistency of style and tone. There is no one-size-fits-all way to approach the task of collaborative revision. Instead, your group should use strategies that are appropriate for your particular situation and purpose.

7. *Establish Explicit Goals for All Revision Sessions.* Whenever your group engages in revision activities, you should articulate specific, concrete goals; doing so will help keep you on track and enable you to make the best use of your time. If you agree to exchange rough drafts, for instance, you should decide whether members will simply comment on or actually revise one another's writing. Similarly, if you are engaged in a group revision session, you should begin by determining the issues you will focus on. As when you write alone, it is generally more efficient to consider global issues involving organization, focus, and content before spending time on such local concerns as sentence structure or word choice. Whether you are evaluating your current draft's organization or looking at the stylistic effectiveness of your essay's introduction, establishing clear goals will ensure a productive work session rather than an unfocused and frustrating free-for-all.

USING ELECTRONIC TECHNOLOGIES TO FACILITATE YOUR COLLABORATIVE EFFORT

Electronic technologies can help make collaborative writing more efficient and productive. Access to email, for instance, can enable members of your group to stay in touch between meetings, while networked computers can simplify drafting and revising. The following guidelines suggest ways your group can make the best use of the electronic technologies that are available to you.

■ GUIDELINES FOR USING ELECTRONIC TECHNOLOGIES IN COLLABORATIVE WRITING

1. *Early in Your Work Together, Take the Time to Discover Group Members' Computer and Online Skills — and Also the Hardware and Software You Will Be Using.* Depending on your personal situations and the resources of your college or university, members of your group may have excellent — or quite limited — access to electronic technologies. During your first meeting, take an inventory of your skills and resources. How many group members own computers or have convenient access to them? Do you all have email accounts? Do you have access to networked computers and to software programs that enable you to generate, revise, and edit text together? If you do not, what electronic resources will you use to share texts? (Will you share computer disks, for instance, or email texts to each other as attachments? If you plan to use attachments and you are not using the same server and email program, are you sure that attachments will be readable?) What word processing programs do group members use? Is text produced via one word processing program easily convertible to another? Answering these questions will enable your group to make the best use of the electronic technologies available to you.

2. *Agree at the Start on the Electronic Technologies That You Will Use and on the Ways That You Will Use Them. If Students in Your Group Vary in Their Computer Skills, Tutor Students Who Need to Learn Essential Procedures.* Electronic technologies can expedite your collaborative writing — but only if you take the time necessary to make sure that all members know how to carry out critical procedures. If one group member uses a desktop publishing software to produce and format her draft and another does not have access to such software, problems can and probably will ensue. So first make certain basic decisions: What hardware and software will you use? Will your group set up an email list to facilitate communication? (Such a list automatically sends emails to all group members.) What common word processing features (such as the SAVE AS feature, which allows files to be saved in different versions and formats) should everyone use?

   All group members need to be able to use the electronic technologies and software programs that best support the project, so

(continued)

(continued)

you may need to tutor those who need help coming up to speed. Given the potential efficiency of being able to email documents to each other, for instance, helping those who do not know how to attach files to an email or how to save files in ASCII text for reading in emails makes sense.

3. *Take the Time to Make Basic Decisions about Document Format and Design.* When you're starting a collaborative project, margin size, font style, and font size can seem like low-priority issues for group discussion. But as group members begin exchanging drafts — and certainly when you begin working toward a final draft — you will be grateful that you made these decisions early on.

4. *Recognize That Electronic Technologies May Require the Development of New Roles and Processes.* If your group is using email extensively, ask one person to serve as the team archivist. Everyone should save important messages, but someone should chronologically organize print and electronic copies of all communications. Group members may also want to take turns summarizing email discussions. After a series of messages on some issue, a summarizer might post a message along these lines: "We discussed the question of whether we should do X or Y. Susan and Jed argued that we should do X. Jason and Andrea recommended Y instead. The consensus seems to be leaning toward Susan and Jed's position, though I think that there might be a possible compromise." Taking time to summarize emails is important because a flurry of email can build up quickly and obscure the major point at issue.

Similar issues can arise when a number of individuals share word processing responsibilities. Suppose that your group does not have good access to email and so decides to use floppy disks to exchange drafts of sections and ongoing revisions of the entire project. At the start of a project, exchanging disks and compiling a master disk with everyone's drafts and revisions are fairly straightforward tasks. But as you move toward the final stages of your writing process, it becomes harder to keep track of the various drafts. For this reason, your group should agree to name files consistently. It should also appoint one member to keep track of file exchanges.

5. *Particularly Where Emails Are Involved, Remember to Practice Good "Netiquette."* This issue is discussed fully in Chapter 7, "Negotiat-

(continued)

(continued)

ing Online Writing Situations," so this guideline serves primarily as a reminder of that discussion. Doing something as simple as writing a subject heading that accurately reflects the content of your email can facilitate communications among group members. Your group will certainly want to avoid flames or other email communications that could impede your group process.

6. *Anticipate — and Prepare for — Possible Electronic Failures and Glitches.* Technology, being a human invention, can and all too frequently does fail. You will encounter power outages, difficulties getting online from a computer at home, accidental deletions of material, corrupted disks, and other problems. Given this fact, your group should plan ahead. Some of this planning represents little more than common sense: Back up copies in more than one location, save files often, and print hard copies to important communications and texts. But your group should also try to anticipate problems that are related to the technologies you are using and establish backup procedures in case the worst happens. If email is central to your collaborative process, for instance, you will want to share phone numbers as well as email addresses in case a server should experience major problems.

Successful collaborative writing, like writing in general, depends on neither luck nor magic. Just as individual writers can learn more efficient, productive, and satisfying ways of managing the writing process, so too can those working on group projects learn how to work — and write — together effectively.

■ ■ ■

FOR THOUGHT, DISCUSSION, AND WRITING

1. To learn more about your group's interactions, tape record a typical meeting. After you have done so, each group member should listen to the tape and respond in writing to the following questions:

   ■ How would you describe your group's interactions? Who spoke most often? Least often? Did gender differences appear in communication patterns (with men speaking more forcefully or frequently, for instance)? Were there cultural differences? What additional observations can you make about the group's conversational patterns and problem-solving strategies?

- What behaviors seemed to be most productive for your group? Least productive? Why?

- What one or two changes in conversational patterns or problem-solving strategies might improve your group's productiveness?

- What most surprised you about your own contributions to the group?

- What one or two changes in your own behavior might improve your group's performance?

After you've all listened to the tape and responded to these questions, meet to discuss the group's responses. Be sure to focus your discussion on ways that the group could improve its interactions, and not on the strengths or weaknesses of specific group members.

2. While working on a collaborative writing project for your composition class — or for another class — keep detailed notes about your experiences. Drawing on these notes and on your analysis of a tape recorded group meeting (as described in the previous activity), write an essay that reflects what you have learned about yourself (as a writer and group participant) as a result of your collaborative experience.

PART FOUR

WRITING ACADEMIC
ARGUMENTS

Understanding Academic Audiences and Assignments

A rhetorical approach to writing calls attention to the fact that all writing is done in a particular context. As Part Two of this book emphasizes, even if you are writing alone at your computer, you are writing in the context of a specific rhetorical situation. By analyzing that situation, you can make appropriate choices about your purpose as writer, the *persona* or "voice" you create in your writing, and your relationship with readers. You can understand which textual conventions are — and are not — appropriate for your writing. And perhaps even more important, you can understand *why* this is the case.

Gaining such an understanding is particularly important when you enter a new community of writers and readers. As a student entering the academic community, you need to develop an insider's understanding of the conventions that characterize academic writing. Some of these conventions are general and apply across the disciplines. Whatever their discipline, for instance, college teachers believe that conclusions expressed in writing must be earned. They must reflect an open, unbiased intellectual engagement with the subject under consideration — whether that subject is a Renaissance painting by Leonardo da Vinci or a particular kind of fungus. Moreover, they believe that both the logic behind these conclusions and the evidence for them must be visible in the writing itself so that readers who wish to understand (and possibly question) the writer's assumptions and conclusions can easily do so.

In an important sense, then, whatever their discipline your instructors believe that — where academic writing is involved at least — everything is an argument. But they have a specific model of argument in mind. This model is less about winning or losing a debate and more about using evidence and reasoning to discover some version of the truth about a particular subject. I use the words "some version" here to emphasize that for your instructors the truth is always in process, always open to further discussion. A political scientist or economist may make a convincing argument about federal government's current policy on harvesting timber in national forests. These scholars know, however, that no matter how convincing their writing is, others will add to, challenge, or refine their comments. Having others respond to their observations is a sign that their writing has been successful, for it means that they have raised questions that others consider important. In this sense, the scholarly work of the academy is like a conversation rather than a debate.

Part Four of *Work in Progress* will enable you to enter the scholarly conversation of the academy and in so doing to write the kinds of essays and reports that will earn approval from your instructors. This chapter describes the values and expectations of academic readers and shows you, as a writer, how to analyze academic writing assignments. Chapter 14 focuses on two important skills required in all academic writing: analysis and argument. And Chapter 15 takes you through the process (via successive drafts of a student's essay) of writing and revising effective academic arguments. It concludes with a miscellany of examples of successful student academic writing.

UNDERSTANDING YOUR AUDIENCE: STUDENTS WRITING, INSTRUCTORS READING

Because your instructors are the primary readers of the writing you do in college, you need to understand their values and goals for you and other students. As I have already indicated, your instructors share a commitment to the ideal of education as inquiry. Whether in business, liberal arts, agriculture, engineering, or other fields, your instructors want to foster your ability to think, write, and speak well. When they read your papers and exams, your instructors are looking for both your knowledge of a specific subject and your ability to think and write clearly and effectively.

This is not to say that your instructors will bring identical expectations to your writing. Methods of inquiry and research questions vary from discipline to discipline, and textual conventions reflect these differing assumptions and practices. A lab report written for your chemistry class will use different kinds of evidence and be organized differently than an essay written for an American literature class. Stylistic expectations also vary among different disciplines. Passive voice (as in "It was discovered . . . ") is more commonly used in the sciences than in the humanities, for instance.

Despite these disciplinary differences, those who teach in colleges and universities generally agree about what it means to be educated, thoughtful, and knowledgeable. They believe, for instance, that perhaps the worst intellectual error is oversimplifying. They want their students to go beyond obvious and stereotypical analysis and arguments to deeper and more complex understandings. Thus a historian might urge students to recognize that more was at stake in the American Civil War than freeing the slaves, and an engineer might encourage students to realize that the most obvious way to resolve a design problem is not necessarily the best.

Most college instructors want their students to be able to do more than memorize or summarize information. Indeed, they strive to develop students' abilities to analyze, apply, question, and evaluate information. They also want students to be able to consider issues from multiple perspectives, to recognize that nearly every issue has at least two sides. Because most intellectual issues are complex, instructors often teach students to limit the issue, question, or problem under discussion. They also believe that arguments should be supported by substantial and appropriate evidence, not emotional appeals or logical fallacies. Various disciplines accept different kinds of evidence and follow different methodologies to ensure that conclusions are as meaningful as possible. But all share the conviction that people arguing a point should support their assertions with more than just an "in my opinion."

Such habits of mind are intrinsically rewarding. The knowledge that you can analyze a complex issue or problem, work through an argument, and develop your own position on a subject brings intellectual satisfaction and confidence. These same habits of thinking also bring extrinsic rewards, for they are — as executives in business and industry emphasize — precisely the habits of mind required to succeed in positions of responsibility in any field. And they also enable you to participate effectively as a citizen of the world.

■ ■ ■

FOR EXPLORATION

Freewrite for five or ten minutes about your experiences so far as an academic writer. What has frustrated or confused you? What has excited you? What questions do you have about the academic rhetorical situation and the conventions of academic writing?

What do instructors look for when they read students' writing? Most broadly, your instructors want writing that demonstrates learning and a real commitment to and engagement with the subject being discussed. In many instances, they want writing that reveals that you are making connections between the issues discussed in class and your life and personal values. And they always want writing that adheres to academic standards of clear thinking and effective communication. Specifically, most instructors hope to find the following characteristics in student writing:

- A limited but significant topic
- A meaningful context for discussion of the topic
- A sustained and full discussion, given the limitations of the topic, time, and length
- A clear pattern of organization
- Fair and effective use of sources (both print and online)

- Adequate detail and evidence as support for generalizations
- Appropriate, concise language
- Conventional grammar, punctuation, and usage

The following essay, written by Hope Leman for a class on politics and the media, meets these criteria. This essay was written in response to the following assignment for a take-home midterm exam:

> Journalists often suggest that they simply mirror reality. Some political scientists argue, however, that rather than mirroring reality journalists make judgments that subtly but significantly shape their resulting news reports. In so doing, scholars argue, journalists function more like flashlights than like mirrors.
>
> Write an essay in which you contrast the "mirror" and "flashlight" models of the role of journalists in American society. Successful essays will not only compare these two models but will also provide examples supporting their claims.

Since Hope was writing a take-home midterm essay, she did not have time to do a formal written analysis of her rhetorical situation. Still, her essay demonstrates considerable rhetorical sensitivity. Hope understands, for instance, that given her situation she should emphasize content rather than employ a dramatic or highly personal style. Hope's essay is, above all, clearly written. Even though it has moments of quiet humor (as when she comments on funhouses at the end of the second paragraph), the focus is on articulating the reasons why the "flashlight" model of media theory is the most valid and helpful for political scientists. Hope knows that her teacher will be reading a stack of midterms under time pressure, so she makes sure that her own writing is carefully organized and to the point. Here is Hope's essay.

THE ROLE OF JOURNALISTS IN AMERICAN SOCIETY: A COMPARISON OF THE "MIRROR" AND "FLASHLIGHT" MODELS

by Hope Leman

The "mirror" model of media theory holds that through their writing and news broadcasts journalists are an objective source of information for the public. This model assumes that journalists are free of bias and can be relied on to provide accurate information about the true state of affairs in the world. Advocates of the "flashlight" model disagree, believing that a journalist is like a person in a dark room holding a flashlight. The light from the flashlight falls briefly on various objects in the room, revealing part — but not all — of the room at any one time. This model assumes that journalists cannot possibly provide an objective view of reality but, at best, can convey only a partial understanding of a situation or event.

In this essay, I will argue that the "flashlight" model provides a more accurate and complex understanding of the role of journalists in America. This model recognizes, for instance, that journalists are shaped by their personal backgrounds and experiences and by the pressures, mores, and customs of their profession. It also recognizes that journalists are under commercial pressure to sell their stories. Newspapers and commercial networks are run on a for-profit basis. Thus, reporters have to "sell" their stories to readers. The easiest way to do that is to fit a given news event into a "story" framework. Human beings generally relate well to easily digestible stories, as opposed to more complex analyses, which require more thought and concentration. Thus, reporters assigned to cover a given situation are likely to ask "What is the story?" and then to force events into that framework. Reality is seldom as neat as a story, however, and life does not always fall into neat compartments of "Once upon a time . . . " "and then . . . " and "The End." But the story framework dominates news coverage of events; thus, the media cannot function as a mirror since mirrors reflect rather than distort reality (except in funhouses).

The "mirror" model also fails to acknowledge that journalists make choices, including decisions about what stories to cover. These choices can be based on personal preference, but usually they are determined by editors, who respond to publishers, who, in turn, are eager to sell their product to the widest possible audiences. Most people tend not to like to read about seemingly insoluble social problems like poverty or homelessness. Thus journalists often choose not to cover social issues unless they fit a particular "story" format.

In addition to deciding what to cover, journalists must also determine the tone they will take in their reporting. If the "mirror" model of media theory were accurate, journalists wouldn't make implicit or explicit judgments in their reporting. But they do. They are only human, after all, and they will inevitably be influenced by their admiration or dislike for a person about whom they are writing, or by their belief about the significance of an event.

From start to finish, journalists must make a series of choices. They first make choices about what to cover; then they make choices about whether their tone will be positive or negative, which facts to include and which to omit, what adjectives to use, etc. Mirrors do not make choices — but a person holding a flashlight does. The latter can decide where to let the light drop, how long to leave it on that spot, and when to shift the light to something else. Journalists make these kinds of choices every day. Consequently, the "flashlight" model provides the more accurate understanding of the role that journalists play in American society, for the "mirror" model fails to take into account the many factors shaping even the simplest news story.

■ ■ ■

FOR GROUP WORK

Working with a group of classmates, respond to these questions about Hope Leman's essay. Appoint a recorder to write down the results of your discussion, which your instructor may ask you to present to the class.

1. Hope begins her essay not by attempting to interest readers in her subject but by defining the "mirror" and "flashlight" models of media theory. In a different context, Hope's introduction might seem abrupt. Given that Hope is responding to a midterm question and is writing under time pressure, why is this an effective way to begin her essay?

2. As Chapter 9 on planning, drafting, and designing documents explains, writers need to have a controlling purpose when they write. Sometimes they signal this purpose to readers by articulating an explicit thesis statement. Sometimes only subtle cues are necessary. In her essay, Hope includes an explicit thesis statement. Identify this statement, and then discuss the reasons that it is necessary in her particular situation.

3. In distinguishing between satisfactory and excellent responses to a question, instructors look for signs that a student has truly grasped the question and its implications. A satisfactory response provides the basic information necessary to address the question. An excellent response in some way reflects on or gives insight into the question itself. Hope Leman's instructors — and most academic readers of student writing — would characterize Hope's essay as excellent. What evidence for this assessment can you point to in her essay?

4. Academic writing is sometimes viewed as dull and lifeless — as, well, academic. And yet even in this essay written under time pressure Hope Leman's writing is not stuffy, dull, or pompous. Examine Hope's essay to identify passages where a personal voice contributes to the overall effectiveness of her essay. How does Hope blend this personal voice with the objective and distanced approach of this essay?

ANALYZING ACADEMIC WRITING ASSIGNMENTS

Understanding the values and goals of the academic community helps you to respond appropriately to the demands of academic writing. In addition, you must know how to analyze academic assignments because assignments (whether presented orally or in writing) provide concrete indications of instructors' expectations. You can improve your understanding of your academic assignments by analyzing each assignment, identifying its assumptions, and developing strategies to increase your commitment to it.

Analyzing an Assignment

All assignments are not alike. Some present broad, unstructured topics. A political science instructor might ask you to write a ten-page research paper discussing an important political consequence of the Vietnam War. Or a psychology instructor might ask you to write a four- to six-page essay exploring how your family background has influenced your attitudes about marriage or parenthood. Broad assignments like these call on you to choose a specific topic and to select an approach to analyzing and presenting your material.

In other instances, instructors offer quite specific assignments. Such assignments may substantially restrict your choice of a topic, and they may include a format or sequence of steps or activities that you must follow. Other assignments may fall halfway between these two extremes.

Whether instructors give broad or limited assignments, the words they use to describe these assignments, especially certain key words, can tell you a great deal about their expectations. These key words — *define, analyze, evaluate, defend, show, describe, review, prove, summarize, classify* — are crucial. An assignment that asks you to *summarize* Freud's Oedipal theory, for instance, is quite different from one that asks you to *criticize* or *evaluate* it. To summarize Freud's Oedipal theory, you need to recount its major features. Criticizing this theory challenges you to identify its strengths and weaknesses and to provide evidence for your assessment.

Identifying the Assumptions behind an Assignment

To complete an assignment effectively, you need to know more than whether it is broad or limited. You need to know the criteria your instructor will use to evaluate the assignment and the processes and resources you can best use as you work on it. Some instructors provide information about these and related matters. If your instructor provides such suggestions, study them with care. If you don't understand how to act on your instructor's suggestions, make an appointment to speak with him or her. Discussing your assignment with other students in your class is another helpful way to test your understanding.

Not all instructors provide this kind of information about assignments, however. They may think that the criteria for evaluation and the processes and resources students might best use to complete an assignment are so obvious that they need not be stated explicitly, or they may believe that students learn more effectively when they take full responsibility for all aspects of an assignment. For this reason, these instructors want students to discover for themselves how they can best work on an assignment and the features that characterize a successful response to an assignment.

You need to "read between the lines" of any assignment, for even detailed suggestions cannot tell you exactly what processes and resources you should use. One way to read between the lines is by thinking about the ways your assignment relates to the objectives, class discussions, and readings for a course. Your instructor may not comment specifically on this connection, but you can be sure that one exists. Considering the questions in the following guidelines should help you recognize such connections and analyze the assumptions inherent in an assignment.

■ GUIDELINES FOR ANALYZING AN ASSIGNMENT

1. How does this assignment reflect the objectives of this course?

2. What general analytical and argumentative strategies does the instructor emphasize during class discussions? In discussions of readings, what organizational, stylistic, and logical qualities does the instructor praise or criticize? How might this assignment represent the instructor's effort to help students develop the critical abilities he or she emphasizes in class?

3. How much class time has the instructor spent on discussions of readings or on activities related to the content or form of this assignment? What has the instructor emphasized in these discussions or activities? How do these discussions and activities relate to this specific assignment?

4. Does this assignment call for a specific type of writing? How can you use your experience with previous writing assignments to help you complete this assignment?

5. To what extent does this assignment require you to follow the methodology and format characteristic of this discipline?

(continued)

(continued)

6. If this is one of several assignments for this course, can you apply comments the instructor has made about earlier essays to this current project?

Building Commitment to an Assignment

Most academic writing is, by definition, *required* writing — writing done to fulfill a requirement. As a student, you often find yourself writing not necessarily because you want to but because you have to. These conditions may make it hard for you to feel a strong sense of "ownership" of your writing. Furthermore, even if you're genuinely interested in your topic, you may feel so pressed by deadlines and other demands that all you can think is "I've just got to get this essay out of the way so I can get ready for biology lab." All writers face these problems.

Successful writers know, however, that they can't write well without being interested in and committed to their subjects. Consequently, they develop strategies to help them build this interest and commitment so that they can transform a required assignment (whether a research paper or a report for the boss) into a question or problem they care about and feel challenged to resolve. This is not to suggest that you must become passionately excited by every writing assignment. That would be unrealistic. But if you can't find some way to interest yourself in an assignment, to view it as an intellectual challenge you want to meet, you're going to have trouble getting beyond stale formulas.

Several strategies can help you build commitment to an assignment. You can, for instance, build your interest by using invention strategies, such as freewriting, looping, brainstorming, and clustering or the more formal journalist's questions, tagmemics, and topical questions (see Chapter 8 for discussions of all these strategies). Keeping a writer's notebook may also help you generate interest in a topic that at first doesn't seem compelling. Suppose, for example, that your economics instructor has asked you to write an essay about the Great Depression. At first you might not find this subject very interesting. After all, the Depression occurred decades ago. You'd rather evaluate some current economic policies. But after brainstorming, freewriting, or writing in your journal, you find that you keep coming back to a single image: the much-reproduced photograph of a businessman in a topcoat selling apples on a street corner. Did this actually happen? How often? How representative is this image of the Depression as a whole? Suddenly you've got a series of related questions — questions that you care about and that can help you limit and focus your topic.

When you build commitment to an assignment, you find reasons to want to write, reasons to "own" the assignment. The following guidelines can enable you to turn a required assignment into an interesting challenge that you want to complete.

■ GUIDELINES FOR GAINING COMMITMENT
TO AN ASSIGNMENT

1. *Use Freewriting, Brainstorming, Journal Writing, or Other Informal Kinds of Writing to Explore What You Already Know about Your Assignment.* Freewriting and brainstorming can help you discover images, questions, contradictions, and problems that turn required assignments into questions you want to answer. You may also find it helpful simply to write or list what you already know about a subject; you may be reassured to discover that you have a surprisingly large fund of information on your subject.

2. *Use the Same Strategies to Explore Your Feelings about an Assignment.* You may find it helpful to freewrite or brainstorm about your feelings about an assignment. While writing in her journal about a required assignment in a journalism class, for instance, Holly Hardin noted that she didn't want to work on a story about whether quarters or semesters are more conducive to learning because it was "just another dead issue." Once she understood the source of her resistance, Holly realized that she should see if her assumption was in fact correct. After interviewing several faculty members on campus, Holly discovered to her surprise that they held widely varying views on this subject. "Once I found a point of conflict," Holly wrote in a later journal entry, "I found a reason to write. From that point on the story was not just easy to work on but interesting."

3. *Work Collaboratively with Other Students in the Class.* Any assignment can seem overwhelming — something to put off rather than to begin — when you're sitting alone in your room or the library thinking about it. A much more productive strategy is to meet with other students in the class to discuss your understanding of the assignment and the processes and resources you are employing to respond to it. I'm not talking about a gripe session or *only* a

(continued)

(continued)

gripe session. You may want to spend a few moments commiserating with one another about how busy you are and how many assignments you need to do, but you should keep your primary goal in focus. By talking about your assignment and about your current efforts to respond to it, you want both to generate enthusiasm for this project and to help each other complete it more effectively.

If you are enrolled in a course you find difficult, you may wish to form a study group of students who will meet on a regular basis. Simply meeting together can provide discipline and intellectual and emotional reinforcement that you can use to your advantage. Your discussions and responses to works in progress can also help stimulate both your interest in the subject and your ability to respond successfully to assignments.

FOR EXPLORATION

Think back to an academic writing experience that was difficult or frustrating for you. To what extent did this problem result from your inability to build a genuine commitment to the assignment? How might you have responded more effectively to this problem? Freewrite for five or ten minutes about this experience.

FOR THOUGHT, DISCUSSION, AND WRITING

1. Interview an instructor who teaches a class you are taking this term or a class in your major area of study. Ask this person to describe his or her understanding of the goals of undergraduate education and the role your particular class or field of study plays in achieving these goals. Discuss the special analytic and argumentative skills required to succeed in this course or field. Ask this person what advice he or she would give to someone, like yourself, who is taking a class in this field or planning to major in it. Be prepared to report the results of this interview to your group so that the group can present its collective findings to the class. Your instructor also may ask you to write an essay summarizing and commenting on the results of your interview.

2. Choose a writing assignment that you are currently working on. Using the suggestions in this chapter, analyze this writing assignment. Begin by analyzing the assignment as it is presented by your instructor. Then

look for the assumptions behind the assignment, and develop strategies to help you build commitment to the assignment. Once you complete the assignment, try to determine if the analysis made your work
easier or more productive. Would you follow this process again?

3. Take a few moments to think about your experiences with academic
writing in college. Have certain kinds of writing assignments been easier or harder to complete successfully? Freewrite for five minutes in
response to this question. Then locate two completed assignments
done either for your composition class or for other courses. If possible,
locate one assignment that your instructor evaluated as successful and
another that your instructor was less satisfied with. After rereading the
assignments and resulting essays, review the discussion of academic
audiences and assignments in this chapter. Does the discussion help
you better understand why your instructors evaluated your writing as
they did? Freewrite for five minutes in response to this question.

Understanding Academic Analysis and Argument

14

As a student, you must respond to a wide range of writing assignments. For your American literature class, you may have to write an essay analyzing the significance of the whiteness of the whale in *Moby Dick*, whereas your business management class may require a collaboratively written case study. You may need to write a lab report for your chemistry class and to critique a reading for sociology.

Although these assignments vary considerably, a close look reveals that they all draw on two related skills: analysis and argument. This chapter will help you strengthen these two important academic skills.

UNDERSTANDING HOW ANALYSIS WORKS

Analysis is the activity of separating something into parts and determining how these parts function to create the whole. When you analyze, you examine a text, an object, or a body of data to understand how it is structured or organized and to assess its effectiveness or validity. Most academic writing, thinking, and reading involve analysis. Literature students analyze how a play is structured or how a poem achieves its effect; economics students analyze the major causes of inflation; biology students analyze the enzymatic reactions that comprise the Krebs cycle; and art history students analyze how line, color, and texture come together in a painting.

As these examples indicate, analysis is not a single skill but a group of related skills. An art history student might explore how a famous painting by Michelangelo achieves its effect, for instance, by *comparing* it with a similar work by Raphael. A biology student might discuss future acid-rain damage to forests in Canada and the United States by first *defining* acid rain and then using *cause-and-effect* reasoning to predict worsening conditions. A student in economics might estimate the likelihood of severe inflation in the future by *categorizing* or *classifying* the major causes of previous inflationary periods and then *evaluating* the likelihood of such factors influencing the current economic situation.

Different disciplines naturally emphasize different analytic skills. But whether you are a history, biology, or business major, you need to understand and practice these crucial academic skills. You will do so most successfully if you establish a purpose and develop an appropriate framework or method for your analysis.

Establishing a Purpose for Your Analysis

Your instructors will often ask you to analyze a fairly limited subject, problem, or process: Mrs. Ramsey's role in Virginia Woolf's *To the Lighthouse,* feminists' criticisms of Freud's psychoanalytical theories, Mendel's third law of genetics. Such limited tasks are necessary because of the complexity of the material being analyzed. Whole books have been written on Woolf's masterpiece and Freud's theories, so you can hardly examine these subjects completely in a brief essay or a research paper. But though you are analyzing a limited topic, the purpose of your analysis is broad: to better understand the material examined. When you analyze a limited topic, you are like a person holding a flashlight in the dark: The beam of light you project is narrow and focused, but it illuminates a much larger area.

Recognizing this larger purpose of analysis can help you make important decisions as you plan, draft, and revise. If your instructor has assigned a limited topic, for instance, you should ask yourself why he or she might have chosen this particular topic. What might make it an especially good means of understanding the larger issues at hand? If you are free to choose your own topic for analysis, your first questions should involve its larger significance. How will analyzing this topic improve your understanding of the larger subject? As you write, ask yourself regularly if your analysis is leading you to understand your topic more deeply. If you can answer yes to this question, you are probably doing a good job of analysis.

Even though the general purpose of your analysis is to understand the larger subject, you still need to establish a more specific purpose for your writing. Imagine, for instance, that your Shakespeare instructor has asked you to write an essay on the fool in *King Lear.* You might establish one of several specific purposes for your analysis:

To explain how the fool contributes to the development of a major theme in *King Lear*

To discuss the effectiveness or plausibility of Shakespeare's characterization of the fool

To define the role the fool plays in the plot

To agree or disagree with a particular critical perspective on the fool's role and significance

Establishing a specific purpose for your analysis helps you define how your analysis should proceed. It enables you to determine the important issues you should address or the questions you should answer. A student analyzing the effectiveness of Shakespeare's characterization of the fool would address different questions, for example, than one who is agreeing with a particular critical perspective on the fool's role and significance.

There are no one-size-fits-all procedures you can follow to establish a purpose for your analysis. Sometimes your purpose will develop naturally as a result of reading, reflection, and discussion with others. In other instances, it may help to draw on the invention strategies described in Chapter 8; freewriting, brainstorming, tagmemics, and the topical questions can help you explore your subject and discover questions that can guide your analysis. You may need to write your way into an understanding of your purpose by composing a rough draft of your essay and seeing, in effect, what you think about your topic. Writing and thinking are dynamically interwoven processes.

Developing an Appropriate Method for Your Analysis

Once you have a purpose, how do you actually analyze something? The answer depends on the subject, process, or problem being analyzed; it also depends, in academic writing, on the discipline within which the analysis is done. The students studying *To the Lighthouse* and Mendel's third law may both use such analytic processes as definition, causal analysis, classification, and comparison to analyze their subjects. But the exact form of the processes each uses — the way each organizes the analysis and the criteria each uses to evaluate it — may well differ. Despite these disciplinary differences, both students must establish some method for analysis if they are to succeed.

There are no hard-and-fast rules for establishing such a method. In general, however, you should look to the methods of inquiry characteristic of the specific discipline for guidance. The questions presented in the following guidelines can help you develop an appropriate method for your analysis.

■ GUIDELINES FOR DEVELOPING AN APPROPRIATE METHOD FOR ANALYSIS

■ How have your instructors approached analysis in class? Do they rely on a systematic procedure, such as case-study or problem-

(continued)

(continued)

solving methodology, or does their analysis vary, depending on the subject under discussion?

■ What kinds of evidence and examples do they draw on?

■ What kinds of questions do your instructors typically ask in class discussions? Why might people in the discipline view these as important questions?

■ What kinds of answers to these questions do your instructors favor? Why might people in this discipline value such responses?

If, after considering these questions and reflecting on your experience in a class, you continue to have difficulty settling on an appropriate method for analysis, meet with your instructor to get help. You might ask him or her to recommend student essays or articles from the field that you can read. Analyzing these texts can help you understand the analytical methods used in the field.

UNDERSTANDING THE RELATIONSHIP BETWEEN ANALYSIS AND ARGUMENT

As I mentioned at the start of Chapter 13, all academic writing has an argumentative edge. Sometimes that edge is obvious. If a student writes a political science essay arguing that the government should follow a particular environmental policy, that student is explicitly arguing that the government should do something. Essays that are organized around the question of whether something should or should not be done are easily recognizable as arguments — probably because they follow the debate format that many associate with argumentation.

But writers can express judgments — can present good reasons for their beliefs and actions — in other ways. A student analyzing the score of a Beethoven sonata for a music theory class may argue that it should be performed in a certain way but also may try to convince her reader, in this case her teacher, that she has a sophisticated understanding of the structure of the sonata she is studying. (She might do this by arguing that the second movement of the particular sonata is more daring or innovative than music historians have acknowledged.) Analysis will play a particularly central role in this student's writing: By identifying specific, concrete details and positing relationships among these details, she will demonstrate her understanding of Beethoven's use of the sonata form.

As this example demonstrates, analysis and argument are mutually inter-dependent. Argumentation depends on analysis, for it is through analysis that writers clarify the logic of their thinking and provide evidence for their judg-ments. (The student arguing that the government should follow a particular environmental policy would certainly have to analyze the potential benefits and disadvantages of that policy and demonstrate that it is workable.) Simi-larly, analysis always carries an implicit argumentative burden. For when you analyze something, you are in effect asserting "This is how I believe X works" or "This is what I believe X means."

Academic analysis and argument call for similar habits of mind. Both encourage writers to suspend personal biases when they undertake academic inquiry. This is not to say that academic writers are expected to be absolutely objective. Your gut feeling that "workfare" programs may not provide employ-ees with adequate support for their children may cause you to investigate this topic for a political science or economics class. This gut feeling is a strength, not a weakness, for it enables you to find a topic of interest to you. Once you begin to explore your topic, however, you need to engage it dispassionately. You need, in other words, to be open to changing your mind.

If you do change your mind about the consequences of workfare pro-grams for children, it will undoubtedly be because the reading and writing you have done have caused you to have a more detailed and specific understanding of the issues at stake in arguments over workfare programs. If the essay you write about this topic is successful, you will not only describe these issues but also analyze their relationships and their implications. You will develop logical connections that make your reasoning — the logic behind your analysis — explicit. In these and other ways you are demonstrating to your readers that you have indeed understood your subject.

The following essay by Jacob Agatucci is a good example of academic analysis. In this essay, Jacob is not arguing that something should or should not be done. Rather, he is attempting to understand the roles that stage direc-tions and cinematic technique play in helping contemporary audiences to better understand Shakespeare's plays. As a consequence, in his essay Jacob focuses on providing clear and specific examples and on analyzing the connections among and the implications of these examples.

DIALOGUE AS IMAGE IN *KING LEAR*
by Jacob Agatucci

What can theater and film directors do to help contemporary audiences appreciate the role of dialogue in Shakespeare's plays? What role can stage directions and cinematic technique play in helping audiences to under-stand the relationships among characters? These are important questions since contemporary audiences often find it difficult to follow the intricacies of Shakespearean dialogue. The language in which Shakespeare wrote is alien to many ears, and the lines are often delivered so quickly that the viewer finds it difficult to remember where a character stands in relation to other characters in a play. *King Lear* is a relevant example. Though the dialogue of the opening act defines the conflicts of the play — estranging loyal daughter from father and suggesting the deception of Goneril, Regan, and Edmund — important elements of this conflict could be lost to the untrained ear. The recent British Broadcasting Company (BBC) production of *King Lear* is a cinematic adaptation that honors Shakespeare's language and intentions but aids in its delivery through visual supplementation.

An example of this supplementation can be found during Act I, Scene 1. It occurs as King Lear derides Cordelia for not equaling her sisters' false expressions of love. The profiles of Lear and Cordelia, facing one another, fill the frame during the scene (see Fig. 1). Their faces are far enough apart to allow a space between them in which Kent is carefully framed — blurred and in the background. Thus the staging and cinematography, in addition to the dialogue, provide a visual representation of the disaffected parties (Lear and Cordelia) and the man (Kent) who seeks to alleviate their estrangement. This cinematic technique neatly encapsu-

Fig. 1

lates the relationship among these three characters and calls attention to an important feature of the plot.

A similar moment occurs when Scene 1 segues into Scene 2. Here, as in the earlier scene, essential characters in *King Lear* are brought together. In this case, however, it is the villains who are brought together. Here (see Fig. 2), the profiles of Regan and Goneril dominate the shot as they reflect on Lear's "long-ingraffed condition" (I. 1.330). Like Kent, Edmund is framed between them and in the background. Just as the former scene linked the protagonists of the play, this scene links its antagonists. This scene also emphasizes Edmund's role in the various deceptions that are central to the plot of *King Lear*. As Regan and Goneril end their exchange, they pull out of the frame to the left and right, and the camera focuses on Edmund, who is in the background (see Fig. 3). Since the next scene (Act I, Scene 2) begins with Edmund's soliloquy, Edmund's destructive ambition is visually linked with Goneril's and Regan's deceit.

Both of these scenes could easily have been shot with Kent and Edmund absent — but then viewers would have had to rely solely on dialogue to link characters and motives. Fortunately, the director chose to structure the play along visual as well as auditory lines. To do so, the director had to go beyond the stage directions included in *King Lear,* which revolve around entrances and exits, to consider the ways in which staging

Fig. 2

Fig. 3

and cinematography could help clarify both the immediate dialogue and future character relations. As a consequence, the BBC adaptation is especially sensitive to the needs of an audience that may not be familiar with Shakespearean dialogue.

Though Shakespeare's language is paramount within his plays, the BBC production of *King Lear* provides an innovative example of how the effective use of visual cues can supplement and clarify dialogue. Through both the physical placement of characters on the stage and careful cinematic technique, the BBC production uses visual cues to reinforce Shakespeare's dialogue. As a result, the experience of the audience is enriched, for they are left not simply with Shakespeare's words but with a synergistic combination of auditory and visual elements.

WORKS CITED

King Lear. Dir. Jonathan Miller. Prod. Shaun Sutton. Videocassette. BBC and Time-Life Films, 1987.

Shakespeare, William. *King Lear. The Complete Works of Shakespeare.* Ed. David Bevington. 4th ed. New York: Longman, 1997. 1167–1218.

■ ■ ■

FOR EXPLORATION

Reread Jacob Agatucci's essay, and then respond in writing to the following:

1. How would you describe the relationship between analysis and argument in Jacob's essay? To what extent does Jacob make a specific argument? What role does analysis play in the development of his ideas?

2. In academic writing, particular value is placed on explicitness and on developing logical connections among ideas. In what ways does Jacob's essay fulfill this expectation?

RESPONDING TO THE DEMANDS OF ACADEMIC ARGUMENT

As the previous discussion has emphasized, whether you are analyzing a subject or taking an argumentative stand in relation to it, your teachers are interested primarily in the quality of your thinking, reading, writing, and researching. In such a situation, the debate model of argumentation proves particularly problematic. Think about the terminology used in debate. Speakers "attack" their "adversaries," hoping to "demolish" their arguments to "win" the judge's assent and claim "victory" in the contest. This model of argument may prevail in forensic and political debates, but it seems less appropriate for academic argument, where the goal is inquiry and not conquest. Your teachers are not interested in whether you can "attack" or "demolish" your opponents. Rather, they value the ability to examine an issue or problem from multiple perspectives. Their commitment is not to winning but to clear reasoning and substantial evidence. For these reasons, academic argument is best conceived of as conversation and dialogue — as inquiry — and not as debate.

Intellectual inquiry is a process that challenges you to explore your topic in the richest and fullest way possible. Your goal is to present good reasons why others should agree with your conclusions and to discuss the reasons why they might not. To reach this goal, you need to determine what is at stake in an argument, what role is played by values and beliefs in argument, what evidence is appropriate, and what counterarguments are possible.

DETERMINING WHAT'S AT STAKE IN AN ARGUMENT

You can't argue by yourself. If you disagree with a recent legislative decision reported in your morning newspaper, you may mumble angry words to yourself at breakfast — but you'd know that you're not arguing. To argue, you must argue with someone. Furthermore, the person with whom you wish to argue must agree with you that an assertion raises an arguable *issue.* If you like rap music, for example, and your friend, who prefers jazz, refuses even to listen to (much less discuss) your favorite CD or tape, you can hardly argue about your friend's preferences. You'll both probably just wonder at the peculiarities of taste.

Similarly, in academic argument you and your reader (most often your instructor) must agree that an issue is worth arguing about if you are to argue successfully. Often this agreement involves sharing a common understanding of a problem, process, or idea. A student who writes an argument on the symbolism of Hester Prynne's scarlet A in *The Scarlet Letter,* for example, begins from a premise, one she believes will be shared by the teacher — that Hester's A has significance for the meaning or theme of the novel. Another example of working from a shared understanding can be found in the essay about the Tacoma Narrows Bridge, reprinted in Chapter 4, in which student Brenda Shonkwiler takes a cue from the ongoing discussion that continues among engineers sixty years after the bridge's collapse and successfully argues that an understanding of the causes underlying the failure is important for preventing future engineering disasters.

All argument, in this sense, begins from shared premises. An important distinction exists, however, between academic arguments and the kind of casual arguments you have with family and friends. Academic arguments, unlike casual arguments, must be structured so that they focus on a limited issue or topic. In a late-night discussion with friends, you may easily slip from a heated exchange over the cause of the national budget deficit to a friendly debate about the best way to remedy bureaucratic inefficiency. In an academic argument, however, you must limit your discussion not just to a single issue but to a single *thesis,* a claim you will argue for. It is not enough, in other words, to decide that you want to write about nuclear energy or the need to protect the wilderness. Even limiting these subjects — writing about the Three Mile Island nuclear reactor or the Forest Service Land Management Plan for the White Mountain National Forest in New Hampshire — wouldn't help much. That's because your thesis must be an assertion — something, in other words, to argue about.

A clear, adequately limited thesis is vital for academic argument because it indicates (for you and for your reader) what's at stake. For this reason, many instructors and writers suggest that academic arguments should contain an explicit thesis statement — a single declarative sentence that asserts or denies something about the topic. The assertion "The United States Forest Service's land management plan for the White Mountain National Forest fails adequately to protect New Hampshire's wilderness areas" is an example of a thesis statement.

Thesis statements serve important functions for writers and readers. Developing a clear, limited thesis statement can help a writer stay on track and include evidence or details relevant to the main point rather than extraneous or only loosely related information. Readers — especially busy readers like your college instructors — also find thesis statements helpful. A clearly worded thesis statement in the introduction of an essay assures readers that the essay will be well organized and clearly written; it also helps them read your writing both more critically and more efficiently.

Here is the first paragraph of an essay written for a class on Latin American history. The student's thesis statement is italicized. Notice how this statement clearly articulates the student's position on the topic, the role of multinational and transnational corporations in Central America:

> Over the past fifty years, Latin American countries have worked hard to gain economic strength and well-being. To survive, however, these countries have been forced to rely on multinational and transnational corporations for money, jobs, and technological expertise. *In doing so, they have lost needed economic independence and have left themselves vulnerable to exploitation by foreign financiers.*

A clear thesis statement can help both writer *and* reader stay on track as they "compose" an essay.

■ ■ ■

FOR EXPLORATION

Look back at the rough draft and revised draft of Todd Carpenter's essay, "Why Isn't There a National Bottle Law?" in Chapter 11. Reread both drafts, and then answer these questions.

1. The rough draft does not contain a clear thesis statement, but the revised draft does. What is the thesis statement in the revised draft? Does this thesis statement help make Todd's essay easier for you as a reader to follow?

2. Todd's analysis of his rhetorical situation, presented on p. 296, demonstrates his awareness of the academic rhetorical situation and of the demands of academic analysis and argument. Todd notes, for instance, that "even if my instructor agrees that there should be a national bottle law, she won't give me a good grade unless I write an effective argument.

In class, my instructor has stressed the importance of looking at both sides of the issue and presenting evidence for my views, so I'll try to do that here." Review Todd's rough and revised drafts, paying particular attention to the ways in which the revised draft responds to these concerns. List at least three of these changes, and write a brief explanation of why they increase the effectiveness of Todd's essay as an academic argument.

3. Suppose that Todd wants to write an essay on bottle laws for members of an ecological group whom he hopes to persuade to support this effort. How might Todd revise his argument to meet the needs and expectations of these readers, who are likely to support the idea of a national bottle law but may not view it as a priority for their particular organization?

If you are like many writers, you will at times have to think — and write — your way to a thesis. You may know the subject you want to discuss, and you may have a tentative or *working thesis* in mind from the start. Sometimes, however, you will find that only by actually writing a rough draft — by marshaling your ideas and ordering your evidence — can you determine what thesis you can support. In situations like this, you will revise your thesis as you write to reflect your increased understanding of your topic and your rhetorical situation.

UNDERSTANDING THE ROLE OF VALUES AND BELIEFS IN ARGUMENT

When you argue, you give reasons and evidence for your assertions. The student arguing against the Forest Service plan might warn that increased timber harvesting will reduce access to the forest for campers and backpackers or that building more roads will adversely affect wildlife. This writer might also show that the Forest Service has failed to anticipate some problems with the plan and that cost-benefit calculations are skewed to reflect logging and economic-development interests. These are all potentially good reasons for questioning the proposed plan. Notice that these reasons necessarily imply certain values or beliefs. The argument against increasing the timber harvest and building more roads, for instance, reflects the belief that preserving wildlife habitats and wilderness lands is more important than the economic development of the resources.

Is this argument flawed because it appeals to values and beliefs? Of course not. When you argue, you can't suppress your own values and beliefs. Your values and beliefs enable you to make sense of the world; they provide links between the world you observe and experience and yourself. They thus play an important role in any argument.

Suppose that you and a friend are getting ready to go out for dinner. You look out the window and notice some threatening clouds. You say, "Looks like rain. We'd better take umbrellas since we're walking. I hate getting soaked." "Oh, I don't know," your friend replies. "I don't think it looks so bad. It usually rains in the mornings in summer. I think we should risk it." Brief and informal as this exchange is, it constitutes an argument. Both you and your friend have observed something, analyzed it, and drawn conclusions — conclusions backed by reasons. Although you each cite different reasons, your conclusions may most strongly reflect your different personal preferences. You're generally cautious, and you don't like getting caught unprepared in a downpour, so you opt for an umbrella. Your friend is more of a risk taker.

If your individual preferences, values, and beliefs shape a single situation like this where only getting wet is at stake, imagine how crucial they are in more complicated and contested situations — situations where the central issue is not whether clouds will bring rain but whether a controversial proposal is right or wrong, just or unjust, effective or ineffective. Argument necessarily involves values and beliefs, held by both writer and reader. These values and beliefs cannot be denied or excluded, even in academic argument, with its emphasis on evidence and reasoned inquiry. The student arguing against the Forest Service plan cannot avoid using values and beliefs as bridges between reasons and conclusions. And not all of these bridges can be explicitly stated; that would lead to an endless chain of reasons. The standards of academic argument require, however, that the most important values and beliefs undergirding an argument be explicitly stated and defended. In this case, then, the student opposing the Forest Service plan should at some point state and support the belief that preserving wildlife habitats and wilderness lands should take priority over economic development.

It's not easy to identify and analyze your own values and beliefs, but doing so is essential in academic argument. Values and beliefs are often held unconsciously, and they function as part of a larger network of assumptions and practices. Your opinions about the best way for the government to respond to unemployed individuals reflect values and beliefs you hold about the family, the proper role of government, the nature of individual responsibility, and the importance of economic security. Thus if your political science instructor asks you to argue for or against programs requiring welfare recipients to work at state-mandated jobs in exchange for economic support, you need to analyze carefully not just these workfare programs but also the role your values and beliefs play in your analysis.

The following guidelines for analyzing your values and beliefs should enable you to respond more effectively to the demands of academic argument.

■ GUIDELINES FOR ANALYZING
YOUR OWN VALUES AND BELIEFS

1. *Use Informal Invention Methods to Explore Your Values and Beliefs about a Subject.* To discover *why* you believe what you believe, you need to consider more than rational, logical arguments: You need to tap into your experiences and emotions. Freewriting, looping, brainstorming, and clustering are excellent ways to explore the values and beliefs that encourage you to adopt a particular stance toward an issue.

2. *After Exploring Your Values and Beliefs, Consider the Degree to Which They Enable You to Argue Effectively about a Subject.* Exploring your own values and beliefs enables you to distance yourself from your habitual ways of thinking and thus encourages the analytical habits of mind your instructors want to foster. Such exploration can also help you discover ways to ground your argument in values and beliefs you share with your readers. (You may wish to review Todd Carpenter's essays, which appear in Chapter 11, to see how he achieves this goal.)

   Sometimes your exploration may enable you to realize that you face special challenges when it comes to writing an effective academic argument on a particular subject. For example, freewriting about your feelings about gun control may help you realize that your convictions about this issue are so deeply rooted in your beliefs and values that you will have to work hard to maintain academic standards of objectivity in an argument about this subject. You might do better, you realize, to choose a different subject for your argument.

3. *Imagine a "Devil's Advocate" Who Holds Different Values and Beliefs.* Becoming aware of your values and beliefs can help you better understand why you have adopted a particular stance toward an issue or a problem. You may nevertheless find it difficult to step outside your way of thinking to consider whether others might reasonably hold differing views — and yet much academic writing demands just this ability. Many writers find it helpful to engage in a silent dialogue with one or more "devil's advocates" — persons whose views differ considerably from their own. If you were writing an essay arguing that the federal government needs to increase funding for college student loans, you might engage in a

(continued)

(continued)

mental or written dialogue with a hard-headed pragmatic congress-person or corporate executive who might resist such an argument because of concerns about the national debt. Their challenges might help you recognize that your assumptions about the need for all students to have access to a college education are not universally shared and that other assumptions — such as the need to reduce the national debt — might reasonably take precedence. Your dialogue has helped you learn that you must make your own assumptions explicit, provide good reasons why those assumptions are valid, and consider competing assumptions as well. Your dialogue might even help you realize that you need to limit or modify your goals for this essay.

4. *Engage in Discussions with Your Classmates.* You're probably already aware from informal discussions that even friends and family members can disagree about complex or controversial subjects. When you discuss current events with your friends or family, for example, they may naturally formulate questions that require you to reconsider not only your stance toward an issue or problem but also the assumptions, values, and beliefs that undergird this position. You can draw on this natural activity of mutual inquiry to help you explore your values, assumptions, and beliefs. This may take the form of informal dinner talk with friends or formal group discussions with classmates. Follow these steps for any formal discussions:

- Decide how much time each student will have to discuss his or her work. Appoint a timekeeper to enforce these limits.

- The writer should begin by describing the controlling purpose or thesis of the essay and then briefly list the values and beliefs that led to this position. The writer should then invite group members to ask questions designed to provide perspectives on these values and beliefs and to explain different views that others might reasonably hold.

- The writer should lead the resulting discussion, asking group members to clarify or elaborate on suggestions. Group members should remember that their goal is not to attack or criticize the writer's values and beliefs but rather to help the writer gain additional perspectives on them.

When you argue, you must consider not only your own values and beliefs but also those of your readers. The student writing about the Forest Service plan would present one argument to the local branch of the Sierra Club and a very different argument to representatives of the Forest Service. In arguing to the Sierra Club, the student would almost assuredly expect agreement and therefore might focus on how the group could best oppose the plan and why members should devote their time and energy to this rather than other projects. The argument to the Forest Service would be quite different. Recognizing that members of the Forest Service would know the plan very well, would have spent a great deal of time working on it, and would be strongly committed to it, the student might focus on a limited number of points, especially those that the Forest Service might be most able and willing to modify. The student might also assume a less aggressive or strident tone to avoid alienating the audience.

In academic argument, of course, your reader is generally your instructor. In this rhetorical situation, the most useful approach is to consider the values and beliefs your instructor holds as a member of the academic community. In writing for an economics or a political science instructor, the student arguing against the Forest Service plan should provide logical, accurate, and appropriate evidence for assertions. He or she should avoid strong emotional appeals and harsh expressions of outrage or bitterness, focusing instead on developing a succinct, clearly organized, carefully reasoned essay.

■ ■ ■

FOR EXPLORATION

Think of an issue that concerns you. Perhaps you are involved with or have been following a campus controversy. You may oppose a decision made recently by your city council or some other elected body. Or you may be committed (or opposed) to broad national movements such as the efforts to provide public child-care facilities, house the homeless, or improve public transportation. After reflecting on this issue, use the guidelines presented earlier in this section to analyze your values and beliefs. Then respond to the following questions.

1. Given your values and beliefs, what challenges would writing an academic essay on this subject pose for you?

2. To what extent did your analysis help you understand that others might reasonably hold different views on this subject? Make a list of the opposing arguments that others might make in response to your subject. Then briefly describe the values and beliefs that might lead readers

to make these counterarguments. How might you respond to these arguments?

3. Now write the major assertions or arguments you would use to support your controlling idea or thesis. Below each assertion, list the values or beliefs your readers must share with you to accept that assertion.

4. How have the guidelines and this application helped you understand how to write an effective academic argument? If you were to write an academic argument on this issue, how would you now organize and develop your ideas? What strategies would you now use to respond to the values and beliefs of your readers?

USING APPROPRIATE EVIDENCE

Whenever you argue, you engage in the process of giving good reasons why your reader should accept your conclusions or judgment. Arguments are not all alike, however. A student reviewing a movie faces different challenges from one advocating laws requiring motorcyclists to wear helmets. These two tasks require different analytic skills — and different kinds of evidence.

Arguments can be characterized in a number of ways, though most systems are somewhat artificial, describing "pure," unmixed arguments. In actuality, many arguments are hybrids. Still, considering your potential argumentative task can help you determine how best to limit your thesis, select appropriate and persuasive evidence or support, and organize your ideas. Professor Annette T. Rottenberg categorizes arguments according to the nature of the thesis or claim. All arguments, she notes, involve *claims of fact, claims of value, or claims of policy.* * Some essays focus on only one of these claims, but more often writers draw on all three approaches to support and develop their ideas.

Claims of Fact

Claims of fact state that something is or will be true. Here are four such claims:

- Eastern European weight lifters consistently outperform their Western counterparts.

- ABC University fails to provide adequate funds for the library.

- Orientation programs for first-year students help them adjust to college life.

---

*Annette T. Rottenberg, *Elements of Argument: A Text and Reader,* 6th ed. (Boston: Bedford/St. Martin's, 2000).

■ When used properly, organic fertilizers and pesticides can be just as effective as their chemical counterparts and much less harmful and expensive.

When arguing about a claim of fact, you often support your thesis by using examples, statistics, and statements by authorities on the subject. Even though you use data to support your claim, however, you must still contextualize and interpret this information. The question of what constitutes "adequate" funds for a university library, for example, is hardly obvious. You should recognize that reasonable people can disagree about just what the facts are. For instance, scientists sometimes disagree about the results of rigorously controlled studies. In academic argument, the distinction between a fact and an inference (a conclusion or an interpretation of a fact) is often subject to debate. Consequently, you should not assume that the facts are obvious. Many facts are open to multiple interpretations; such interpretations play a crucial role in academic argument.

Claims of Value

Claims of value assert a judgment. For example:

■ Doctor-assisted suicide is a humane alternative to the pain suffered by patients with terminal illnesses.

■ None of the *Star Trek* movies has matched the original television series for wit and originality.

■ Maslow's psychological theories describe the nature of human motivation better than do those of Freud or Pavlov.

■ The news media's obsession with the private lives of politicians is harmful to the practice of democracy.

Claims of value attempt to prove that something is right or wrong, just or unjust, effective or ineffective, well crafted or poorly constructed. If you go to a movie with a friend and then argue about how well the actors performed, you are arguing about a claim of value.

Your experience arguing about movies may help you understand an essential requirement for a claim of value: acceptable criteria for judgment. You could hardly defend the merits of a movie because you liked the color of the heroine's dress or because you think that gangster movies set in Chicago are always good. Even if you've never studied film or read movie reviews, you know that if you want your opinion to be taken seriously by others, you need to base your arguments on such commonly accepted criteria as the quality of the acting, the script, and the direction; the significance of the theme; or the movie's ability to draw you into the action. When writing an academic essay about a claim of value, you need to be especially concerned with identifying criteria or standards for your analysis. Otherwise, you may be charged with focusing on trivial issues or with relying on mere opinion rather than informed judgment.

Claims of Policy

Claims of policy assert that something should or should not exist or occur. Here are four policy claims:

- Student fees should not be used to support this college's athletic program.

- The federal government should direct more funds to public transportation and less to constructing new highways.

- American executives should pay as much attention to ethics as they do to profits and other bottom-line issues.

- Students should boycott the *Playboy* photographer who will visit campus this term to recruit models.

When you assert a claim of policy, you are implicitly arguing that some current problem must be remedied. Better child care would not be needed, for example, if current services were adequate. Essays making claims of policy often begin with necessary background information. Next, the proposed policy must be carefully explained and supported. The support for a claim of policy often comes from statistics and similar forms of evidence. A student advocating increased support of child-care programs might cite the number of children needing child care as well as the number of placements available or include the comments of a noted child psychologist on the need for high-quality care.

Beliefs and values often play a crucial role in arguments about a claim of policy. They do so because they strongly influence how you (and your readers) interpret data. Two individuals reviewing statistics about the number of children needing child care might draw very different conclusions. "This is evidence," the first might think, "of the need for our state to provide public child-care facilities." The second might conclude, "This is evidence of the breakdown of the traditional American family. We need to convince mothers that staying home and caring for children is the most important job possible."

■ ■ ■

FOR EXPLORATION

Think again about the issue you wrote about in response to the Exploration on pp. 370–71. Formulate a tentative or working thesis statement that reflects your current position on this issue. Identify whether this thesis statement asserts a claim of fact, of value, or of policy, and then list the major evidence you would use to support this thesis. Finally, write a brief statement explaining why this evidence is appropriate, given your thesis statement and the kind of claim it makes.

ACKNOWLEDGING POSSIBLE COUNTERARGUMENTS

Academic argument is modeled on inquiry and dialogue rather than debate. Your task in an academic argument is not to persuade your instructor to agree with you but to demonstrate that you can reason, and write, in a logical, coherent manner. This approach requires that you consider multiple "sides" of an issue. Discussing and responding to counterarguments in your essay is one of the most effective ways to demonstrate that you have seriously analyzed an issue from a number of perspectives — that you have drawn reasonable conclusions.

Earlier sections of this chapter provided a number of ways to discover counterarguments. For instance, you could dialogue with one or more "devil's advocates," or you could discuss your subject with a group of classmates. You might even decide to interview someone who holds a position different from your own. Being aware of your own values and beliefs can also help you identify possible counterarguments. The student arguing against the Forest Service plan might consider the views of someone with different values, perhaps someone who believes in the importance of economic development, such as the owner of a lumber company. Finally, reading and research (both print and online) can expose you to the ideas and arguments of others.

How you use the counterarguments that you identify will depend on your subject and your rhetorical situation. In some instances, these counterarguments can play an important structural role in your essay. After introducing your essay and indicating your thesis, for example, you might present the major counterarguments to your position, refuting each in turn. You might also group these counterarguments, responding to them all at once at an appropriate point.

■ ■ ■

FOR GROUP WORK

This activity will help you recognize possible counterarguments to the thesis you have been writing about in this chapter. To prepare for this group activity, be sure that you have a clear, easy-to-read statement of your tentative or working thesis and of the major evidence you would use to support this thesis in an academic essay. Now spend five to ten minutes brainstorming a list of possible counterarguments to your working thesis.

Bring these written materials to your group's meeting. Determine how much time the group can spend per person if each student is to get help. Appoint a timekeeper to be sure that the group stays on time. Then have each writer read his or her working thesis, evidence, and possible counterarguments, followed by members of the group suggesting additional counterarguments that the writer has not considered. Avoid getting bogged down in specific arguments; instead, focus on generating as many additional counterarguments as possible. Continue this procedure until each student's work has been discussed.

When you enter a college or university, you join an academic community with unique values, beliefs, and methods of inquiry. Yet few members of that community will discuss these directly with you. Instead, your history instructor explores the impact of printing on the Renaissance imagination, and your political science instructor focuses on recent events in the Middle East. Your instructors leave it to you to understand the academic rhetorical situation and to master the skills necessary to succeed in their courses. You don't have to face this challenge alone, however. Your composition instructor and your classmates, acting as both coaches and supporters, can help you understand and develop the critical thinking, reading, and writing skills necessary for success in school. What is at stake in your composition course, then, is not just earning a passing grade or fulfilling a requirement but becoming a fully participating and successful member of the academic community.

■ ■ ■

FOR THOUGHT, DISCUSSION, AND WRITING

1. Chapter 3 presents a number of readings on cyberspace, including Robert J. Samuelson's "The Internet and Gutenberg" and a diverse selection of readings at the end of the chapter. Evaluate the strengths and weaknesses of the arguments in these earlier readings.

2. Read a daily newspaper for a week. (You may want to read one of the national newspapers, such as the *Christian Science Monitor* or the *Wall Street Journal.*) Paying particular attention to the editorials, look for examples of arguments making claims of fact, value, and policy. Analyze the effectiveness of these arguments. Be prepared to bring examples of each kind of argument to class for discussion. Try also to find at least two or three examples of mixed arguments — arguments that focus on more than a single claim. How do these arguments differ from those that focus on a single claim?

3. This chapter has presented activities designed to improve your under-standing of academic argument. The Exploration on pp. 370–71, for instance, asks you to identify the values, assumptions, and beliefs that have led you to hold strong views on an issue. The one on p. 373 asks you to formulate a tentative or working thesis and to list the major evi-dence you would use to support it. Finally, the group activity on p. 374 encourages you to acknowledge possible counterarguments to your thesis.

Drawing on these activities, write an essay directed to an academic reader on the topic you have explored, revising your working thesis if you need to do so.

Putting It All Together: Writing Academic Arguments

One of the best ways to understand a complex process is to see that process in action. An aspiring chef who wants to learn how to make croissants can read recipe after recipe and yet not quite grasp the technique required to make these rich, crescent-shaped rolls. Observing someone who is actually making croissants — someone demonstrating critical elements of the technique — can make a world of difference. So it is with writers. This chapter provides an opportunity for you to take an in-depth look at one writer's process in action. Though you will not be able to sit next to this writer as she composes, you will be able to observe — and learn from — the three drafts of a single essay that are presented here. With each draft, this writer clarifies and strengthens her argument.

The writer is Beth Runciman, a student at Smith College in Northampton, Massachusetts. For an American literature survey course, Beth was assigned to write an essay analyzing a poem by Emily Dickinson, a nineteenth-century American writer. As a first step in her composing process, Beth wrote an analysis of her rhetorical situation. Here is Beth's analysis:

> This assignment calls for a formal argument, so I will need to follow the conventions of an academic essay, with a clear introduction and conclusion and a logical order to the organization. The assignment asks us to demonstrate that we understand what's going on in the poem we choose to write about — that we locate the poem in its historical context and that we talk about the literary techniques the author is using to make her point. I'll want to make sure that the argument I present is grounded in evidence from the poem itself and that I'm able to quote specific lines from the poem to support what I say. I'll also want to use the vocabulary we've studied in class — terms like image, metaphor, meter, and line break.
>
> The audience for this essay is my professor. I know that she appreciates Dickinson's poetry, but what she'll be looking for in my essay isn't so much appreciation as understanding. To help convey that understanding, I need to adopt a tone of objectivity and authority.

Notice how in these comments Beth moves from a general assessment of her assignment — "I need to follow the conventions of an academic essay, with a clear introduction and conclusion and a logical order to the organization" — to consideration of the conventions of the discipline for which she is writing, in this case literary criticism. Beth understands that when instructors read student writing they do so from the perspective of their disciplinary training. Given this, Beth recognizes that her goal is to demonstrate her ability to analyze and interpret Dickinson's poem and not to persuade her teacher to believe or do something.

Beth's understanding of her rhetorical situation will influence the choices she makes as a writer. To become more self-conscious about these choices, Beth concluded her analysis by considering how her essay might best address Aristotle's three appeals: the appeal to *logos*, or reason; to *pathos*, or emotion; and to *ethos*, or the credibility of the writer. (If you wish to review Aristotle's three appeals, see p. 156.)

> *Logos:* I'll appeal most strongly to *logos* when writing this essay. To be successful, I've got to show my teacher that I can analyze the poem in detail and draw conclusions from my analysis.

> *Pathos:* Emotional appeals won't play a strong role in my essay. Dickinson's poem is very emotional, but my analysis needs to focus on its technique and content. I do want to appeal to *pathos* in one way, though: I want to encourage the reader to appreciate Dickinson's skill and daring.

> *Ethos:* I want my teacher to see me as being fully in control of my ideas and their presentation. If my analysis *(logos)* is effective, my teacher will view me as a credible writer.

Beth's analysis has helped prepare her to meet the demands of her assignment. This analysis has reminded Beth that even when an assignment is relatively broad and open-ended, as hers is, her teacher nevertheless has specific expectations about how students can best complete it. In this instance, Beth's teacher expects that successful students will write essays demonstrating their ability to "talk the talk and walk the walk" of literary criticism.

BETH'S FIRST DRAFT: ANALYZING EMILY DICKINSON'S POEM #48

As mentioned earlier, Beth worked her way through three drafts before she arrived at an essay that satisfied her. According to Beth, each draft had a slightly different purpose. "In my first draft," she said, "I was trying to analyze the poem itself and understand how Dickinson's choices of meter, rhythm, imagery, and syntax made the poem what it was. I wrote this draft to talk to myself about all the ways the poem was working. I knew I would need to know it inside out to write a formal argument about it."

Beth wrote this comment, by the way, in a writing-process journal that she kept while working on her essay. Beth was taking a first-year writing class at the same time that she was enrolled in her American literature survey class, and her writing instructor had asked her students to choose a writing assignment from a different class and keep detailed notes about their writing process. You may find it helpful to undertake similar self-study. (See pp. 33–34 for directions for a case study of your own writing process.)

Here is Beth Runciman's first draft of her essay. It is preceded by the Emily Dickinson poem that Beth chose to analyze.

ANALYSIS OF EMILY DICKINSON'S POEM #48 [FIRST DRAFT]

by Beth Runciman

> Once more, my now bewildered Dove
> Bestirs her puzzled wings
> Once more her mistress, on the deep
> Her troubled question flings —
>
> Thrice to the floating casement
> The Patriarch's bird returned,
> Courage! My brave Columba!
> There may yet be Land!

In poem #48 ("Once more, my now bewildered Dove"), Dickinson talks about feelings of hope and feelings of desperation, and she uses the story of Noah and the end of the flood as a metaphor to do so. In the story, Noah releases a dove from the ark three times near the end of the flood. He knows that if the bird cannot see land, it will return to the ark. If land is in sight, however, the bird will fly toward it, showing Noah the direction in which to sail. Dickinson builds the whole poem around this image. She replaces "The Patriarch," Noah, with a female speaker; we know this from the word "mistress." This speaker's tone is desperate, as Noah's would be as well — an ark can hold only so much food, and if the bird does not direct Noah to land soon enough, all living creatures will perish.

Dickinson's rhythm and word choice create a frantic and desperate tone in the first stanza. We know this from the progression of the speaker's adjectives, from "bewildered" to "puzzled" to "troubled," in which each adjective is more severe than the preceding one. The verb "flings" at the end of the stanza is a desperate action as well, drawing attention to the speaker's urgency. Working against this urgency metaphorically, however, is the time the speaker has had to endure simply waiting. We get this sense in the poem's first phrase, "Once more," as well as in the stanza's rhythm. The speaker talks in iambs, making the reader wait for the stressed syllable. In this way, the speaker creates in the reader a feeling similar to what she is experiencing.

This desperation is not unchecked, however. The speaker's attention in the poem is focused on the dove, a symbol of hope. Here Dickinson uses the image of Noah releasing and waiting for the dove. From this image we infer that Noah is watching the bird carefully and earnestly as it flies. In the biblical story, if Noah loses sight of the bird and it does not return, he will not know which way to sail, and eventually everything on his boat will perish. The speaker in this poem is trying to ignore her own desperation and pay attention only to her hope, as symbolized by the bird. Dickinson's syntax as well as her imagery support this idea of hopeful attention. We know from the word "my" in the first line that this poem is written in the first person. In the second and third lines, however, the speaker refers to herself in the third person as "her mistress," the mistress of the dove. The speaker is so focused on the dove that the sense of the bird replaces the speaker's sense of self as a valid reference point. The bird is so important that it makes sense for the speaker to talk about herself only in relation to it.

The second stanza serves to clarify the speaker's imagery about the flood and to change the poem's tone. "Thrice to the floating casement / The Patriarch's bird returned," is a direct reference to Noah's experience as told in the Bible. In the last two lines of this stanza, the voice of the speaker and the voice of Noah merge together. Instead of desperation, both these voices encourage the dove in its search for land and thus encourage the spirit of hopefulness within themselves. By ending the poem with the assertion "There may yet be Land!" the speaker shows the reader that her circumstances have not gotten the better of her. In this way, Dickinson uses the poem as a way of presenting an emotional process or progression — in this case, from the heavy and urgent feelings of fear to the strong and self-assured experience of hope and faith.

Even in this early version, Beth Runciman's essay has a number of strengths. Perhaps most impressive is her ability to read Dickinson's poem with care and to make specific and detailed comments about the meaning of the poem and Dickinson's craft as a writer. Beth uses the vocabulary of literary criticism (terms like "stanza," "iambs," and "image") to good effect. And she draws on her previous knowledge of the Bible to clarify some of the references in the poem. Nevertheless, when Beth looked closely at her draft, she saw some limitations. "There's a lot of specific information in this draft," she wrote in her process journal. "But it doesn't add up. There's not a clear enough point. I end with a kind of assertion about how the poem works, but it's pretty general. It could probably apply to a number of other poems by Dickinson." Beth's last comment is particularly telling, for if her comments could apply to other Dickinson poems, then she is writing at a fairly general level and needs to sharpen both her analysis and her argument.

BETH'S SECOND DRAFT: DEVELOPING A THESIS

The next time Beth worked on her essay, she decided to begin by freewriting about her goals for this drafting session. Writing in her process journal, Beth commented, "I think I understand how this poem works, but I'm not doing enough with it. I've got to figure out exactly what I want to argue in my essay. I think that I could do more with the biblical references that Dickinson uses. In my first draft I talk about these references, but I don't really explain how important they are to the poem's meaning. I'll try to do that now." Here is the draft that Beth wrote in response to this goal setting.

AN EXPLORATION OF EMILY DICKINSON'S POEM #48 [SECOND DRAFT]
by Beth Runciman

> Poets often write for an audience that shares a certain background or knowledge base. They build their poems assuming that readers will be familiar enough with their references to understand the work. Writing in the late nineteenth century, Emily Dickinson frequently used biblical allusions in her poetry. In this essay, I explore how such an allusion works in Dickinson's poem #48 ("Once more, my now bewildered Dove"). I closely read the poem, describing the poetic techniques Dickinson uses, and I demonstrate that the reader's knowledge of the story of Noah and the Ark plays a crucial role in the poem's communication with the reader.
>
> According to the biblical story, Noah released a dove from the ark three times near the end of the great flood. Noah knew that if the bird could not see land, it would return to the ark. If land were in sight, however, the bird would fly toward it, showing Noah the direction in which to sail. Dickinson builds her whole poem around the image of this third release. In poem #48, she writes:
>
>> Once more, my now bewildered Dove
>> Bestirs her puzzled wings
>> Once more her mistress, on the deep
>> Her troubled question flings —

> Thrice to the floating casement
> The Patriarch's bird returned,
> Courage! My brave Columba!
> There may yet be Land!

The first and second lines of the second stanza refer directly to Noah's experience as told in the Bible. However, in this poem Dickinson also selectively edits this biblical scene, making the story her own. She replaces "The Patriarch," Noah, with a female speaker; we know this from her choice of the word "mistress." Throughout the poem, Dickinson draws on her reader's knowledge of the end of the flood to talk about the feelings of hope and feelings of desperation that belong to her unique speaker.

Dickinson's rhythm and word choice create a frantic and desperate tone in the first stanza. We know this from the progression of the speaker's adjectives, from "bewildered" to "puzzled" to "troubled," in which each adjective is more severe than the preceding one. The verb "flings" at the end of the stanza is a desperate action as well, drawing attention to the speaker's urgency. These choices underscore the desperation implicit in the biblical story. Noah's ark can hold only so much food, and if the bird does not direct Noah to land soon enough, all living creatures will perish.

Working against this urgency metaphorically, however, is the time the speaker has had to endure simply waiting. We get this sense in the poem's first phrase, "Once more," as well as in the stanza's rhythm. The speaker talks in iambs, making the reader wait for the stressed syllable. In this way, Dickinson creates in the reader a feeling similar to what her speaker is experiencing, waiting and watching for the bird.

The speaker's desperation is not unchecked, however. Her attention throughout the poem is focused on the dove, a traditional symbol of hope. Here, Dickinson draws on the image of Noah releasing and waiting for the dove; in the story, we infer that Noah is watching the bird carefully and earnestly as it flies. If Noah loses sight of the bird and it does not return, he will not know which way to sail, and eventually everything on his boat will perish. By structuring her poem around this image, Dickinson suggests that her speaker is trying to ignore her own desperation and pay attention only to her hope, as symbolized by the bird.

The syntax in the poem supports this idea of hopeful attention. We know from the word "my" in the first line that this poem is written in the first person. In the second and third lines, however, the speaker refers to herself in the third person as "her mistress," the mistress of the dove. The speaker is so focused on the dove that the sense of the bird replaces the speaker's sense of self as a valid reference point. The bird is so important that it makes sense for the speaker to talk about herself only in relation to it.

In the last two lines of this stanza, the voice of the speaker and the voice of Noah merge. Instead of desperation, both these voices seek to encourage the dove in its search for land and thus encourage the spirit of hopefulness within themselves. By ending the poem with the assertion "There may yet be Land!" the speaker shows the reader that her circumstances have not gotten the better of her.

In this poem, then, Dickinson uses the biblical image as a way of presenting an emotional progression within her speaker, from the heavy and urgent feelings of fear to the strong and self-assured experience of hope and faith. She draws on changes in tone, supported by her choices of rhythm and syntax, to support the emotional process the biblical scene suggests. She also edits the image to serve her purposes, and she depends on the reader's prior knowledge of the biblical version for her changes to be meaningful. Dickinson's poem is an excellent example of an author drawing on and interpreting a shared cultural story in a piece of poetry.

This second draft improves Beth's earlier effort in several important ways. The new introduction provides background information that leads directly to a statement of purpose: "In this essay, I explore how such an allusion works in Dickinson's poem #48 ("Once more, my now bewildered Dove"). I closely read the poem, describing the poetic techniques Dickinson uses, and I demonstrate that the reader's knowledge of the story of Noah and the Ark plays a crucial role in the poem's communication with the reader." Included in this statement of purpose is a thesis statement: "the reader's knowledge of the story of Noah and the Ark plays a crucial role in the poem's communication with the reader." Also helpful is Beth's comment that she will "closely read the poem" — for what those in the discipline of English studies call "close reading" is a specific way of reading texts. In using this term here, Beth is signaling to her teacher that she understands the importance of this method for analyzing literary texts and will employ it in her essay.

The next two paragraphs of Beth's second draft generally follow the lines of her first draft — but with one important difference. Beth revises the first draft's straightforward observation (that Dickinson "replaces 'The Patriarch,' Noah, with a female speaker") with the stronger and more pointed comment that "in this poem Dickinson also selectively edits this biblical scene, making the story her own." In addition to this change, Beth significantly develops the conclusion to her essay. Beth's first draft ended with the observation that "Dickinson uses the poem as a way of presenting an emotional process, or progression, in this case from the heavy and urgent feelings of fear to the strong and self-assured experience of hope and faith." This sentence now begins a new paragraph that builds on many of the observations Beth has made about how the poem achieves its effect. The final sentence of this draft — "Dickinson's poem is an excellent example of an author drawing on and interpreting a shared cultural story in a piece of poetry" — demonstrates that Beth not only understands the poem but can generalize from it to other literary efforts.

BETH'S FINAL DRAFT: CLARIFYING AND EXTENDING HER ARGUMENT

After completing the second draft of her essay, Beth waited a day before rereading it. "I need to have time between drafts," she wrote in her process journal. "I either love or hate my writing right after I've written something. Either way, there's no point in trying to work with it then." When Beth did return to her draft, she saw that she had improved her essay. But she was still dissatisfied with her overall argument. "What frustrates me," Beth wrote, "is that I haven't been able to convey how gutsy Dickinson is being in this poem." In an effort to clarify her ideas, Beth spent some time rereading Dickinson's poem and brainstorming and freewriting about it. She also reviewed notes she had taken during class discussions of Dickinson's poetry. And, finally, she returned to her original analysis of her rhetorical situation (p. 377). "There's nothing wrong with this analysis," Beth wrote in her process journal. "But it's pretty general. Maybe if I force myself to be more specific I can work out what I want to do." So Beth wrote a new second paragraph for her analysis:

> In class, we talked about how subversive Emily Dickinson's poetry was for her historical moment, and I remember being surprised at the critical edge that laced much of her work. For this assignment I want to explore not only how #48 works as a poem but also how it challenges certain norms of nineteenth-century New England society. I want my reader to come away from my essay with an appreciation of Dickinson's method for critiquing the culture in which she lived her life, as well as with an appreciation for her poetic skills.

As Beth noted in her process journal, this was a critical moment in her writing. She was finally able to see what she wanted to be at stake in her argument. She didn't want just to show that Dickinson was a good poet who knew how to use biblical allusions effectively. She wanted to demonstrate that Dickinson was a subversive poet. As Beth explained in her process journal, this insight was important in several ways. "I saw I had the hook that I needed to give my argument zip," she wrote. "But even better I reconnected with my passion for Dickinson. I'm a rebel, and I was really drawn to the rebel in Dickinson — but I couldn't find a way to get that into my writing. Now I can."

Did Beth succeed in demonstrating that Dickinson's poem #48 "challenges certain norms of nineteenth-century New England society"? You can decide for yourself as you read the third and final draft of her essay.

THE MATRIARCH'S BIRD [FINAL DRAFT]
by Beth Runciman

> Once more, my now bewildered Dove
> Bestirs her puzzled wings
> Once more her mistress, on the deep
> Her troubled question flings —
>
> Thrice to the floating casement
> The Patriarch's bird returned,
> Courage! My brave Columba!
> There may yet be Land!

Poets often write for an audience that shares a certain background or knowledge base, and they build their poems assuming that readers will be familiar enough with their references to understand their work. Writing in the late nineteenth century, Emily Dickinson frequently used allusions to biblical stories in her poetry. In this essay, I explore how such an allusion works in Dickinson's poem #48 ("Once more, my now bewildered Dove"). I closely read the poem, describing the techniques Dickinson uses to communicate through it, and I argue that the reader's knowledge of the story of Noah and the Ark plays a crucial role in this communication.

More is going on in this poem, however, than a simple reference to a shared cultural story. Dickinson selectively edits the details of this tale, and she retells it with her own unique and, I would argue, subversive slant. Instead of calling to mind the familiar story of Noah and reinforcing traditional nineteenth-century values, Dickinson changes the tale to suggest a radical revision of nineteenth-century ideals. The fact that the text she revises is held sacred by most of her audience makes this revision all the more startling and gives the poem its subversive appeal.

According to the Bible, Noah released a dove from the ark three times near the end of the flood. He knew that if the bird could not see land, it would return to the ark. If land were in sight, however, the bird would fly toward it, demonstrating to Noah the direction in which to sail. In poem #48, Dickinson builds her entire poem around the image of this third release. "Thrice to the floating casement / The Patriarch's bird returned" is a direct reference to Noah's experience as told in the Bible. Dickinson's poem depends on her readers' recognition of the biblical story from these brief lines. The tone in both of her stanzas — the tone she sets up to match Noah's emotional state during the releasing of the dove — reinforces this recognition.

In the first stanza, her rhythm and word choice create a frantic and desperate tone. We know this from the progression of the speaker's adjectives.

Each adjective — from "bewildered" to "puzzled" to "troubled" — is more emphatic than the preceding one. The verb "flings" at the end of the stanza is a desperate action as well, drawing attention to the speaker's urgency. These choices underscore the desperation implicit in the biblical story. Noah's ark can hold only so much food, and if the bird does not direct Noah to land soon enough, all living creatures will perish.

Working against this urgency metaphorically, however, is the time the speaker has had to endure waiting for the dove to return. We get this sense in the poem's first phrase, "Once more," as well as in the stanza's rhythm. The speaker talks in iambs, making the reader wait for the stressed syllable. In this way, Dickinson creates in the reader a feeling similar to what her speaker is experiencing.

There is something unexpected about this speaker, however. Dickinson replaces the figure of "The Patriarch," Noah, with a female speaker; we know this from her choice of the word "mistress" and by the female possessive pronoun that appears in "*her* troubled question." To Dickinson's contemporaries, this would have been a scandalous revision indeed. At that time in New England, biblical laws were invoked to uphold the father as the rightful ruler of the family and to maintain separate spheres of work for men and women. Women were expected to be obedient wives, to stay home, and to raise children, and stories from the Bible were frequently told to ensure that they did so. To suggest that a woman could have done the work that Noah did — responding to the very voice of God and saving all living creatures from certain death — would disrupt the assumptions on which society was built. Not only was Dickinson suggesting that women could do men's work; she was using the same text her contemporaries frequently called on to suggest exactly the opposite.

So of course Dickinson takes particular care to ground the reader in the biblical tale, despite the fact that the speaker is female. While the poem opens with a desperate and frantic tone, the speaker's desperation is not unchecked. Throughout the poem, her attention is focused on the dove, a traditional symbol of hope. If Noah loses sight of the bird and it does not return, he will not know which way to sail, and eventually all living creatures on his boat will perish. Drawing on this shared cultural knowledge, Dickinson suggests that her speaker, like Noah, is trying to ignore her own desperation and pay attention only to her hope, as symbolized by the bird. By structuring her poem around the exact emotional dimensions of this moment, Dickinson reinforces the idea that her speaker is, in fact, the same Noah as in the biblical story.

Dickinson's syntax works to communicate her speaker's hopeful attention. We know from the word "my" in the first line that this poem is written in the first person. In the second and third lines, however, the speaker refers to herself in the third person as "her mistress," the mistress of the dove. The speaker is so focused on the dove that the bird replaces the speaker's self as a reference point. In the last two lines of this stanza, the voice of the speaker and the voice of Noah merge. Instead of desperation, both these voices seek to encourage the dove in its search for land and thus encourage the spirit of hopefulness within themselves. By ending the poem with the assertion "There may yet be Land!" the speaker shows the reader that her circumstances have not gotten the better of her. These are the most subversive lines in the poem: In them, Dickinson's speaker becomes Noah and speaks with his voice. There is no longer any room for doubt about who this speaker is or about the fact of Dickinson's substitution of a female for Noah. By speaking out in the voice of Noah, one of the most important men in the sacred biblical text, Dickinson's female speaker becomes impossible for her reader to dismiss.

Several things are going on in this poem, then. Dickinson presents her readers with a poem that documents an emotional progression, from the heavy and urgent feelings of fear to the strong and self-assured experience of hope and faith. She draws on changes in tone, supported by the careful use of rhythm and syntax, to support this progression. Dickinson builds this progression around a well-known biblical tale and depends on her readers' shared cultural knowledge of the Bible. However, she edits the tale to convey a more subversive message. By substituting a female speaker for Noah, Dickinson challenges fundamental assumptions of sex-segregated nineteenth-century society; further, her challenge is based in the very text on which those assumptions were thought to rest. Thus does Dickinson's poem quietly — but effectively — challenge the cultural norms of her day.

The first thing you might have noticed about Beth's draft is that it now has a title: "The Matriarch's Bird." This titles provides important cues to the reader about the focus of her essay, for the term "matriarch" calls to mind the related term "patriarch." This is a term used in the Old Testament to refer to such important male figures as Adam and Noah. A "matriarch," then, is a female figure of great importance in her society. Beth's title thus prepares readers for her discussion of Dickinson's subversion of the biblical story of Noah and the Ark.

There are other important additions to Beth's essay. After the introduction, which resembles that of the previous draft, Beth added a new second paragraph:

More is going on in this poem, however, than a simple reference to a shared cultural story. Dickinson selectively edits the details of this tale, and she retells it with her own unique and, I would argue, subversive slant. Instead of calling to mind the familiar story of Noah and reinforcing traditional nineteenth-century values, Dickinson changes the tale to suggest a radical revision of nineteenth-century ideals. The fact that the text she revises is held sacred by most of her audience makes this revision all the more startling and gives the poem its subversive appeal.

This paragraph adds complexity and significance to Beth's interpretation of Dickinson's poem. While her earlier drafts focused primarily on how Dickinson's poem works — how it is put together and achieves its effect — this draft goes beyond analysis to argument. It demonstrates that Beth can read a poem with care, place that poem in its historical context, and make claims about its contemporary significance.

In the sixth paragraph, Beth further develops and supports her position. She does so by building on an observation that has appeared in all three drafts: that Dickinson replaces the figure of Noah with a female speaker. But here for the first time she considers the cultural context of this change and provides explicit links that connect evidence with larger generalizations:

> To Dickinson's contemporaries, this would have been a scandalous revision indeed. At that time in New England, biblical laws were invoked to uphold the father as the rightful ruler of the family and to maintain separate spheres of work for men and women. Women were expected to be obedient wives, to stay home, and to raise children, and stories from the Bible were frequently told to ensure that they did so. To suggest that a woman could have done the work that Noah did — responding to the very voice of God and saving all living creatures from certain death — would disrupt the assumptions on which society was built. Not only was Dickinson suggesting that women could do men's work; she was using the same text her contemporaries frequently called on to suggest exactly the opposite.

Here, and again in the closing paragraphs of her essay, Beth effectively argues that Dickinson not only grounds her poem in her readers' knowledge of the Bible but subverts the biblical story for her own purposes.

Thanks to her three drafts, Beth was able to write her way to an effective academic argument. In her final process journal entry, Beth commented on this experience, observing, "In this essay, I didn't know exactly what I was going to argue until the final draft — but I wouldn't have been able to see that argument and make it work if I hadn't studied the poem by writing the other drafts first." With each draft, Beth's argument became clearer, and the links between her evidence and her generalizations became both more explicit and more fully developed.

■ ■ ■

FOR EXPLORATION

The preceding analysis has focused primarily on global changes that Beth Runciman made as she worked on her essay. But in addition to revising the approach and organization of her essay, Beth made many small, local changes. After rereading the second and third drafts of Beth's essay, identify at least three local (word- or sentence-level) revisions that Beth made that in your view improved her writing.

LEARNING FROM YOUR READING OF BETH'S THREE DRAFTS

To write a successful essay on Dickinson's poem #48, Beth Runciman drew on her understanding of writing and of the writing process as well as on her rhetorical awareness of the demands of academic argument. By giving herself the time to write three drafts of her essay, Beth demonstrated her control over the composing process. But as Beth noted in her journal, this process was hardly perfect: Beth had hoped to arrange for a peer-response session with her study group — but she ran out of time. "I know my essay would be even better if someone else had been able to read it," Beth wrote in her process journal. "Once I've wrestled my way through to getting the big things working, I have a lot of trouble seeing smaller things like awkward sentences and errors."

As I'm sure you will agree, Beth did indeed do a good job of attending to "the big things." She took time at the start of her writing process, for instance, to think long and hard about the demands of her assignment. (Many students neglect to do this seemingly obvious step, and their writing often suffers as a result.) Because Beth's assignment was general and open-ended, she needed to make a number of inferences about her teacher's expectations. As her analysis of her rhetorical situation demonstrates, Beth drew both on her knowledge of the conventions of academic writing and her understanding of literary criticism to do so.

Once Beth began drafting, she moved back and forth from analysis to argument. Her first draft about Dickinson's poem was primarily analytical: It focused on how the poem "works," how it achieves its effect. But Beth quickly recognized that without an argumentative "edge" her observations lacked force. Once she was able to determine what was at stake in her analysis — in this case the subversiveness of Dickinson's poem — she was able to clarify and extend her argument. Equally important was Beth's exploration of her own values and beliefs as they relate to Dickinson. A bit of a rebel herself, Beth was emotionally as well as intellectually drawn to Dickinson's nonconformity. She was able to use that connection to her advantage in her writing.

Beth also understood that literary criticism calls for certain kinds of claims — and certain kinds of evidence. As you may recall, the previous chapter presented three kinds of argumentative claims developed by Professor

Annette T. Rottenberg (and discussed on pp. 371–73): claims of fact, claims of value, and claims of policy. In her essay, Beth drew on claims of fact and claims of value. When Beth makes observations about Dickinson's use of rhyme and meter, she is making claims of fact, for she is asserting that Dickinson uses these conventions of poetry in specific ways. Those who are knowledgeable about rhyme and meter can determine whether Beth is correct or incorrect in her analysis. At those moments where Beth is making judgments about Dickinson's poem — that it is intentionally subversive of contemporary gender roles, for instance, and that this subversiveness is praiseworthy — Beth is making claims of value.

Because of the nature of her inquiry, Beth quite reasonably does not spend much time addressing possible counterarguments to her reading of Dickinson's poem #48. But Beth does acknowledge that potential counterarguments exist. At the beginning of her final paragraph, for instance, she observes, "Poems are often viewed as the expression of an *individual's* emotions and ideas." In so doing, Beth recognizes that some readers might prefer to read Dickinson's poem from another perspective and argue, for example, that the poem serves only to express the writer's individual feelings. Against this view, Beth develops what is clearly a feminist reading of the poem that views the poem both as a personal expression of feeling and a challenge to the situation of nineteenth-century women.

■ ■ ■

FOR EXPLORATION

Reread the final draft of Beth Runciman's essay, keeping the preceding analysis in mind. As you read, focus particularly on these questions: Would Beth's essay be stronger if she specifically acknowledged that she was undertaking a feminist reading of Dickinson's poem? Should Beth have addressed possible counterarguments to her reading more explicitly and fully, or does her brief allusion to possible counterarguments suffice?

FOR GROUP WORK

Bring your response to the previous Exploration to class. Working together with a group of classmates, discuss your response to the questions presented there. Be prepared to discuss your conclusions with your classmates.

FURTHER EXPLORATIONS OF ACADEMIC WRITING: A MISCELLANY OF STUDENT ESSAYS

One of the most important ways to learn about writing is through reading. As Chapter 6, "Thinking about Communities and Conventions," emphasized, you can learn a good deal by studying examples of various kinds of writing. In that chapter, for instance, you read three essays by psychologist John H. Flavell and observed the ways in which he adapted his writing to the needs and expectations of readers of three different journals, including the popular magazine *Psychology Today* and the scholarly journal *Cognitive Psychology*. In the final section of this chapter, you will read a variety of examples of student writing across the disciplines — from anthropology to chemistry to ethnic studies. These essays are not intended to serve as models in any strict or rigid sense, for assignments given in different disciplines can vary considerably. But these essays can give you a sense of the kinds of writing that you can expect to undertake as you continue your studies.

Before presenting these essays, I would like briefly to discuss other opportunities available to you as a beginning college writer. Almost certainly, for instance, your college or university offers writing classes in addition to the one that you are now taking. These classes may or may not be required — but if you are serious about writing you should consider taking additional course work in this area. You may be able to supplement these classes by consulting with writing assistants at your campus writing center. Not all colleges and universities provide such centers, but many do.

Various departments across campus are increasingly recognizing how important writing is to student success and so are offering writing-intensive courses. Sometimes these courses are part of a writing-across-the-curriculum requirement. At Oregon State University, for instance, students must take at least one writing-intensive course in their major before they graduate. If your school has such a requirement or offers such courses as electives, be sure to take this course sooner rather than later. Better yet, take several such courses in disciplines related to your major.

Finally, you may find it helpful to consult writing textbooks designed for students taking courses in particular disciplines. Some of these textbooks are available through national publishers. Bedford/St. Martin's, for instance, publishes the following discipline-based textbooks: *Writing Papers in the Biological Sciences,* by Victoria E. McMillan (2nd ed., 1996); *Thinking and Writing about Philosophy,* by Hugo Bedau (1996); *Writing in the Sciences: Exploring Conventions of Scientific Discourse,* by Ann M. Penrose and Steven B. Katz (1998); and *A Student's Guide to History,* by Jules R. Benjamin (7th ed., 1998). In addition, you may have access to a guide for writers developed by a department at your local college or university. The philosophy department at Oregon State University, for instance, developed and published a helpful guide for students taking philosophy courses. This publication, *Writing Philosophy: A Student Guide* (Dubuque: Kendall-Hunt, 1997), discusses various forms of philosophical writing (self-discovery writing, class journals, summaries, essays, case studies, dialogues, and research papers) and provides examples of each.

I hope you will both enjoy and learn from the examples of successful academic writing in the following collection of student writing in the disciplines.

THE DEBT OF JUSTICE
by Jon Dorbolo

> *The first essay in this section's miscellany of student writing appeared in the OSU philosophy department's* Writing Philosophy: A Student Guide. *This essay, by Jon Dorbolo, is presented as a successful example of an essay that tests a hypothesis. As the guide explains, "Hypothetical reasoning involves deriving and testing the consequences of some supposition — that is, a claim supposed to be true for the purposes of the inquiry. The basic idea is to test the truth of the supposition by seeing whether consequences which follow from it turn out to be true or false."*

In *The Republic,* a dialogue by Plato, Socrates begins a discussion with several people at a party about what they believe that "justice" is. He gets several answers, the first of which comes from the party host, Cephalus. Cephalus gives a long answer citing his honesty and wise management of money. Socrates interprets this answer to mean that justice is "to speak the truth and to pay your debts." That is, if you are honest in dealing with others and pay back what you owe, then you are a just person. Cephalus agrees that is his meaning.

Socrates rejects this theory, arguing that speaking the truth and repaying debts cannot be all there is to justice. I agree. There are certainly situations in which honesty in word and deed are not sufficient to make you a just person.

Consider, for example, the slave owners of the American South in the 19th century. Many of these men may well have dealt with one another honorably in business and other matters. Some of them may have been entirely truthful and scrupulous in repaying all debts. Such persons may think, according to Cephalus' theory of justice that they were very just indeed. But they were also slave owners. They denied millions of people the most basic rights a human has. They destroyed families by selling off children as objects for profit. Slavery is an entirely unjust institution. It harms the slave in innumerable ways physically, morally, and spiritually. No human being with a sense of self-worth, including the slave owners, would choose to live as a southern plantation slave. By forcibly subjecting people to a condition of living they themselves would not choose, the slave owners show the deep injustice in their characters. No amount of truth telling and debt repaying can change that. So, I conclude that the slave owners were unjust even if they satisfied the conditions of Cephalus' theory.

To emphasize the point that honesty alone cannot guarantee justice, consider the case of *Huckleberry Finn,* by Mark Twain. The book's main character, a young boy named Huck, runs away from home with an escaped slave, Jim. While floating down the Mississippi river on a raft, a group of men pass by in a boat and call out to Huck. "Is there anyone else on board?" they ask. Huck answers that his friend Jim is asleep under a blanket. "Is he a white man or a black man?" they ask. Huck realizes that if he answers truthfully, they will capture Jim and return him to slavery. His conscience bothers him, though, for he realizes that under the law Jim is another man's property. If he were to follow Cephalus' theory of justice, he would tell the truth and return the property to its owner. But Huck does not. He lies and says that Jim is a white man. The boat goes on its way searching for other escaped slaves.

In this case it is clear that following Cephalus' theory would not result in justice. It would only return Jim to an unjust situation, slavery. According to that theory we will have to say that Huck is unjust. He lies and fails to return property. But in reading this story, that is not the judgment it is natural to make. It seems clear that Huck has done the right thing. He prevented an injustice. As Socrates points out, Cephalus is wrong. Justice is not simply truth-telling and debt-repaying.

"EVERYDAY EXPOSURE TO TOXIC POLLUTANTS"
by Hannah Grubb

> *The assignment to which Jon Dorbolo responded was quite precise. Philosophers follow a particular method for testing hypotheses. Often, however, students are given much more general and open-ended assignments. This was the case with the essay by Hannah Grubb, presented below. Hannah is a student at the University of Oregon, and she wrote this essay for an introductory chemistry class. Hannah's teacher asked students to select an article from a recent issue of* Scientific American *that in some way involved chemistry. Students were to demonstrate their understanding of the article by summarizing and responding to it. Hannah chose to write about an article titled "Everyday Exposure to Toxic Pollutants" by Wayne R. Ott and John W. Roberts. This article appeared in the February 1998 issue of* Scientific American.

Pollutants are everywhere. Walking down a busy street, I inhale car exhaust, gas fumes, secondhand smoke, and other toxic substances. Flying into Los Angeles to visit friends, I notice that the sky over the city is a distinctly different color than the beautiful clean air over the Pacific Ocean. Opening the newspaper, I read debates about the use of pesticides and news of the war on pollution. Like many people, I worry about the effects of pollution on my health. But rarely have I thought about the toxins that I could be breathing in my very own home.

"Everyday Exposure to Toxic Pollutants" examines those toxins and considers their relative concentrations indoors and outdoors. After reading this article by Wayne R. Ott and John W. Roberts, I now know that I have more to worry about sitting in my own home than when I go jogging through city streets. Their study discusses the presence of volatile organic compounds, carbon monoxide, pesticides, and dangerous particles within and outside of homes across America. One surprising finding is that even in cities where industrial and chemical processing plants have a major presence, the air outside is generally cleaner than the air indoors. The source of this indoor pollution, according to Ott and Roberts, is ordinary consumer products, such as air fresheners and cleaning compounds, and various building materials. Another major pollutant, tetrachloroethylene, is found on clothes that have been dry cleaned. This chemical has been found to cause cancer in laboratory animals. Chloroform, a gas that also causes cancer in laboratory animals, is a by-product of showers, boiling water, and clothes washers.

Dust particles, which are continually around us (whether we can see them or not), also carry toxic particles into our lungs. I might pick up particles of insecticides on my shoes, for instance, and carry these particles into my home where they can settle and mix in with other dust. This is especially dangerous for small children, who spend most of their time on or near the ground and who are still developing. But adults are at risk also. Ott and Roberts state that "pesticides and volatile organic compounds found indoors cause perhaps 3,000 cases of cancer a year in the U.S., making these substances just as threatening to nonsmokers as radon . . . and second-hand tobacco smoke" (90). Ott and Roberts conclude that the main sources of indoor pollution are such run-of-the-mill products that most people don't even think to question whether they should or shouldn't use them. Because the effect of indoor pollutants is not as noticeable as, say, the exhaust from an old car, few people are aware of their dangers. But they should be, as this analogy from Ott's and Roberts's article suggests: "If truckloads of dust with the same concentrations of toxic chemicals as is found in most carpets were deposited outside, these locations would be considered hazardous-waste dumps" (91).

"Everyday Exposure to Toxic Pollutants" by Ott and Roberts is a relevant and informative discussion of problems that many people don't even realize exist. It certainly puts general concerns about pollution in perspective. Recently there have been campaigns about the use of pesticides in our residence hall cafeterias. And as I went jogging the other day, I cringed as I passed a smoker, and I purposely ran through quiet neighborhoods to get away from cars and their pollution. Perhaps I should have been worrying about inhaling chloroform every time I make a cup of tea.

FIELD MEASUREMENTS OF PHOTOSYNTHESIS AND TRANSPIRATION RATES IN DWARF SNAPDRAGON (*CHAENORRHINUM MINUS* LANGE): AN INVESTIGATION OF WATER STRESS ADAPTATIONS

by Tara Gupta

Here is another essay written by a student in the sciences. The student, Tara Gupta from Colgate University, wrote the following as an application for a summer research fellowship at her university. Note that Tara uses headings to mark the various sections of her application. She also uses the documentation style required by the Council of Biology Editors. For details on this reference style, consult their handbook, Scientific Style and Format: The CBE Manual for Authors, Editors, and Publishers. *The current edition, the sixth, was published in 1994 (Cambridge).*

Application for Summer Research Fellowship

Colgate University

INTRODUCTION

Dwarf snapdragon (*Chaenorrhinum minus*) is a weedy pioneer plant found growing in central New York during spring and summer. Interestingly, the distribution of this species has been limited almost exclusively to the cinder ballast of railroad tracks,[1] a harsh environment characterized by intense sunlight and poor soil water retention. Given such environmental conditions, one would expect *C. minus* to exhibit anatomical features similar to those of xeromorphic plants (species adapted to arid habitats).

However, this is not the case. T. Gupta and R. Arnold (unpublished) have found that the leaves and stems of *C. minus* are not covered by a thick, waxy cuticle, but rather with a thin cuticle that is less effective in inhibiting water loss through diffusion. The root system is not long and thick, capable of reaching deeper, moister soils; instead, it is thin and diffuse, permeating only the topmost (and driest) soil horizon. Moreover, in contrast to many xeromorphic plants, the stomata (pores regulating gas exchange) are not found in sunken crypts, or cavities in the epidermis that retard water loss from transpiration. Despite a lack of these morphological adaptations to water stress, *C. minus* continues to grow and reproduce when morning dew has been its only source of water for up to five weeks (R. Arnold, personal communication). Such growth involves fixation of carbon by photosynthesis, and requires that the stomata be open to admit sufficient carbon dioxide. Given the dry, sunny environment, the time required for adequate carbon fixation must also mean a significant loss of water through transpiration as open stomata exchange carbon dioxide with water. How does *C. minus* balance the need for carbon with the need to conserve water?

AIMS OF THE PROPOSED STUDY

The above observations have led me to an exploration of the extent to which *C. minus* is able to photosynthesize under conditions of low water availability. It is my hypothesis that *C. minus* adapts to these conditions by photosynthesizing in the early morning and late afternoon, when leaf and air temperatures are lower and transpirational water loss is reduced. During the middle of the day, its photosynthetic rate may be very low, perhaps even zero on hot, sunny afternoons. Similar diurnal changes in photosynthetic rate in response to midday water deficits have been described in crop plants.[2,3] There appear to be no comparable studies on noncrop species in their natural habitats.

Thus, the research proposed here should help explain the apparent paradox of an organism that thrives in water stressed conditions despite a lack of morphological adaptations. This summer's work will also serve as a basis for controlled experiments in a plant growth chamber on the individual effects of temperature, light intensity, soil water availability, and other environmental factors on photosynthesis and transpiration rates. These experiments are planned for the coming fall semester.

METHODS

Simultaneous measurements of photosynthesis and transpiration rates will indicate the balance *C. minus* has achieved in acquiring the energy it needs while retaining the water available to it. These measurements will be taken daily at field sites in the Hamilton, NY, area, using an LI-6220 portable photosynthesis system (LICOR, Inc., Lincoln, NE). Basic methodology and use of correction factors will be similar to that described in related studies.[4–6] Data will be collected at regular intervals throughout the daylight hours, and will be related to measurements of ambient air temperature, leaf temperature, relative humidity, light intensity, wind velocity, and cloud cover.

BUDGET

1 kg soda lime, 4–8 mesh	$70
(for absorption of CO_2 in photosynthesis analyzer)	
1 kg anhydrous magnesium perchlorate	$130
(used as desiccant for photosynthesis analyzer)	

SigmaScan software (Jandel Scientific Software, Inc.) (for measurement of leaf areas for which photosynthesis and transpiration rates are to be determined)	$195
Estimated 500 miles travel to field sites in own car @ $0.28/mile	$140
CO_2 cylinder, 80 days rental @ $0.25/day (for calibration of photosynthesis analyzer)	$20
TOTAL REQUEST	$555

REFERENCES

1. Wildrlechner MP. Historical and phenological observations of the spread of *Chaenorrhinum minus* across North America. Can J Bot 1983;61:179–87.

2. Boyer JS. Plant productivity and environment. Science 1982;218:443–8.

3. Manhas JG, Sukumaran NP. Diurnal changes in net photosynthetic rate in potato in two environments. Potato Res 1988;31:375–8.

4. Doley DG, Unwin GL, Yates DJ. Spatial and temporal distribution of photosynthesis and transpiration by single leaves in a rainforest tree, *Argyrodendron peralatum*. Aust J Plant Physiol 1988;15:317–26.

5. Kallarackal J, Milburn JA, Baker DA. Water relations of the banana. III. Effects of controlled water stress on water potential, transpiration, photosynthesis and leaf growth. Aust J Plant Physiol 1990;17:79–90.

6. Idso SB, Allen SG, Kimball BA, Choudhury BJ. Problems with porometry: measuring net photosynthesis by leaf chamber techniques. Agron 1989;81:475–9.

LINCOLN'S PRESIDENCY AND PUBLIC OPINION

by Elizabeth Ridlington

In-class essay exams are a common form of academic writing. Essay exams pose special challenges for writers, for you must be able both to recall information and to present it in a clearly organized — and concise — manner. The following essay exam meets these goals. During a midterm for a course in American history at Harvard University, student Elizabeth Ridlington had fifty minutes to respond to this question: "During his presidency, did Lincoln primarily respond to public opinion, or did he shape public opinion more than he responded to it?" This is what she wrote.

This essay argues that Lincoln shaped public opinion more than he responded to it and examines the issues of military recruitment, northern war goals, and emancipation as examples of Lincoln's interaction with public opinion.

At the start of the war Lincoln needed men for the military. Because of this, he could hardly ignore public opinion. But even as he responded in various ways to public opinion, he did not significantly modify his policy goals. Lincoln's first call for seventy-five thousand soldiers was filled through militias that were under state rather than federal control. As the war progressed, the federal government took more control of military recruitment. The government set quotas for each state and permitted the enlistment of African American soldiers via the Militia Act. Kentucky, a slave state, protested, and Lincoln waived the requirement that blacks be enlisted so long as Kentucky still filled its quota. In so doing, Lincoln responded to public opinion without changing his policy goal. Another example of this strategy occurred when the first federal draft produced riots in New York City. When the riots occurred, Lincoln relented temporarily and waited for the unrest to quiet down. Then he reinstated the federal draft. Again, Lincoln responded to a volatile situation and even temporarily withdrew the federal draft. But he ultimately reinstated the draft.

Lincoln's efforts to shape public opinion in the north in favor of the war provides another example of his proactive stance. Whenever he discussed the war, Lincoln equated it with freedom and democracy. Northerners linked democracy with their personal freedom and daily well-being, and therefore Lincoln's linkage of the Union with democracy fostered northern support for the war even when the conflict was bloody and northern victory was anything but assured. After the emancipation, Lincoln continued his effort to influence public opinion by connecting the abolition of slavery with democracy. The image of a "new birth of freedom" that Lincoln painted in his Gettysburg address was part of this effort to overcome northern racism and a reluctance to fight for the freedom of blacks.

The process that led to the emancipation provides perhaps the clearest example of Lincoln's determination to shape public opinion rather than simply respond to it. Lincoln's views on slavery were more progressive than those of his contemporaries. These views caused him personally to wish to abolish slavery. At the same time, Lincoln knew that winning the war was his highest priority. Consequently, retaining the border states early in the war was more important to Lincoln than emancipation, and for this reason he revoked Freemont's proclamation in the summer of 1861. In explaining this decision privately to Freemont, Lincoln admitted that he was concerned about public opinion in Kentucky since it would determine if Kentucky stayed with the Union. However, in a letter that Lincoln knew might be made public, Lincoln denied that he had reacted to Kentucky's pressure and claimed that emancipation was not among his powers — a clear effort to gain public approval. Even when others such as Frederick Douglass (in a September 1861 speech) demanded emancipation, Lincoln did not change his policy. Not until July 1862 did Lincoln draft the preliminary emancipation proclamation. Rather than releasing it then, at the advice of his cabinet he waited for a time when it would have a more positive impact on public opinion.

Lincoln realized that the timing of the Emancipation Proclamation was crucial. While he was waiting for an opportune time to release the document, Horace Greeley published his "Prayer of Twenty Million," calling on Lincoln to abolish slavery. Lincoln's response, a letter for publication, emphasized the importance of the Union and the secondary importance of the status of slavery. By taking this position, Lincoln hoped to shape public opinion. He wanted northerners to believe that he saw the Union cause as foremost, so that the release of the proclamation would create as few racial concerns as possible. The Emancipation Proclamation was released on January 1, 1863. Once it was released, Lincoln stood by it despite strong public opposition. In 1864, when Democrats called for an armistice with the south, Lincoln stood by his decision to abolish slavery. He defended his position on military grounds, hoping voters would approve in the 1864 election.

As the examples I have just discussed indicate, Lincoln could not ignore public opinion, and at times he had to respond to it. But when Lincoln did so, this was always part of a larger effort to shape public opinion and to ensure Union victory.

BETWEEN CULTURES

by Monica Molina

The personal essay is another common form of academic writing, particularly in the humanities. Students in philosophy, for instance, are sometimes asked to write personal essays that, as Writing Philosophy Papers: A Student Guide *indicates, encourage them to "search for meaning" about a specific topic, such as the nature of truth or beauty. Here is a personal essay written by Monica Molina, a student at Oregon State University. Monica wrote this essay for an ethnic studies class. Her assignment was to write an essay that in some way reflected on her ethnic heritage.*

Opening the door and peering curiously around the room full of brown faces, I felt nervous and awkward. My fears were soon eased, however, as cheerful voices welcomed me to an Oregon State University Hispanic Student Union meeting. Although I wasn't sure what the meeting would be about, I felt suddenly comfortable — almost like I was among family. But then some students in the corner began speaking in Spanish, their crescendo building with excitement as they shared a story. Soon it seemed that everyone was adding bits of information. I sat quietly, just getting the gist of what they were saying. Then everyone broke into laughter. Everyone but me, that is; I had missed the punchline.

*   *   *

Spanish sounds like a song to me, one that is beautiful and rich, but one I can't quite catch the words to. I ache for the foreign sounds to roll off my tongue, but instead only a few words stumble out, flat and anglicized. I studied Spanish for three years in high school, and for one year in college, but learning a language in a classroom from textbooks is different from hearing it spoken by your parents at home. My father is Mexican, and his native language is Spanish. But he has never spoken anything other than English with my mother, sisters, and me.

I was surrounded by Anglo culture as I grew up, and I assimilated easily, not even knowing what I was missing. Educated in mainstream schools and raised in a predominantly white neighborhood, I accepted the images I saw on television and in the movies. Most of the time, I took it for granted that we would speak English at home. When my friends learned that my father was Mexican and asked me if I spoke Spanish, or if we spoke it at home, I always answered "no," feeling a sudden sense of confusion and loss.

At times as I was growing up, I wondered why my father never spoke Spanish with us. Recently, I decided to ask him about it. My dad seemed surprised by my question and replied that he didn't know; perhaps it was because he was too busy to teach us. He didn't seem to want to talk about this subject. I could tell that he didn't understand why I asked the question or what it might mean to me. I didn't push my question, for I realized that it really doesn't matter why my father didn't speak Spanish with us. What matters is how I feel about this now — now that I realize I know only the Anglo side of my heritage and not the Mexican side. What matters is my desire to connect with my father's culture, with the Mexican heritage that has been ignored and silenced.

When I was a child, I asked innocent questions about life in Mexico that annoyed my father, questions like "Do they have ice cream in Mexico?" My dad would shake his head in disbelief at these questions and not even answer. Now I realize that the questions reminded him too much of snobby Anglos asking if the water was OK to drink in Mexico. My father must have found it hard to realize how little I knew about Mexican culture. Moreover, he probably felt there was no point in teaching us about a culture we would never embrace as our own.

My father struggled to learn to speak English and to make a place for himself in this country. But my father's English reminds my mom, sisters, and me that he is different from us. Dad's English is distinct in that he has created his own pronunciations and vocabulary. His words and phrases have become part of our family language, and we sometimes tease him about them. One of his favorite phrases is "You crazy!"; now we all say that to each other. We also mimic the exasperated way he says "What?!" Sometimes my father realizes that we are teasing him and laughs, but other times he gets angry. His anger reminds me how easy it is to forget his struggles with English and with Anglo culture, just as it is hard for my father to sense my need to connect with his Mexican way of life.

As a fifth grader, I remember my father coming to me with business letters to check for grammar and spelling. As I gently explained to my dad why a tense was wrong or a word misspelled, I knew it must be hard for him to ask his daughter for help. My father's lack of English skills coupled with my limited knowledge of Spanish highlighted the gap between our Anglo and Mexican cultures. I felt this gap most strongly when my dad called his family in Mexico. Calling home was a pretty big event, and my mom would tell us to be quiet so dad could hear. We would sit listening to the unfamiliar language, fascinated with the quick sounds and changes in expression. After my father hung up, we would rush to him and ask what he had said.

As a teenager, and now as a college student, I have made attempts to learn about my father's culture. Sometimes I try to explain my longing to connect with my Mexican heritage to my father, but he doesn't seem to understand why this is important to me. He also doesn't understand why some people would question my identification with Mexico and its cultural heritage. When I told my dad that people sometimes ask whether I am Mexican and are surprised when I say "yes" since I can't speak Spanish very well, he says it's none of their business and "to hell with them." Lately

I'm beginning to think that my father may be right. Other people may worry if I don't fit into predetermined ethnic categories. But I think I can identify with both Mexican and Anglo cultures as long as I define what that means for me.

*   *   *

I come home from another Hispanic Student Union meeting, excited about the possibility of attending my first MECHA (Movimiento Estudiantil Chicano de Azatlan) conference. Entering my house, I notice that the answering machine light is on and push the button. My father begins the message he has left for me. Because his voice is so familiar, I don't usually hear my father's accent. But today it rings out as a reminder of the ways in which we're both similar and different. As I listen to my dad telling me what time he'll pick me up for a quick trip home, I think of how different my world is from his. My father came to a new country and had to work hard to support a family; he had to believe that he was gaining more than he was giving up. Because my father has struggled, I have more opportunities. In some ways, my success will be his. But unlike my father, I may not have to choose between two cultures. For me, gaining something new may not have to mean leaving something else behind.

THE HOPI WORLD VIEW: A CYCLIC MODEL OF BALANCE AND DUALITY
by Eric Hill

> *This next essay was written by Eric Hill, a student at the University of Southern California. Eric wrote this essay as a take-home midterm for an anthropology class. The assignment to which he responded was as follows: "In a succinct and clearly organized essay, describe the Hopi world view, and relate it to other cultural world views." (In case you are not familiar with the term* cosmography, *it means a description of a particular world or universe.)*

One of the most striking characteristics of Hopi myth and cosmography is the repetition of specific themes and metaphors. A theme that appears consistently throughout Hopi thought and that seems to be at the heart of their complex symbology is a cyclical view of the universe. This cyclical view is reflected not only in Hopi ceremonies and beliefs but also in their secular activities. It forms the basis of their culture and dictates much of their daily behavior — including rituals for birth and death.

The Hopi's cyclical view of the universe is both like and unlike Western views. It is like Western views in that it has a definite sense of duality. But it is not the kind of polarized duality found in most Western religious and cultural models, where body and soul, mind and spirit, are at odds. Reading about the Hopi, I was surprised to discover that much in Hopi thought seems essentially Taoist in nature. Like Taoists, the Hopi reconcile life and death by viewing them as two halves of the same whole. When a child is born into a Hopi household, a ritual is performed in which the infant is named and covered in corn meal. The ritual for the dead is carried out in much the same manner: the deceased is given a new name, and the body is washed and then covered in corn meal. In the Hopi's cyclical view of the universe, opposites exist to create a sense of balance *through* their polarization.

It is no coincidence that the Hopi view of life directly parallels the path of the sun across the sky. Just as the human emerges from the womb into this life, the sun emerges from the horizon in the east. Both the sun and human being enter this world via the navel or entrance from the underworld. Both must "set" at the end of their cycle and then enter once again into the underworld. This mythical image of emergence and reemergence gives Hopi thought a distinctly Eastern rather than Western flavor.

This cyclical dance of duality is made even more apparent by the significance of corn in Hopi life. Besides being the most important staple in their diet, corn is also essential to their ceremonial life. In nature, corn must die to seed the ground so that more corn can be produced. With the growing of corn, as with other aspects of Hopi life and culture, the life-death-life cycle is clearly delineated. As this example indicates, corn is the embodiment of many symbols, concepts, and practices essential to Hopi thought. This is evident in their view of the corn mother, who is androgynous: the tassel or pollen stem is male, while the ear is female. Here, as elsewhere in Hopi thought, the necessity of coexisting opposites is emphasized. Male and female qualities share equal importance in the life cycle.

As these examples indicate, from the Hopi perspective birth and death, male and female, are opposites (in the sense that they are two different ends or aspects of reality); yet they nevertheless emerge (and reemerge) together into life here, above, and below. The Hopi world view is unique; it reflects Hopi culture and history. But it also looks both to the East and the West. Like Western cosmographies, it is based on dualisms. But like Eastern cosmographies, it sees these dualisms as interdependent aspects of reality that emerge (and reemerge) as part of larger processes.

LAYING IT ON THE LINES
by Chris Bowman

College students are often asked to read and respond to one or more books. Chris Bowman, a student at Oregon State University, was asked to do just this in an ethnic studies course on narratives of Latino migration. Here is the essay that Chris wrote in response to her assignment. The book Chris read is Between the Lines: Letters Between Undocumented Mexican and Central American Immigrants and Their Families and Friends. *This book was edited by Larry Siems and published in 1992 by the University of Arizona Press.*

To read *Between the Lines* is to begin to understand the *lives* of migrant Latinos in America. I emphasize the word *lives* because it is often automatic to think with singularity: *the* migrant worker. In this book, a collection of letters between immigrants to the United States and their families and friends in Mexico and Central America, multiple stories emerge. These stories provide powerful insights into the many complex relationships that are affected when Latinos come to the United States.

The letters collected in *Between the Lines* are from husbands and wives, daughters and sons, in-laws, nieces, uncles, sisters, fathers, and mothers. Friends write to friends. Priests write for those who cannot write themselves. Surprisingly, the letters from illiterate Latinos — letters that, in the case of those who speak indigenous languages, have been translated twice — have a refreshingly emotional style that feels like conversation. But whether the authors wrote or dictated their thoughts, through almost every letter there winds a thread of love and longing for those who are far away.

In many letters, writers implore their loved ones to write, send photos, send news. To encourage response, the writers send their own news — about health, children, finance. They also share gossip, advice, and hopes for the future. In this respect, these migrants and their families are like any other ordinary "American" family. And yet they are clearly not ordinary. These writers lead difficult lives, more difficult than those of many Americans. In the very first letter, the writer tells of his deep sadness when he realized how much he would have to endure to get to America. Another letter writer describes her disappointment when friends give her a chilly reception when she comes to the United States. Worried that she has done something wrong, she discovers that her friends were both sad and angry that she would now be subjected to the hardships that they had endured.

As these examples indicate, the letters in *Between the Lines* are very powerful. And they are powerfully arranged by Larry Siems, the editor of this collection. Siems has organized the letters to suggest the process that migrants and their loved ones experience as the migrants acculturate. The first letters are from those who have recently arrived in this country, and while they speak of hardship, there is an underlying tone of hopefulness. The next section is comprised of letters from those who have been left behind. These letters convey faith in and encouragement for the migrants, as well as fears and advice about how to negotiate new situations. The next three sections are from close friends, spouses, and families. It is clear from the letters in these sections that the writers have been apart for some time — but that the letters continue to nurture their relationships. The final section includes a mix of letters that emphasize the complexity and difficulty of the lives of migrants. They also demonstrate the reasons that people continue to risk these difficulties to come to the United States.

Between the Lines contributes to an understanding of the lives of Latino migrants in America because it tells a different story than that portrayed in the media. The media often portray migrants as people who impulsively leave one country for another. As these letters reveal, the decision to leave family and friends is heart-wrenching. One man writes of how he hid when his friend came to tell him goodbye because he could not bear the parting. Many apologize to their families for leaving but state that this is the only way that they can help their families.

Between the Lines also corrects many popular misconceptions about the lives of Latino migrants. These are not people on public assistance. These are workers who are sending money home to loved ones and saving what little they can for their future. The letters tell stories of migrants who are exploited by employers who refuse to pay them after a job has been completed, knowing full well that the undocumented worker has no recourse in such a situation. Letters also tell (time and time again) of migrants being scorned because they do not speak English. One writer describes how "here one feels like a sad lost dog. . . . [in Mexico] one has freedom even to scream in his house and do in his house whatever he pleases, and here if you do all this the first to arrive are the police because the neighbors call them" (299).

For most who come, the United States is not like they thought it would be. So maintaining a link with their families and friends is vital to their existence. Not that they entirely leave their past behind. The letters in *Between the Lines* indicate that many migrants move to neighborhoods where they know at least one person from their home country — or even village. The letters that go back and forth from the United States to home thus participate in an ongoing neighborhood grapevine that discourages misbehavior.

Clearly, as Larry Siems indicates in his comments on the letters in this collection, these are individuals attempting to lead ordinary lives. They are also people who are deeply misunderstood and shamelessly abused. It's heartbreaking to read of vigilante groups who look on border crossings as opportunities for target practice. How ironic that many citizens in the United States are concerned about such practices as bilingual education but can't see the many ways that Latino migrants are mistreated in our country.

Between the Lines tells the story of human beings who are striving to provide for themselves and for their families. This should be a familiar story — but in this case it is not. These people know what it's like for their families to go hungry. Many know the horrors of war. And all know what it's like to be forced to leave the ones they love in order for them (and often for their families) to survive. That's what this book is about.

TACOMA NARROWS BRIDGE FAILURE: PROGRESS REPORT

The final essay in this miscellany is by a student whose writing you have already read, Brenda Shonkwiler. Chapter 4, "Understanding the Research Process," includes a research paper that Brenda, a student at Oregon State University, wrote for her first-year writing class. Chapter 9, "Strategies for Planning, Drafting, and Document Design," reproduces the proposal that Brenda presented to her teacher, Carole Ann Crateau, at the start of her project. Here is a report that Brenda wrote for Ms. Crateau when she was two-thirds of the way through her project. As the subject heading indicates, it serves as a progress report on her work.

March 8, 1999

To: Carole Ann Crateau

From: Brenda Shonkwiler

Subject: Tacoma Narrows Bridge Failure — Interviews and Progress Report

The Tacoma Narrows Bridge was built to span Puget Sound. At the time, it was the only fixed roadway connecting the Washington mainland and the Olympic Peninsula. When it was built, the Narrows Bridge was praised as the epitome of artistry in bridge construction. However, the bridge soon earned the nickname "Galloping Gertie" because of its rolling, undulating motion. People drove hundreds of miles to drive across Gertie's center span. Despite the obvious oscillations of the bridge's roadbed, many people, including bridge officials, were confident in the structure. A bank near the Tacoma end of the bridge even had a billboard advertisement that boasted "Safe as the Narrows Bridge." However, only four months after completion, the bridge collapsed in a windstorm due to wind-induced vibrations. The oscillating and twisting motions had become too strong for the bridge to withstand.

The bridge failure initiated research on the aerodynamic stability of bridges. A special wind tunnel was built at the University of Washington to test three-dimensional models. Several years were spent researching and testing before the second Tacoma Narrows Bridge was constructed. Ten years after Galloping Gertie collapsed, the new bridge was completed. This new bridge is of major significance because of its numerous unique design features. This was the first time a research program was implemented to investigate the aerodynamic effects of wind action on a bridge. This effort provided significant information to suspension bridge engineers nation-wide and had an important effect on all suspension bridge designs that followed.

To learn more about the topic, I set up two interviews. One was with P. C. Klingeman, a professor in the civil engineering department at Oregon State University (OSU). The other interview was with Albert Stetz, a physics instructor at OSU. These interviews assisted in my research efforts.

In this report I summarize these interviews and describe my progress on my project.

STRUCTURAL ASPECTS

To learn more about Gertie's structural problems and how bridges are now designed to prevent problems from wind-related vibrations, I decided to interview my strengths-of-materials teacher, P. C. Klingeman. He is a pro-fessor in the civil engineering department and knows about structures, so I thought he would be a good resource. When I told Professor Klingeman about my project, he loaned me a three-minute video showing the col-lapse of the Tacoma Narrows Bridge. I could see how much the bridge twisted torsionally and oscillated vertically. In one clip, a person got out of his car and tried to run off of the bridge while it shook violently.

In the interview, I asked Professor Klingeman about the flexibility of the concrete. At maximum twisting, one side of the bridge deck was 28 feet above the other. I did not realize that concrete was that flexible. Professor Klingeman explained that there was a steel mesh within the concrete that helped hold the bridge together. The violent motion of the bridge had caused stress fractures in the concrete. This allowed the bridge deck to twist and oscillate as much as it did. The steel reinforcements are what kept the bridge from crumbling right away.

We then discussed the depth of the stiffening girders, which was eight feet. I wanted to know what this told us about the bridge and how it affected structural stability. Professor Klingeman said that it was the thickness of the center span. Because the stiffening girders were solid, no air could pass through them. This created a tremendous amount of wind resistance. The new Tacoma Narrows Bridge was built without solid stiffening girders. The depth of the girders was increased while the wind resistance was decreased, resulting in a more stable structure.

In my preliminary research, I discovered that the bridge was oscillating even while it was being constructed. I was curious as to why nothing had been done to stiffen the bridge before it collapsed. Professor Klingeman told me that at the time people did not know enough about wind's effect on bridges. As it turns out, a few modifications were made to the bridge, but they were not very effective. Many people believed that the bridge was safe and were confident that it would remain standing.

Then I asked how the collapse of the Tacoma Narrows Bridge has affected the way bridges were currently designed. I discovered that the collapse generated much research on aerodynamics. Bridge models were tested in wind tunnels. This helped bridge designers learn about the effects of wind on bridges.

Professor Klingeman spent the remainder of the time explaining to me how bridges are built. I had gone to the library before the interview. One of the books I checked out, *Bridging the Narrows,* had many pictures showing how the two Tacoma Narrows Bridges were constructed. Professor Klingeman explained the whole process, using the pictures to illustrate it.

This interview was very informative. Many of my questions were answered, and I learned about the process of bridge construction.

ROLE OF RESONANCE

To understand the role that resonance had in the collapse of the Tacoma Narrows Bridge, I interviewed Albert Stetz, a physics professor at OSU. I had read in my physics book that all structures have a natural frequency, so I asked Professor Stetz about that topic. He explained that a simple harmonic oscillator could be used as a base model. The equation to model simple harmonic motion can be derived from the Taylor series.[1] I had learned about the Taylor series last year in calculus, so I knew what he was talking about. When the oscillations are small, the first term of the Taylor series can be used for a fairly accurate approximation. However, as the oscillations increase, the approximation becomes less accurate. When the oscillations become violent, some of the other terms of the Taylor series start to apply. At this point, the motion is no longer simple harmonic motion. This explanation was interesting to me because it tied together things I had learned in calculus and in physics. Professor Stetz's explanation helped me understand how complicated Galloping Gertie's motion

---

[1]Taylor series: $f(x) = f(0) + \dfrac{f'(0)}{1!}x + \dfrac{f''(0)}{2!}x^2 + \ldots$

was, and why it was so difficult to predict. Professor Stetz used examples, such as the motion of earthquakes and metronomes, to illustrate the variety of applications of the Taylor series to physics.

This interview was interesting and informative. I learned some fascinating things about resonance and oscillations and gained helpful background information on what happened to Galloping Gertie.

IMPACT OF INTERVIEWS

The information I gained from the two interviews increased my background knowledge of the subject. Because of my interview with Professor Klingeman, I have a much better understanding of the way bridges are put together, how wind causes torsion and oscillations, and how it is possible that problems with the bridge were overlooked. The interview with Professor Stetz helped me understand the impact of resonance.

The interviews helped me look at my topic from various perspectives and enabled me to widen my research. The cause of the Tacoma Narrows Bridge collapse is complicated. There were several factors that eventually led to the failure. After the interviews, I was able to conduct research on such topics as *suspension bridges, vortex-induced vibrations, long-span bridges, bridge aerodynamics, turbulence,* and *wind tunnels.*

WORK STATUS

My project is coming along nicely. I have been able to find a variety of sources, mostly from the Internet. Now it is just a matter of looking through the information, deciding what is important, and putting it all together. I still have not looked for newspaper articles from 1940 to see what was written when the bridge collapsed. That would be a good source that could add interest to my discussion of the collapse of the Tacoma Narrows Bridge.

I found a short video in the Valley Library that I plan to use in my oral presentation. The video is similar to the one Professor Klingeman loaned to me, but it includes a few more scenes. This video will be a great visual aid. I am glad I found it.

CONCLUSION

Through videos, research, and interviews, I have learned a great deal about the failure of the Tacoma Narrows Bridge. The two interviews I conducted were informative and helped me widen my research. I now better understand how such a catastrophe could have occurred and what is being done in current bridge design to prevent similar failures from happening in the future.

■ ■ ■

FOR EXPLORATION

As a college student you undoubtedly have more experience in some kinds of academic writing than in others. Think about a kind of academic writing that you feel particularly confident about. (This might be analyses of literary or historical texts, lab reports in the sciences, case studies in the social sciences, and so on.) Now take five minutes to freewrite about a specific analytical technique required in this kind of writing. What specific writing abilities does this technique call for?

FOR GROUP WORK

Meet with a group of classmates to discuss your responses to the preceding Exploration. (Appoint a member of the group to act as a recorder so you can share the results of your discussion with the rest of the class.) Begin by having each student read his or her freewriting. Then answer these questions:

1. How many different kinds of writing did group members write about?

2. Did some of these kinds of writing require similar analytical and writing skills?

3. In what ways did the demands of these kinds of writing differ?

FOR THOUGHT, DISCUSSION, AND WRITING

1. Take a few minutes to think about your work thus far in your writing course. With what aspects of this work are you most — and least — pleased? In thinking about this question, be sure to think about both product and process. You may feel that several of your essays could be stronger in one or another way, for instance, and yet you could feel satisfied about the effort you put into your writing. After some thought, freewrite or brainstorm a list of observations.

2. Now take a few minutes to look to the future. Think about the course of study you hope to undertake. If you don't know the specific major you will have, you probably have a sense of the general area of focus

you wish to pursue. What writing demands will your studies make of you? How prepared do you feel to respond to these demands? What additional steps can you take to become the strongest, most efficient writer possible? After reflecting on these questions, freewrite or brainstorm a second list of observations.

3. Drawing on the two previous activities, write an essay in which you consider your development as a writer. As you do so, consider both your development as a writer to this point and the future demands you face.

WRITERS' REFERENCES

MLA Documentation Guidelines

MLA documentation style, developed specifically for those writing about literature and related areas, is used in a number of other disciplines in the humanities as well. This section provides examples of the most common forms of documentation. For further information, consult the fifth edition of the *MLA Handbook for Writers of Research Papers* (published in 1999) or the MLA online style guide: <http://www.mla.org/style/style_index.htm>.

In-Text Citations

MLA style requires documentation in the text of an essay for every quotation, paraphrase, and summary as well as other material requiring documentation. In-text citations document material from other sources with both signal phrases and parenthetical citations. Signal phrases introduce the material, often including the author's name. Keep your parenthetical citations short, but include the information your readers need to locate the full citation in the list of works cited at the end of the text.

Place a parenthetical citation as near the relevant material as possible without disrupting the flow of the sentence, as in the following examples.

1. AUTHOR NAMED IN A SIGNAL PHRASE

Ordinarily, you can use the author's name in a signal phrase — to introduce the material — and cite the page number(s) in parentheses.

```
Herrera indicates that Kahlo believed in a "vitalistic
form of pantheism" (328).
```

2. AUTHOR NAMED IN PARENTHESES

When you do not mention the author in a signal phrase, include the author's last name before the page number(s) in the parentheses.

In places, de Beauvoir "sees Marxists as believing in subjectivity" (Whitmarsh 63).

3. TWO OR THREE AUTHORS

Use all the authors' last names in a phrase or in parentheses.

Gortner, Hebrun, and Nicolson maintain that "opinion leaders" influence other people in an organization because they are respected, not because they hold high positions (175).

4. FOUR OR MORE AUTHORS

Use the first author's name and *et al.* ("and others"), or name all the authors in a phrase or in parentheses.

Similarly, as Belenky, Clinchy, Goldberger, and Tarule assert, examining the lives of women expands our under-standing of human development (7).

5. ORGANIZATION AS AUTHOR

Give the full name of a corporate author (or a shortened form of it if it is long).

Any study of social welfare involves a close analysis of "the impacts, the benefits, and the costs" of its poli-cies (Social Research Corporation iii).

6. UNKNOWN AUTHOR

Use the full title, if it is brief, in your text — or a shortened version of the title in parentheses.

"Hype," by one analysis, is "an artificially engendered atmosphere of hysteria" ("Today's Marketplace" 51).

7. AUTHOR OF TWO OR MORE WORKS

If your list of works cited has more than one work by the same author, include a shortened version of the title of the work.

> Gardner shows readers their own silliness in his descrip-
> tion of a "pointless, ridiculous monster, crouched in the
> shadows, stinking of dead men, murdered children, and
> martyred cows" (<u>Grendel</u> 2).

8. TWO OR MORE AUTHORS WITH THE SAME LAST NAME

Always include the authors' first *and* last names in the signal phrases or in the parenthetical citations for their works.

> Children will learn to write if they are allowed to
> choose their own subjects, James Britton asserts, citing
> the Schools Council study of the 1960s (37–42).

9. MULTIVOLUME WORK

Note the volume number first and then the page number(s).

> Modernist writers prized experimentation and gradually
> even sought to blur the line between poetry and prose,
> according to Forster (3: 150).

If you name only one volume of the work in your list of works cited, you need include only the page number.

10. LITERARY WORK

Because literary works are often available in many different editions, cite the page number(s) from the edition you used followed by a semicolon, and, in addition, give other identifying information that will lead readers to the passage in any edition — such as the act and scene in a play (37; sc. 1). For a novel, indicate the part or chapter (175; ch. 4).

> In utter despair, Dostoyevsky's character Mitya wonders
> aloud about the "terrible tragedies realism inflicts on
> people" (376; bk. 8, ch. 2).

For poems, cite the part (if there is one) and line(s). If you are citing only line numbers, use the word *line(s)* in the first reference (lines 33–34).

> On dying, Whitman speculates, "All goes onward and out-
> ward, nothing collapses. / And to die is different from
> what anyone supposed, and luckier" (6.129–30).

For verse plays, give only the act, scene, and line numbers.

> As <u>Macbeth</u> begins, the witches greet Banquo as "Lesser
> than Macbeth, and greater" (1.3.65).

11. WORK IN AN ANTHOLOGY

For an essay, short story, or other piece of prose reprinted in an anthology, use the name of the author of the work (not the editor of the anthology) and the page number(s) from the anthology.

> Narratives of captivity play a major role in early writ-
> ing by women in the United States, as demonstrated by
> Silko (219).

12. BIBLE

Identify quotations by giving the title of the Bible, the book, and the chapter and verse separated by a period. In your text, spell out the names of books. In parenthetical citations, use abbreviations for books with names of five or more letters (*Gen.* for *Genesis*).

> He ignored the admonition "Pride goes before destruction,
> and a haughty spirit before a fall" (<u>New Oxford Annotated</u>
> <u>Bible</u>, Prov. 16.18).

13. INDIRECT SOURCE

Use the abbreviation *qtd. in* to indicate that you are quoting from someone else's report of a conversation, interview, letter, or the like.

> As Arthur Miller says, "When somebody is destroyed
> everybody finally contributes to it, but in Willy's case,
> the end product would be virtually the same" (qtd. in
> Martin and Meyer 375).

14. TWO OR MORE SOURCES IN THE SAME CITATION

Separate the information with semicolons.

> Economists recommend that <u>employment</u> be redefined to
> include unpaid domestic labor (Clark 148; Nevins 39).

15. ENTIRE WORK OR ONE-PAGE ARTICLE

Include the reference in the text without any page numbers or parentheses.

```
Michael Ondaatje's poetic sensibility transfers beauti-
fully to prose in The English Patient.
```

16. WORK WITHOUT PAGE NUMBERS

If a work has no page numbers or is only one page long, you may omit the page number. If a work uses paragraph numbers instead, use the abbreviation *par(s).*

```
Whitman considered their speech "a source of a native
grand opera," in the words of Ellison (par. 13).
```

17. NONPRINT OR ELECTRONIC SOURCE

Give enough information in a signal phrase or parenthetical citation for readers to locate the source in the list of works cited. Usually give the author or title under which you list the source. Specify a source's page, section, paragraph, or screen numbers if numbered.

```
Describing children's language acquisition, Pinker
explains that "what's innate about language is just a way
of paying attention to parental speech" (Johnson, sec. 1).
```

Explanatory and Bibliographic Notes

MLA style allows explanatory notes for information or commentary that does not readily fit into your text but is needed for clarification or further explanation. In addition, MLA style permits bibliographic notes for citing several sources for one point and for offering thanks to, information about, or evaluation of a source. Use superscript numbers in the text to refer readers to the notes, which may appear as endnotes (typed under the heading *Notes* on a separate page after the text but before the list of works cited) or as footnotes.

1. SUPERSCRIPT NUMBER IN TEXT

```
Stewart emphasizes the existence of social contacts in
Hawthorne's life so that the audience will accept a dif-
ferent Hawthorne, one more attuned to modern times than
the figure in Woodberry.[3]
```

2. NOTE

³ Woodberry does, however, show that Hawthorne <u>was</u> often an unsociable individual. He emphasizes the seclusion of Hawthorne's mother, who separated herself from her family after the death of her husband, often even taking meals alone (28). Woodberry seems to imply that Mrs. Hawthorne's isolation rubbed off onto her son.

List of Works Cited

A list of works cited is an alphabetical list of the sources you have referred to in your essay. (If your instructor asks you to list everything you have read as background, call the list *Works Consulted.*) Here are some guidelines for preparing such a list.

- Start your list on a separate page after the text of your essay and any notes.
- Continue the consecutive numbering of pages.
- Type the heading *Works Cited,* not underlined, italicized, or in quotation marks, centered one inch from the top of the page.
- Start each entry flush with the left margin; indent subsequent lines one-half inch (or five spaces if you are using a typewriter). Double-space the entire list.
- List sources alphabetically by author's last name. If the author is unknown, alphabetize the source by the first major word of the title.

The sample works cited entries that follow observe the MLA's advice to underline words that are often italicized in print. Although most computers can generate italics easily, the MLA recommends that "you can avoid ambiguity by using underlining" in your research essays. If you wish to use italics instead, first check with your instructor.

BOOKS

The basic entry for a book includes three elements, each followed by a period: the author's name, last name first; the title and subtitle, underlined or (if your instructor permits) italicized, with all major words capitalized; and the city of publication, a shortened version of the publisher's name, and the date of publication.

1. ONE AUTHOR

deCordova, Richard. <u>Picture Personalities: The Emergence
    of the Star System in America</u>. Urbana: U of Illinois
    P, 1990.

2. TWO OR THREE AUTHORS

Appleby, Joyce, Lynn Hunt, and Margaret Jacob. <u>Telling
    the Truth about History</u>. New York: Norton, 1994.

3. ORGANIZATION AS AUTHOR

American Chemical Society. <u>Handbook for Authors of Papers
    in the American Chemical Society Publications</u>. Wash-
    ington: American Chemical Soc., 1978.

4. UNKNOWN AUTHOR

<u>The New York Times Atlas of the World</u>. New York: New York
    Times Books, 1980.

5. TWO OR MORE BOOKS BY THE SAME AUTHOR(S)

Lorde, Audre. <u>A Burst of Light</u>. Ithaca: Firebrand, 1988.
---. <u>Sister Outsider</u>. Trumansburg: Crossing, 1984.

6. EDITOR(S)

Wall, Cheryl A., ed. <u>Changing Our Own Words: Essays on
    Criticism, Theory, and Writing by Black Women</u>. New
    Brunswick: Rutgers UP, 1989.

7. AUTHOR AND EDITOR

James, Henry. <u>Portrait of a Lady</u>. Ed. Leon Edel. Boston:
    Houghton, 1963.

8. WORK IN AN ANTHOLOGY OR CHAPTER IN A BOOK WITH AN EDITOR

Gordon, Mary. "The Parable of the Cave." <u>The Writer on
    Her Work</u>. Ed. Janet Sternburg. New York: Norton,
    1980. 27-32.

9. TWO OR MORE ITEMS FROM AN ANTHOLOGY

Include the anthology itself in your list of works cited. Then list each selection separately by its author and title, followed by a cross-reference to the anthology.

```
Donalson, Melvin, ed. Cornerstones: An Anthology of
     African American Literature. New York: St. Martin's,
     1996.
Baker, Houston A., Jr. "There Is No More Beautiful Way."
     Donalson 856-63.
```

10. TRANSLATION

```
Zamora, Martha. Frida Kahlo: The Brush of Anguish. Trans.
     Marilyn Sode Smith. San Francisco: Chronicle, 1990.
```

11. EDITION OTHER THAN THE FIRST

```
Kelly, Alfred H., Winfred A. Harbison, and Herman Belz.
     The American Constitution: Its Origins and Develop-
     ment. 6th ed. New York: Norton, 1983.
```

12. ONE VOLUME OF A MULTIVOLUME WORK

```
Foner, Philip S., and Ronald L. Lewis, eds. The Black
     Worker. Vol. 3. Philadelphia: Lippincott, 1980.
     8 vols.
```

13. TWO OR MORE VOLUMES OF A MULTIVOLUME WORK

```
Foner, Philip S., and Ronald L. Lewis, eds. The Black
     Worker. 8 vols. Philadelphia: Lippincott, 1980.
```

14. PREFACE, FOREWORD, INTRODUCTION, OR AFTERWORD

```
Schlesinger, Arthur M., Jr. Introduction. Pioneer Women:
     Voices from the Kansas Frontier. By Joanna L. Strat-
     ton. New York: Simon, 1981. 11-15.
```

15. ARTICLE IN A REFERENCE WORK

List the author of the article. If no author is identified, begin with the title. For a well-known encyclopedia, just note the edition and date. If the entries in the reference work are in alphabetical order, you need not give volume or page numbers.

```
Johnson, Peder J. "Concept Learning." Encyclopedia of
    Education. 1971.
"Traquair, Sir John Stewart." Encyclopaedia Britannica.
    11th ed. 1911.
```

16. BOOK THAT IS PART OF A SERIES

```
Moss, Beverly J., ed. Literacy across Communities. Writ-
    ten Language Series 2. Cresskill: Hampton, 1994.
```

17. GOVERNMENT DOCUMENT

Begin with the author, if identified. Otherwise, start with the name of the government, followed by the agency and any subdivision. Use abbreviations if they can be readily understood. Then give the title. For congressional documents, cite the number, session, and house; the type (*Report, Resolution, Document*), in abbreviated form; and the number of the material. If you cite the *Congressional Record,* give only the date and page number. Otherwise, end with publication information; the publisher is often the Government Printing Office (*GPO*).

```
United States. Cong. House. Report of the Joint Subcom-
    mittee on Reconstruction. 39th Cong., 1st sess.
    H. Rept. 30. 1865. New York: Arno, 1969.
U.S. Bureau of the Census. Historical Statistics of the
    United States, Colonial Times to 1870. Washington:
    GPO, 1975.
```

18. PAMPHLET

```
Why Is Central America a Conflict Area? Opposing View-
    points Pamphlets. St. Paul: Greenhaven, 1984.
```

19. PUBLISHED PROCEEDINGS OF A CONFERENCE

```
Martin, John Steven, and Christine Mason Sutherland, eds.
    Proceedings of the Canadian Society for the History
    of Rhetoric. Calgary: Canadian Soc. for the History
    of Rhetoric, 1986.
```

20. TITLE WITHIN A TITLE

Do not underline or italicize the title of a book within the title of a book you are citing. Underline or italicize and enclose in quotation marks the title of a short work within a book title.

```
Gilbert, Stuart. James Joyce's Ulysses. New York: Vintage-
     Random, 1955.
Renza, Louis A. "A White Heron" and the Question of a
     Minor Literature. Madison: U of Wisconsin P, 1984.
```

PERIODICALS

The basic entry for a periodical includes the following elements: the author's name, last name first; the article title, in quotation marks; and the publication information, including the periodical title (underlined or italicized), the volume and issue numbers (if any), the date of publication, and the page number(s). Each of the three elements ends with a period (which in the article title goes *inside* the closing quotation marks).

21. ARTICLE IN A JOURNAL PAGINATED BY VOLUME

```
Norris, Margot. "Narration under a Blindfold: Reading
     Joyce's 'Clay.'" PMLA 102 (1987): 206-15.
```

22. ARTICLE IN A JOURNAL PAGINATED BY ISSUE

Follow the volume number with a period and the issue number.

```
Lofty, John. "The Politics at Modernism's Funeral." Cana-
     dian Journal of Political and Social Theory 6.3
     (1987): 88-96.
```

23. ARTICLE IN A MONTHLY MAGAZINE

```
Weiss, Philip. "The Book Thief: A True Tale of Biblio-
     mania." Harper's Jan. 1994: 37-56.
```

24. ARTICLE IN A NEWSPAPER

After the author and title of the article, give the name of the newspaper as it appears on the front page but without any initial *A, An,* or *The.* Add the city in brackets after the name if it is not part of the title. Then give the date and edition if one is listed, and add a colon. Follow the colon with a space, the section number or letter (if given), and then the page number(s). If the article appears on discontinuous pages, give the first page followed by a plus sign.

> Bruni, Frank, and B. Drummond Ayers Jr. "Bush Moving
>   toward Center." New York Times 8 Mar. 2000, natl.
>   ed.: A1+.

25. EDITORIAL OR LETTER TO THE EDITOR

> Magee, Doug. "Soldier's Home." Editorial. Nation 26 Mar.
>   1988: 400–01.

26. UNSIGNED ARTICLE

> "The Odds of March." Time 15 Apr. 1985: 20+.

27. REVIEW

List the reviewer's name and the title of the review, if any, followed by *Rev. of* and the title and author or director of the work reviewed. Then add the publication information for the periodical in which the review appears.

> Solinger, Rickie. "Unsafe for Women." Rev. of Next Time,
>   She'll Be Dead: Battering and How to Stop It, by Ann
>   Jones. New York Times Book Review 20 Mar. 1994: 16.

ELECTRONIC SOURCES

Electronic sources such as CD-ROMs, World Wide Web sites, and email differ from print sources in the ease with which they can be — and the frequency with which they are — changed, updated, or even eliminated. In addition, as the *MLA Handbook for Writers of Research Papers* notes, electronic media "so far lack agreed-on means of organizing works" so that it is often hard to identify information that can direct a reader to the source. In recommending the following guidelines for some of the most common kinds of electronic sources, the *Handbook* adds, "writers must often settle for citing whatever information is available to them." Further guidelines for citing electronic sources can be found in the *Handbook* and online at <http://www.mla.org>.

Note that MLA style requires that electronic addresses, or URLs, in a Works Cited list be broken only after a slash.

28. CD-ROM, PERIODICALLY REVISED

Include the author's name; publication information for the print version, if any, of the text (including its title and date of publication); the title of the database; the medium (CD-ROM); the name of the company producing it; and the electronic publication date.

> Natchez, Gladys. "Frida Kahlo and Diego Rivera: The
>   Transformation of Catastrophe to Creativity."
>   Psychotherapy-Patient 4.1 (1987): 153-74. PsycLIT.
>   CD-ROM. SilverPlatter. Nov. 1994.

29. SINGLE-ISSUE CD-ROM, DISKETTE, OR MAGNETIC TAPE

> "Communion." The Oxford English Dictionary. 2nd ed.
>   CD-ROM. Oxford: Oxford UP, 1992.

30. ONLINE SCHOLARLY PROJECT OR REFERENCE DATABASE

To cite an online scholarly project or reference database, begin with the title followed by the name of the editor, if given. Supply the electronic publication information, including version number, date, and name of the sponsoring organization. End with the date of access and URL.

> The Orlando Project: An Integrated History of Women's
>   Writing in the British Isles. 1997. U of Alberta.
>   9 Oct. 1977 <http://www.ualberta.ca/ORLANDO/>.

To cite a poem, essay, or other short work within a scholarly project or database, begin with the author's name and the title of the work, and give the URL of the short work.

> Scott, Walter. "Remarks on Frankenstein, or the Modern
>   Prometheus: A Novel." Romantic Circles. Ed. Neil
>   Fraistat, Steven Jones, Donald Reiman, and Carl
>   Stahmer. 1996. 15 Apr. 1998 <http://www.udel.edu/
>   swilson/mws/bemrev.html>.

To cite an anonymous article from a reference database, include the article title and URL.

> "Sasquatch." The Encyclopedia Mythica. Ed. Micha F. Lin-
>   demans. 1998. 31 Mar. 1998 <http://www.pantheon.org/
>   mythica/areas/folklore/>.

31. PROFESSIONAL OR PERSONAL WORLD WIDE WEB SITE

Give the author's name, if known, or start with the title of the site. Include the date of publication or the latest update and the name of any institution or organization associated with the site. End with the date of access and the URL.

> Bowman, Laurel. Classical Myth: The Ancient Sources. 24
>   June 1999. Dept. of Greek and Roman Studies, U of
>   Victoria. 7 Mar. 2000 <http://web.uvic.ca/grs/
>   bowman/myth>.

If no title exists, include a description such as *Homepage.*

> Kim, Angela. Homepage. 9 Oct. 1999 <http://
>   www.cohums.ohio-state.edu/english/people/
>   kim.1/>.

32. ONLINE BOOK

Provide the author's name or, if only an editor, a compiler, or a translator is identified, the name of that person followed by *ed., comp.,* or *trans.* Then give the title and the name of any editor, compiler, or translator not listed earlier, preceded by *Ed., Comp.,* or *Trans.* Include the publication information (city, publisher, and year) for the print version, if given, or the date of electronic publication and the sponsoring organization. End with the date of access and the URL.

> Riis, Jacob A. How the Other Half Lives: Studies among
>   the Tenements of New York. Ed. David Phillips. New
>   York: Scribner's, 1890. 26 Mar. 1998 <http://
>   www.cis.yale.edu/amstud/inforev/riis/
>   title.html>.

If you are citing a poem, essay, or other short work within a book, include its title after the author's name. Give the URL of the short work, not of the book, if they differ.

> Dickinson, Emily. "The Grass." Poems: Emily Dickinson.
>   Boston, 1891. Humanities Text Initiative American
>   Verse Collection. Ed. Nancy Kushigian. 1995. U of
>   Michigan. 9 Oct. 1997 <http://www.planet.net/
>   pkrisxle/emily/poemsOnline.html>.

33. ARTICLE IN AN ONLINE PERIODICAL

Begin with the author's name, if known; the title of the work or material, in quotation marks; the name of the periodical; the volume or issue number, if any; the date of publication; and the page or paragraph numbers, if given. End with the date of access and the URL.

```
Browning, Tonya. "Embedded Visuals: Student Design in Web
     Spaces." Kairos: A Journal for Teachers of Writing
     2.1 (1997). 9 Oct. 1997 <http://english.ttu.edu/
     kairos/2.1/index_f.html>.
Gwande, Atul. "Drowsy Docs." Slate 9 Oct. 1997. 10 Oct.
     1997 <http://www.slate.com/MedicalExaminer/
     97-10-09/MedicalExaminer.asp>.
```

34. WORK FROM AN ONLINE SUBSCRIPTION SERVICE

To cite an article from an online service to which you subscribe personally, such as America Online, begin with the author's name, if known, and the title of the work. Give the title of the online service, along with the date of access and the word *Keyword,* followed by the keyword used.

```
Weeks, W. William. "Beyond the Ark." Nature Conservancy
     Mar.-Apr. 1999. America Online. 2 Apr. 1999. Key-
     word: Ecology.
```

For a work from an online service to which a library subscribes, list the information about the work, followed by the name of the service, the library, the date of access, and the URL of the service.

```
"Breaking the Dieting Habit: Drug Therapy for Eating Dis-
     orders." Psychology Today Mar. 1995: 12+. Electric
     Lib. Main Lib., Columbus, OH. 31 Mar. 1999 <http://
     www.elibrary.com/>.
```

35. POSTING TO A DISCUSSION GROUP

To cite a posting to an online discussion group such as a listserv or Usenet newsgroup, give the author's name; the document title, in quotation marks; the description *Online posting*; and the date of posting. For a listserv posting, then give the name of the listserv; the number of the posting, if any; the date of access; and the URL of the listserv or the email address of its moderator. For a newsgroup posting, end with the date of access and the name of the newsgroup.

```
Martin, Jerry. "The IRA & Sinn Fein." Online
     posting. 31 Mar. 1998. 1 Apr. 1998
     <news:soc.culture.irish>.
```

You should always cite an archival version of a posting, if one is available.

```
Chagall, Nancy. "Web Publishing and Censorship." 2 Feb.
     1997. Online posting. ACW: The Alliance for Comput-
     ers and Writing Discussion List. 10 Oct. 1997
     <http://english.ttu.edu/acw-1/archive.htm>.
```

36. EMAIL MESSAGE

Include the writer's name; the subject line of the message, in quotation marks; a description of the message that mentions the recipient; and the date of the message.

```
Lunsford, Andrea A. "New Documentation Examples." Email
     to Kristin Bowen. 26 Jan. 1999.
```

37. SYNCHRONOUS COMMUNICATION (MOOs, MUDs)

In citing a posting in a forum such as a MOO, MUD, or IRC, include the name(s) of any specific speaker(s) you are citing; a description of the event; its date; the name of the forum; the date of access; and the URL. Always cite an archived version of the posting if one is available.

```
Patuto, Jeremy, Simon Fennel, and James Goss. The Myti-
     lene Debate. 9 May 1996. MiamiMOO. 28 Mar. 1998
     <http://moo.cas.edu/cgi-bin/moo?look+4085>.
```

38. OTHER ONLINE SOURCES

In citing other online sources, follow the guidelines given on pp. 434–37, but adapt them as necessary. Here are examples of citations for a work of art, an interview, and a film clip, accessed online.

```
Aleni, Giulio. K'un-yu t'u-shu. ca. 1620. Vatican, Rome.
     28 Mar. 1998 <http://www.ncsa.uiuc.edu/SDG/
     Experimental/vatican.exhibit/exhibit/full-images/
     i_rome_to_china/china02.gif>.
```

```
Dyson, Esther. Interview. Hotseat 23 May 1997
     <http://www.hotwired.com/packet/hotseat/97/20/
     index4a.html>.
Face/Off. Dir. John Woo. 1997. Hollywood.com. 8 Mar. 2000
     <http://www.hollywood.com/multimedia/movies/
     faceoff/trailer/mmindex.html>.
```

39. WORK IN AN INDETERMINATE ELECTRONIC MEDIUM

If you are not sure whether material accessed through a local network is stored on a central computer's hard drive, on a CD-ROM, or on the Web, use the label *Electronic*. Include any publication information that is available, the name of the network or of its sponsoring organization, and the date of access.

```
"Communion." The Oxford English Dictionary. 2nd ed.
     Oxford: Oxford UP, 1992. Electronic. OhioLink. Ohio
     State U Lib. 15 Apr. 1998.
```

OTHER SOURCES

40. UNPUBLISHED DISSERTATION

Enclose the title in quotation marks. Add the identification *Diss.*, the name of the university or professional school, and the year the dissertation was accepted.

```
LeCourt, Donna. "The Self in Motion: The Status of the
     (Student) Subject in Composition Studies." Diss.
     Ohio State U, 1993.
```

41. PUBLISHED DISSERTATION

Cite a published dissertation as a book, adding the identification *Diss.* and the name of the university. If the dissertation was published by University Microfilms International, add *Ann Arbor: UMI* and the year, and list the UMI number at the end of the entry.

```
Botts, Roderic C. Influences in the Teaching of English,
     1917-1935: An Illusion of Progress. Diss. Northeast-
     ern U, 1970. Ann Arbor: UMI, 1971. 71-1799.
```

42. ARTICLE FROM A MICROFORM

Treat the article as a printed work, but add the name of the microform and information for locating it.

```
Sharpe, Lora. "A Quilter's Tribute." Boston Globe 25 Mar.
     1989. Newsbank: Social Relations 12 (1989): fiche 6,
     grids B4-6.
```

43. INTERVIEW

```
Schorr, Daniel. Interview. Weekend Edition. Natl. Public
     Radio. WEVO, Concord. 26 Mar. 1988.
Beja, Morris. Personal interview. 2 Oct. 1997.
```

44. LETTER

If the letter was published, cite it as a selection in a book, noting the date and any identifying number after the title.

```
Frost, Robert. "Letter to Editor of the Independent." 28
     Mar. 1894. Selected Letters of Robert Frost. Ed.
     Lawrance Thompson. New York: Holt, 1964. 19.
```

If the letter was sent to you, follow this form.

```
Anzaldúa, Gloria. Letter to the author. 10 Sept. 1997.
```

45. FILM OR VIDEOCASSETTE

In general, start with the title; then name the director, the distributing company, and the date of release. Other contributors, such as writers or actors, may follow the director. If you cite a particular person's work, start the entry with that person's name. For a videocassette, include the original film release date (if relevant) and the label *Videocassette.*

```
Face/Off. Dir. John Woo. Perf. John Travolta and Nicholas
     Cage. Paramount, 1997.
The Star. Dir. Lawrence Pitkethly. Videocassette. CBS/Fox
     Video, 1995.
Weaver, Sigourney, perf. Aliens. Dir. James Cameron. 20th
     Century Fox, 1986.
```

46. TELEVISION OR RADIO PROGRAM

In general, begin with the title of the program. Then list the narrator, writer, director, actors, or other contributors, as necessary; the network; the local station and city, if any; and the broadcast date. If you cite a particular person's work, begin the entry with that person's name. If you cite a particular episode, include any title, in quotation marks, before the program's title. If the program is part of a series, include the series title (not underlined, italicized, or in quotation marks) before the network.

> Box Office Bombshell: Marilyn Monroe. Narr. Peter Graves. Writ. Andy Thomas, Jeff Schefel, and Kevin Burns. Dir. Bill Harris. A&E Biography. Arts and Entertainment Network. 23 Oct. 1997.

47. SOUND RECORDING

Begin with the name of the composer, performer, or conductor, depending on whose work you are citing. Next give the title of the recording, which is underlined or italicized, or the title of the composition, which is not. End with the manufacturer and the year of issue. If you are not citing a compact disc, give the medium before the manufacturer. If you are citing a particular song, include its title, in quotation marks, before the title of the recording.

> Grieg, Edvard. Concerto in A-minor, op. 16. Cond. Eugene Ormandy. Philadelphia Orch. LP. RCA, 1989.
> Kilcher, Jewel. "Amen." Pieces of You. A&R, 1994.

48. WORK OF ART

> Kahlo, Frida. Self-Portrait with Cropped Hair. Museum of Modern Art, New York.

49. LECTURE OR SPEECH

> Lu, Min-Zhan. "The Politics of Listening." Conference on College Composition and Communication. Palmer House, Chicago. 3 Apr. 1998.

50. PERFORMANCE

List the title, other appropriate details (such as composer, writer, or director), the place, and the date. If you cite a particular person's work, begin the entry with that person's name.

> Frankie and Johnny in the Clair de Lune. By Terrence McNally. Dir. Paul Benedict. Westside Arts Theater, New York. 18 Jan. 1988.
> Watson, Emily, perf. The Mill on the Floss. Masterpiece Theatre. PBS. WNET, New York. 2 Jan. 2000.

51. MAP OR CHART

<u>Pennsylvania</u>. Map. Chicago: Rand, 1985.

52. CARTOON

Trudeau, Garry. "Doonesbury." Cartoon. <u>Philadelphia
      Inquirer</u> 9 Mar. 1988: 37.

53. ADVERTISEMENT

Dannon Yogurt Advertisement. <u>TV Guide</u> 4 Dec. 1999: A14.

APA Documentation Guidelines

The APA documentation style was established by the American Psychological Association and is used broadly in the social sciences. For further information, consult the fourth edition of the *Publication Manual of the American Psychological Association,* published in 1994. The APA has also established a Web site with information about APA Electronic Style Guidelines: <http://www.apa.org/journals/webref.html>.

In-Text Citations

APA style requires parenthetical citations in the text to document quotations, paraphrases, summaries, and other material from a source. These in-text citations correspond to full bibliographic entries in a list of references at the end of the text.

1. AUTHOR NAMED IN A SIGNAL PHRASE

Generally, use the author's name in a signal phrase to introduce the cited material, and place the date, in parentheses, immediately after the author's name. For a quotation, the page number, preceded by *p.,* appears in parentheses after the quotation. For electronic texts or other works without page numbers, paragraph numbers may be used instead. Position the page reference in parentheses two spaces after the final punctuation of a long, set-off quotation.

```
Key (1983) has argued that the placement of women in
print advertisements is subliminally important.

As Briggs (1970) observed, parents play an important role
in building their children's self-esteem because "chil-
dren value themselves to the degree that they have been
valued" (p. 14).
```

2. AUTHOR NAMED IN PARENTHESES

When you do not mention the author in a signal phrase in your text, give the name and the date in parentheses.

```
One study has found that only 68% of letters received by
editors were actually published (Renfro, 1979).
```

3. TWO AUTHORS

Use both names in all citations. Use *and* in a signal phrase, but use an ampersand *(&)* in parentheses.

```
Murphy and Orkow (1985) reached somewhat different con-
clusions by designing a study that was less dependent on
subjective judgment than were previous studies.
```

```
A recent study that was less dependent on subjective
judgment resulted in conclusions somewhat different from
those of previous studies (Murphy & Orkow, 1985).
```

4. THREE TO FIVE AUTHORS

List all the authors' names for the first reference.

```
Belenky, Clinchy, Goldberger, and Tarule (1986) have sug-
gested that many women rely on observing and listening to
others as ways of learning about themselves.
```

In subsequent references, use just the first author's name plus *et al.*

```
From this experience, observed Belenky et al. (1986),
women learn to listen to themselves think, a step toward
self-expression.
```

5. SIX OR MORE AUTHORS

Use only the first author's name and *et al.* in *every* citation.

```
As Mueller et al. (1980) demonstrated, television holds
the potential for distorting and manipulating consumers
as free-willed decision makers.
```

6. ORGANIZATION AS AUTHOR

If the name of an organization or a corporation is long, spell it out the first time, followed by an abbreviation in brackets. In later citations, use the abbreviation only.

FIRST CITATION (Centers for Disease Control [CDC], 1990)
LATER CITATION (CDC, 1990)

7. UNKNOWN AUTHOR

Use the title or its first few words in a signal phrase or in parentheses (in this example, a book's title is underlined).

The school profiles for the county substantiated this trend (Guide to Secondary Schools, 1983).

8. TWO OR MORE AUTHORS WITH THE SAME LAST NAME

If your list of references includes works by different authors with the same last name, include the authors' initials in each citation.

G. Jones (1984) conducted the groundbreaking study of retroviruses.

9. TWO OR MORE SOURCES WITHIN THE SAME PARENTHESES

List sources by different authors in alphabetical order by author's last name, separated by semicolons: (Chodorow, 1978; Gilligan, 1982). List works by the same author in chronological order, separated by commas: (Gilligan, 1977, 1982).

10. SPECIFIC PARTS OF A SOURCE

Use abbreviations (*chap., p.,* and so on) in a parenthetical citation to name the part of a work you are citing.

Montgomery (1988, chap. 9) argued that his research yielded the opposite results.

11. EMAIL AND OTHER PERSONAL COMMUNICATION

Cite any personal letters, email, electronic bulletin-board correspondence, telephone conversations, or interviews with the person's initial(s) and last name, the identification *personal communication,* and the date. Note, however, that APA recommends not including personal communications in the reference list.

> J. L. Morin (personal communication, October 14, 1999) supported with new evidence the claims made in her article.

12. WORLD WIDE WEB SITE

To cite an entire Web site, include its address in parentheses in your text (http://www.gallup.com); you do not need to include it in your list of references. To cite part of a text found on the Web, indicate the chapter or figure, as appropriate. To document a quotation, include the page or paragraph numbers, if available, or you may omit them if they are not available.

> Shade argued the importance of "ensuring equitable gender access to the Internet" (1993).

Content Notes

APA style allows you to use content notes to expand or supplement your text. Indicate such notes in your text by superscript numerals. Type the notes themselves on a separate page after the last page of the text, under the heading *Footnotes,* centered at the top of the page. Double-space all entries. Indent the first line of each note five spaces, but begin subsequent lines at the left margin.

SUPERSCRIPT NUMERAL IN TEXT

> The age of the children involved was an important factor in the selection of items for the questionnaire.[1]

FOOTNOTE

> [1] Marjorie Youngston Forman and William Cole of the Child Study Team provided great assistance in identifying appropriate items.

List of References

The alphabetical list of the sources cited in your document is called *References.* (If your instructor asks that you list everything you have read as background — not just the sources you cite — call the list *Bibliography.*) Here are some guidelines for preparing such a list.

- Start your list on a separate page after the text of your document but before any appendices or notes.

- Type the heading *References,* neither underlined nor in quotation marks, centered one inch from the top of the page.

- Begin your first entry. Unless your instructor suggests otherwise, do not indent the first line of each entry, but indent subsequent lines one-half inch or five spaces. Double-space the entire list.

- List sources alphabetically by authors' last names. If the author of a source is unknown, alphabetize the source by the first major word of the title.

For print sources, the APA style specifies the treatment and placement of four basic elements — author, publication date, title, and publication information.

- *Author*   List all authors with last name first, and use only initials for first and middle names. Separate the names of multiple authors with commas, and use an ampersand before the last author's name.

- *Publication date*   Enclose the date in parentheses. Use only the year for books and journals; use the year, a comma, and the month or month and day for magazines; use the year, a comma, and the month and day for newspapers. Do not abbreviate.

- *Title*   Underline titles and subtitles of books and periodicals. Do not enclose titles of articles in quotation marks. For books and articles, capitalize only the first word of the title and subtitle and any proper nouns or proper adjectives. Capitalize all major words in a periodical title.

- *Publication information*   For a book, list the city of publication (and the country or postal abbreviation for the state if the city is unfamiliar), a colon, and the publisher's name, dropping *Inc., Co.,* or *Publishers.* For a periodical, follow the periodical title with a comma, the volume number (underlined), the issue number (if appropriate) in parentheses and followed by a comma, and the inclusive page numbers of the article. For newspapers and for articles or chapters in books, include the abbreviation *p.* ("page") or *pp.* ("pages").

The following sample entries are in a hanging indent format, in which the first line aligns on the left and the subsequent lines indent one-half inch or five spaces. This is the customary APA format for final copy, including student papers. Unless your instructor suggests otherwise, it is the format we recommend. Note, however, that for manuscripts submitted to journals, APA requires the reverse (first line of each entry indented, subsequent lines flushed left), assuming that the citations will be converted by a typesetting system to a hanging indent. Similarly, APA allows for the substitution of italics for underlining in student papers; check which format your instructor prefers.

BOOKS

1. ONE AUTHOR

Lightman, A. (1993). <u>Einstein's dreams.</u> New York: Warner Books.

2. TWO OR MORE AUTHORS

Newcombe, F., & Ratcliffe, G. (1978). <u>Defining females: The nature of women in society.</u> New York: Wiley.

3. ORGANIZATION AS AUTHOR

Institute of Financial Education. (1983). <u>Income property lending.</u> Homewood, IL: Dow Jones-Irwin.

Use the word *Author* as the publisher when the organization is both the author and the publisher.

American Chemical Society. (1978). <u>Handbook for authors of papers in American Chemical Society publications.</u> Washington, DC: Author.

4. UNKNOWN AUTHOR

<u>National Geographic atlas of the world.</u> (1988). Washington, DC: National Geographic Society.

5. EDITOR

Hardy, H. H. (Ed.) (1998). <u>The proper study of mankind.</u> New York: Farrar, Straus.

6. SELECTION IN A BOOK WITH AN EDITOR

West, C. (1992). The postmodern crisis of the black intellectuals. In L. Grossberg, C. Nelson & P. Treichler (Eds.), <u>Cultural studies</u> (pp. 689–705). New York: Routledge.

7. TRANSLATION

Durkheim, E. (1957). <u>Suicide</u> (J. A. Spaulding & G. Simpson, Trans.). Glencoe, IL: Free Press of Glencoe.

8. EDITION OTHER THAN THE FIRST

Kohn, M. L. (1977). <u>Class and conformity: A study in values</u> (2nd ed.). Chicago: University of Chicago Press.

9. ONE VOLUME OF A MULTIVOLUME WORK

Baltes, P., & Brim, O. G. (Eds.). (1980). <u>Life-span development and behavior</u> (Vol. 3). New York: Basic Books.

10. ARTICLE IN A REFERENCE WORK

Ochs, E. (1989). Language acquisition. In <u>International encyclopedia of communications</u> (Vol. 2, pp. 390–393). New York: Oxford University Press.

If no author is listed, begin with the title.

11. REPUBLICATION

Piaget, J. (1952). <u>The language and thought of the child.</u> London: Routledge & Kegan Paul. (Original work published 1932)

12. GOVERNMENT DOCUMENT

U.S. Bureau of the Census. (1975). <u>Historical statistics of the United States, colonial times to 1870.</u> Washington, DC: U.S. Government Printing Office.

13. TWO OR MORE WORKS BY THE SAME AUTHOR(S)

List two or more works by the same author in chronological order. Repeat the author's name in each entry.

Goodall, J. (1991). <u>Through a window.</u> Boston: Houghton-Mifflin.

Goodall, J. (1999). <u>Reason for hope: A spiritual journey.</u> New York: Warner Books.

PERIODICALS

14. ARTICLE IN A JOURNAL PAGINATED BY VOLUME

Shuy, R. (1981). A holistic view of language. <u>Research in the Teaching of English, 15,</u> 101–111.

15. ARTICLE IN A JOURNAL PAGINATED BY ISSUE

Maienza, J. G. (1986). The superintendency: Characteristics of access for men and women. <u>Educational Administration Quarterly, 22</u>(4), 59–79.

16. ARTICLE IN A MAGAZINE

Gralla, P. (1994, April). How to enter cyberspace. <u>PC Computing,</u> 60–62.

17. ARTICLE IN A NEWSPAPER

Browne, M. W. (1988, April 26). Lasers for the battlefield raise concern for eyesight. <u>New York Times,</u> pp. C1, C8.

18. EDITORIAL OR LETTER TO THE EDITOR

Russell, J. S. (1994, March 27). The language instinct [Letter to the editor]. <u>New York Times Book Review,</u> 27.

19. UNSIGNED ARTICLE

What sort of person reads <u>Creative Computing?</u> (1985, August). <u>Creative Computing,</u> 8, 10.

20. REVIEW

Larmore, C. E. (1989). [Review of the book <u>Patterns of moral complexity</u>]. <u>Ethics, 99,</u> 423–426.

21. PUBLISHED INTERVIEW

McCarthy, E. (1968, December 24). [Interview with Boston
    Globe Washington staff]. <u>Boston Globe,</u> p. B27.

ELECTRONIC SOURCES

The APA's Web site, <http://www.apa.org/journals/webref.html>, includes current guidelines for citing various electronic sources, updating the information given in the fourth edition of the *Publication Manual of the American Psychological Association.* However, with the exception of guidelines for citing email, Web sites, articles and abstracts from electronic databases, and software, the APA does not offer guidelines for citing some common electronic sources. The following formats include these additional electronic sources, adapted from APA style and based on guidelines from *Online! A Reference Guide for Using Internet Sources,* 2000 edition, by Andrew Harnack and Eugene Kleppinger.

    The basic entry for most sources you access via the Internet should include the following elements:

- *Author*   Give the author's name, if available.

- *Publication date*   Include the date of Internet publication or of the most recent update, if available.

- *Title*   List the title of the document or subject line of the message, neither underlined nor placed in quotation marks.

- *Publication information*   For documents from databases or other scholarly projects, give the city of the publisher or sponsoring organization, followed by the name. For articles from online journals or newspapers, follow the title with a comma, the volume number (underlined), the issue number (if appropriate) in parentheses and followed by a comma, and the inclusive page numbers of the article.

- *Retrieval information*   Type the word *Retrieved* followed by the date of access and retrieval method (for example, *from the World Wide Web*), followed by a colon. End with the URL or other retrieval information and no period.

22. WORLD WIDE WEB SITE

    To cite a whole site, give the address in a parenthetical citation (p. 441).

    To cite a document from a Web site, include information as you would for a print document, followed by a note on its retrieval.

```
Mullins, B. (1995). Introduction to Robert Hass. Readings
    in Contemporary Poetry at Dia Center for the Arts.
    Retrieved April 24, 1997 from the World Wide Web:
    http://www.diacenter.org/prg/poetry/95-96/
    interhass.html
Shade, L. R. (1993). Gender issues in computer network-
    ing. Retrieved January 28, 2000 from the World Wide
    Web: http://www.0.delphi.com/woman/text3.html
```

23. FTP (FILE TRANSFER PROTOCOL), TELNET, OR GOPHER SITE

After the retrieval statement, give the address (substituting *ftp, telnet,* or *gopher* for *http* at the beginning of the URL) or the path followed to access information, with slashes to indicate menu selections.

```
Korn, P. (October 1994). How much does breast cancer
    really cost? Self. Retrieved May 5, 1997: gopher://
    nysernet.org:70/00/BCIC/Sources/SELF/94/how-much
```

24. LISTSERV MESSAGE

Provide the author's name; the date of posting; the subject line from the posting; the retrieval statement; and the listserv address.

```
Lackey, N. (1995, January 30). From Clare to here.
    Retrieved May 1, 1997 from the listserv:
    nanci@world.std.com
```

To cite a file that can be retrieved from a list's server or Web address, include the address or URL from the list's archive.

```
Lackey, N. (1995, January 30). From Clare to here.
    Retrieved May 1, 1997 from the listserv: http://
    www.rahul.net/frankf/Nancy/archives/95130.html
```

25. NEWSGROUP MESSAGE

Include the author's email address. After the subject line from the posting, give a retrieval statement that ends with the name of the newsgroup.

```
Sand, P. <psand@unh.edu> (1996, April 20). Java disabled
    by default in Linux Netscape. Retrieved May 10, 1996
    from the newsgroup: keokuk.unh.edu
```

26. EMAIL MESSAGE

The APA's *Publication Manual* discourages including email in a list of references and suggests citing email only in text as personal communication (p. 440).

27. SYNCHRONOUS COMMUNICATION (MOOs, MUDs)

To cite postings in MOOs, MUDs, and IRCs, provide the speaker's name, if known, or the name of the site; the date of the event; the title of the event, if appropriate; and the kind of communication (*Group discussion, personal interview*) if not indicated elsewhere. Include a retrieval statement with the address using a URL or other Internet address.

```
Cohen, S. (2000, March 15). Online Collaboration. [Group
     discussion]. Retrieved March 17, 2000 from the World
     Wide Web: http://moo.du.org:8000
```

28. MATERIAL FROM A CD-ROM DATABASE

```
Natchez, G. (1987). Frida Kahlo and Diego Rivera: The
     transformation of catastrophe to creativity
     [Abstract]. Psychotherapy-Patient, 8, 153–174.
     Retrieved from SilverPlatter (PsycLIT, CD-ROM, 1999
     release, Item 76-11344)
```

29. MATERIAL FROM AN INFORMATION SERVICE OR ONLINE DATABASE

```
Belenky, M. F. (1984). The role of deafness in the
     moral development of hearing impaired children.
     In A. Areson & J. De Caro (Eds.), Teaching, learn-
     ing and development. Rochester, NY: National Insti-
     tute for the Deaf. Retrieved January 20, 2000 from
     ERIC online database (No. ED 248 646)
```

30. MATERIAL FROM A DATABASE ACCESSED VIA THE WEB

```
Pryor, T., & Wiederman, M. W. (1998). Personality fea-
     tures and expressed concerns of adolescents with
     eating disorders. Adolescence, 33, 291–301. Re-
     trieved February 7, 2000 from Electric Library data-
     base on the World Wide Web: http://www.elibrary.com
```

31. SOFTWARE OR COMPUTER PROGRAM

McAfee Office 2000. Version 2.0 [Computer software].
        (1999). Santa Clara, CA: Network Associates.

OTHER SOURCES

32. TECHNICAL OR RESEARCH REPORTS AND WORKING PAPERS

Wilson, K. S. (1986). <u>Palenque: An interactive multimedia
        optical disc prototype for children</u> (Working Paper
        No. 2). New York: Center for Children and Technol-
        ogy, Bank Street College of Education.

33. PAPER PRESENTED AT A MEETING OR SYMPOSIUM, UNPUBLISHED

Cite the month of the meeting if it is available.

Engelbart, D. C. (1970, April). <u>Intellectual implications
        of multi-access computing.</u> Paper presented at the
        meeting of the Interdisciplinary Conference on Multi-
        Access Computer Networks, Washington, DC.

34. DISSERTATION, UNPUBLISHED

Leverenz, C. A. (1994). <u>Collaboration and difference in
        the composition classroom.</u> Unpublished doctoral dis-
        sertation, Ohio State University, Columbus.

35. POSTER SESSION

Ulman, H. L., & Walborn, E. (1993, March). <u>Hypertext in
        the composition classroom.</u> Poster session presented
        at the Annual Conference on College Composition and
        Communication, San Diego.

36. FILM OR VIDEOTAPE

Hitchcock, A. (Producer & Director). (1954). <u>Rear window</u>
        [Film]. Los Angeles: MGM.

37. TELEVISION PROGRAM, SINGLE EPISODE

Begin with the names of the script writers, and give the name of the director, in parentheses, after the episode title.

```
Kuttner, P. K., Moran, C., & School, E. (1994, July 19).
     Passin' it on (W. Chamberlain, Executive Director).
     In D. Zaccardi (Executive Producer), P.O.V. New
     York: Public Broadcasting Service.
```

38. RECORDING

Begin with the name of the writer or composer followed by the date of copyright. Give the recording date if it is different from the copyright date.

```
Colvin, S. (1991). I don't know why. [Recorded by
     A. Krauss and Union Station]. On Every time you say
     goodbye [Cassette]. Cambridge, MA: Rounder Records.
     (1992)
```

Web Resources

The World Wide Web hosts numerous sites useful to students. The following sites provide a starting point (and only a starting point) for exploring the riches of the Web.

General Web Resources

The Library of Congress (LOC) homepage provides access to the catalogues, collections, exhibitions, special programs, and research services of the Library of Congress. The LOC's National Digital Library Program offers access to documents, films, photos, and sound recordings in the American Memory Historical Collections.
<http://lcweb.loc.gov>

The Internet Public Library Web site provides a large collection of easily searched online serials, newspapers, and texts. It also includes materials designed to encourage more effective and efficient searching of the Web.
<http://www.ipl.org/>

Purdue University Libraries' Virtual Reference Desk provides an array of online resources, including dictionaries, thesauri, acronyms, and almanacs; general works on information technology; maps and travel information; phone books and area codes; selected government documents; and other reference sources.
<http://thorplus.lib.purdue.edu/ reference/index.html>

The WWW Virtual Library is a rich resource for information on the following subjects: agriculture, business and economics, computer science, communications and media, education, engineering, humanities, information management, international affairs, law, recreation, regional studies, science, and society. Tim Berners-Lee, who created html and the Web, founded this site.
<http://vlib.org/>

The Argus Clearinghouse provides a selective collection of topical guides for the following subjects: arts and humanities, business and employment, communication, computers and information technology, education, engineering, environment, government and law, health and medicine, places and peoples, recreation, science and mathematics, and social sciences and social issues.
<http://www.clearinghouse.net>

The California State University System's Global Campus Web site contains a variety of materials (including images, sounds, text, and video) to be used for educational purposes. Topics covered include business, fine arts, engineering, liberal arts, library, and science.
<http://www.csulb.edu/~gcampus/info/ index.html>

The Educational Resources Information Center, which is sponsored by the National Library of Education, provides access to the ERIC database, the largest source of educational information in the world. It also provides links to ERIC clearinghouse sites, resources, and special projects.
<http://www.accesseric.org/>

The Official U.S. Executive Branch Web Sites provide links to all existing Web sites of the executive branch of the U.S. government.
<http://lcweb.loc.gov/global/executive/ fed.html>

The United States Legislative Branch Web Sites provide links to a number of sites directly or indirectly related to the U.S. Congress. They include links for congressional mega sites, which are rich resources for information on current legislative initiatives, as well as links to congressional members, committees, organizations, schedules, calendars, floor proceedings, records and journals, votes, and other information.
<http://lcweb.loc.gov/global/legislative/ congress.html>

The Federal Judiciary Homepage provides a variety of resources about the federal judiciary system. These include information about the U.S. courts and various judicial system publications and directions. Links are provided to current news releases and reports, as well as to items about the judiciary in various news sources.
<http://www.uscourts.gov/>

Web Resources for Writers

The National Writing Center Association's Resources for Writers Web page is a rich source of online help for all aspects of writing. The page includes links to a grammar hotline directory, handouts, online tutor-

ing, and miscellaneous resources, such as punctuation guides, MLA and APA citation formats, and tips for technical writers.
<http://departments.colgate.edu/diw/ NWCA/Resources.html>

Roget's II Web site enables writers to find just the right word — and to do so online.
<http://www.bartleby.com/index.html>

The American Heritage Dictionary (4th edition) Web site provides all the resources of traditional print dictionaries.
<http://www.bartleby.com/index.html>

Online Writing Labs (OWLs) and Centers

The National Writing Center Association's Directory of Online Writing Centers provides links to the many online writing centers throughout North America. Some of these online writing centers will assist all writers; others provide services only to students at their university. These and other policies are clearly stated on each center's homepage.
<http://departments.colgate.edu/diw/ NWCAOWLS.html>

The following list includes some particularly well-developed online writing centers. The first such center in the United States was developed by Muriel Harris at Purdue University. Purdue's center remains one of the most valuable online resources for writers.

Purdue University's Online Writing Lab
<http://owl.english.purdue.edu/>

The Writers' Workshop at the University of Illinois, Champaign–Urbana
<http://www.english.uiuc.edu/cws/ wworkshop/index.htm>

Washington State University's Online Writing Lab
<http://owl.wsu.edu/index.asp>

Oregon State University's Online Writing Lab
<http://osu.orst.edu/dept/writing-center/owl.html>

The Writer's Center at Colorado State University
<http://www.colostate.edu/Depts/WritingCenter/>

Resources for ESL (English as a Second Language) Students

The Online English Grammar, maintained by Anthony Hughes, provides multiple resources for ESL students, including extensive information about various aspects of English, practice pages, a grammar clinic, and a learning center.
<http://www.edunet.com/english/grammar/>

Dave's ESL Café Web site provides a rich array of resources for ESL writers — from a quiz center to handouts, message exchanges, and chat central.
<http://www.eslcafe.com/>

George Washington University's ESL Study Hall provides links to resources for reading, writing, vocabulary, conversation, grammar, and listening.
<http://gwis2.circ.gwu.edu/~gwvcusas/>

The Frizzy University Network Web site provides assistance with grammar and with online reference materials (both general and specific to ESL). It also provides links to ESL discussion lists, to information about studying in the United States, and Web site construction.
<http://thecity.sfsu.edu/%7Efunweb/>

Karin's ESL PartyLand Web site includes seventy-five interactive quizzes, fifteen discussion forums, interactive lessons on a variety of topics, a chat room, and links to a variety of online ESL resources.
<http://www.eslpartyland.com/>

Resources for the Humanities and Fine Arts

Carnegie-Mellon University's **The English Server** comprises a diverse collection of online literary and cultural resources, including art, architecture, drama, fiction, poetry, history, political theory, cultural studies, philosophy, women's studies, and music.
<http://english-www.hss.cmu.edu/>

The University of California's **Voice of the Shuttle,** which is maintained by Alan Liu, is a particularly rich site for humanities research. In addition to listing resources on a wide variety of topics in the humanities, it includes extensive information on Web searching. Other resources include lists of highly ranked Web sites; guides to evaluating Internet resources; and humanities texts, archives, journals, and discussion lists and newsgroups.
<http://vos.ucsb.edu/shuttle/general.html>

Project Gutenberg originated in 1971, when Michael Hart decided that the best use of the Internet was to make public domain works available to the public. Project Gutenberg provides access to hundreds of downloadable (and, in the case of public domain texts, reproducible) texts — from Shakespeare and Lewis Carroll to Poe and Dante.
<http://promo.net/pg/>

Worldwide Internet Music Resources is a service provided by the William and Gayle Cook Music Library, Indiana University. The site includes links to a wide range of

resources on both classical and contemporary music.
<http://www.music.indiana.edu/ music_resources/>

Valdosta University's Home Page of Philosophy Resources provides links to numerous and diverse resources related to all branches of classical and contemporary philosophy. Representative links include Tuft's Greek Library, the Internet Encyclopedia of Philosophy, the Markkula Center for Applied Ethics, and homepages sponsored by various teachers and students of philosophy.
<http://www.valdosta.peachnet.edu/ ~rbarnett/phi/resource.html>

Art History Resources on the Web, a site maintained by Chris Witcombe of Sweet Briar College, includes an extensive array of links. All periods of art history — from prehistoric to the present — are covered, as are all mediums. The site also includes links to general research resources and to museums and galleries around the world.
<http://witcombe.sbc.edu/ ARTHLinks.html>

Horus's Web Links to History Resources, sponsored by the University of California, Riverside history department, provides links to historical sites organized according to time, place, and area within history. It also lists online services about history, research tools, and general resources.
<http://www.ucr.edu/h-gig/ horuslinks.html>

Resources for the Social Sciences

The American Psychological Association homepage includes research links to news articles, publications, and a for-fee searchable database; guidelines on library research and tips on APA documentation style; and informational content on parenting, mental health, and other topics.
<http://www.apa.org/>

The American Psychological Society, an international association of professionals in psychology, publishes the APS *Observer* online, a bimonthly journal offering in-depth articles on current topics in psychological science, noteworthy research, and issues that are affecting the field. It also provides links to psychology departments, psychological societies and organizations, government agencies, and related sites.
<http://www.psychologicalscience.org>

Psych Web offers a wealth of information on psychology and the social sciences, including thousands of links to psychology homepages of universities around the world, journals in psychology and the social sciences, psychology-related Web sites, APA style guides, and even complete versions of two classic texts in psychology, Sigmund Freud's *The Interpretation of Dreams* and William James's *The Varieties of Religious Experience.*
<http://www.psywww.com/index.html>

The Society of Professional Journalists, the largest journalism organization in the United States, offers a Web site with in-depth information on such issues as ethics in journalism, the Freedom of Information Act, student journalism, cameras in court, privacy, reporter's privilege, online challenges, the Supreme Court and the media, and trial coverage.
<http://www.spj.org>

IDEAS (Internet Documents in Economics Access Service) is a storehouse of articles in the field of economics, including published articles from hundreds of journals, author information, institution homepages, software information, and papers in prog-

ress, all classified by journal title or the *Journal of Economic Literature* codes.
<http://www.csufresno.edu/speechcom/wscalink.htm>

THOMAS is a service of the Library of Congress that provides legislative information on the Internet, including the status and history of bills, the congressional record, committee information, background materials on the legislative process, copies of historical documents, and much more.
<http://thomas.loc.gov>

Foreign Government Resources on the Web, sponsored by the University of Michigan, provides links to foreign government Web sites and background information on foreign countries, including leader biographies, human rights records, politics and election data; information on constitutions, laws, treaties, and embassies; and current news via links to international newspapers.
<http://www.lib.umich.edu/libhome/Documents.center/foreign.html>

The U.S. Census Bureau, part of the United States Department of Commerce, offers census information from Census 2000 and earlier, including data on population size broken down by state, county, and city; business-related figures; and information on income, poverty, minorities, genealogy, housing, and foreign trade.
<http://www.census.gov>

The Department of History at Tennessee Technological University offers links to databases and sites related to issues in the social sciences, including international affairs, the global environment, the Internet, demographics, policy analysis, government, political organizations, and social development.
<http://www.tntech.edu/www/acad/hist/data.html>

The **SocioWeb** is an unaffiliated guide to Web resources in the field of sociology, with links arranged by the following topics: Net indexes and guides, commercial sites, giants of sociology, journals and zines, learning sociology, sociological associations, sociology in action, sociological theory, surveys and statistics, topical research, university departments, and writings.
<http://www.socioweb.com/~markbl/socioweb>

The Department of Sociology and Anthropology at Trinity University hosts this Sociological Tour through cyberspace, a site featuring opinions, data analyses, essays, and links arranged by the following categories: general sociological resources, sociological theory, data resources and Web tools, and methods and statistics.
<http://www.trinity.edu/~mkearl/index.html>

The University of Iowa Department of Communication Studies **LINKS to Communication Studies Resources** is organized around the following subject areas: advertising; cultural studies and popular culture; digital media, hypertext, cybernetics, cyborgs, and virtual realities; film studies; gender, ethnicity, and race in mass communication; general communication resources; health and science communication; journalism and mass communication; media studies; political communication; rhetorical studies; social science resources; speeches and speechmakers; and visual communication/visual rhetorics.
<http://www.uiowa.edu/~commstud/resources/>

Resources for the Sciences and Mathematics

The **Math Archives Undergrads' Page** provides links to the following topics: societies,

undergraduate projects and research, summer programs, competitions, careers, undergraduate publications, and other Web sites.
<http://archives.math.utk.edu/ undergraduates.html>

The **Math on the Web** site, maintained by the American Mathematics Society, includes links on the following topics: literature guides, mathematics online, mathematics organized, people, reference literature, servers, and related resources.
<http://www.ams.org/mathweb/>

Biology Links, maintained by Harvard University's department of molecular and cellular biology, provides links to resources on specific topics within molecular and cellular biology, as well as to general Internet resources for biology, banks and tables, selected model organism and biological databases, and biological software directories.
<http://mcb.harvard.edu/BioLinks.html>

The National Human Genome Research Institute Web site serves as a clearinghouse for research on this important project. Topics include the ethical, legal, and social implications of the human genome project; policy and public affairs issues; and genomic and genetic resources.
<http://www.nhgri.nih.gov/index.html>

The National Institutes of Health (NIH) Web site includes news, health information, and links to scientific resources and to NIH suborganizations. The NIH is the central government organization dealing with health issues.
<http://www.nih.gov/>

Indiana University's **ChemInfo** site provides resources to a wide range of online resources in chemistry. The site offers both alphabetical and keyword searches.
<http://www.indiana.edu/~cheminfo/ cisindex.html>

BioChemNet is a Web site devoted to biology and chemistry resources. It includes subject directories in the following areas: general biology, general chemistry, organic chemistry, biochemistry, molecular genetics, teaching science, science careers, science clip art, among others. It also provides links to a variety of related science news journals.
<http://schmidel.com/bionet.cfm>

ICE: Internet Connections for Engineering is a Web site maintained by the Engineering Library at Cornell University. Though ICE specializes in the engineering disciplines, it also includes links for chemistry, math, physics, and other "hard" sciences.
<http://www.englib.cornell.edu/ice/ ice-index.html>

Physics News, maintained by the Brown University Physics Department, presents news and information related to physics and public policy, current work in physics, science news from wire services, and links to other journals and magazines.
<http://www.het.brown.edu/news/ index.html>

Developing a Portfolio of Your Written Work

Increasingly, writing teachers are integrating portfolios into course work. Sometimes, portfolios serve primarily to organize and store work in progress; such portfolios are often called *working* portfolios. In other cases, portfolios serve a more public purpose; these *presentation* portfolios highlight a writer's strengths and accomplishments. In writing classes, presentation portfolios often play a role in assessment, including end-of-term grading. Both types of portfolios can provide you with an excellent opportunity to reflect upon your writing process, progress, and future goals.

Whether your teacher asks you to develop a working portfolio or a presentation portfolio, the following guidelines can help you benefit from the process.

■ GUIDELINES FOR KEEPING A WRITING PORTFOLIO

1. *Understand the Purpose and Requirements of Your Portfolio.* The first thing you need to know is whether you are developing a working or a presentation portfolio — or both. A working portfolio exists primarily for your personal use, though your teacher may also ask to review it. A presentation portfolio serves a public function. Your teacher may ask you to develop both a working and a presentation portfolio. In this situation, your working portfolio serves as a source of materials for your presentation portfolio, which you will develop at the end of (and maybe during) the term. A presentation portfolio will include some or all of the materials in your working portfolio, organized according to a particular format. Your teacher may also ask you to write additional commentary,

(continued)

(continued)

such as a cover letter for your portfolio, introductions to individual projects, and analyses of your growth as a writer.

Portfolios can vary considerably in their purpose and requirements. If your teacher asks you to develop a portfolio, you should be sure you know the answers to the following questions:

What primary function does my portfolio serve? If I am developing both a working and a presentation portfolio, what is the relationship between them?

What should my portfolio include?

If I am able to select some or all of the materials in my portfolio, what criteria should govern my selection?

How should my portfolio be organized?

Will my portfolio be evaluated? When, by whom, and according to what criteria?

What role does this evaluation play in determining my final course grade?

Will I be asked to write descriptive or reflective statements about my portfolio? What kind of information might I need to gather during the term to prepare to write these comments?

Is there anything else I need to know to develop an effective portfolio? Do I need to use a specific binder, for instance? Do all materials need to be typed or printed, or are handwritten materials acceptable? What role do neatness and other aspects of visual presentation play in the evaluation of my portfolio? Are there any other requirements I must follow?

2. *Make the Fullest Possible Use of Your Portfolio.* Portfolio development takes time and care, so you might be tempted to look upon it as a burden, something to expend minimal energy on. And yet the process of gathering, organizing, and reflecting upon your writing can be a powerful aid to learning and can also help you gain confidence as a writer — if you take this process seriously. If you save drafts of your essays but never take the time to review them, you may fulfill the minimal requirement for developing a portfolio, but you will have failed to take advantage of a valuable opportunity to learn more about your strengths and weaknesses as a writer.

(continued)

(continued)

3. *Organize Materials for Your Portfolio as You Produce Them.* A few simple but effective organizational strategies can help you to keep track of materials for a portfolio.

> Identify all drafts, whether print or electronic, with a date and with a brief heading.

> Develop a system for organizing your drafts. You may want to keep all drafts for a single project in one envelope. If you are composing on-screen, you might set up a directory or folder for each project, taking care to name and save all versions of drafts as you work on them. (In most cases, you will also want to print and organize electronically generated drafts. Even if you submit your portfolio on disk, you should still print backups in case of hardware or software problems.)

> Begin each drafting session by reviewing previous work on your project. Doing so will make it easier for you to keep your notes and drafts in order. This practice brings additional benefits, for it will help you reimmerse yourself in your project. It may also remind you that sections that you discarded from earlier versions might work well in your current draft.

> Organize your materials at the end of each drafting session. If you have been drafting on a computer, print the current version of your draft and clip or staple it together, then add it to earlier drafts of this essay.

4. *Keep Notes about Your Composing Process.* Teachers sometimes ask students to include reflections on their composing process in their portfolio. Sometimes these reflections are general; in other instances they focus upon projects you have done during the term. Keeping process notes about your writing will enable you to respond to such an assignment, and thus gain a richer understanding of yourself as a writer.

Acknowledgments

Text

cle of Higher Education. Reprinted by permission of The Chronicle of Higher Education and the author.

Art

ACLU Homepage. <www.aclu.org>. Copyright © 2000 American Civil Liberties Union. Reproduced by permission.

Scott Adams. Two *Dilbert* cartoons, 2/3/97; 5/5/97. Copyright © 1997 United Features Syndicate, Inc. Reprinted by permission of United Features Syndicate, Inc.

ASPCA Homepage. <www.aspca.org>. Copyright © 2000 The American Society for the Prevention of Cruelty to Animals. Reproduced by permission.

King Lear. Three scenes from the BBC/Time-Life Films *King Lear* videocassette, 1987. Courtesy of the BBC.

MasterCard Homepage. <www.mastercard.com>. Copyright © 1994–2000. Courtesy of MasterCard International Incorporated. All rights reserved.

Oregon State University Homepage. <www.orst.edu/>. Reproduced by permission of OSU Web Coordinator, Computer Network Services.

James Porto/*WIRED*, December 1999. *WIRED*/Conde Nast Publications, Inc. All rights reserved. Reprinted by permission.

Index